Favourite Hymns

Love the Words, Love the Music

An introduction to well-known Hymns & Hymnists

giving in a few pages:

the story of the Author, the Translator,

the original Text and some of the alterations;

the usual Setting(s) and the Composer(s);

as part of the Background,

there are details of the Source, Anecdotes,

and sundry Comments to add enjoyment

- also some extra information.

John King   **mmxxii**

Acknowledgements

Thanks to my wife Naomi for advising on this project, much proofreading and proof-reading – and saying she was impressed even with the first draft.

Thanks also to those who have assisted, given explanations or useful commentary; these include Professor Watson (University of Durham; Lead co-Editor of the Canterbury Dictionary of Hymnology)

Nicholas Markwell, a fellow member and on the Committee of The Hymn Society of Great Britain and Ireland.

Canon Rosalind Brown (Durham Cathedral)

Members of the Hymn Singing Society

Members of the Prayer Book Society;

Members of the Hymn Society of Great Britain and Ireland;

 -especially their Vintage Hymn offshoot– led by Philip Price and Nicholas Markwell;

Members of All Saints Church, Monkland and nearby Leominster Priory;

Members of the Mennonite Church at Craven Arms, Shropshire;

Anne O'Nimmus of the University of Limerick

Sarah N'Dipiti of the Hymn Society of Sri Lanka

Annder Wyfe of the Hymn Singing Society

Publishing data   JK Enterprises

© J P King   mmxxii

Introduction

I tried to resist the temptation. But here I adapt, in 18th century style, Wesley's Preface to his Select Hymns of 1761, exactly 100 years before Hymns Ancient and Modern's first edition was delivered at the hands of Sir H W Baker and his colleagues in 1861 – now some 160 years ago.

Over the years, many books and now websites have been devoted to the study and description of hymns and hymnists. Nevertheless, this modest volume is, I declare, different from all others that have come before. As its author I cannot declare it better, although the structure and form has moved away from being solely concerned with words, music or biblical source alone. Similarly, in allowing well-chosen description and even anecdote, I believe that all unprejudiced persons will judge that it exceeds, beyond all degrees of available comparison with any work that has gone before.

The Public may be surprised to find there is another attempt to publish such a book when there are such numbers already extant and several of them have so lately made their appearance; but I flatter myself that the style and format herein will have some weight to it receiving a favourable reception.

As is true with any collection, the choice is rarely objective. For my usual preference, there are but two or three modern hymns which catch and hold my attention. The older hymns are subjectively better. Therefore, there will be moments of pleasure at the inclusion of some, and astonishment at the exclusion of others. The truth is – authors get to make choices. I have had immense enjoyment at putting this work together. I truly hope that others will gain from the reading of the pieces collected here.

Rather obviously and implicitly my background is white, anglo-saxon and Protestant – labellings which I cannot avoid or evade. In addition I am very middle. Middle-class, middle-aged (when this idea was conceived), middle-of-the-road (in my own view), maybe not middle-educated. I cannot apologise for any of this but, in these days of the new vociferous minority oft succeeding in pressing back against their erstwhile (allegedly oppressing) majority or some other competing minority, I durst accept relevant critique.

This book is for dipping into rather than reading as one large piece. A hymn will catch the attention, a phrase, a name – and here are hundreds of facts about 'Great Hymns'. Some are MY favourites, some may be your favourites. But once you begin, there is a great deal of useful, general information about some of the hymns you love.

While the words above in italics have been edited and paraphrased since the 18th century, the intent here is still exactly as stated so many years ago. This book is original. This book is different from any on the same area. This book, in its format, style and approach, is unique. The choice of hymns may be 'the old favourites', the so-called 'Great Hymns', but nowhere else can you find, without an full encyclopaedic article, the basic details of the author, the translator, the composer, the best tunes and the background stories.

All of this is set in brief articles that are easy to read and easy to see where more and deeper interest might take you. The opportunities for serendipity are excellent. Where else would you find out about the man who translated Latin-to-English hymns back into his own version of the Latin – for which, thank you Bishop Bingham. There are stories I never knew about Wesley, and Blake as authors and Sullivan and Vaughan-Williams as composers.

Here are some of the great names of English literary and musical history – albeit in the smaller scope of hymns and song rather than the larger arenas of literature or music.

Why should you read this book?

If you are of a 'certain age' then you grew up with these hymns and they are a deep, sometimes hidden, fragment of your childhood. But when the time comes, you know the tunes, you know the opening line(s) and it makes you feel wonderful, joyful, eager when you sing.

On those occasions when you do go to church, and for some this will be for hatches, matches and despatches plus Christmas, there will be opportunities to sing – and doesn't it feel great to sing a hymn you remember from long ago with a bit of enthusiasm. These are the hymns you will find in this book: the great hymns, the favourites.

But there are not so many about the details, the how and the why of each hymn. For some, the why is obvious – it's a Christmas hymn, an Easter hymn, a song about Joy, Sadness, Birth and the rest. If you sit and glance at a hymnbook, many of them will have an index of Special Days, Special Events, Important Topics, the almost forgotten Saints Days and the useful General. Scattered among them will be the words you remember; and sometimes a name like Wesley, Milton, Bunyan, Haydn or Sullivan.

When a carol is played on the radio, on those rare occasions when a hymn is heard outside a church – don't you wonder about it just a little. Who wrote it? Why is it so familiar? Is there some sort of story about it, or the author? Some background?

There's all that and more in this book.

Who is going to read it?

With these pages, a hand is extended to those who feel that the world of Christianity is not for them. Here are words, ideas and music designed to enhance the text which, over the years, has inspired some to interest, and some to true belief and certainty.

Older hymns have many of the traits of great poems – rhyme, rhythm, emotion and love; expressing the feelings and thoughts which many find difficult to put into daily language. Many of these favourites spring from deep personal experience. But it is part of their being 'favourites' that they be shared and enjoyed, not just as powerful poems, but as a joint endeavour. There are books of hymns, thousands of them.

To know a little of the context, historical and theological, from which each one develops greatly enriches the apparently simple act of congregational singing.

Sadly, there is no room for the music. The book would have been so much bigger and aiming at a more specific audience rather than the hymn-interested generalist.

How did this book come to be written?

Some friends got excited about hymn-singing. They decided to run a hymn-singing event. Then the actual planning began. How many hymns? Which hymns? Where? When?

'We can't just keep singing, we'll have to have a pause now and again'.

'Yes – how about an introduction to each hymn, y'know 60, 90 seconds or so'.

That's how it all began.

'Mmmm, well, so, about 10 or 15 lines of text. I'll see what I can find'.

Later 'I can't just pull out the 'most interesting' lines as a hymn introduction – I'm going to have to do a page or so and only then I can decide what's most interesting. And which ones are we going to do'.

Having written the first draft purely as a set of personal and casual notes in order to be able to give a brief chat at a friend's planned hymn festival … suddenly, I was close to delivering a book. This book. With details of the author, the translator when there was one, the tune used for it (often more than one) so more than one composer. The changes, amendments and rewrites by different people with their own aims as to what the hymn should say. The background, the anecdotes. The relevant verses or lines from the Bible.

Then barely days later, I was looking for better sources for my comments; topics that would make my document that bit more interesting or suitable for a different audience than a 'mere book about hymns'. And while there is still nothing like this book, there are some which are exceeding useful as sources for useful comment or snippet.

As every author in the 18th century and ever since has said *'this modest volume is, I declare, different from all others that have come before'*. Certainly I have found nothing like this document. I have looked at books about hymns; books about hymn-writers; books of the Biblical background and inner meaning of hymns; books about 'why I like hymns'. Many books. And still, as far as I can see, there is nothing like this one.

One of the interesting things about this project is, that having looked at a whole range of hymn books and books about hymns, almost the most fascinating part of each one is the introduction. The effort put in by the editors to prove that their choices have some form of objective judgement – when the truth is that any comparison between two or three items has to be subjective.

Serendipity plays its part, most especially with a reference book as large and interestingly opinionated as Julian's Dictionary of Hymnology. Julian may have a defect for me in that he has barely a mention of tunes for hymns, or the composers thereof. But his book has been the bible for hymnists for over 100 years. It is full of useful facts written in delicious language. Quotes are repeatedly taken from there as his prose is so splendid.

What can I say now ….

I never meant to write a book – but here we are. As has been mentioned, there is nothing exactly like this book with the original or early text and a reasonable amount of background. On the other hand, I will not pretend that the story presented here is complete or encyclopaedic.

Writing a book of any sort has to be a work delivering the author's interest and enthusiasm for the subject – otherwise it's just a job. I can promise that almost every stage of this has been fun and interesting. I have met some fascinating people along the way. All I can hope is that you will enjoy what is delivered here. Happy Hymning. Happy Singing.

John King   mmxxii

Notes

Showing the majority of entries as a two-page spread is deliberate, if unusual. Set out this way each article is easily readable. The intent is to give the ORIGINAL or an early text rather than any of the versions currently sung – as the modern text will be available in whichever hymnal is to hand.

Generally, the fourth page in such a set will have pictures relevant to the whole or, on occasion, there will be an extra piece of related information of more general interest.

The choice of hymns, hymnists and extra topics is by choice and sometimes chance, when a topic seems particularly appropriate.

The **Header** of each hymn is factual, even if occasionally adjusted as to layout. It identifies the Author and Translator and the early publishing date; and the number of Verses; then the most common Setting(s) and their Composer, relevant dates and the Metre. If a particular bible verse is clearly identified then this is included.

> **Verses** – as you read the text, it will become clear how often verses are added, removed, altered, re-sorted and just not sung. An attempt is made to show this variation in the heading.
>
> **Settings** – similarly, the preferred TUNE can often vary accoring to what the organist, cleric and congregation are used to. The statement 'this is THE tune' is not always accurate.

The **Detailed Index of Hymns summarises** this key information, arranged so that at an easy glance, the hymn title, author and source; setting and composer is identified.

As regards layout and to ensure the 2-page layout for several hymns – on a few occasions a hymn text will have its two lines laid out across the page with a divider … as shown :

> Receive instead of Palm-boughs, … Our victory o'er the foe,
> That in the conquerer's triumph … This strain may ever flow.

'§' is a marker that the hymn or person so marked has a full section in the book. Generally, if such an entry is referenced, a repeat in the same article is not annotated.

Usage of Capital letters and some spellings do vary even through to the Victorian era; so almost every apparent error will be more likely due to the original document – rather than this author's mistake.

Apology : This is an amateur book, that is – done for love rather than in an attempt to deliver academic quality or to make money. It grew from a casual idea to this first fruition very quickly and with no intent for more than personal use as a text for brief introductions to some two dozen hymns. It has grown mightily but references, attributions and the like have crept alarmingly out of reach, although never with intent to avoid giving relevant or due acknowledgement. If I could track and trace each of these, then I would have tried to do so. Whatever the aim, there will also be slippage, errors and omissions.

I trust that before a second edition or an e-book that there will be a quantity of feedback and suggestions for correction and improvement.

Hymns and Hystories Contents

Introduction
Illustrations   5
Favourite Hymns Detailed Index   6
Abide with Me   8
All Glory, Laud, and Honour   12
All People that on Earth do Dwell   16
All Things Bright and Beautiful   20
Amazing Grace   24
    In passing – Why do you sometimes get the 'wrong' music   27
And can it be, that I should gain   28
And did those feet in ancient time   32
    William Blake   1757-1827   35
Angel-Voices, Ever Singing   36
Angels, From the Realms of Glory   38
Angels we have heard on High   42
At the name of Jesus   44
    Rev Sir Henry Williams Baker   1821-1877   46
Blessed City, Heavenly Salem   (Urbs Beata)   48
Breathe on me, Breath of God   52
    In passing – Catholic Hymns
Crown Him with many crowns   54
    Digression: The Common Doxology
Dear Lord and Father of mankind   58
    John Bacchus Dykes   1823-1876   62
Eternal Father, strong to save   66
Father, hear the prayer we offer   68
Fight the good fight   70
For all the Saints   72
Glorious things of Thee are spoken   74
God be in my head   77
God moves in a mysterious way   78
God save our gracious Queen   80
Good Christian men rejoice   (In Dulci Jubilo)   84
    In passing – Bishop Bingham goes back to Latin   87
Guide me, O thou great Jehovah / (Redeemer)   88

In passing – Welsh Song	
Hail the day that sees Him rise	92
Hark!! the Herald-Angels sing	94
Bishop Heber 1783-1826	96
Holy Holy Holy! Lord God Almighty	98
How great Thou art	100
Hymns Ancient and Modern 1861	104
Immortal, Invisible, God only wise	108
Jesus Christ is risen today (Surrexit Hodie)	112
Joy to the world	114
Jesus shall reign where'er the sun	116
John Julian 1839-1913	118
King of Glory, King of Peace	122
Lead, kindly Light amid th'encircling gloom	124
Lead us, heavenly Father, lead us	126
In passing – the influence of German (Lutheran) hymn	
Let all the world in every corner sing	128
Lift up your hearts! We lift them, Lord, to thee	130
Lo, He comes with clouds descending	132
Love Divine, all loves excelling	134
Martin Luther 1483-1546	137
Henry Francis Lyte 1793-1847	138
Mine eyes have seen the glory of the Coming of the Lord / Battle Hymn of the Republic	140
William Henry Monk 1823-1889	144
James Montgomery 1771-1854	146
John Mason Neale 1816-1866	148
Now thank we all our God	150
O come, all ye faithful (Adeste Fideles)	152
In passing – Carols	
O for a Thousand tongues to sing	155
In passing – Hymns or Gospel Songs	
O God, our help in ages past	158
O praise ye the Lord	163
O Thou who camest from above	164
O worship the King all glorious above	166
Onward, Christian soldiers	168
In passing – The verse of Lord Calvin	171
Psalms	172
Praise, O praise my God and King	176
In passing – Local names for hymns	177

Praise, my soul, the King of heaven	178
Praise the Lord ! ye heavens adore him	180
In passing – The Ten Commandments - in verse	181
Praise to the holiest in the height (Gerontius)	182
Digression: Cardinal Newman	
Digression: The Dream of Gerontius	
Digression: Dante's 'Divine Comedy'	
Praise to the Lord, the Almighty	186
Ride on! ride on, in majesty	188
Rock of Ages, cleft for me	190
Soldiers of Christ, arise	192
The Church's one Foundation	194
The day thou gavest, Lord, is ended	196
The King of love my Shepherd is	198
The Lord's my shepherd	200
There is a green hill far away	202
Thine be the glory, ris'n conquering Son	204
Isaac Watts 1674-1748	206
Digression: Logick	
We plough the fields and scatter	210
Charles Wesley 1707-1788	212
When I survey the wond'rous cross	216
Who would true valour see	218
Ye holy Angels bright	222
References – Publications and Websites	224
Afterwords	226
Chambers Encyclopedia 1892 – on Hymns	226
Oxford Dictionary of Music - Scholes – Hymns	228
Canterbury (online) Dictionary of Hymnology	229

Illustrations

Front Cover

1	18th Century – Isaac Watts, John & Charles Wesley, John Newton,	p11
2	H W Baker, J B Dykes; W H Monk; J M Neale;	p15
#3	Psalm 100 - 3 early examples (2 from the 'Old Version')	p19
#4	4 Women Hymnists - Alexander; Howe; Winkworth; Irvine	p23
#5	Frontispiece of Olney Hymns 1779; John Newton; William Cowper	p29
#6	Wesley's handwritten text; Title Page	p31
#7	Victorian Hymnists – Murray, Newman; Howe, Montgomery	p41
#8	Manuscript of Urbs Beata	p51
#9	Parry, Vaughan Williams, Stainer, Stanford,	p61
#10	1861 Front Cover of Hymns Ancient and Modern	p65
#11	Collage of Royal Arms	p83
#12	Manuscript of In Dulci Jubilo	p87
#13	Singing at Cardiff	p91
#14	Old Choirs & New	p105
#15	John Julian	p118
#16	Russian & German Army	p143
#17	The Ten Commandments in Verse	p179
#18	Pilgrim's Progress	p221

Favourite Hymns' Detailed Index

Title	Author/ Translator	Tune	Composer
Abide with me, fast falls the Eventide	H F Lyte	Eventide	W H Monk
All glory, Laud and Honour to thee,	Theodulf of Orleans : J M Neale	St.Theodulf	adap M Teschner
All people that on Earth do dwell	Genevan Psalter trans Kethe	Old 100th	L Bourgeois
All things bright and beautiful	C F Alexander	per Title	W H Monk
Amazing Grace	John Newton	New Britain	L Chapin
And can it be that I should gain	Charles Wesley	Sagina	T Campbell
And did those feet in ancient time	William Blake	Jerusalem	C H Parry
Angels from the realms of Glory;	James Montgomery	Regent Square	H Smart
Angel voices ever singing	F Pott	per Title	E G Monk
Angels we have heard on high	trans James Chadwick	Gloria	E S Barnes
At the name of Jesus every knee	Caroline Noel	Evelyns	W H Monk
Blessed City, Heavenly Salem	trans. J M Neale	Urbs Beata	(Sarum)
Breathe on me, breath of God	E Hatch	Trentham	R Jackson
Crown him with many crowns	Matthew Bridges	Diademata	G J Elvey
Dear Lord and Father of mankind	J G Whittier	Repton	C H Parry
Eternal Father, strong to save	W Whiting	Melita	J B Dykes
Father hear the prayer we offer	Love Maria Willis	Marching	M Shaw
Fight the Good Fight	James Monsell	Duke Street	J Hatton
For all the Saints	W Walsham How	Sine Nomine	R Vaughan Williams
Glorious things of thee are spoken	John Newton	Austrian Hymn	J Haydn
God be in my head	Latin / French 1497	per Title	H Walford Davies
God moves in a mysterious way	William Cowper	Dundee	A Hart
God save our gracious Queen	uncertain 1745	uncertain 1744	(Bull)
Good Christian Men, rejoice	trans J M Neale	Gelobt sei Got	trad.German
Guide me, O thou great Redeemer	J Williams	Bread of Heaven/Cwm Rhondda	J Hughes
Hail the day that sees him rise	Charles Wesley	Llanfair	R Williams
Hark! The herald angels sing	Charles Wesley	Festgesang	F Mendelssohn
Holy, holy, holy, Lord God .Almighty	Bishop Heber	Nicaea	J B Dykes
How great thou art	C Boberg	O Store Gud	Swedish
I vow to thee my country	C Spring Rice	Thaxted (Jupiter)	adap. Holst
Immortal, invisible, God only wise	W Chalmers Smith	St Denio	trad. Welsh
Jesus Christ is risen today, Alleluia	Lyra Davidica 1708	Easter Hymn	anon
Jesus shall reign where'er the sun	Isaac Watts	Truro	T Williams
Joy to the World	Isaac Watts	Comfort	Rider,Hawkes
King of Glory, King of Peace	George Herbert	Gwalchmai	J Jones

Hymn	Author	Tune	Composer
Lead, kindly light, amidst th'encircling gloom	John H Newman	Lux Benigna	J B Dykes
Lead us, Heavenly Father lead us	J Edmeston	Mannheim	F Filitz
Let all the World, in every corner sing	George Herbert	Luckington	B Harwood
Lift up thy hearts, we lift them Lord	H Montagu Butler	Woodlands	W Greatorex
Lo! He comes with clouds descending	Charles Wesley	Helmsley	T Olivers
Love divine, all loves excelling,	Charles Wesley	Beecher	J Zundel
Mine eyes have seen the Glory	Julia Lowe	Canaan's Shore	US folk
Now thank we all our God	Luther/Rinkart trans Winkworth	Nun danket	Cruger
O Come all ye faithful	J F Wade	tune included	J F Wade
O Come, O come, Emmanuel	trans. J M Neale	Veni Emmanuel	15C
O for a Thousand tongues to sing	Charles Wesley	Lyngham	Jarman
O God our help in ages past	Isaac Watts	St Anne	W Croft
O Jesus, I have promised	J E Bode	Wolvercote	W Ferguson
O praise ye the Lord, praise him	H W Baker	Laudate Dominum	C H Parry
O thou who camest from above	Charles Wesley	Hereford	S S Wesley
O worship the King, all glorious above	Robert Grant	Hanover	W Croft
Onward Christian Soldiers	S Baring-Gould	St Gertrude	A Sullivan
Praise, my soul, the King of heaven	H F Lyte	Lauda Anima	John Goss
Praise, O praise, our God and King	H W Baker	Monkland	J Antes
Praise the Lord, ye Heavens adore him	Foundling Hospital	Austria	J Haydn
Praise to the holiest in the height	J H Newman	Gerontius	J B Dykes
Praise to the Lord, the Almighty	Neander tr. Winkworth	Praxis Pietatis 1665	trad German
Soldiers of Christ arise	Charles Wesley	St Ethelwald	W H Monk
Ride On, Ride on, in majesty	H H Milman	Winchester New	G Wittwe
Rock of Ages, cleft for me	A M Toplady	Petra	R Redhead
The Church's one foundation	S J Stone	Aurelia	S S Wesley
The day thou gavest, Lord is ended	J Ellerton	St Clement	C Scholefield
The King of Love my shepherd is	H W Baker	Dominus regit me	J B Dykes
The Lord's my Shepherd	Scottish Psalter (Rous)	Crimond	D Grant
There is a green hill far away	C F Alexander	Horsley	W Horsley
Thine be the glory, risen, conquering son	Budry trans R B Hoyle	Maccabaeus	G F Handel
We plough the fields and scatter	M Claudius trans J M Campbell	Wir pflugen	J Schulz
When I survey the wondrous cross	Isaac Watts	Rockingham	E Miller
Who would true valour see	John Bunyan	Monks Gate	R Vaughan Williams
Ye Holy Angels bright	R Baxter & J Gurney	Darwall's 148th	Darwall arrgd WH Monk

Abide with Me;

| | Henry Francis Lyte § | 1793-1847 | 1847 | 8(5) verses |
| EVENTIDE | William Henry Monk§ | 1823-1899 | 1861 | 10.10.10.10 |

Luke 24:29   "Abide with us: for it is toward evening, and the day is far spent"

'Abide with Me' is an astonishingly well-known hymn by Somerset-born Henry Francis Lyte. The final or at least the most familiar text was written by him in 1847 as he was dying from tuberculosis and he also wrote his own setting for it, although this was later replaced.

Tennyson ranked this hymn 'among the really perfect poems' in English, endorsing the view that Lyte's facility with language was appreciated by the Victorian literary establishment. A later commentator wrote 'The verses are intensely personal, freely using 'I' and 'me', and with the best aspects of Victorian sentiment. The hymn is also helped by having a tune specifically composed for the text.'

There are significant instances where 'Abide with me' has been adopted into popular culture and treated as a secular piece. For instance, there is the current practice of singing it at the English Football Association Cup Final, begun in 1927 at the suggestion of the secretary, Sir Alfred Wall, and with the approval of King George V and Queen Mary, who shared a particular affection for Lyte's hymn. The institution of this tradition may partly be explained by the hymn's encapsulating of a shared national sense of loss and remembrance resulting from vivid memories of the recent First World War. Interestingly, the hymn was parodied by soldiers in the trenches of Flanders, who sang 'We've had no beer, we've had no beer today'.

There is some controversy as to the exact dating of the text to 'Abide with Me'. An article in *The Spectator*, 3 Oct. 1925, says that Lyte composed the hymn in 1820 while visiting a dying friend. It was related that he was staying with the Hore family in County Wexford and had visited an old friend, William Augustus Le Hunte, who was dying. As Lyte sat with the dying man, William kept repeating the phrase 'abide with me…'. After leaving William's bedside, Lyte wrote the hymn and gave a copy of it to Le Hunte's family.

The second version is that twenty-seven years later in 1847when Lyte felt his own end approaching at the age of 54, as his tuberculosis advanced, he recalled the lines he had written so many years before in County Wexford. Using his friend's more personal phrasing 'Abide with Me', the hymn was composed. His daughter, Anna Maria Maxwell Hogg, recounts the story of how 'Abide with Me' came out of that context.

The summer was passing away, and the month of September (that month in which he was once more to quit his native land) arrived, and each day seemed to have a special value as being one day nearer his departure. His family were surprised and almost alarmed at his announcing his intention of preaching once more to his people. His weakness and the possible danger attending the effort urged all to try to prevent it, but in vain. 'It was better', as he used to say often playfully, when in comparative health, 'to wear out than to rust out'. He felt that he should be enabled to fulfil his wish, and feared not for the result. He did preach, and amid the breathless attention of his hearers, gave them a sermon on the Holy Communion. That evening he placed in the hands of a near and dear relative the little hymn, 'Abide with Me', with an air of his own composing, adapted to the words.

Just weeks later, on 20 November 1847 in Nice then in the Kingdom of Sardinia, he died, and the hymn was sung for the very first time at his funeral.

The author was an Anglican minister, born in 1793, he was first a curate in County Wexford from 1815 to 1818. Later Lyte was vicar of All Saints' Church in Brixham, Devon, England. For most of his life he suffered from poor health, and he would regularly travel abroad for relief, as was customary at that time.

The hymn is a prayer for God to remain present with the speaker throughout life, through trials, and through death. The opening line is taken from Luke 24:29 and the penultimate verse draws on text from 1Corinthians 15:55, 'O death, where is thy sting? O grave, where is thy victory?' The hymn is now particularly associated with funeral services, but has had wide appeal in secular contexts as well, for evenings and endings of various sorts.

The piece appeals widely in a religious context because it illustrates effectively, in the interplay of light and dark, the contrast between the degeneration of earthly things and the permanence of God's care and love.

W H Monk's setting EVENTIDE is very much the one most often used with this hymn. Monk was both a well-known organist and church musician. According to some sources, he wrote the tune in just ten minutes. As one story goes, he was attending a hymnal committee meeting for the 1861 edition of Hymns Ancient and Modern of which he was music editor. Apparently believing that this particular text had no available tune, Monk sat down at the piano and composed EVENTIDE According to his wife, it was written, 'at a time of great sorrow' when they had been watching a glorious sunset. The tune has become famous and much loved, and may be partly responsible for the deep affection in which this hymn is held.

Being such a strong tune and in a simple 10.10.10.10 metre, many new texts have been written to suit. 'Not worthy, Lord to gather up the crumbs'; 'An upper room with evening lamps ashine' by Timothy Dudley-Smith; 'We turn to god when we are sorely pressed' by Dietrich Bonhoeffer; and apparently more than 50 others, some not even in English.

Over and above, new texts for the tune, there are of course alternative tunes for the text. These include: ABIDE WITH ME – the author's own original setting in 1847;

CHANTE TROYTE No.1 or TROYE'S CHANT; OLD 124Th; MORECAMBE, Frederick C. Atkinson, 1870; PENITENTIA Edward Dearle, 1874; and an unnamed setting by Samuel Liddle (1867-1951), published in 1896 which was the version favoured by the well-known singer Dame Clara Butt; as well as and WOODLANDS, Walter Greatorex, 1916. More recently, settings such as ORISONS; SWANTON; ELLERS and DORLAND MOUNTAIN have found favour.

The principal theme of the fourth movement of Gustav Mahler's Symphony No. 9 is often noted for its similarity to Monk's melody.

Vaughan-Williams composed for the Hereford Festival of 1936 an orchestral prelude *Two Hymn-Tune Preludes 1. Eventide.* Charles Ives, the American composer wrote a setting in 1890 which was only published in his collection *Thirteen Songs* in 1958, four years after his death.

One commentator wrote : 'These missing stanzas 3,4,5 illustrate a more personal relationship between God and humankind. Those emotive phrases 'Familiar, condescending [in its old meaning, 'disregarding superiority'], patient, free', 'Tears for all woes, a heart for every plea' and smiling on early youth, though it is 'rebellious and perverse' all emphasise the truly personal message in Lyte's words.

Lyte delivered his own adjustments so this is an early version of the text. Sometimes there are variations of punctuation as the only indicator; elsewhen the changes are larger, most especially in the thou-you interference of recent times. Since the original there have, as usual, been many variations, small and large.

1   Abide with me! fast falls the eventide;
    The darkness deepens; Lord, with me abide!
    When other helpers fail, and comforts flee,
    Help of the helpless, O abide with me!

2   Swift to its close ebbs out life's little day;
    Earth's joys grow dim, its glories pass away;
    Change and decay in all around I see;
    O Thou who changest not, abide with me!

3   Not a brief glance I beg, a passing word,   (generally omitted)
    But as Thou dwell'st with Thy disciples, Lord,
    Familiar, condescending, patient, free,
    Come not to sojourn, but abide with me!

4   Come not in terrors, as the King of kings,   (sometimes omitted
    But kind and good, with healing in Thy wings;
    Tears for all woes, a heart for every plea.
    Come, Friend of sinners, thus bide with me.

5   Thou on my head in early youth didst smile,   (sometimes omitted)
    And though rebellious and perverse meanwhile,
    Thou hast not left me, oft as I left Thee.
    On to the close, O Lord, abide with me!

6   I need Thy presence every passing hour.
    What but Thy grace can foil the Tempter's power?
    Who, like Thyself, my guide and stay can be?
    Through cloud and sunshine, O abide with me!

7   I fear no foe, with Thee at hand to bless:
    Ills have no weight, and tears no bitterness.
    Where is death's sting? Where, grave, thy victory?
    I triumph still, if Thou abide with me.

8   Hold then Thy cross before my closing eyes;
    Shine through the gloom, and point me to the skies.
    Heaven's morning breaks, and earth's vain shadows flee;
    In life, in death, O Lord, abide with me!

Many hymnals omit certain verses, especially verse 5 beginning 'Thou on my head in early youth didst smile;' for being in some way too personal. What this means is not made clear.

STOP PRESS – There has been heated discussion in the Indian Army at the dropping of Abide with Me from their Beating the Retreat ceremony after 70 years.

18C hymnists; Watts; John & Charles Wesley; Newton

Isaac Watts 1674-1748
- Jesus shall reign where'er … 1719
- Joy to the world 1719
- O God, our help n ages past 1708
- (Jesu, lover of my Soul) 1707

John Wesley 1703-1791 (translator)

John Newton 1725-1807
- Amazing Grace 1779
- Glorious things of thee 1779
- (How sweet the name of Jesus sounds)

Charles Wesley 1797-1788
- And can it be that I should gain 1747
- Hark! The herald angels sing 1739
- Lo! He comes, with clouds … 1752
- Love Divine, all loves excelling 1747
- O For a thousand tongues 1780
- O Thou who camest from above 1762
- Soldiers of Christ, arise 1747

All Glory, Laud, and Honour

    Theodulf of Orleans c 820   trans. J M Neale §   1818-1866   1851   8,7,6 verses
ST.THEODULF   adapted M Teschner   fl 1600   1615   7.6.7.6 (D)
Psalm 8:2   "Out of the mouths of babes and sucklings thou hast perfected praise …"

This is famous as a Palm Sunday hymn; the principal theme is praising Christ's triumphal entry into Jerusalem as made clear in the refrain. In a shortened form from the original 39 verses, it became used in Palm Sunday processions in medieval breviaries. In some Uses or Cathedral routines it was by choirboys, either strategically stationed in the church or at points along the procession route. As a reminder, Palm Sunday is the weekend before Easter and, thus, the first day of Holy Week when Jesus made his entry into Jerusalem.

The biblical source best describing Palm Sunday is Matthew 21:1–11 but the words of the text do not equate; to do so would require a very casual usage. There is, in particular and rather surprisingly, no reference there directly to Glory or Laud or Honour or Redeemer, rather Hosanna and Blessed. 'And the multitudes …cried, saying, 'Hosanna to the Son of David: Blessed is he that cometh in the name of the Lord; Hosanna in the highest'. Matthew 21:9 There is an interesting change of emphasis for 'Hosanna' between Old and New Testaments: it used to mean 'Lord Save me' but became 'Praise' – very different.

The hymn is an English translation by the Anglican clergyman John Mason Neale§ of the Latin hymn 'Gloria, laus et honor, tibi sit, rex Christi redemptor', which was written by Theodulf of Orléans in 820 He became the Bishop of Orléans under Charlemagne. When Charlemagne died and Louis the Pious became the emperor of the Holy Roman Empire, due to Theodulf's opposition to icons and Louis' suspicion that he supported an Italian rival to the throne, he was removed from the bishopric and placed under house arrest at a monastery in Angers on the Loire during the power struggle following Louis' ascension.

While under arrest, Theodulf this hymn wrote for Palm Sunday. Although unlikely, a 16th-century story asserted that Louis heard the prisoner sing these words one Palm Sunday, and was so inspired that he released the bishop and ordered that the hymn be sung thereafter on every Palm Sunday. As John Julian§, the hymn historian, pointed out, this could not have been true: the date given for what he calls 'this pretty story' is 821, but Louis the Pious is not known to have visited Angers after 818.

A Middle English translation was delivered by William Herebert (c1270-1333): The first lines 'translate' as 'Wealth, Praise and Worship be to Christ who saved us / to whom great Hosannas from innocent children.' The first line shows two old-english characters … Wele herizyng and worshype boe to crist that doere ous bought.

Wele heriȝyng and worshype boe to crist þat doere ous bouhte.

To wham gradden 'Osanna' children clene of thoughte.
Thou art king of Israel and of Davides kunne,
Blessed king that comest till ous withoute wem of sunne.

> Transliterated
> Glory, praise and honour be to Christ who dear us bought,
> To whom cried 'Hosanna' children pure of thought.
> You are the king of Israel and of David's kin,
> Blessed King who comes to us without the stain of sin.

All that is in hevene thee herieth under on,
And all thine owne hondewerk and euch dedlich mon.
The folk of Jiwes with bowes comen ayeinest thee,
And we with bedes and with song meketh ous to thee.

> All that is in heaven praises you as one,
> And all your own handiwork and every mortal man.
> The Jewish people with boughs came to meet you,
> And we with prayers and with songs humble ourselves to you.

He kepten thee with worshiping, ayeinst thou shuldest deye,
And we singen to thy worshipe, in trone that sittest heye.
Here wil and here mekinge thou nome tho to thonk;
Queme thee thenne, milsful King, oure offrings of this song.

> They attended you with honour, at the time when you should die,
> And we sing to your honour, who in throne sits on high.
> Their will and their humility you accepted graciously then;
> So may please you, merciful King, our offering of this song.

AClerkofOxford [sic / website] tells us 'As always, Herebert produces a creative translation, a fluid and confident reworking of the Latin hymn into an English idiom. The first verse also plays effectively on the similarity between the English words king and kin, and the two lines of each verse are neatly linked to each other by alliteration as well as by rhyme: king/kunne/comest, hevene/herieth/hondewerk, bowes/bedes, etc. Since several of the verses are carefully structured as parallels - the first line describes what the people of Jerusalem did, the second what 'we' do on Palm Sunday - linking them through alliteration works to re-enforce the parallels between, for instance, their bowes and our bedes. [palm-boughs and prayers]

The commonly used tune of the hymn, titled ST THEODULF or originally VALET WILL ICH DIR GEBEN, was composed in 1603 by Melchior Teschner (1584-1635). In A&M it is set to 8-line stanzas which requires the final refrain to conclude the hymn at a fine point half way through the tune; but that has not prevented this hymn from remaining perhaps the best known of all hymns for Palm Sunday. 'Valet will ich dir geben,' was a hymn for the dying written by Valerius Herberger. Teschner composed the tune in two five-voice settings, published in the leaflet *Ein andächtiges Gebet* in 1615. It is also known as MELCHIOR or KRONSTADT.

ST THEODULF is linked with the majority of the published hymnals; some five other settings account for the remainder, although a great many more are tunes used only in one hymnal. The major others include :-   HELDER (by Helder);   HIEROSOLYMA; EULOGIA; WIE SOLL ICH DICH EMPFANGEN; and MUNICH (by Mendelssohn).

In addition, there are a huge number of tunes which can be used for a metre such as this of 7.6.7.6 D – not that metre is the only constraint for a rhythmic piece.

As is common with other well-known settings, ST THEODULF is used for other texts; including 'O Lord, how shall I meet thee'; 'By all your saints still striving'; 'O Jesus, King of Glory'; 'Hail to the Lord's anointed'; 'Light of the Gentile nations' and some 90 more.

The original Latin words are used by Roman Catholics and are thus often printed alongside the English translation in a double-column. In 1851, John Mason Neale§ translated the hymn from Latin into English to be published in his *Medieval Hymns and Sequences*, in a form which kept to the Latin rhythm with 'Glory, and laud, and honour'. A trial edition of A&M (1859) altered the first line to a more singable metre 'All glory, laud, and honour', and the First Edition (1861) printed a text in just 6 eight-line stanzas. The first stanza is used as a refrain after each stanza that follows. There is an additional stanza:

> Receive instead of Palm-boughs, ... Our victory o'er the foe,
> That in the conquerer's triumph ... This strain may ever flow.

This is the 1854 text and shows twenty-two Biblical verses that have been referenced.

54 PALM SUNDAY.   H.N. 76
MORNING.

Gloria, laus, et honor.

1. ᵃ GLORY, and laud, and honour,
    ᵇ To Thee, Redeemer King !
    ᶜ To Whom the lips of children
      Made sweet Hosannas ring.

2. ᵈ Thou art the King of Israel,
    ᵉ Thou, David's Royal Son,
    ᶠ Who in the LORD's Name comest,
    ᵍ The King and Blessed One.

3. ʰ The Company of Angels
      Are praising Thee on high,
    ⁱ And mortal men, and all things
      Created, make reply.

4. ᵏ The people of the Hebrews
      With Palms before Thee went;
    ˡ Our praise and prayer and anthems
      Before Thee we present.

5. ᵐ Thou wast hast'ning to Thy Passion,
      When they raised their hymns of praise :
    ⁿ Thou art reigning in Thy glory,
      When our melody we raise.

6. ᵒ Thou didst accept their praises ;
    ᵖ Accept the prayers we bring,
    ᵠ Who in all good delightest,
    ʳ Thou good and gracious King !

7. ˢ Receive, instead of Palm-boughs,
      Our victory o'er the foe,
    ᵗ That in the Conqueror's triumph
      This strain may ever flow :

8.   Glory, and laud, and honour,
      To Thee, Redeemer King !
     To Whom the lips of children
      Made sweet Hosannas ring.

ᵃ S. John xii. 13.   ᵇ Psalm lxxxix. 19. Psalm cxviii. 26.   ᵐ S. Luke xii. 50.   ⁿ Acts vii. 55.
ᶜ Psalm viii. 2. S. Matt. xxi. 15.   ᵒ S. Luke xix. 40.
ᵈ S. Matt. xxvii. 37.   ᵉ S. Matt. xxii. 42.   ᵖ Psalm cxix. 108.   ᵠ Psalm xi. 6.
ᶠ S. John v. 43.   ᵍ 1 Tim. vi. 15.   ʳ Psalm cxix. 68. Psalm lxxiv. 13.
ʰ Rev. v. 11.   ⁱ Rev. v. 13.   ˢ Psalm l. 14.   ᵗ Rev. iv. 4.
ᵏ S. John xii. 12, 13.   ˡ Psalm liv. 6.

Neale noted that one stanza (which he omitted) was sung until the 17th century 'at the pious quaintness of which we can scarcely avoid a smile' :

> Be Thou, O Lord, the rider,   ... And we the little ass;
> That to God's Holy City ... Together we may pass.

Four 1861 hymnists   Baker; Dykes; Monk; Neale;

Henry Williams Baker   1821-1877
Editor of Hymns Ancient and Modern   1861
    O Praise ye the Lord   1875
    Praise, o praise my God and King   1861
    The King of Love my shepherd is   1868

John Bacchus Dykes (in full regalia)   1818-1866
    ST ANDREW …   1862   Christian dost thou …
    MELITA   1860   Eternal Father,
    LUX BENIGNA   1865   Lead, kindly light
    DOMINUS REGIT   1868   The King of Love
    GERONTIUS   1868   Praise to the holiest …

William H Monk   1823-1899
    EVENTIDE   1861   Abide with Me
    ALL THINGS BRIGHT   1887   All things bright and ….
    EVELYNS   1875   At the name of Jesus
    MONKLAND   1861   Praise, o praise, my god
    ST ETHELWALD   1861   Soldiers of Christ arise

John Mason Neale (Translator) 1818-1866
    All Glory, Laud and Honour   1851
    Blessed City, Heavenly Salem   1851
    Christian, dost thou see them   1862
    O come, O come, Emmanuel   1861
    (Good King Wenceslas)
    (Good Christian men, rejoice)
    and many others

All People that on Earth do Dwell

Genevan Psalter 1561 Psalm 100   trans Kethe dc1593   1560   5 verses
OLD HUNDREDTH   L Bourgeois   c1510-1559   1561   8.8.8.8 ie LM
Psalm 100:1   "Make a joyful noise unto the Lord, all ye lands"   Jubilate Deo

---

This piece is an old hymn and known as the Old Hundredth, the wording used is based on the Genevan Psalter of 1561. This set of versified and translated Psalms was compiled over several years at Geneva, then a centre of Protestant activity. The hymn is strongly linked to Calvin and his teaching that communal singing of psalms in the vernacular was a foundation of the new church's life.

William Kethe is identified as the translator [from Latin to English] and he wrote the first line as 'All People that on earth do dwell'. A Protestant, Kethe fled to the continent from Queen Mary of England's persecution of English Protestants in the late 1550s. He lived in Geneva for some time but travelled to Basel and Strasbourg to maintain contact with other English refugees. Kethe's paraphrase of 1560-1 in 'the old black-letter text of the period' began as follows:

Al people yt on earth do dwel,
sing to ye lord, with chereful voice
Him serve wt fear, his praise forth tel,
come ye before him and reioyce.

In truth, Kethe's work is as much a paraphrase or rewrite as an actual translation from the Latin. It was first published in five stanzas in an early collection entitled *Four Score and Seven Psalmes of David in English Mitre* [sic] and published in two versions with slight differences in 1561 which was appended to *The forme of prayers and ministration of the sacraments, &c. vsed in the English Congregation at Geneua* (1561).

In the publishing tumult of the period, it is not clear when the other 63 were added; there were many different, overlapping and underlapping volumes. In the 1562 *'Old Version' Whole Booke of Psalmes'* Kethe's version disappeared. In 1563 it re-appeared as one of two versions.

The spelling, phrasing and words show with astonishing clarity how English of 1560 is only just understandable, yet within 40 years we have the works of Shakespeare and the King James Bible which are easily read by modern people with only the rare difficulty. Elsewhere there are examples in earlier English and these are yet more surprisingly divergent. In the Protestant world, it is the only metrical psalm from the that period still in use. It has thus become an iconic emblem of the worship inspired by the Protestant exiles, for whom 'We are his folk' (verse 2,2) may have had a particular resonance – even if originally a misprint for 'flock'.

Kethe is thought to be one of the scholars who translated and published the English-language *Geneva Bible* (1560), a version favoured over the *King James Bible* by the Pilgrim Fathers. The twenty-five psalm versifications he prepared for the *Anglo-Genevan Psalter* of 1561 are found also in the *Scottish Psalter* of 1565. This versification of Psalm 100 is the only one that has found its way into modern psalmody. Kethe died in about 1593.

During the tumultuous religious upheaval of the Reformation, a group of British Protestants migrated to Geneva, mostly for the purpose of escaping the wrath of Queen Mary I (reigned 1553–1558). In Geneva, these English Protestants learned from the French disciples and colleagues of Calvin, (1509–1564), who had been preparing a complete metrical paraphrase of the Psalms. For the English edition, the Reformers used the work of Thomas Sternhold, a former 'groom of robes' of King Edward VI (reigned 1547–1553). Jean Calvin's influence was such that these melodies were intended to be sung as plainsong in the church but harmonized when in the home, as some home-churches still do.

The King James Bible has the translation of Psalm 100 as follows :-

100 v1 Make a joyful noise unto the Lord, all ye lands.
v2 Serve the Lord with gladness: come before his presence with singing.
v3 Know ye that the Lord he is God: it is he that hath made us, and not we ourselves; we are his people, and the sheep of his pasture.
v4 Enter into his gates with thanksgiving, and into his courts with praise: be thankful unto him, and bless his name.
v5 For the Lord is good; his mercy is everlasting; and his truth endureth to all generations.

Psalm 100 completes a collection of psalms that celebrate the Lord's righteous rule over all creation (Ps. 93, 95-99). Like the others, taking one historic-theological view, the original psalm was composed to be sung by the Levites at a high religious festival that annually celebrated the Lord's kingship over the entire world (perhaps the Feast of Tabernacles). Psalm 100 is thus a Hebrew equivalent of a vibrant call to worship the Lord with joyful song (verse 1, 3): the Lord is the one true God who made us to be 'the sheep of his pasture' (verse 2), and God's love and faithfulness never fail (verse 4).

Being such a significant Psalm, others have produced hymns from the text. Isaac Watts has two: 'Sing to the Lord with cheerful voice' as well as 'Before Jehovah's awful throne'. Rinkart has 'Now thank we all our God §'; another German, Neander has 'Praise to the Lord the Almighty §'; George Herbert 'Let all the world in every corner sing §'; yet another of the hymns in this collection is H W Baker's Praise, O Praise, my God and King §' … Hymnary.org lists an almost astonishing 297 but this includes several not in English and many for which Psalm 100 is not the major reference. In the 'minor reference' group are such as . 'O for a 1000 songs to sing §' & 'O God our help in ages past §'. Analysis can be overdone.

The most common tune for this is, surprisingly, also known as the Old Hundredth. The first half of the tune is a musical phrase which is found in various combinations both before and after that time; but the latter part of the tune, and its overall form, is the work of Loys Bourgeois. Guillaume Franc is named by some due to his being the editor of the *French Genevan Psalter*. The *Psalter Hymnal* includes both an English and a French versification.

Loys Bourgeois' melody was first used for Psalm 134 in the *Genevan Psalter* for which the best-known words for that are actually French. It is a very short psalm shown here.

'Vous, saints ministres du Seigneur,
Qui, devoues a son honneur,
Veülez la nuit dans sa maison,
presentez lui votre oraison'.

Or, in an English translation :

You faithful servants of the Lord,
sing out his praise with one accord,
while serving him with all your might
and keeping vigil through the night.

Bourgeois' setting then became used for this 'All People' text; and for other texts as well including that known as the Common Doxology §. The tune is used in some German Lutheran chorales; Bach wrote one called 'Herr Gott, dich loben alle wir' BWV 130.

While the Old 100th and GENEVAN 100 tunes are hugely the most common, there are so many others which fit the LM form. Hymnary lists another 12 including DUKE STREET; WILLS; PRAISE; ROCKINGHAM.

Another hymn commonly sung to Old 100th is 'Praise God, from Whom All Blessings Flow §,'; the finale is often referred to as the Doxology, written in 1674 by Bishop Thomas Ken; and it began as the final verse of a longer hymn 'Awake my soul and with the Sun'.

The traditional text for this finale is :-

> *Praise God, from Whom all blessings flow;*
> *Praise Him, all creatures here below;*
> *Praise Him above, ye heavenly host;*
> *Praise Father, Son, and Holy Ghost.*

The *Historical Companion* gives SIX harmonizations from the 16thC and the 17thC just for the Old 100th and there are many more LM settings which may or may not fit with the contour of the music. And, obviously, God knows how many alternatives of text, tune and combination have come since. An early version of the text is :-

1 All people that on earth do dwell,
   sing to the LORD with cheerful voice;
   Him serve with fear, his praise forth tell,
   come ye before him, and rejoice!

   [Refrain]   *Praise God, from Whom all blessings flow;*
   Praise Him, all creatures here below;
   Praise Him above, ye heavenly host;Praise Father, Son, and Holy Ghost.

2 The Lord, ye know is God indeed;
   Without our aid he did us make;
   We are the flock, he doth us feed,   *Note - some have 'folk'*
   And for his sheep he doth us take.   [Refrain]

3 O enter then his gates with Praise,
   Approach with joy his courts unto;
   Praise, laud, and bless his Name always,
   For it is seemly so to do.   [Refrain]

4 For why? The LORD our God is good;
   his mercy is for ever sure;
   His truth at all times firmly stood,
   and shall from age to age endure.   [Refrain]

4 To Father, Son and Holy Ghost,
   The God, whom heav'n and earth adore,
   From men and from the angel-host
   Be praise and glory evermore.   [Refrain]

Psalm 100: from the 17th Century

Psalme 100

He exhorteth all to serve the Lord, who hathe chosen us, and preserved us, and to entre into his assemblies to praise his Name.

Jubilate Deo. Pſal. c. J. H.

ALL people that on earth do dwell,
    ſing to the Lord with cheerful voice:
2 Him ſerve with fear, his praiſe forth tell,
    come ye before him and rejoice.
3 The Lord ye know is God indeed;
    without our aid he did us make;
We are his flock he doth us feed;
    and for his ſheep he doth us take.
4 O enter then his gates with Praiſe,
    approach with joy his Courts unto:
Praiſe, laud and bleſs his Name always,
    for it is ſeemly ſo to do.
5 For why? the Lord our God is good,
    his mercy is for ever ſure;
His truth at all times firmly ſtood.
    and ſhall from age to age endure.

Another of the ſame, by J. H.

IN God the Lord be glad and light,
    praiſe him throughout the earth
2 Serve him and come before his ſight
    with ſinging and with mirth.
3 Know that the Lord our God he is,
    he did us make and keep,
Not we our ſelves: for we are his
    own flock and paſture ſheep.
O go into his gates always,
    give thanks within the ſame
Within his courts ſet forth his praiſe,
    and laud his holy Name.
5 For why? the goodneſs of the Lord
    for evermore doth reign;
From age to age throughout the world
    his truth doth ſtill remain.

All Things Bright and Beautiful

	C F Alexander	1818-1895	1848	(7) 6 verses
per title	W H Monk§	1823-1889	1887	7.6.7.6
or ROYAL OAK	arrgd Martin Shaw	1875-1958	1916	

Genesis 1:31   "And God saw every thing that he had made, and, behold, it was very good."

The text was written by Cecil Frances Alexander (1818-1895) - despite the spelling of the names, Cecil was a girl as was Frances. She became the wife of the Bishop of Derry. In *Hymns for Little Children (*1848), Alexander wrote a set of 12 based the articles of the Creed for her godson. Here the line extracted from the Creed is 'Maker of Heaven and Earth'. The hymn has seven verses that expand this and build the simple creationist view of the natural world. From this dozen hymns from the Creed are two well-known pieces: 'Once in royal David's city (based on 'Conceived by the Holy Spirit,' etc.), and 'There is a green hill far away'§ (based on 'Suffered under Pontius Pilate,' etc.). The nine others are all less well-known. Mrs Alexander wrote several other sets of hymns, including ones based on the Baptism service, the Lord's Supper and the Ten Commandments.

For many centuries, the Apostles' Creed has been a vital tool for instruction in Christian doctrine. For just as long, it has been sung, either in chanted form in Latin or versified metrically into other languages. Metrical hymns based on the Creed sometimes encapsulate the entire text in a single hymn, or they are made in an extended form, with separate hymns for each of the twelve articles of the Creed. Mrs Alexander's set is not the only one.

Yet another inspiration could come from Coleridge's 1798 *Rime of the Ancient Mariner* 'He prayeth best, who loveth best; All things great and small; For the dear God who loveth us; He made and loveth all.' An equally old reference is to William Paley's *Natural Theology* of 1802, who cites wings and eyes as complex designs delivered by God the designer.

Despite, or perhaps because of being hymn for 'children' – some have tried to link the text or phrases to a huge number of biblical verses mentioning 'All things'; 'God Made'; 'How great is God' and similar. In the same way as noted later for 'purple-headed mountains' – analysis to such detail can be overdone.

In his book *The Gospel in Hymns*, Albert Bailey writes of this particular one, "For once Mrs. Alexander has forgotten her theology and lost herself in the beauty of nature". There may be truth in this; it is not difficult to get dazzled or even lost in the beauty of God's creation – in hill or valley, shore or plain, in daylight, twilight or starry night are wonders.

This hymn is available in an astonishing variety of hymnals, across the world. In the church world, especially amongst organists who are asked to play this very often, this hymn is often referred to as ATBB. Nowadays, ATBB is enjoyed by some; others feel is too childish. The original seven stanzas are now trimmed to 6 primarily because of what Percy Dearmer, the noted Christian Socialist, in 1933 called 'the appalling lines' of verse 3:

The rich man in his castle,   ... The poor man at his gate,
God made them high or lowly,   ... And ordered their estate.

Modern views are that this implies that God is responsible for inequality in the economic and social system – extremely unlikely to be the intended mid-Victorian sentiment which would ideally have pressed for the equality of rich and poor in the eyes of God. Such simplicity is, for some, too childish but the hymn's easy and timeless appeal is still much loved and enjoyed.

These lines have been interpreted as an expression of the theological view that society is ordered and upheld by Divine providence. Or that this view of social strata comes out of Alexander's identity as Anglo-Irish thus affirming the existing social order in the midst of the Irish potato famine. A milder interpretation of the third verse holds that Alexander was expressing the equality of rich and poor in the eyes of God. This is endorsed by a comparable text in her *Verses for Holy Seasons* (1846) 'The poor man in his straw-roofed cottage,/ The rich man in his lordly hall' and states that their prayers to God are of equal importance: 'He listens, and He answers all'.

Nevertheless, the sentiments of this verse are generally considered to be outdated and many later versions and performances of 'All Things Bright and Beautiful' omit this third verse. As noted, Percy Dearmer omitted the verse; his sympathy with Christian Socialism came to the fore and he wrote that the words reflected the "passivity and inertia at the heart of the British Establishment in the face of huge inequalities in Edwardian society". Dearmer then questioned whether Alexander had considered the parable of the Rich Man and Lazarus [Luke 16:19-31] and attributed her view of the world to her having 'been brought up in the atmosphere of a land-agent on an Irish estate'.

A less critical view of Mrs Alexander describes her thus 'She showed her concern for disadvantaged people by traveling many miles each day to visit the sick and the poor, providing food, warm clothes, and medical supplies. She and her sister founded a school for the deaf. She was much influenced by the Oxford Movement and by Keble's *Christian Year*. Her first book of poetry, *Verses for Seasons*, was an equivalent, a 'Christian Year' for children.'

Keble's 1827 book *'The Christian Year'* was hugely popular; a book of poems for the Sundays and feast days of the church year. It was very effective in spreading his devotional and theological views and became 'his great contribution to the Oxford Movement'.

Individual lines such as 'purple-headed mountain' have been 'identified' with specific locations such as Monmouthshire or Blorenge or Benevenagh (or surely indeed any heather-topped hill). Analysis can easily be taken further than is sensible.

Many will have noticed that the vet stories of James Herriott published in the 1970s used titles from this text: *All Creatures Great and Small; All Things Bright and Beautiful; All Things Wise and Wonderful* as well as *The Lord God Made Them All*. 'All Creatures' was also used for the (two) TV series and the 1993 film.

The hymn is commonly sung to the setting ALL THINGS BRIGHT AND BEAUTIFUL, composed by W H Monk in 1887. Another popular tune is ROYAL OAK which traces its first few bars back to the 17th-century English folk-tune '29th of May' [the date of the arrival in London of Charles II after the removal of the Commonwealth]. This was first published in *The Dancing Master* of 1686 and the tune was then arranged by Martin Shaw in 1916. Other settings and adaptations have come from John Rutter, John Stainer and Sir Frederick Ouseley.

Hymnary identifies the Monk and ROYAL OAK versions as much the most common settings. In addition, amongst the 20 or more tunes listed for this text are BREIDDEN; EDEN; GREYSTONE and SPOHR. The number of settings in 7.6.7.6 is numerous.

ATBB originally had seven stanzas and began 'All things bright and beauteous', with line 3 as 'All things wise and wondrous'. By the time of the 4th edition (1850) this had been changed to the present familiar opening. There is no stated intent for the first stanza was to repeat as a refrain, although that is now common practice.

There are different versions of the words - one heard on BBC Gardener's Time includes and which has been sung at gardeners' funerals.

> *All things spray and swattable ... Disasters great and small.*
> *All things paraquatable ... The Lord God made them all.*
> *The fungus on the goosegogs, ... The club root on the greens,*
> *The slugs that eat the lettuce ... And chew the aubergines!*

There are other parodies: The Monty Python's adaptation has

> *All things dull and dangerous, ... All creatures short and squat,*
> *All things rude and nasty, ... The Lord God made the lot.*
> *Each little snake that poisons, ... Each little wasp that stings,*
> *He made their brutish venom. ... He made their horrid wings.*

Alexander's final version of the text with all seven verses reads:

1. All things bright and beautiful, ... All creatures great and small,
   All things wise and wonderful, ... The Lord God made them all. *as Refrain*

2. Each little flower that opens, ... Each little bird that sings,
   He made their glowing colours, ... He made their tiny wings.

3. The rich man in his castle, ... The poor man at his gate,   (omitted)
   God made them, high or lowly, ... And ordered their estate.

4. The purple headed mountain, ... The river running by,
   The sunset and the morning, ... That brightens up the sky;

5. The cold wind in the winter, ... The pleasant summer sun,
   The ripe fruits in the garden, ... He made them every one;

6. The tall trees in the greenwood, ... The meadows where we play,
   The rushes by the water, ... We gather every day;

7. He gave us eyes to see them, ... And lips that we might tell
   How great is God Almighty, ... Who has made all things well.
   (Amen)

An extra verse can be inserted with American overtones :

> The Rocky Mountain splendour,   ... the lone wolf's haunting call,
> the Great Lakes and the prairies,   ... the forest in the fall.

Without considerable extra research, the existence of equivalent African, Indian, Australian verses across the English-speaking world is uncertain. With the enormous spread of this delightful child-oriented piece, there can be little doubt many schoolchildren have been asked to deliver equivalent extra lines. Fitting in koala, kangaroo and platypus is a task for others.

C F Alexander; Julia Howe; C Winkworth; J Irvine

Mrs C F Alexander   1818-1895
     All things bright and beautiful   1848
     (Once in Royal David's city)   1848
     There is a green hill far away   1848

Julia Howe   1819-1910
     Mine eyes have seen the Glory   1861

Mrs Catherine Winkworth   (Translator)   1827-1878
     Now thank we all our God   1858
     Praise to the Lord, the Almighty   1863

Jessie Irvine   1836 – 1887
     CRIMOND The Lord's my Shepherd 1871

Amazing Grace

| | John Newton | 1725-1807 | 1779 | 6 verses |
| NEW BRITAIN | Lucius Chapin | 1760-1842 | 1829 | 8.6.8.6 |

I Chronicles 17:16-17   "Faith's review and expectation"   as per *Olney Hymns No.53*

The key themes in these Newton verses are faith in salvation, wonder at God's grace, his love for Jesus, and his cheerful exclamations of the joy he found in his faith. Newton wrote the words from personal experience. Growing up without any particular religious conviction, his life held a wild variety of twists and coincidences. Pressed (conscripted) into service in the Royal Navy, later, he worked in the Atlantic slave trade. Newton often openly mocked the captain with obscene poems and songs about him, which became so popular that the crew began to join in. His disagreements with several colleagues resulted in his being starved almost to death, imprisoned while at sea, and chained like the slaves they carried.

While aboard the ship Greyhound, Newton gained notoriety as being one of the most profane men the captain had ever met. In a culture where sailors habitually swore, Newton was admonished several times for not only using the worst words the captain had ever heard, but creating new ones to exceed the limits of verbal debauchery.

In 1748, a violent storm battered Greyhound off the coast of Ireland, so severely that he called out to God for mercy – and began his conversion. He continued slaving until 1754 or 1755, when he ended his seafaring altogether. In between voyages, he married Polly in 1750, despite her family's concern at what they knew of Newton. He found it more difficult to leave her at the beginning of each trip. After three more shipping voyages in the slave trade, Newton was promised a position as ship's captain with cargo unrelated to slavery. But at the age of thirty, he collapsed and never sailed again.

In 1756 in Liverpool, Newton began to teach himself Latin, Greek, and theology. He and Polly immersed themselves in the church community, and Newton's passion was so impressive that his friends suggested he become a priest in the Church of England. Turned down at first, he wrote about his experiences in the slave trade and his conversion. This was sufficient for him to be allowed to study for the priesthood.

Newton began studying Christian theology further and later became an abolitionist. Ordained in 1764, Newton became curate in Buckinghamshire at Olney. There he began to wrote hymns with the poet William Cowper. 'Amazing Grace' was written to accompany the sermon on New Year's Day of 1773. Unless there was suitable music – and that is unknown – it would likely have been chanted by the congregation.

In the parish of some 2,500 people, Newton's preaching was unique in that he shared many of his own experiences from the pulpit; many clergy preached from a distance, not admitting any intimacy with temptation or sin. Newton was involved in his parishioners' lives and was much loved, although his writing and delivery were sometimes unpolished. But his devotion and conviction were apparent and forceful, and he often said his mission was to 'break a hard heart and to heal a broken heart'.

The sermon preached by Newton was among the last of those that William Cowper heard in Olney, since Cowper's mental instability returned shortly thereafter. One author suggests Newton may have had his friend in mind, employing the themes of assurance and deliverance from despair for Cowper's benefit.

The New Testament is the basis for many of the lyrics of 'Amazing Grace'. The first verse, for example, can be traced to the story of the Prodigal Son as described by Luke. The father says, 'For this son of mine was dead and is alive again; he was lost, and is found'.

With the message that forgiveness and redemption are possible regardless of sins committed and that the soul can be delivered from despair through the mercy of God, 'Amazing Grace' is one of the most recognisable songs in the English-speaking world. The *Olney Hymn Book* itself links the hymn with 1 Chronicles 17: 16-17, where David exclaims in humble wonder at what the prophet, Nathan, has just said about God's care for him from his early days. Newton implicitly applies this to his own experience of divine grace.

Newton wrote in 1779, "*How industrious is Satan served. I was formerly one of his active undertemptors and had my influence been equal to my wishes I would have carried all the human race with me. A common drunkard or profligate is a petty sinner to what I was. … Like an unwary sailor who quits his port just before a rising storm, I renounced the hopes and comforts of the Gospel at the very time when every other comfort was about to fail me*".

One modern critic wrote about Newton, specifically referring to 'Amazing Grace', as an 'unashamedly middlebrow lyricist writing for a lowbrow congregation', noting that only twenty-one of the nearly 150 words used in all six verses have more than one syllable.

The Dictionary of American Hymnology writes rather: 'Amazing Grace' is Newton's spiritual autobiography in verse'.

Contrastingly, John Julian§, the hymn historian, bluntly said in 1892 'outside of the United States the song was unknown and it was far from being a good example of Newton's work.'

First published in Book 1 of *Olney Hymn*s in 1779, 'On select Passages of Scripture', it had six Common Metre verses with the title 'Faith's Review and Expectation'. The lyrics there were arranged by their association to the Biblical verses that would be used by Newton and Cowper in their prayer meetings. The impact of their Olney Hymns was immediate. Scholars appreciated Cowper's poetry more than Newton's plaintive and plain language although this better fitted his forceful personality.

Mid 17th century hymnbooks did not contain music and were simply small books of religious poetry. The first time Newton's lines were joined to music was in 1808 in *A Companion to the Countess of Huntingdon's Hymns* using the tune HEPHZIBAH by English composer John Husband.

The effect of the lyrical arrangement, according to Bruce Hindmarsh, allows an instant release of energy in the exclamation 'Amazing grace!', to be followed by a qualifying reply in 'how sweet the sound'. One analyst says 'Newton's use of an exclamation at the beginning of his verse is 'crude but effective' in an overall composition of 'a forceful, if simple, statement of faith'. Grace is used three times in the second verse, building to Newton's most personal story of his conversion, underscoring the use of his private testimony with his parishioners.

While the hymn was forgotten in England, in the USA it was treasured. 'Amazing Grace' became a popular song used by Baptist and Methodist preachers as part of their evangelizing, especially in the South, during the Second Great Awakening of the early 19th century. It was quickly associated with more than 20 melodies; including EVAN; PISGAH; PRIMROSE and IN THE PINES. All suit the Common Metre used by the majority of the repertoire. The 8.6.8.6 metre fits settings such as Carl Glazer's AZMON; WARWICK; Arne's ARLINGTON and many others.

In about 1829 it was partnered with the American folk melody by Lucius Chapin now known as NEW BRITAIN. This setting was a melding of GALLAHER and ST MARY. William Walker is mentioned here – but he was only the editor of an 1835 collection.

The joining of the words with NEW BRITAIN was, according to author Steve Turner, a 'marriage made in heaven … the music behind 'amazing' had a sense of awe to it. The music behind 'grace' sounded graceful. There was a rise at the point of confession, as though the author was stepping out into the open and making a bold declaration'.

Taken from the Olney Hymns facsimile – the original words are as follows:

1   Amazing grace! how sweet the sound   ... That sav'd a wretch like me!
    I once was lost, but now am found,   ... Was blind, but now I see.

2   'Twas grace that taught my heart to fear, ... And grace my fears reliev'd;
    How precious did that grace appear   ... The hour I first believ'd!

3   Thro' many dangers, toils, and snares   ... I have already come;
    'Tis grace hath brought me safe thus far, ... And grace will lead me home.

4   The Lord has promis'd good to me,   ... His word my hope secures;
    He will my shield and portion be   ... As long as life endures.

5   Yes, when this flesh and heart shall fail, ... And mortal life shall cease,
    I shall possess, within the veil,   ... A life of joy and peace.

6   The earth shall soon dissolve like snow, ... The sun forbear to shine;
    But God, who call'd me here below,   ... Will be forever mine.

Harriet Beecher Stowe's 1852 anti-slavery novel *Uncle Tom's Cabin* has three verses sung by Tom in his hour of deepest crisis. Stowe added another verse, not written by Newton, that had come down orally in African-American communities for some 50 years. It was one of some 70 verses from 'Jerusalem, My Happy Home', in a 1790 *Collection of Sacred Ballads*. Strangely, the most verses I can find is a mere 25.

When we've been there ten thousand years,   ... Bright shining as the sun,
We've no less days to sing God's praise,   ... Than when we first begun.

For many African Americans it is taken as the 'paradigmatic Negro spiritual' because it expresses the joy felt at being delivered from slavery and worldly miseries.
===

In Passing – why does it seem you sometimes get the 'wrong' music?

As these notes make clear, some texts have more than one 'well-known' tune; and organists are human. They may move from church to chapel to cathedral as their work demands – but they know the tunes they've been taught. And the cleric at each site knows what they want. Sometimes a particular congregation or cleric will 'know' what the correct tune is. But they can differ as to their choice – and as a mere congregant or even as a chorister being led by the choir-master – there is little choice but to listen and deliver.

It's embarrassing for everyone when there's a hiccup. Even at my own father's funeral! But it's never deliberate – it actually shows there is choice.

Olney Hymns 1779 : Frontispiece 1795; Newton, Cowper,

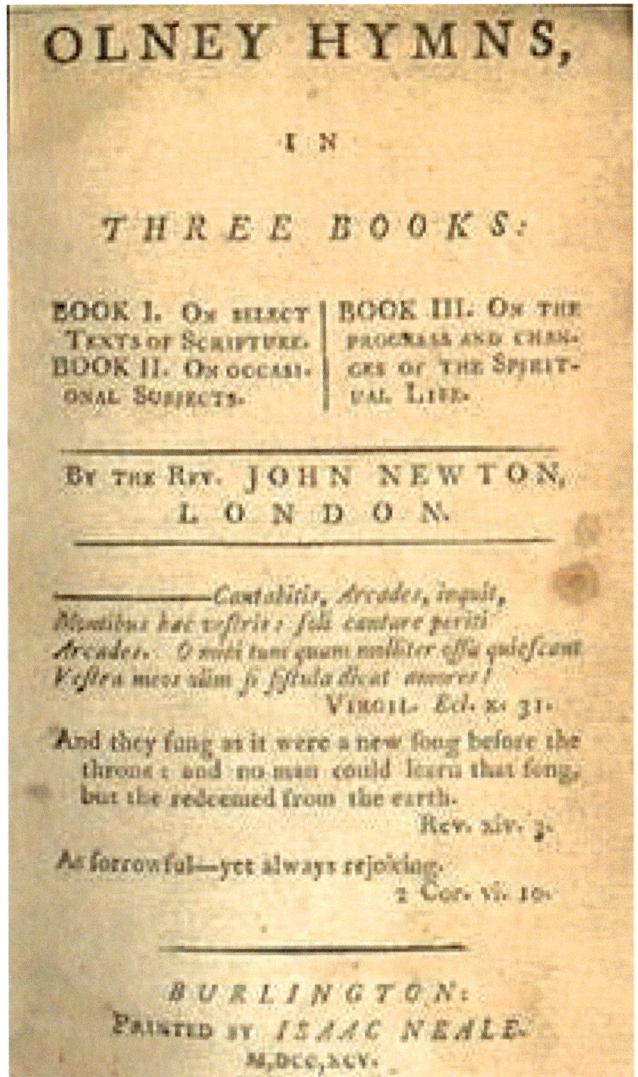

Newton's handwritten original text for #256 'Father Forgive them'

"Father forgive", (the Savior said,) They know not what they do"

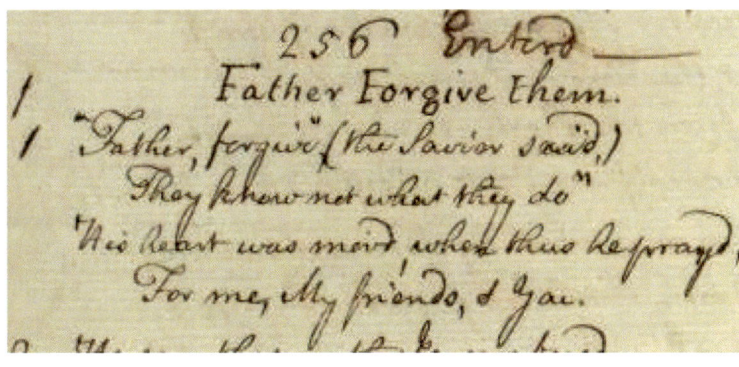

And can it be, that I should gain

	Charles Wesley§ 1707-1788	1747	5 verses
SAGINA	T Campbell 1800-1876	1825	8.8.8.8.8.8

The first draft was finished – and there were several Wesley hymns already included – and someone said 'if Wesley is that important, you could add 'And can it be' so that one of his should be the first entry too'. And, yea, verily, so it came to pass – near the beginning.

First published in *Hymns and Sacred Poems* (1739) in five 6-line stanzas, with the title 'Free Grace', it was thought Charles Wesley§ wrote this at the time of his conversion, but now, the belief is it was rather 'Where shall my wond'ring soul begin' which seems more apposite. 'And can it be', using the same 8x6 metre, is now taken as following shortly after.

They share the same message of personal salvation through the death and resurrection of Jesus. Wesley wrote a series of spiritual-autobiographical hymns in this period, and few enable the singer to share in the author's wonder and thankfulness as deeply as this. His diary of the date gives minute details of the mental and spiritual struggles through which he passed, evidences of which and the final triumph, are [for experts] clearly traceable in both hymns.

As often with Wesleyan pieces, it is the text and the tune and the meaning all together that makes it a whole. And thus it is still a very popular Methodist hymn. The hymn is in the 20th-century hymn books of almost all nonconformist denominations.

In John Wesley's 1780 *Collection of Hymns for the Use of the People called Methodists* verse 5 was omitted. It has been customary to omit that verse in most books since that time:

> Still the small inward Voice I hear,
>   That whispers all my Sins forgiv'n;
> Still the attoning Blood is near,   [a printing error for 'atoning']
>   That quench'd the Wrath of hostile Heav'n:
> I feel the Life his Wounds impart;
> I feel my Saviour in my Heart.

In a compact poetic manner, this text exclaims the mystery of God's grace extended to sinners who turn to Christ in faith. These sinners receive the righteousness of Christ and can approach the Lord's throne in confidence. Such is the amazing love of God in Christ!

The whole hymn succeeds in conveying the 'amazing love' of the Free Grace of the poem's title. That love is so profound and amazing that even the first-born Seraph (almost certainly the seraph of light, from Milton, *Paradise Lost Book III* line 1) cannot comprehend it.

The first three stanzas of this hymn explore both the contrast between the glory of heaven that Christ came from and the suffering He endured on earth, and the mystery of the love that motivated Him to make that journey. The final stanza is a jubilant celebration of our new state in Christ and the privilege of communion with God that we enjoy.

John Julian§ summarises very tidily: in 1716, aged 9, Charles Wesley went to Westminster School, being provided with a home and board by his elder brother Samuel, then usher at the school, until 1721, when he was elected King's Scholar, and as such received his board and education free. In 1726 he was elected to a Westminster studentship at Christ Church, Oxford, where he took his degree in 1729, and became a college tutor. In the early part of the same year his religious impressions were much deepened, and he became one of the first band of 'Oxford Methodists'.

On April 8, 1749, he married Miss Sarah Gwynne. His marriage, unlike that of his brother John, was a most happy one; his wife was accustomed to accompany him on his evangelistic journeys, which were as frequent as ever until the year 1756, when he ceased to itinerate, and mainly devoted himself to the care of the Societies in London and Bristol. Bristol was his headquarters until 1771, when he removed with his family to London, and, besides attending to the Societies, devoted himself much, as he had done in his youth, to the spiritual care of prisoners in Newgate.

As a hymn-writer Charles Wesley was unique. He is said to have written no less than 6500 hymns, and though, of course, in so vast a number some are of unequal merit, it is perfectly marvellous how many there are which rise to the highest degree of excellence. His feelings on every occasion of importance, whether private or public, found their best expression in a hymn. His own conversion, his own marriage, the earthquake panic, the rumours of an invasion from France, the defeat of Prince Charles Edward at Culloden, the Gordon riots, every Festival of the Christian Church, every doctrine of the Christian Faith, striking scenes in Scripture history, striking scenes which came within his own view, the deaths of friends as they passed away, one by one, before him, all furnished occasions for the exercise of his divine gift. Nor must we forget his hymns for little children, a branch of sacred poetry in which the mantle of Dr. Watts seems to have fallen upon him.

It would be simply impossible within our space to enumerate even those of the hymns which have become really classic. The saying that a really good hymn is as rare an appearance as that of a comet is falsified by the work of Charles Wesley; for hymns, which are really good in every respect, flowed from his pen in quick succession, and death alone stopped the course of the perennial stream; [direct quotes from Julian's 1892 *Dictionary of Hymnology*].

Thomas Campbell made little impact apart from this tune; born in Sheffield, Yorkshire in 1800, he died there in 1876. In 1825 he published *The Bouquet*: a collection of tunes composed and adapted to Wesley's Hymns which included 23 tunes, all of which were given botanical names; the most well-known is SAGINA (PEARLWORT). Actually, SAGINA was written for another hymn by Wesley – a translation of a German hymn 'Thee will I love, my strength, my tow'r' from 'Ich will dich lieben, meine Stärke'.

The setting has been fitted to other texts including – 'Behold the servant of the Lord'; 'Ancient of Days! The years roll on'; 'Object of all our knowledge here'; 'How shall the young direct their way' and others. Musicologist Percy Scholes views this type of tune as 'Old Methodist' and considers that its style was influenced by the choruses of G F Handel.

Attempts have been made to provide alternatives to this rumbustious tune; ABINGDON by Erik Routley; DIDSBURY by Cyril Taylor; as well as others, none has taken over.

Earlier tunes in the 100 years before SAGINA, included SURREY by Henry Carey; CRUCIFIXION by Samuel Akeroyde; and another called BIRMINGHAM from 1786.

No Bible verse is attached to the text, so interested parties have taken it upon themselves to link verses to phrases as they will – some dealing with spiritual or mental rebirth or others who write of resurrection.

An early version of the text, with an extra verse added later, is as follows :
In some hymnals, the first verse's last two lines are the refrain, in others each verse's last lines are repeated.

    1   And can it be, that I should gain
         An int'rest in the Saviour's blood?
         Died He for me, who caus'd His pain?
         For me, who Him to death pursu
    2   ed?
         Amazing love! how can it be
         That Thou, my God, should die for me?
             Refrain: Amazing love! how can it be
                           That Thou, my God, should die for me!

    2   'Tis mystery all! Th'Immortal dies!
         Who can explore His strange design?
         In vain the first-born seraph tries
         To sound the depths of love divine!
         'Tis mercy all! let earth adore,
         Let angel minds inquire no more.   [Refrain]

    3   He left His Father's throne above -
         So free, so infinite His grace -
         Emptied Himself of all but love,
         And bled for Adam's helpless race:
         'Tis mercy all, immense and free;
         For, O my God, it found out me!   [Refrain]

    4   Long my imprisoned spirit lay
         Fast bound in sin and nature's night;
         Thine eye diffused a quick'ning ray, -
         I woke, the dungeon flamed with light;
         My chains fell off, my heart was free,
         I rose, went forth, and followed Thee.   [Refrain]

    5.   Still the small inward voice I hear,   [Later addition]
         That whispers all my sins forgiven;
         Still the atoning blood is near,
         That quenched the wrath of hostile Heaven.
         I feel the life His wounds impart;
         I feel the Saviour in my heart.   [Refrain]

    6   No condemnation now I dread;
         Jesus, and all in Him, is mine!
         Alive in Him, my living Head,
         And clothed in righteousness divine,
         Bold I approach th'eternal throne,
         And claim the crown, through Christ my own. [Refrain] Amen.

Wesley's handwritten copy of 'Christ, the Lord is ris'n today' with the heading Hymn for our Lord's Resurrection.

and the Title Page from a 1739 edition of the *Hymns and Sacred Poems*.

And did those feet in ancient time

	William Blake	1757-1827	1808	2 verses
JERUSALEM	C H Parry	1848-1918	1916	8.8.8.8

Revel 21:2   "And I, John, saw the holy city, new Jerusalem …."

Despite the power of the words, it is unlikely that it would have become so famous without the setting by Hubert Parry, which carries the words so powerfully. Perhaps because the rhythm is so complex, there is no other significant setting. Walford Davies' motet of 1907 is now nigh-on forgotten.

If you look up 'Blake' and 'Jerusalem' you can easily be taken to a poem called *Jerusalem, the Emanation of the Giant Albion*. It is quite confusing that this hymn is referred to as 'Jerusalem' as the name is only mentioned once. In addition, the correct source is Blake's *Milton: a Poem in two Books* of 1808 being the last but one of his Prophetic Books. *Milton* is shorter and more specific in scope than *Jerusalem, the Emanation*.

The exact original text is in the Preface to Book 1 and is found following the strange heading beginning "The Stolen and Perverted Writings of Homer & Ovid: of Plato & Cicero, which all Men ought to contemn: …" Blake's verse follows before he writes "Would to God that all the Lord's people were prophets!" a quote from Numbers 11:29 which does not seem an immediate fit. The poem has Milton returning to preach the message of Christ crucifed and the importance of self-sacrifice and forgiveness.

Bypassing the long-ago mis-labelling, these two verses are Blake at his most inspired and prophetic, as the demand for the chariot of fire suggests. He is recalling England in its ideal state as a green and pleasant land in which the holy Lamb of God could be found and the Divine Countenance could shine; to a time before the Fall; in which the City of God, Jerusalem itself, might have existed, in the minds of men and women if not in stone.

Now there are the dark Satanic mills, perhaps the factories of the Industrial Revolution, but also symbolic as a mill (like the flour mill near his childhood home) that grinds down the individual human spirit and reduces it to slavery or like the Church tries to squeeze out all attempts at dissension or non-conformity. This is why he resolves never to cease from mental fight, and never to let his sword become idle: he wants to restore his own country to a state in which it is once again an ideal place, where Jerusalem, the holy city, is to be found. The poem is a magnificent vision of an ideal.

The piece in Milton that is used for this hymn was inspired by the unlikely tale that the young Jesus was brought to England by Joseph of Arimathea. The British folklore scholar A W Smith made it clear he thought there was little evidence of such a story or even of any oral tradition before the early twentieth century.

The obvious references in the text are to the Book of Revelation and the Second Coming where Jesus establishes the New Jerusalem [Revel 3:12 & 21:2]. The Church of England has often allowed Jerusalem as a metaphor for Heaven - a place of universal love and peace.

The complex text allows for great deal of analysis and interpretation. The standard view is that Blake was referring to the Industrial Revolution and a hoped-for new Renaissance from the wealth which drove the nation to a wonderful new position. Blake asks questions at the beginning. Was there a Divine visit? Was there briefly Heaven in England?

The second verse is a riposte; an exhortation to create an ideal society. It is certain that Blake despised the repressive ideology and the effective enslavement of his countrymen.

The non-conformists saw the great enemy, the dark, as the Church of England. Their view being based on their dislike, even disapproval, of the 'official' preaching of a doctrine of conformity to the established social order and class system, in contrast to Blake.

There are yet other interpretations: When Blake's Milton poem notes Stonehenge and other megaliths - do they relate somehow to the oppressive power of priestcraft in general?

The line from the poem 'Bring me my Chariot of fire!' links to 2 Kings 2:11 where the Old Testament prophet Elijah is taken directly to heaven: "And it came to pass, as they still went on, and talked, that, behold, there appeared a chariot of fire, and horses of fire, and parted them both asunder; and Elijah went up by a whirlwind into heaven".

The final phrase 'green and pleasant land' is now a standard metaphor for an identifiably English landscape or society – as a complete contrast to the earlier 'dark, satanic mills'.

It was Parry's setting that began to turn the whole into something approaching a national anthem. Indeed the work has become criticised as a 'national anthem' although how Jerusalem is such a link is unclear – other than in these particular lines.

C H Parry (1848-1918) was born in Bournemouth - grandson of a wealthy director of the East India Company until its dissolution in 1874. His mother died of consumption 12 days after his birth; his father remarried when he was three, and his stepmother favoured her own children over her stepchildren, so he and his two siblings were sometimes left out.

At the age of 13 in 1861 he studied with S S Wesley and went to the Three Choirs Festival' in Hereford, where works by Mendelssohn, Mozart, Handel, and Beethoven were performed. That left a great impression on him. It also sparked the beginning of a lifelong association with the festival. That year, his brother was disgraced at Oxford for drug and alcohol use, and his sister, Lucy, died of consumption. Both events saddened Hubert. However, he began study at Eton College and distinguished himself at both sport and music. He also began having heart trouble, that would plague him the rest of his life.

Eton was not known for its music program, and although some others had interest in music, there were no teachers there that could help Hubert much. He turned to George Elvey, organist of St George's Chapel, Windsor Castle, and started studying with him in 1863. Hubert eventually wrote some anthems for the choir of St George's Chapel, and eventually earned his music degree. While still at Eton, Hubert sat for the Oxford Bachelor of Music exam, the youngest person ever to have done so. His exam exercise, a cantata: 'O Lord, Thou hast cast us out' astonished the Heather Professor of Music, Sir Frederick Ouseley, and was triumphantly performed and published in 1867.

In 1918 he contracted Spanish flu during the global pandemic and died at Knightscroft, Rustington, West Sussex. In 2015 they found 70 unpublished works of Parry's hidden away in a family archive, some never performed. The documents were sold at auction for a large sum.

Parry worked with George Grove, first as a contributor to the *Dictionary of Music* in the 1870s and '80s, and then in 1883 as professor of composition and musical history at the Royal College of Music, of which Grove was the first head. In 1895 Parry succeeded Grove, remaining as head until his death. He wrote several books about music and music history, the best-known of which is probably his 1909 study of J S Bach. He also wrote the setting REPTON for 'Dear Lord and Father of Mankind'. Even in his lifetime and later, Parry's reputation and critical standing have varied.

Blake's poem, which had fallen out of memory during the century which followed its writing, was included in the 1916 patriotic anthology of verse The Spirit of Man, edited by Robert Bridges, then Poet Laureate. The anthology was aimed at helping against the decline in morale because of the high number of casualties in World War I and the perception that there was no end in sight.

Under these circumstances, Bridges, found the poem an appropriate hymn text to "brace the spirit of the nation [so as to] accept with cheerfulness all the sacrifices necessary". He asked Sir Hubert Parry to put it to music for a Fight for Right campaign meeting in London's Queen's Hall. Bridges asked Parry to supply "suitable, simple music to Blake's stanzas – music that an audience could take up and join in", and added that, if Parry could not do it himself, he might delegate the task to Parry's friend, George Butterworth.

Parry determined on turning the text into two eight-line verses. There is a four-bar introduction to each verse and a coda echoing motifs in the song. He did also alter 'these' to 'those' dark satanic mills'.

Due to late reluctance at supporting such an ultra-patriotic event, Parry handed the task of conducting to his former student Walford Davies. The concert was a huge success, but again Parry had concerns. Fortunately, the National Union of Women's Suffrage took up the anthemic hymn and Parry was delighted. After this second concert, Millicent Fawcett, leader of NUWS, asked the composer if it might become the Women Voters' Hymn. Parry wrote back, "I wish indeed it might become the Women Voters' hymn, as you suggest".

> And did those feet in ancient time
> Walk upon England's mountains green?
> And was the holy Lamb of God
> On England's pleasant pastures seen?
>
> And did the Countenance Divine
> Shine forth upon our clouded hills?
> And was Jerusalem builded here
> Among these dark Satanic Mills?
>
> Bring me my bow of burning gold!
> Bring me my Arrows of desire!
> Bring me my Spear! O clouds, unfold!
> Bring me my Chariot of Fire!
>
> I will not cease from Mental Fight,
> Nor shall my Sword sleep in my hand,
> Till we have built Jerusalem
> In England's green & pleasant Land.

F W Bateson, the mid-20th century critic noted how "the adoption by the Churches and women's organizations of this anti-clerical paean of free love is an amusing evidence of the carelessness with which poetry is read".

Alternatively, "The ideal of social justice and the good society has never been better expressed than in these verses". With complex interpretation there is always a choice of view.

In modern times, Billy Bragg, the socialist singer, asked what we would find now in modern Britain and he wrote a new verse to make clear his feelings.

William Blake   1757 - 1827

Blake was an English poet, artist, illustrator, painter, and printmaker. His idiosyncratic lifestyle and belief in 'self' made him very interesting to the Victorian Romantics and to the New-Elizabethans. His visual artistry led 21st-century critic J Jones to say 'far and away the greatest artist Britain has ever produced'. Largely unrecognised during his life, Blake is now considered a seminal figure in the British poetry and art.   Consistency, foolish or otherwise, is one of Blake's chief preoccupations, just as 'self-contradiction' is always one of his most contemptuous comments.

Blake's prophetic books are a series of lengthy, interrelated poetic works are linked by Blake's own personal mythology. This schema is largely Biblical in inspiration and it has been extensively debated for both its political and religious content.

The 12 pieces have been described as forming 'what is in proportion to its merits the least read body of poetry in the English language'. While Blake worked as a commercial illustrator, these books were ones that he produced, with his own engravings, as an extended and largely private project. These works concluded with the epic *Jerusalem, the Emanation of the Giant Albion.* The previous book *Milton,* an epic poem, written and illustrated between 1804 and 1810. Its hero is John Milton, who returns from Heaven and unites with Blake to explore the relationship between living writers and their predecessors, and to undergo a mystical journey to correct his own spiritual errors. This *Milton* was printed in his unique combination of etched text and illustration enhanced by watercolour.

Although Blake was considered mad by contemporaries for his idiosyncratic views, he is held in high regard by later critics for his expressiveness and creativity, and for the philosophical and mystical undercurrents within his work. His paintings and poetry have been characterised as part of the Romantic movement and as 'Pre-Romantic'. A committed Christian who was hostile to the Church of England (indeed, to almost all forms of organised religion), Blake was influenced by the ideals of the French and American revolutions.

Since his death, William Blake has been claimed by those of various movements who apply his complex and often elusive use of symbolism and allegory to the issues that concern them. Blake was critical of the marriage laws of his day, and generally railed against traditional Christian notions of chastity as a virtue. It is true that, partly due to Catherine's apparent inability to bear children, he did suggest bringing a second wife into the house. His work also says that external demands for marital fidelity reduce love to mere duty rather than authentic affection, and he decries jealousy and egotism in marriage.

Blake's later writings show a renewed interest in Christianity, although he radically reinterprets Christian morality in a way that embraces sensual pleasure, there is little of the sexual libertarianism of some early poems, and there is advocacy of 'self-denial', though his abnegation must be inspired by love rather than authoritarian compulsion.

While Blake had a significant role in the pre-Raphaelite world, it was in the Modernist period that this work began to influence a wider set of writers and artists.

What remains of his work is remarkable. Sadly, his friends destroyed quantities of his papers: Tatham after conversion to the fundamentalist Irvingites where the conservative members deemed the work heretical (to them); D G Rossetti's brother destroyed ones if he judged them lacking quality; Linnell because of the sexual content. Blake said he had written 20 unpublished works 'as long as Macbeth' – none survive.

𝔄ngel-𝔙oices, 𝔈ver 𝔖inging

	Francis Pott	1832-1909	1861	5 verses
per Title	E G Monk	1819-1900	1861	8.5.8.5.8.4.3

Ecclesiasticus 51:22 "The lord hath given me a tongue …and I will praise Him therewith".

There is no clear Bible verse stating when, where or how much the angels sing – though a great many verses do mention singing to God, or for God and similar. Certainly, little is said in reference to the Medieval puzzle about Angels atop a needle, nor anything as to whether they sang at that time. The verse attributed to this hymn in the *Hymns Ancient and Modern* is from in the Apocrypha, therefore it is not linked to any part of the Christmas story.

This hymn is the work of Francis Pott born 1832 and died in 1909. It was written in 1861 for his friend and contemporary at Brasenose College, Oxford, William Kenneth Macrorie, who was then Perpetual Curate of Wingates, Bolton-le-Moors, Lancashire. Written for the dedication of a new organ, it was first entitled 'For the Dedication of an Organ or for a Meeting of Choirs'. It was published in the Second Edition of Pott's 1866 collection *Hymns fitted to the Order of Common Prayer'* and rapidly became popular. One commentator writes 'Despite criticism, (it is not clear about what!) the hymn remains constant in many books.'

More precisely, the 1861 book was *'Hymns fitted to the Order of Common Prayer, and Administration of the Sacraments, and other Rites and Ceremonies of the Church, According to the Use of the Church of England, To which are added Hymns for Certain Local Festivals.'*

On this occasion, the tune came before the text. The tune, ANGEL VOICES, was written by E G Monk, another of Macrorie's friends; both taught at St Peter's College, Radley. Pott and Monk may therefore have worked together on the piece for their friend. E G Monk is no relation of the better known W H Monk and so is linked only as a friend of friends and working on hymns.

The wording has been occasionally altered, most frequently in verse 4 where in the last line 'Psalmody' appears as 'Melody' in an 1872 hymn book. Some books begin verse 3, 'Yea, we know…', with 'Lord, we know', making it easier for the hymn to be started at that point.

Musically, Pott writes a complex metre (8.5.8.5.8.4.3) and an equally complex rhyming scheme (ababccb) and what the Canterbury Dictionary of Hymnology calls 'numerous enjambements'. This required Monk to produce a tune of equal inventive merit. Several others which cope with the this complex metre have the names EIDE, MAIQUEZ, ARTHOG and MIDHURST. Generally these grace but a single hymnal, sometimes two.

One commentator writes 'Lines one and two work together as a musical unit reach the first melodic climax at 'ever ringing; lines three and four also make a unit. The last three irregular lines - 8.4.3. - which reflect the Tractarian fondness for refrains are distinctive for their dissonant sequence.' While the text may appear to be the most important component of a hymn, the setting, rhythm, metre and overall structure of the music can make the difference between dull, ordinary and wonderful.

In 1872, Arthur Sullivan wrote a separate tune, which was also called 'Angel Voices' for the hymn. Though it gained popularity in the United States and was published with it, Pott did not like Sullivan's tune and banned it from being published alongside his words.

Pott stated quite vigorously "*I am afraid that some of its popularity arose from Sullivan having, contrary to my desire, set it in The Hymnary to a pretty, trivial but altogether unfit tune of his own – which caught the ear of people who did not trouble themselves to see that the hymn was of quite another character. In giving permission since for the printing of the hymn I have always made it a condition that Sullivan's tune shall not be in any way referred to"*.

An early version of the text is as follows :

1. Angel voices ever singing
round Thy throne of light,
angel harps, forever ringing,
rest not day nor night;
thousands only live to bless Thee
and confess thee Lord of might.

2. Thou who art beyond the farthest
mortal eye can scan,
can it be that Thou regardest
songs of sinful man?
Can we feel that Thou art near us
and wilt hear us? Yea, we can.

3. Yea, we know Thy love rejoices   [Alternative start]
o'er each work of Thine;
Thou didst ears and hands and voices
for Thy praise combine;
craftsman's art and music's measure
for Thy pleasure didst design.

4. Here, great God, today we offer
of Thine own to Thee;
and for Thine acceptance proffer,
all unworthily,
hearts and minds, and hands and voices
in our choicest melody.

5. Honor, glory, might, and merit
Thine shall ever be,
Father, Son, and Holy Spirit,
blessed Trinity:
of the best that Thou hast given
earth and heaven render Thee.

Angels, from the Realms of Glory

	James Montgomery §	1771-1854	1816	6, 5, 6 verses
REGENT SQUARE	H Smart	1813-1879	1860	8.7.8.7 & Refrain

Luke 2:13   "And suddenly there was with the angel ….the heavenly host praising God".

Rather obviously, this is based on the section in the Gospel of Luke where the shepherds are outside Bethlehem and encounter a multitude of angels singing and praising the new-born Christ child. Perhaps because he knew the psalms so well, Montgomery§ expresses a cosmic sense in this text: he reaches from Christ's incarnation to the final great day. The text successively incorporates all creatures–the angels (verse 1), the shepherds (verse 2), the wise men (verse 3), saints (verse 4), sinners [all people] (verse 5), and all nations (verse 6) –in the call to 'come and worship Christ, the newborn King!'

This hymn was first published in Montgomery's newspaper, *The Sheffield Iris* on Christmas Eve 1816, in five 6-line stanzas, entitled 'Nativity'. In 1825 it was slightly altered by him, and re-titled 'Good tidings of great joy to all people'.

Of the original five verses, many hymnals now delete the fifth and others, as here, deliver a replacement. It is, what some see as, the severe opening of the 5th verse which has caused many editors to omit it:

> Sinners, wrung with true repentance, … Doomed for guilt to endless pains,
> Justice now revokes the sentence,   … Mercy calls you; break your chains

This is frequently replaced by a stanza beginning 'Though an infant now we view him' from another hymn in the Religious Tract Society's publication *'The Christmas Box or New Year's Gift'* of 1825.

Verses 1-3 are from the original text, which was inspired by the Christmas stories in Luke 2 and Matthew 2. Verse 4 comes from another Montgomery carol inspired by Philippians 2. Verse 6 is a doxology (not written by Montgomery) from the *Salisbury Hymn Book* (1857), as a final stanza it echoes Psalm 85: 10: 'Mercy and truth are met together; righteousness and peace have kissed each other'. These many changes offer many different choices.

But this piece is not just a carol as it can be delivered anytime anywhere as a joyous piece. It may surprise some to learn that carols never used to be restricted solely to Advent and Christmas time, although by their words some are self-restricted to specific days and events.

Bishop Bingham put this, too, back into Latin 'Angeli, sancta regione lucis' for his *Hymnologia Christiana Latina* of 1871 [available via archive.org]

James Montgomery was born in 1771 and died 1854. His parents worshipped as Moravians, a group which derived from the Hussite Reformation, 60 years before Luther in the Kingdom of Bohemia (now approximately central Czech Republic). The change was led by Jan Hus. Montgomery's story is given a much more detail in a separate article.

The group is equally well-known as the Unity of Brethren. In simple terms, their style can be described as placing a high value on a personal conversion to Christ (called the New Birth), piety, good works, pacifism, ecumenism, pacifism and evangelism – especially the establishment of missions), and music. There is no overlap or linkage with the 'Unitarians': which is very different as a liberal Christian theological movement known for its belief in the unitary nature of God, and for its rejection of the doctrines of the Trinity, original sin, predestination, and of biblical inerrancy.

The Moravian beliefs, like much of the later Protestant Reformation, had a distinct touch of Puritanism. As an indicator, their main tenets, barely changed since 1800, are as follows :-

> I. We will know no other God, but the one only true God, who made us and all creatures, and came into this world in order to save sinners; to Him alone we will pray.
>
> II. We will rest from work on the Lord's Day, and attend public service.
>
> III. We will honour father and mother, and when they grow old and needy we will do for them what we can.
>
> IV. No person shall get leave to dwell with us until our teachers have given their consent, and the helpers (native assistants) have examined him.
>
> V. We will have nothing to do with thieves, murderers, whoremongers, adulterers, or drunkards.
>
> VI. We will not take part in dances, sacrifices, heathenish festivals, or games.
>
> VII. We will use no Tschappish [meaning is unknown] or witchcraft when hunting.
>
> VIII. We renounce and abhor all tricks, lies and deceits of Satan.
>
> IX. We will be obedient to our teachers and to the helpers who are appointed to order our meetings in the town and fields.
>
> X. We will not be idle nor scold, nor beat one another, nor tell lies.
>
> XI. Whoever injures the property of his neighbour shall make restitution.
>
> XII. A man shall have but one wife—shall love her and provide her and his children. A woman shall have but one husband, be obedient to him, care for her children, and be cleanly in all things.
>
> XIII. We shall not admit rum, or any other intoxicating liquor into our towns.
>
> XIV. No one shall contract debts with traders, or receive to sell for traders, unless the helpers give their consent.

Its first setting in 1774 was LEWES by J Randall; others include FENITON COURT by E J Hopkins as well as HAPPY ZION. T Hastings and W B Gilbert both provided settings labelled as the title 'Angels from the realms'. In the USA, however, the normal setting is REGENT SQUARE, by the English Henry Smart. One source states that although this was written in 1860, it did not become attached to this hymn until 1928. No explanation is given.

Smart (1813-1879) gave up a career in the legal profession for one in music. Although largely self-taught, he became proficient in organ playing and composition, and he was a music teacher and critic. He was organist at St. Luke's, Old Street (1844-1864), and then St. Pancras (1864-1869). He was famous for his extemporizations and for his accompaniment of congregational singing. He became completely blind in 1865 at the age of fifty-two, but his remarkable memory enabled him to continue playing the organ. Though once highly rated as a composer by his English contemporaries, Smart is now largely forgotten, save for this.

REGENT SQUARE is used for over 100 hymns; these additional texts have included 'Praise my soul, the King of Heaven'§; 'Lo he comes with clouds, descending'§; 'Christ is made the sure foundation'; 'Lord dismiss us with thy blessing'; 'Light's Abode, Celestial Salem', and so many more.

H E Fosdick greatly admired REGENT SQUARE, and wrote his own 'God of Grace and God of Glory' specifically in the hope that it would be generally sung to that tune. He was horrified when, in 1935, the *Methodist Hymnal* instead set the lyrics to Vaughan Williams CWM RHONDDA.

An early version of the text :

1. Angels, from the realms of glory,
Wing your flight o'er all the earth;
Ye who sang creation's story,
Now proclaim Messiah's birth:
    Refrain: Come and worship, Come and worship
              worship Christ, the newborn King.

2. Shepherds, in the fields abiding,
Watching o'er your flocks by night,
God with man is now residing,
Yonder shines the infant light: Refrain.

3. Sages, leave your contemplations,
Brighter visions beam afar;
Seek the great Desire of nations,
Ye have seen his natal star: Refrain.

4. Saints before the altar bending,
Watching long in hope and fear,
Suddenly the Lord, descending,
In his temple shall appear.   Refrain.

5. Sinners, wrung with true repentance,   [often omitted]
Doomed for guilt to endless pains,
Justice now revokes the sentence,
Mercy calls you—break your chains: Refrain.

6. Though an infant now we view him,   [replacement]
He shall fill his Father's throne,
Gather all the nations to him;
Every knee shall then bow down: Refrain.

7. All creation, join in praising   [added as a Doxology]
God the Father, Spirit, Son,
Evermore your voices raising,
To th'eternal Three in One: Refrain.

8. Lord of Heaven, we adore Thee,
God the Father, God the Son,
God the Spirit, One in glory,
On the same eternal throne.
    Hallelujah! Hallelujah!
Lord of Heaven, Three in One.

Some other important later Victorian faces

Rev. F H Murray   1820-1902
Proprietor of Hymns Ancient & Modern 1861

(Cardinal) J Newman 1801-1890
    Lead, Kindly Light   1833
    Praise to the Lord, the Almighty 1865

James Montgomery   1771-1854
    Angels from the realms of glory   1816

W Walsham How   1823-1897
    For all the Saints   1864
    Soldiers of the Cross, arise 1864

Angels we have heard on High

'Les Anges dans nos campagnes' trans. J Chadwick	1813-1882	1862	3,4 verses
GLORIA	arrgd E S Barnes	1887-1958	1937	7.7.7.7

Not surprisingly, this carol is based on the song of the Angels at the birth of Christ in Bethlehem at Christmas according to the Gospel of Luke. The refrain 'Gloria in excelsis Deo' is the Latin which translates to 'Glory to God in the Highest', being the first line of their song. it is one of the few Latin phrases in common use in Protestant churches.

While the text is rather obviously based on the birth of Jesus and the proclamation of the Angels, there is no specific verse attached to the text. It could be Luke 2:13 – 'And suddenly there was with the angel, the heavenly host praising God' but several others do suit.

The refrain has become the identifying feature of the piece with the 'o' of 'Gloria' fluidly sustained through 16 notes of a rising and falling melodic sequence; such a sequence on a single syllable is technically 'melismatic'.

The English lyrics were loosely translated by James Chadwick in 1862 and the whole text significantly abbreviated. The French original 'Les anges' is a French noel (from the Languedoc region), its text and tune were first well-known via the *Nouveau Recueil de Cantiques* in 1855. Of the original eight-stanza French text, stanzas 1, 2, and 4 are translated, so most modern hymnals usually include three verses. The full French text is not yet available in translation. HymnologyArchive gives the detail to clear up much uncertainty as to origin and setting. The first publication, therefore it may be older, is headed "L'echo des montagnes de Bethleem', in *Choix cantiques sur nos airs nouveaux* in 1842 with an opening line 'Les anges, dans nos campagnes' all arranged by Louis Lambillotte in 10 verses of 4 lines. It is a French Latin mix so 'macaronic'. This version then already had the now well-known extended 'Gloria'. There is an unevidenced statement that it is believed to date from the eighteenth century.

Surprisingly, the English carol quickly became popular in the West Country and it was given the label 'Cornish' and listed in a collection of *Dorset Carols*. It has been translated into other languages, and is widely sung and published.

James Chadwick, the translator, (1813-1882) came from a Lancashire Catholic family which had moved to Ireland. His father had been fined and imprisoned in 1745 for siding with Prince Charles, 'Bonnie Prince Charlie'. By 1825, James was in North England and he never left the area; ordained in 1836 he was made Bishop of Newcastle and Hexham in 1866.

His translation was 1860, and he added a word at the beginning of every line which changes the rhythm and therefore tune. The extra unstressed syllable makes it iambic, no longer the better-known trochaic, thus requiring a pickup note to accommodate the new text' and actually a different tune in 8.8.8.8. A revision in 1862 still has it at just 4 verses but also still as '**The** angels we have heard on high'.

The music for this was by Henri Heny (1818-1888) with a single vocal line. The usual music is by the US Composer Edward Shippen Barnes (1887-1958) with a distinctive counterpoint texture especially in the refrain, which was first seen in 1937 and called IRIS. The tune is very similar to one from 1891 by the American C H Hutchins with one 'Gloria'. This traces back to a tune by G P Grantham for Chope's 'When the crimson sun had set' in 1875. One source suggests that Barnes based his tune on a different carol.

The bifurcation of the name is due to the Mennonites calling it GLORIA; the name IRIS comes from it being first used for Montgomery's 'Angels from the realms of glory §'.

As has already been noted, the tune GLORIA / IRIS has been linked to more than one text; and the text links to more than one tune. There are actually many different tunes with the 7.7.7.7 measure which could or might suit until one looks at the internal rhythm of the words and the pace, tone and, as mentioned, the contour. A few of the alternatives are LEWES; LARKIN; KENSINGTON NEW; WESTMINSTER ABBEY; and a few less known – PLEASANT PASTURES; SICILIAN MARINERS. Some near-equivalents offer 'Come and Worship' or 'Alleluia' as the refrain. In Hymnary's list of over 200, less surprisingly, many of these secondary combinations occur in only a very few hymnals.

The French version, whether of 10 verses or 8 begins as its first verse as :-

Les anges dans nos campagnes	The angels in our countryside
Ont entonné l'hymne des cieux,	have sung the hymn of heaven
Et l'écho de nos montagnes	and the echo from our mountains
Redit ce chant mélodieux	makes a melodious song.

As well as the relaxed translation, then almost every hymnbook available shows some differences; words are edited, tweaked, amended or even revised. The earliest known example in English is as follows :

1   Angels we have heard on high,
    sweetly singing o'er the plains,
    and the mountains in reply
    echoing their joyous strains.
Refrain: Glo-o-o-o-o-o-o-o-o-o-o-o-o-o-o-o-ria in excelsis Deo, gloria in excelsis Deo.

2   Shepherds, why this jubilee?
    Why your joyous strains prolong?
    What the gladsome tidings be
    which inspire your heav'nly song? [Refrain]

3   Come to Bethlehem and see
    him whose birth the angels sing;
    come, adore on bended knee
    Christ the Lord, the newborn King. [Refrain]

There are versions with a fourth verse; still some way short of the 10 verse French original.

    See him in a manger laid
    Whom the angels praise above;
    Mary, Joseph, lend your aid,
    While we raise our hearts in love.

At the Name of Jesus

	Caroline Noel	1817-1877	1870	8,7,6,5,4, verses
EVELYNS	W H Monk§	1823-1899	1875	11.11.11.11

Philip. 2:10 "….At the name of Jesus, every knee shall bow"   similar to Isaiah 45:23

'At the name of Jesus' is an 1870 hymn with lyrics written by Caroline Maria Noel. Born in 1817, the daughter of an Anglican clergyman and hymn writer, she began to write poetry in her late teens and again after a long gap. She suffered frequent bouts of illness and eventually became an invalid. To encourage both herself and others who were incapacitated or ill, Noel began to write devotional verse again. Miss Noel, in common with Miss Charlotte Elliott, writer of 'Just as I am' and others, was a great sufferer, and many of her verses were the outcome of her days of pain. As the collection says, they are often aimed 'for the Sick and Lonely' and were written rather for private meditation than for public use, despite their later use as such. Despite her poor health, she lived to just over 60, dying in 1877.

Her first hymn, 'Draw nigh unto my soul' (Indwelling), was written when she was 17 with a dozen more in the next three years: from 20 years of age to 40 she wrote nothing; then in the next 20 years she wrote more. Her works were later published in *The Name of Jesus, and other Verses for the Sick and Lonely* (1861 & 1870), this grew over the years, and by 1878 contained 78 pieces. This hymn was there entitled 'Ascension Day'; so it was not this poem that titled the volume, but another actually called 'The Name of Jesus' (without the 'at').

This is her best known hymn and its 8 verses can be used as a Processional for Ascension Day. There are various versions of the text. One example has four verses, with a new verse 2 replacing verses 2-4 and verse 6 starting 'Brothers' rather than 'Christians'.

It is based on Philippians 2: 5-11, and sets forward very clearly the great themes of Creation and Redemption, Christ's Ascension and his Second Coming. In some books, the hymn begins 'In the Name of Jesus' rather than 'At'; being taken from the Revised version (1881) of the Bible rather than the Authorized.

Alterations have been made to the text in recent years to avoid what some see as overt and blatant use of non-inclusive language. These amendments being : 'Name him, brothers, name him' (verse 5) and 'Brothers, this Lord Jesus' (verse 7).

As is far too common – and often due to taking care to ensure copyright - there are numerous versions of the text. The concept of 'ecclesiastical copyright' adopted by Hymns Altered and Modified has long passed.   Their view seemed too often to be 'we can borrow, edit and publish your text or music – but others shouldn't do it with what we publish.'

W H Monk wrote EVELYNS which fitted the irregular iambic line, 'With love as strong as death', a curious decision as the editors changed the next line of verse 6, 'But with awe and wonder' to be more conforming. Erik Routley called this 'one of Monk's most successful tunes'. Trickett said 'It is a strong tune, capable of interpreting these words with great effectiveness'. Dykes§' MARY MAGDALENE and Ferguson's CUDDESDON are amongst the many that will suit the metre. By 1903, PRINCETHORPE by W Pitts was being used.

In 1925, Vaughan Williams composed KING'S WESTON for this text; the title refers to a manor house on the Avon River near Bristol, England. The combination of text and tune in a festive hymn-anthem, based on the 1533 LAUS TIBI CHRISTE is a favourite of many church choirs. It is a great tune marked by distinctive rhythmic structures and a soaring climax in the final two lines. Like many of Vaughan Williams' tunes, it is best sung in unison although the vigorous melody has a lovely anthemic descant for verse 4.

    The original 8 verses are given here :

        1   At the name of Jesus every knee shall bow,
              every tongue confess him King of glory now;
              'tis the Father's pleasure we should call him Lord,
              who from the beginning was the mighty Word.

        2   Mighty and mysterious;   In the highest height,   (usually omitted)
              God from everlasting, Very Light of Light:
              In the Father's bosom, With the Spirit blest,
              Love, in Love eternal, Rest, in perfect rest.

        3   At his voice creation sprang at once to sight,
              all the angel faces, all the hosts of light,
              thrones and dominations, stars upon their way,
              all the heavenly orders, in their great array.

        4   Humbled for a season, to receive a name
              from the lips of sinners unto whom he came,
              faithfully he bore it spotless to the last,
              brought it back victorious when from death he passed:

        5   Bore it up triumphant with its human light,
              through all ranks of creatures, to the central height,
              to the throne of Godhead, to the Father's breast;
              filled it with the glory of that perfect rest.

6.   Name Him, brothers, name Him, with love strong as death,   (often omitted)
              But with awe and wonder, and with bated breath;
              He is God the Saviour, He is Christ the Lord,
              Ever to be worshipped, trusted, and adored.

        7   In your hearts enthrone him; there let him subdue
              all that is not holy, all that is not true:
              Crown him as your captain in temptation's hour
              let his will enfold you in its light and power.

        8   Brothers, this Lord Jesus shall return again,
              with his Father's glory, with his angel train;
              for all wreaths of empire meet upon his brow,
              and our hearts confess him King of glory now.

Rev Sir Henry Williams Baker   1821-1877

Sir Henry Williams Baker, was the driving force behind the arrival of *Hymns Ancient and Modern* in 1861. His success is made clear by its sales of 200 million copies in the last 160 years. He did all the necessary work in deeply rural Monkland near Hereford – hugely assisted by the train (Leominster station opened in 1857) and the postal service (1840). He was a hymn writer, translator and rector of All Saints Church, Monkland from 1852 until his death.

Young Henry went to Trinity College, Cambridge for his BA and took holy orders in 1844. After a curacy at Great Horkesley in Essex with the Rev W Edwards, where they both were rivals for the hand of Miss Laetitia Bonner – and Baker's suit failed. Edwards went to Orleton where the east windows are in her memory. Edwards' nephew wrote 'There was no further friendly communication between the vicarages'. Sir Henry was firmly in favour of the celibacy of clergy; it would be simplistic to say that this attitude arose in any way from his setback.

The family became noticeable with the baronetcy to Sir Robert Baker in 1796. His son Henry Loraine Baker served with distinction at Guadeloupe in 1815 and became a Vice Admiral; he married Louisa Anne Williams of Dorset. Their son, Henry Williams Baker was born in 1821 in Dorset. He was given, as was common at the time, the mother's maiden name as a second forename.

Rev Baker was appointed as vicar to All Saints Church at Monkland near Hereford in 1852 aged just 30; he remained there until his death in 1877 aged 57. In 1859, he inherited the baronetcy and needless to say had no children. The baronetcy passed to a kinsman.

On succeeding Rev Jelinger Symons and his 3 communions a year; Rev Baker aimed for many more and asked for 6 bottles of wine for each event. The church officers decided 4 was enough and also soon set limits on laundry and cleaning; but they did double the levy for church repairs from twopence to fourpence.

Sir Henry was an early participant in planning the proposed *Hymns Ancient and Modern*. He had been planning his own collection – like many others – at the low price of sixpence. From 1858, Sir Henry was Chairman of the Proprietors or Committee for compiling *Hymns Ancient and Modern* 'H A&M' and 'A&M'. The first edition came out in 1861, just 3 years from the very first discussions. Sir Henry was also responsible for the Appendix in 1868 and the second edition in 1875.

He was skilled at adapting the work of others as well as at translating. He adapted such texts as Neale's§ 'Of the Father sole-begotten' to become 'Of the Father's love begotten'. Other translations include what became 'On this day, the first of days'; 'Jesu, grant me this I pray'; 'Captains of the saintly band' as well as 'O sacred head, surrounded' which had begun as Gerhardt's 'O Haupt voll Blut und Wunden'.

Sir Henry composed many hymns; for the rededication of the church he wrote 'Lord, Thy word abideth'. Perhaps his most famous is 'The King of Love my Shepherd is §'. The A&M hymnal was compiled to meet the wants of churchmen of all schools despite his own high-church views. Certes, the hymns of Wesley§ took a very minor place compared to other collections and especially more modern hymnals which do recognise their power.

He inherited his baronetcy in 1859 and, implicitly, funds to begin to repair, rebuild and enhance his church and village. Baker built his own Vicarage (Horkesley House – named after his curacy) as well as a school with places for 60 children. Once his A&M began to sell so well, further money quickly arrived. As well as having generously donated to the rebuilding of the church by first replacing the Chancel and then backing the rebuilding, Sir Henry gifted the organ. Said to be 'the finest in any country church'. It was designed by Sir Henry and Sir Frederick Ouseley and built by Walkers, now of Devizes. His hymn 'Praise, O Praise Our God and King', is sung at Harvest throughout the country to the tune 'Monkland'. Wilkes, its author, played it at the dedication service at Monkland for the new organ in 1866.

Enhancing the organ, Sir Henry trained an excellent choir. He also gave much time and support for the choirs to Leominster & Hereford.

Hatfield in 1884 described him thus : "Sir Henry distinguished himself principally in the line of hymnology. Some of his hymns were written as early as 1852. To the first Hymns A&M he contributed twelve original hymns and at least ten translations. He developed not only particular facility in versification, but remarkable skill in adapting his compilation to the prevailing tastes of the Church of England. His churchmanship is everywhere apparent, especially in his hymn on Baptism: 'Tis done, that new and heavenly birth / Which re-creates the sons of earth, / And cleanses from the guilt of sin / The souls whom Jesus died to win".

"Of his translations, four were then still of value by 1884: 'On this day, the first of days,' etc., is a translation of 'Die parente temporum', etc., from the *LeMans Breviary*. 'Blessed Trinity! from mortal sight', etc., is a successful version of 'O luce, quae tua lates', etc., a hymn in the Paris Breviary, credited to Santolius Maglorianus. Another Latin hymn by the same author, 'Prome vocem, mens canoram', etc., was versified by Chandler and reconstructed by Sir Henry in the form now so extensively in use, 'Now, my soul! thy voice upraising', etc. 'Jesus! grant me this, I pray', etc., is a version of a Latin hymn of four stanzas, 'Dignare me, O Jesu! rogo te', etc., taken from one of the later French missals, and of uncertain origin."

"Among the earliest of his poetical essays is the hymn, 'Oh! what, if we are Christ's', etc. It was written in 1852, and celebrates the faith of the martyrs. 'Oh, praise our God today', etc., 'There is a blessed home', etc., were written in 1852."

Sir Henry was also the author of *Daily Prayers, for the Use of Those Who Have to Work Hard;* also a similar Daily Text-Book for hard workers, and a few short tracts.

Rev Baker was, from his Cambridge days, a strong supporter of the Tractarian, high-church views and beliefs. This is evident in his hymns and more visibly in the adornments he saw necessary for his church. One such hymn was addressed to the Virgin Mary, 'Shall we not love thee. Mother dear?' Such a Marian approach was typical of many Anglo-catholics; so many strong objections were made.

By his death in 1877 sales of Hymns A&M had reached some 8 million and the government had even issued copies to every ship in the Royal Navy. His obituary included '…the beautifully restored church, the excellent choir, the crowded services and the efficient school bear witness to his zeal and devotion…' and '…. His true memorial will be found in the work Hymns Ancient and Modern'.

It is reported that on his deathbed, the last words he spoke were the third verse :
>Perverse and foolish oft I strayed … But yet in Love he sought me
>And on his shoulder gently laid … And home rejoicing brought me.

Sir Henry's remains are buried in Monkland near the wicket-gate, The Good Shepherd on a cross is his headstone. His colleagues on the committee donated the East window.

John Julian§, the hymnologist, writes a tribute to his art as a hymnwriter, 'a tender sadness brightened by a soft calm peace was the epitome of his poetical life'.

𝕭lessed 𝕮ity, 𝕳eavenly 𝕾alem (Urbs Beata)

6th-7th-8th Century   trans. J M Neale§   1818-1866   1851   9 verses
URBS BEATA (per Sarum Use)   13th C   8.7.8.7.8.7
Revel 21:2   "And I, John, saw the holy city, new Jerusalem …."

There are a number of hymns which trace their origins back to the Latin and the early church where hymns, or perhaps more accurately sacred singing, was an essential part of the service and ritual. This text relates to the Roman Catholic service for the 'Office of the Dedication' for a new church. It dates back to the 7th or 8th century. The text is most obviously inspired by Revelation 21 and the arrival of the new Jerusalem out of heaven, and there are also clear references to Ephesians 2:20 and 1 Peter 2:5. Not too surprising, these verses also reference 'And did those feet in ancient time §', better known to many as Jerusalem.

The Latin words 'Urbs beata Hierusalem, dicta pacis visio, quae construitur in coelo'
translate to 'Blessed city of Jerusalem, called vision of peace, built out of living stone;' from this Neale§ obtains

>Blessed City, Heavenly Salem, Vision dear of Peace and Love,
>Who, of living stones upbuilded, Art the joy of Heav'n above,

and then A&M amends it further; especially in the second and third verses.

The original translation had 8 verses as well as the typical doxology or finale of praise. Neale's full translation was first published in his own *Mediaeval Hymns and Sequences* (1851), in nine verses. Neale's version used 'Laud' rather than the later 'Praise'.

Originally, the first four stanzas of 'Urbs beata Jerusalem' were usually done, in the Office of the Dedication of a Church, at Vespers and Matins, while the last four were given to Lauds. Neale's later split of his translation into two 4-verse hymns matches this Catholic division.

A second hymn has been created beginning at verse 5 with 'Angularis fundamentum' or 'Square cornered and basic' - and thence becoming in translation 'Christ is made a sure Foundation'. Both hymns end with the words 'Praise and Honour to the Father'.

Yet more complicated, some hymnals have taken the 7th verse 'Hoc in templo, summa Deus' and the 8th as a separate section for a third hymn.

Strangely, Neale translated a different hymn, 'O beata Jerusalem', and began his translation with the same first line but a different second line: 'Blessed City, Heav'nly Salem,/ Land of glory, land of rest'. This is found in the *Hymnal Noted* Part II (1854). The Latin text begins 'O beata Jerusalem,/ Praedicanda civitas'. The hymn is thought to be of Mozarabic origin (the period when southern Spain 'Al-Andalus' was ruled by the Moslems).

There are other translations, Julian's§ *Dictionary of Hymnology* lists several. The best known after Neale is by John Chandler in his *Hymns of the Primitive Church* (1837) with the first line beginning 'Christ is our corner-stone'.

John Julian makes a fascinating comment "One point strikes us as very remarkable in these hymns, and indeed in all Dr. Neale's poetry, viz., its thorough manliness of tone. Considering what his surroundings were (with the almshouses and convent), one might have expected a feminine tone in his writings. Dr. Littledale, in his most vivid and interesting sketch of Dr. Neale's life, to which the present writer is largely indebted, has remarked the same with regard to his teaching: 'Instead of committing the grave error of feminising his sermons and counsels [at St. Margaret's] because he had only women to deal with, he aimed at showing them the masculine side of Christianity also, to teach them its strength as well as its beauty."

This masculine side was however not enough for him to accept the provostship of St Ninian's Cathedral in Perth, the climate being too cold for him to be willing.

An early version of the words is as follows, with the first Latin verse also shown.

Blessed city, heavenly Salem,	Coelestis Urbs Ierusalem,
vision dear of peace and love,	Beata pacis visio,
who of living stones art builded	Quæ celsa de viventibus
in the height of heaven above,	Saxis ad astra tolleris,
and with angel hosts encircled,	Sponsæque ritu cingeris
as a bride dost earthward move!	Mille Angelorum millibus.

From celestial realms descending,
bridal glory round thee shed,
meet for him whose love espoused thee,
to thy Lord shalt thou be led;
all thy streets and all thy bulwarks
of pure gold are fashioned.

Bright thy gates of pearl are shining,
they are open evermore;
and by virtue of his merits
thither faithful souls do soar,
who for Christ's dear name in this world
pain and tribulation bore.

Many a blow and biting sculpture
polished well those stones elect,
in their places now compacted
by the heavenly Architect,
who therewith hath willed for ever
that his palace should be decked.

    Doxology
Laud and honour to the Father,
laud and honour to the Son,
laud and honour to the Spirit,
ever Three, and ever One,
consubstantial, co-eternal,
while unending ages run.

Other contributors have, over time, added verses. Three of these begin

    5. Grant that all Thy faithful people   ... May Thy truer temple be;

    6. Come Thou now, and be among us,   ... Lord and Maker, while we pray;

    7. Glory to thy royal Bridegroom,   ... Salem, sing rejoicingly;

Strangely, the earliest known printed source is H A Daniel's *Thesaurus Hymnologicus* of 1856 ie after both Chandler and Neale had done their translation. This Latin text had 8 three line verses; Neale expands these into 8 6 line verses.

Neale's original full translation continues from 'Angularis fundamentum' producing a second hymn with 4 verses as follows:

> Christ is made the sure foundation,
> Christ the Head and comer-stone,
> chosen of the Lord, and precious,
> binding all the church in one,
> Holy Sion's help for ever,
> and her confidence alone.
>
> All that dedicated city,
> dearly loved of God on high,
> in exultant jubilation
> pours perpetual melody,
> God the One in Three adoring
> in glad hymns eternally.
>
> To this temple, where we call thee,
> come, O Lord of Hosts, to-day;
> with thy wonted loving-kindness
> hear thy servants as they pray,
> and thy fullest benediction
> shed within its walls alway.
>
> Here vouchsafe to all thy servants
> what they ask of thee to gain,
> what they gain from thee for ever
> with the blessed to retain,
> and hereafter in thy glory
> evermore with thee to reign.

There is an old plainsong setting, surprisingly called URBS BEATA; Caspar Ett has the setting ORIEL; there is also URBS COELESTIS by H E Hobson written in 1872, two named after the title Blessed City; or indeed Michael Haydn's [Josef's brother] DULCE CARMEN / TANTUM COELIS.

Purcell (1659-1695) was the author of WESTMINSTER ABBEY, and this is the usual setting for the second hymn 'Christ is made the sure foundation'. Obviously, this also links to the same range of settings as 'Blessed City'.. Then you look to see which hymns each tune has been used for … and the interweaving paths of texts and tunes travel onward.

Urbs Beata Ierusalem

Breathe on me, Breath of God

	E Hatch	1835-1890	1876	4 verses
TRENTHAM	Robert Jackson	1842-1914	1878	6.6.8.6
Job 33:4	"The breath of the Almighty hath given me life"			

It is not just metre and rhythm which make a setting of tune and text truly satisfactory. One writer says of TRENTHAM, one of the less common settings for these words, that 'it fits the words very beautifully'. Opinion can vary however: later, TRENTHAM was criticised by hymnologist Donald Webster in 1980: 'One might conclude from [this tune] and the way it is sung that the breath of God was an anaesthetic, not a 'Giver of Life'.'.

Edwin Hatch had a non-conformist childhood before being ordained into the Church of England. In 1876 he wrote 'Breathe on Me, Breath of God' and published it privately in a pamphlet entitled *Between Doubt and Prayer*. giving it the Latin title of 'Spiritus Dei' (Spirit of God). The hymn was later published into the public sphere in 1886 in Henry Allon's *The Congregational Psalmist Hymnal*. It was then republished posthumously by Hatch's widow in 1890 in *Towards Fields of Light: Sacred Poems* still entitled 'Spiritus Dei'.

There is an oft-quoted statement about Hatch's faith being 'as simple and unaffected as a child; being also an appropriate description of the hymn. Later, a Methodist writer said 'The simplicity of this profound hymn belies the education and knowledge of its author'. Hatch knew that though he had written the hymn using simple words, they had profound meaning with references to creation of man by God in Genesis and then in the spiritual breath of God which came to humanity at Pentecost via Jesus.

Recently, it has been amended by the 'you' treatment ('Till I am wholly yours...etc '). There is also now a translation into French, 'Souffle du Dieu vivant' by Suzanne Bidgrain.

There seems to be a clear choice about which verse in the bible is being referenced – Genesis or New Testament John. But Ancient and Modern offers Job 33:4. There is a very clear Old Testament line in Genesis where God 'breathes life' into his various creations.

But equally suitable is the source being from the New Testament and there are several clear references. The hymn stands as a prayerful meditation on John 3:3-8, where Christ, speaking to Nicodemus, identifies the relationship that exists between the creating breath of God (Genesis 2: 7) 'Then the LORD God formed a man from the dust of the ground and breathed into his nostrils the breath of life, and the man became a living being, and the breath of the Holy Spirit in the new creation.' Second, there is the New Testament which has Jesus' preaching about how one must be born again and born of water and the Spirit, leading to John 20:33 is the verse, 'When he [Jesus] had said this, he breathed on them and said to them, 'Receive the Holy Spirit'.

Watson and Trickett further suggest a much deeper progression through the whole poem: 'Verse 1- the Spirit brings new life; Galatians 2:20 and 5:22. Verse 2- purity and obedience, Psalm 51:10, Mark 13:13. Verse 3- surrender and inspiration, Acts 2:3-4; and in Verse 4- eternal life, 1 Peter 5:10.

It has been sung to many SM [Short Metre] 6.6.8.6 tunes. The most commonly used ones have been John Chetham's 1718 AYLESBURY – surprisingly also known as FETTER LANE, WIRKSWORTH, and BRENTFORD. There is also CARLISLE by the then-blind London organist Charles Lockhart, he was also renowned for his training of chirlen's choirs. Other tunes include VENI SPIRITUS was by Sir John Stainer. Gauntlett, Lowell Mason, and HAMPTON by Aaron Williams are also known. As mentioned above there is TRENTHAM by Robert Jackson; even if the latter was originally for H W Baker's text 'O perfect life of love'.

As with almost every hymn, there are textual tweaks and amendments. And since the original does have the occasional 'thou' the you-brigade will have exerted their influence thereabouts. An early version of the text (although noting one well-known amendment) :

1	Breathe on me, Breath of God, ... Fill me with life anew,	
	That I may love what Thou dost love,	... And do what Thou dost do.
2	Breathe on me, Breath of God,	... Until my heart is pure,
	Until with thee I will one will,	... To do and to endure.
3	Breathe on me, Breath of God,	... Blend all my soul with Thine,
	Until this earthly part of me	... Glows with Thy fire divine.
4	Breathe on me, Breath of God;	... So shall I never die,
	But live with Thee the perfect life	... Of Thine eternity.

In Passing: What about the Catholic Hymns :

There are Catholic hymns but … not with the quantity and intent of the Protestant oeuvre.

It has been said by a fellow Cathoic 'We don't sing hymns because we don't know how to' as well as 'too many are all goopy, modernist, sentimental trash about walking on the beach with Jesus and eagles and 'gathering together' or equally bad 'the hymns are archaic, incomprehensible, overly theological Victorian lyrics put to thumping old hymn tunes that nobody likes any more'. This is a very simple view – and Catholics do sing. But differently.

In 1969 to promote music in English it was decided to allow hymns for use at the Introit, Offertory and Communion, This endorsed the new four-hymn Mass, with such singing being merely 'religious music' and so did not violate the ban on liturgical music at a low Mass.

In 1995, a detailed article bemoaned the loss of favorite hymns since the Vatican II reforms and the changes to the 'low' Mass; 'in the good old days 'goose flesh would break out all over you as you and the congregation sang with all your lungs the great hymns of Catholic spirituality'. Liturgical or sacred music belonged to the sung or high Mass and consisted of two parts, the ordinary and the proper. The proper includes the varying texts of the day, the Introit, Gradual, Alleluia, Offertory and Communion. The ordinary includes the invariable texts, the Kyrie, Gloria, Credo, Sanctus and Agnus Dei. All this is now sung more rarely.

The hymns sung nowadays have suffered an inflow of the most popular non-Catholic pieces especially by means of Funerals and Weddings. According to Cardinal Ratzinger, later Benedict XVI, '[we have] witnessed the increasingly grim impoverishment which follows when beauty for its own sake is banished from the Church and all is subordinated to the principle of 'utility', lackluster, banal and boring'.

Crown Him with many crowns

	Matthew Bridges	1800-1894	1851	6 & 6	
DIADEMATA	G J Elvey	1816-1893	1868	6.6.8.6	x2

Revel 19:12   "On his head [were] many crowns."

In its original form, the hymn has a smooth progression through the attributes of Christ (from Revelation 5:11-13) :- beginning :

1	Crown him with many crowns	God in his several forms ...
2	Crown Him the Virgin's Son,	The God Incarnate born ...
3	Crown Him the Lord of Love;	Behold his Hands and Side ...
4	Crown Him the Lord of Peace,	Whose power a sceptre sways ...
5	Crown Him the Lord of Years,	The Potentate of time ...

And finally, the hymn returns to the beginning, with Christ in glory.

6	Crown Him the Lord of Heaven!	One with the Father known ...

Matthew Bridges wrote this for the 1851 second edition of *Hymns of the Heart for the use of Catholics*. Aged 51 and having converted to Catholicism in 1848, this is his most famous hymn. He died in 1894 after writing many more hymns. His hymn joined the 1868 Appendix to the first edition of A&M. In a time of some Anglican v Catholic, erm, disagreement, the use of this hymn in an Anglican book is quite surprising.

The Roman Catholic tendencies of the hymn are revealed in its Latin title in *Hymns of the Heart*, 'in capito eius diademata multa' (Revelation 19:12). In a later printing in Bridges' *The Passion of Jesus* (1852) it was entitled 'Third Sorrowful Mystery, Song of the Seraphs'. The author began as a staunch critic of Rome but later was heavily influenced by the Tractarian Anglo-Catholic view, sufficient unto his conversion.

In the 1868 *H A&M*, it was joined with the splendid tune DIADEMATA ('Crowns') written for it by (Sir) George Job Elvey. He was organist at St Georges Chapel, Windsor from 1835 to 1882. One critic says "His style was stately, a la Handel which by the 1850s was often being seen as old-style and dated." There are numerous alternatives, for example, CORONA by Hylton Stewart from 1927.

The hymn has been used in almost every English-language hymn book, but only after having been subjected to an extraordinary number of textual alterations. The extreme is a complete rewrite of 6 new verses by Godfrey Thing (1823-1903) at the instigation of Rev H W Hutton who asked him to write this variant hymn in 1874. Thring had begun to make changes of his own in 1871, beginning with 'Crown him with crowns of gold'.

Like others, Thring wrote sets of hymns. His series of *Hymns on the Creation*, all in the same metre (8.8.8.8.8.6), is described as 'certainly very fine'. The first lines are:-

When o'er the water's misty deep.	Sunday.
The earth in robes of light arrayed.	Monday.
With azure girdle circled round.	Tuesday.
So grass, and herb, and fruitful tree.	Wednesday.
Four days had come and gone to rest.	Thursday.
The last great day of work had come.	Friday.
And now, 'mid myriad worlds enthroned.	Saturday.

Thring later compiled *A Church of England Hymn Book, adapted to th Daily Services of the Church throughout the year* (1880) in an attempt to produce a book which would be free from the factional bias which he perceived in existing Church of England collections. He was 'a churchman who kept to the centre among the controversies of the Victorian church'.

John Julian noted: "Prebendary Thring's hymns are more fully represented in his own collection than elsewhere, yet a good many are found in a other hymnbooks. His hymns are of a strong and decided character. His descriptive and narrative hymns are very few, and Passiontide and the two Sacraments of the Church are almost untouched. In some of his finer hymns his tone is high and his structure massive, in several others his plaintiveness is very tender, whilst very varied, and his rhythm is almost always perfect. The prominent features throughout are a clear vision, a firm faith, a positive reality, and an exulting hopefulness."

A great many of Prebendary Thring's hymns are annotated under their respective first lines. Thus his 1874 'Crown Him' text had the comment: "This new version was written at the request of the Reverend H.W. Hutton, to supply the place of some of the stanzas in Matthew Bridges' well-known hymn, of which he and others did not approve; it was then thought better to rewrite the whole, so that the two hymns might be kept entirely distinct".

Hutton was a Prebendary of Lincoln and worked on several supplementary hymn books. It is not clear what caused this disapproval, although Bridges' conversion to Roman Catholicism, and his reference to the 'mystic Rose' in stanza 2, may have raised Protestant hackles in an age of ecclesiastical controversy and church rivalry. 'Mystic Rose' is a well-known reference to the Virgin Mary: Jesus is both the 'fruit' of the rose and the stem, so his mother is, in an intricate medieval tradition, the daughter of her own son, *figlia del suo figlio.*

The socialist Dearmer, editor of the *English Hymnal*, added his own disapproval and penned another new verse 'Crown him upon the throne', A E Bailey said, 'It emphasizes the social rather than the theological reasons why Christ should be crowned'.

There are now 2 completely separate versions – 6 verses by Bridges and 6 by Thring; sharing the sme theme, melody and theological references – but difffent only in wording.

An early version of the Bridges text is as follows:

Crown him with many crowns,	... The Lamb upon his throne;
Hark! how the heav'nly anthem drowns	... All music but its own:
Awake, my soul, and sing	... Of him who died for thee,
And hail him as thy matchless king	... Through all eternity.
Crown him the Virgin's Son!	... The God Incarnate born,-
Whose arm those crimson trophies won	... Which now his brow adorn:
Fruit of the mystic Rose,	... As of that Rose the Stem;
The Root, whence mercy ever flows,-	... The Babe of Bethlehem!
Crown him the Lord of love:	... Behold his hands and side,
Those wounds yet visible above	... In beauty glorified:
No angel in the sky	... Can fully bear that sight,
But downward bends his burning eye	... At mysteries so bright!

Crown him the Lord of peace, ... Whose power a sceptre sways
From pole to pole, that wars may cease, ... Absorbed in prayer and praise:
his reign shall know no end, ... And round his piercéd feet
Fair flowers of paradise extend ... Their fragrance ever sweet.

Crown him the Lord of years! ... The Potentate of time,
Creator of the rolling spheres, ... Ineffably sublime.
Glassed in a sea of light, ... Where everlasting waves
Reflect his throne --the Infinite, ... Who lives --and loves --and saves.

Crown him the Lord of heaven! ... One with the Father known,
And the blest Spirit through him given ... From yonder triune throne:
All hail, Redeemer, Hail! ... For Thou hast died for me!
Thy praise shall never, never fail ... Throughout eternity!

    Thring :
Crown him with crowns of gold, ... All nations great and small,
Crown him, ye martyred saints of old, ... The Lamb once slain for all;
The Lamb once slain for them ... Who bring their praises now,
As jewels for the diadem ... That girds his sacred brow.

Crown him the Son of God ... Before the worlds began,
And ye, who tread where He hath trod, ... Crown him the Son of Man;
Who every grief hath known ... That wrings the human breast,
And takes and bears them for His own, ... That all in him may rest.

Crown him the Lord of light, ... Who o'er a darkened world
In robes of glory infinite ... His fiery flag unfurled.
And bore it raised on high, ... In heaven--in earth--beneath,
To all the sign of victory ... O'er Satan, sin, and death.

Crown him the Lord of life ... Who triumphed o'er the grave,
And rose victorious in the strife ... For those he came to save;
His glories now we sing ... Who died, and rose on high.
Who died, eternal life to bring ... And lives that death may die.

Crown him of lords the Lord, ... Who over all doth reign
Who once on earth, the incarnate Word, ... o'er ransomed sinners slain,
Now lives in realms of light, ... Where saints with angels sing
Their songs before him day and night, ... Their God, Redeemer, king.

Crown him the Lord of heaven, ... Enthroned in worlds above;
Crown him the king, to whom is given ... The wondrous name of Love,
Crown him with many crowns, ... As thrones before him fall.
Crown him, ye kings, with many crowns, ... For He is King of all.

Digression: The Common Doxology

A Doxology is defined as a hymn of praise to God. There are three pieces commonly labelled Doxologies. Being based on the description by Luke of the angels singing at the Nativity, this is also known as the 'Gloria in Excelsis':

Glory to God in the highest, and on earth peace to people of good will.
We praise you, we bless you, we adore you, we glorify you, we give you thanks for your great glory, Lord God, heavenly King, O God almighty Father.
Lord Jesus Christ, Only Begotten Son, Lord God, Lamb of God, Son of the Father, you take away the sins of the world, have mercy on us; you take away the sins of the world, receive our prayer; you are seated at the right hand of the Father, have mercy on us (etc).

There is the shorter Gloria Patri as follows :
Glory be to the Father and to the Son and to the Holy Ghost
As it was in the beginning, and now, and always, and into the ages of ages. Amen.

The third doxology in widespread use in English, in some Protestant traditions is commonly referred to simply as The Doxology or The Common Doxology:

Praise God, from whom all blessings flow;
Praise Him, all creatures here below;
Praise Him above, ye heavenly host;
Praise Father, Son, and Holy Ghost. Amen.

These last words were written in 1674 by Thomas Ken (1637-1711) as the final verse of a both of a pair of hymns, 'Awake, my soul, and with the sun' (14 verses) and 'Glory to thee, my God, this night,' (12 verses) intended for morning and evening worship at Winchester College. There is mention of a Midnight hymn in 13 verses – with no indication of how many boys sang at that time of night.

In the first edition of *Hymns A&M*, these two were the first and the tenth hymns. Later 'Awake, my soul' became linked with the dedication of Alms or offerings at Sunday worship. The evening hymn was retitled without the Bishop's approval and can still be found with the alternate title 'All praise to thee, O God, this night'.   The first verse of 14 with the long measure of 8.8.8.8 is :-

    Awake, my soul, and with the sun   ... Thy daily stage of duty run;
    Shake off dull sloth, and joyful rise   ... To pay thy morning sacrifice.

It is usually sung to the tune MORNING HYMN by F H Barthelemon (1741-1808).

The final verse, can be separated from its proper hymns and is sung to the tune 'OLD 1OOTH, DUKE STREET, LASST UNS ERFREUEN or the EIGHTH TUNE by Thomas Tallis. The chosen setting can be used for any hymn text in long metre (often abbreviated simply to LM), that is, with four lines of eight syllables in iambic feet.

Other texts include: 'From all that dwell below the skies' by Isaac Watts§ which paraphrases Psalm 117, again with the Doxology as the final verse; 'O Come, Loud Anthems Let Us Sing', a metrical paraphrase of Psalm 95 from Tate and Brady's *A New Version of the Psalms of David* and others.

The popular Hawaiian version Hoʻonani i ka Makua mau was translated by the Victorian bishop, Hiram Bingham and is published in relevant hymnals.

Dear Lord, and Father of Mankind

	J G Whittier 1807-1895 / G Horder		1884	6 verses
REPTON	C H Parry	1848-1918	1888	8.6.8.8.6

Startlingly, this hymn arrives via the American Quaker poet, John Greenleaf Whittier, from an Indian source writing about religious drugs. The words of this are lines taken from the end of an astonishing and peculiar 17-verse longer poem, 'The Brewing of Soma' by Whittier in 1872. The adaptation into a hymn was made by Garrett Horder in 1884. Somehow these words became a hymn, but Quakers do not use hymns. It must have been galling to him to find so many of his works turned into hymns. Even more so as he and his fellows had a strong antipathy towards tub-thumping, hearty gospel songs and highly emotional religion.

Whittier would have been appalled at his words being used so; and the huge enthusiasm with which the song is squeaked and growel at public schools in England. His intent was to compare the misuse of drugs in certain Eastern religions both with the over-fervent excitement of much Christian worship with the third way of quiet unassisted contemplation.

Soma was a drink sacred to the Vedic religion, going back to about 2000 BC and the proto-Indo-Iranian times. It would seem to have had hallucinogenic properties; perhaps based on the Fly Agaric Amanita mushroom (red with white spots). The poem opens with a quote from the *Rigveda*, attributed to Vasishtha:

> *These libations mixed with milk have been prepared for Indra:*
> *offer Soma to the drinker of Soma.* (Rigv. vii. 32, trans. Max Müller).

The storyline in the first 6 verses is of Vedic priests preparing and drinking Soma in an attempt to experience divinity by trance-like ecstatic states. It then describes everyone getting drunk on Soma. It compares this to some Christians' use of *'music, incense, vigils drear, and trance, to bring the skies more near, or lift men up to heaven!'* But all such is in vain - it is mere intoxication.

These are meant to be the 'foolish ways' that we are asking God to forgive; but, taken out of context, our foolish ways become more generalised, and also more personal

Whittier ends by describing the only true method for contact with the divine, as practised by Quakers. This way is 'Sober lives dedicated to doing God's will, seeking silence and selflessness in order to hear the 'still, small voice', of I Kings 19:11-13 as the authentic voice of God, rather than earthquake, wind or fire'.

Müller's *Sacred Books of the East* included one of the most ancient and famous scriptures of the Hindu prophet Vashishta. The drinking of Soma, an intoxicating drug, was part of Vedic ritual, 'the Soma's sacred madness' (stanza 4). In his poem Whittier describes this with a fine intensity, and then introduces the idea that there is an equivalent intoxication in some kinds of Christian worship. He includes incense, and even music:

> As in that child-world's early year,
>   Each after age has striven
> By music, incense, vigils drear,
> And trance, to bring the skies more near,
>   Or lift men up to heaven! (stanza 8)

Whittier's Quaker self, brought up on silence and serious contemplation, uses Soma as a metaphor for elaborate ritual with distinct pagan overtones.

> And yet the past comes round again,

>   And new doth old fulfil;
>   In sensual transports wild as vain
>   We brew in many a Christian fane
>   The heathen Soma still! (stanza 11)

This is immediately followed by 'Dear Lord and Father of mankind', and the six stanzas that are familiar to users of most modern hymnbooks. It was Garrett Horder in 1884 who saw the possibility of making a hymn from the last six stanzas of this strange poem, though with a number of alterations.

Since that time, the stanzas have become Whittier's best-known hymn, and the only one of his hymns in some major books. The vocabulary is that of 'purer lives' and 'deeper reverence', the 'simple trust' of those who listened to Jesus beside the sea and in the calm of the hills. These are they who have heard 'the silence of eternity', and the 'noiseless' blessing, and who have felt the still dews of quietness, and the beauty of peace. The overall effect is one in which the last rhymes, 'balm' and 'calm', sum up, in sound and sense, the commendation of the simple and Quaker-like life. It is given scriptural backing by the apt use of 1 Kings 19 in the final stanza, with its account of the earthquake, wind and fire, followed by the still, small voice.

Despite the rather strong godly and Christian references in the title, the author adduced no link to any particular bible verse until much later. Despite the very clear God, Father – there is no verse in the bible which has these words. As ever, thorough research can find lines which do have echoes in the bible. One might, for example, equate 'after the fire came a gentle whisper' I Kings 19:11-13, with 'a still small voice of calm'. The text does rather obviously seem to be taken from the New rather than the Old Testament.

One author states that the whole poem is a polemic designed to disparage other Christian traditions, and raise up the Quaker way of silent listening to the Holy Spirit. It is therefore of interest as to why this hymn should be so popular among so many Christian traditions today. Of course, there is Hubert Parry's majestic music, which builds to a climax before the quiet resolution of the repeated last line. But the appeal in the last verse for 'cool, balm, still, small, calm' is a call to quietness in a time and a world of frenzy.

In the United Kingdom, the hymn is usually sung to the setting REPTON by Hubert Parry. This tune is adapted from an aria in Act 1 of his opera Judith. It comes after the line 'Long since in Egypt's plenteous land'. If sung to Parry's tune the last line of each stanza is repeated. The naming REPTON comes from it having been used in 1924 at Repton School by G G Stocks for this text.

S S Wesley delivered a setting called ENGEDI; but this was originally, as so often, for another text 'Eternal Light! Eternal Light! How pure the soul must be'. In the US, the prevalent tune is REST by Frederick Maker of Bristol (1844-1927); even if originally for a different hymn 'There is an hour of peaceful rest' by William Tappan.

Other settings include HAMMERSMITH by W H Gladstone, the son of the Liberal Prime Minister; and ELEGY FOR DUNKIRK by Dario Marianelli.

The American composer Charles Ives took stanzas 14 and 16 of The Brewing of Soma ('O Sabbath rest…/Drop Thy still dews…') and set them to music in 1919 as the song 'Serenity'; however Ives quite likely extracted his two stanzas from the hymn rather than from the original poem.

An early version of the text appears below. Some hymnal editors omit the fourth stanza or reorder the stanza so that the fifth stanza as printed here comes last.

>Dear Lord and Father of mankind,
>Forgive our foolish ways!
>Reclothe us in our rightful mind,
>In purer lives Thy service find,
>In deeper reverence, praise.
>
>In simple trust like theirs who heard,
>Beside the Syrian sea,
>The gracious calling of the Lord,
>Let us, like them, without a word
>Rise up and follow Thee.
>
>O Sabbath rest by Galilee!
>O calm of hills above,
>Where Jesus knelt to share with Thee
>The silence of eternity,
>Interpreted by love!
>
>With that deep hush subduing all
>Our words and works that drown
>The tender whisper of Thy call,
>As noiseless let Thy blessing fall
>As fell Thy manna down.
>
>Drop Thy still dews of quietness,
>Till all our strivings cease;
>Take from our souls the strain and stress,
>And let our ordered lives confess
>The beauty of Thy peace.
>
>Breathe through the heats of our desire
>Thy coolness and Thy balm;
>Let sense be dumb, let flesh retire;
>Speak through the earthquake, wind, and fire,
>O still small voice of calm!

It is often the modern custom, when singing the final stanza as printed here, to gradually sing louder from 'Let sense be dumb...', reaching a crescendo on '...the earthquake, wind and fire', before then singing the last line 'O still, small voice of calm' much more softly.

Parry;   Vaughan Williams;   Stainer;   Stanford

C H Parry   1848-1918
JERUSALEM   1916   And did those feet
REPTON   1888   Dear Lord and Father …
LAUDATE DOM.   1894   O Praise ye the Lord …

Ralph Vaughan-Williams   1872-1958
MONKS GATE   1906   He who would valiant
SINE NOMINE   1906   For all the Saints,
SUSSEX   Father, hear the prayer
KING'S WESTON   At the name of Jesus

C V Stanford   1852-1924
Composer; Critic of Victorian hymn-tunes

John Stainer   1840-1901
Composer; Critic of Victorian hymn-tunes

John Bacchus Dykes   1823-1876

John Bacchus Dykes was a clergyman and hymnwriter with a very unusual middle name. There seems to be no well-documented reason for his forename of 'Bacchus' as part of an evangelical background – recent calculations suggest it may derive as a maternal surname, going back to perhaps Backhouse thence Bakehouse. His definitely non-pagan tunes have proved remarkably resilient, with NICAEA, MELITA, DOMINUS REGIT ME and GERONTIUS continuing to find a place in modern hymnals.

By the age of 10, he was de facto assistant organist – there is no record of any formal appointment – at St John's Church in Myton, Hull. His father's father was vicar; his uncle was organist. After the Proprietary School at Wakefield, he went to St. Catharine's College), Cambridge, as the second 'Dikes Scholar' (an endowment in honour of his grandfather).

Although his paternal grandfather and father were firmly evangelical; once he had left Hull, Dykes went towards the Anglo-Catholic, ritualist, wing of the Church of England during his Cambridge years. He definitely sympathised with the Oxford Movement's views.

There, as an extra-curricular subject, he studied music under Thomas Walmisley, whose madrigal society he joined. He also joined the Peterhouse Musical Society (later renamed the Cambridge University Musical Society) and became its fourth President.

Having graduated in 1847, he was appointed to the curacy of Malton, North Yorkshire, in 1847. He was ordained Deacon at York Minster within the year. The following year he was appointed a minor canon at Durham Cathedral, an appointment which he held until his death. In 1862 he relinquished the precentorship (to the dismay of his friend Sir Frederick Ouseley) as he was then appointed to the living of St Oswald's Durham, situated almost in the shadow of the Cathedral, where he remained until his death in 1876.

It was also in 1860 that he heard, by chance, of the work being done to create Hymns Ancient and Modern. He offered several pieces, all of which were well received.

At Durham he took his responsibilities as precentor very seriously. He established choir discipline (the choir was reckoned to be one of the finest in England under his stewardship), proper dress (which included cassocks and surplices), and rehearsals for Lay Clerks; he was a supporter of the movement to introduce special 'orchestral' services with music from oratorios. In 1861 Durham University conferred on him the degree of DMus, and in 1863 he conducted a grand festival of music in the cathedral. He was a regular visitor to the Three Choirs Festival, and was a friend of Ouseley, Sullivan and Stainer.

At this time, antagonism between the evangelical and Anglo-Catholic wings of the Church of England was heated and sometimes violent. One fragment of shrapnel hit Dykes.

A very traumatic episode of his ministry was in his last years at St Oswald's when he entered into a dispute with the Bishop of Durham, Charles Baring, in 1873. Forbidden to wear coloured stoles and to turn eastwards during the celebration of Communion (a practice which led such as Liddon, Purchas, Gregory, Mackonochie and others into similarly public dispute at their Bishops) Dykes saw this as an unreasonable attack on high church or ritualistic practices in the Durham diocese. With his allies, he defied his Bishop, who refused to license further curates to St Oswald's. An appeal to the Court of the Queen's Bench was made in January 1874, but, not wishing to interfere in ecclesiastical matters, the judges dismissed the case.

Dykes' defeat was followed by a gradual deterioration in his physical and mental health, necessitating absence (which was to prove permanent) from St. Oswald's from 1875. Rest and the bracing Swiss air proving unavailing, Dykes eventually went to recover on the south coast of England where, on 22 January 1876, he died aged just 52.

The popular image of Dykes is that he was a quiet, thoughtful, cautious man who recoiled from abrasiveness or pugnacity. Yet, surviving documents reveal that he could be highly assertive, argumentative and outspoken. As a high churchman he embraced the 'consubstantial' view of the Eucharist (rather than the 'transubstantiation' of Wilberforce), a sacrament he promoted with alacrity at St Oswald's; and he felt a kinship with Keble's teachings on the early church (rather than Newman's understanding of the doctrine of the church). He resisted attacks on the low-church evangelicals and dissenters but, during the controversy on the writings of Bishop Colenso, called unequivocally for his deposition.

He is buried in the 'overflow' churchyard of St. Oswald's, a piece of land for whose acquisition and consecration he had been responsible a few years earlier. Touchingly, he shares a grave with his youngest daughter, Mabel, who died, aged 10, of scarlet fever in 1870. Dykes' grave is now the only marked one in what, in recent years, has been transformed into a children's playground.

His works display both erudition and wit (as well as a penchant for damnation by faint praise and gentle sarcasm). He wrote on the Apocalypse, the Psalms, and the function of music and ritual for the church. He composed over 200 hymn-settings. Of great significance was his speculative submission in 1860 of settings to the music editor (W.H. Monk) for the new venture: Hymns Ancient and Modern. His reputation as a hymn-writer was established after this first contribution. With W H Monks, his music became a crucial part of the A&M repertoire. This amounted initially to seven tunes shown below; all of which became well known, and most still are.

DIES IRAE	(Day of wrath O day of mourning) [now rarely sung];
HOLLINGSIDE	(Jesu, lover of my soul);
HORBURY	(Nearer, my God, to Thee);
MELITA,	(Eternal Father, strong to save);
NICAEA	(Holy, holy, holy! Lord God Almighty!), a tune which bears striking similarities to John Hopkins' TRINITY, from 1850 for the same words.
ST. CROSS	(O come and mourn with me awhile);
ST. CUTHBERT	(Our blest Redeemer, ere He breathed).

Later, tunes include GERONTIUS (Praise to the Holiest in the height), taken from Cardinal Newman's poem The Dream of Gerontius,;

    LUX BENIGNA   (set to Newman's poem Lead, Kindly Light);
    STRENGTH AND STAY (O strength and stay, upholding all creation.
    DOMINUS REGIT ME (The King of Love my shepherd by W H Baker)

He harmonised WIR PFLÜGEN   (We plough the fields, and scatter),
as well as   MILES LANE   (All hail the power of Jesu's name)
and   O QUANTA QUALIA   (O, what their joy and their glory must be).

'O perfect love, all human thoughts transcending' by Dorothy Gurney was inspired by Dykes' tune STRENGTH AND STAY. The author wrote "The tune by John B. Dykes was my sister's favourite, but that hymn's text (by Ellerton and Hort) included the line 'the brightness of a holy death-bed', which in my view made it inappropriate for a wedding." So, being challenged to write a new text, just 15 minutes later, she had succeeded. When it was used at the wedding of Princess Louise in 1889, it gained huge popularity.

For the 1868 Appendix, W H Monk invited Dykes to deliver 17 more tunes. For the 1875 edition, a further 32 were accepted bringing his total to 56, one eighth of the entire collection. In the 1904 edition, a reaction against the Victorian hymn (in favour of the desire to 'elevate popular taste') was measured by a decrease in the number of Dykes' tunes to 38, though, after the failure of that edition, his presence once again rose.

The end of his century brought a widespread reaction against much of the Victorian aesthetic, and his music did not escape a censure which was often vituperative. In particular, one wrote "Though much of his work has fallen into disuse in recent years, some deservedly so, although the Burial Service is a minor gem."

Speaking of Victorian hymn-tunes generally, but evidently with Dykes in his sights Vaughan Williams wrote of "the miasma of the languishing and sentimental hymn tunes which so often disfigure our services."

Scholars in recent years have questioned this criticism which so condemned Dykes' music out of hand. Several, especially Prof Dibble have noted the importance of his pioneering work in moving hymn-tunes from the bland and four-square long metre tunes which had been the staple of Tate and Brady's New Version of the Psalms. "A…characteristic element of [Dykes'] style is his use of imaginative diatonic and chromatic harmony. Dykes was thoroughly aware of the rich reservoir of continental harmonic innovation in the music of Schubert, Mendelssohn, Weber, Spohr, Schumann, Chopin, Liszt and early Wagner and he had absolutely no compunction in using this developed harmonic vocabulary in his tunes both as a colourful expressive tool and as a further means of musical integration."

While changing tastes in music have seen a steady decline in the use of Victorian hymn tunes generally, including those by Sir Arthur Sullivan, Sir John Stainer, Sir Joseph Barnby and Lowell Mason, despite the decades of criticism a good number of Dykes' tunes have actually proved remarkably resilient and continue to find a place in twenty-first century hymnals. In the 1950 *A&MR* he was still prominent, with 31 tunes, and in *A&MCP* there are 21 original tunes and one harmonization by him.

By the mid-19th century, Victorian composers, Dykes among them, had departed from the older manner of harmonic motion governed by individual syllables of the text and instead had developed a sophisticated and more liberal approach. Harmony was thus independent of the individual syllables and took a much more important and musically integral role. Therefore the congregation became part of a more elaborate artistic composition where the four voices of the choir (invariably appreciable in size) and a generous organ became vital factors in a more homogeneous equation. This is powerfully evident in the first line of NICAEA 'Holy, holy, holy, Lord God Almighty'.

Dykes was, along with Gauntlett – almost unknown now - a hugely prolific Victorian composer of hymn tunes. In 1902 a volume containing no less than 276 numbers was published by Novello and edited by his son, Edward (with assistance from Stainer, who died before its publication). It showed that Dykes had contributed to a very wide range of hymnals but that he had 70 or more tunes which were then unpublished.

It is a very considerable surprise that he is omitted from Julian's§ 1892 *Dictionary of Hymnology* – until one realizes he is 'only a composer' He does have a piece in the (American) *Chambers Encyclopedia* of the same year.

As well as his legacy of hymns, he and his wife Susannah had 3 sons and 5 daughters.

First Edition of Hymns Ancient and Modern 1861
Inside Front Cover

Note that W H Monk is the only name displayed!

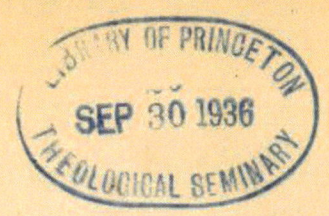

HYMNS,

ANCIENT AND MODERN,

FOR USE IN THE SERVICES OF THE CHURCH,

WITH

ACCOMPANYING TUNES,

COMPILED AND ARRANGED

UNDER THE MUSICAL EDITORSHIP OF

WILLIAM HENRY MONK,

ORGANIST AND DIRECTOR OF THE CHOIR AT KING'S COLLEGE, LONDON.

"Young men and maidens, old men and children, praise the Name of the Lord."

LONDON:
J. ALFRED NOVELLO,
69, DEAN STREET, SOHO, AND 35, POULTRY.

𝔈ternal 𝔉ather, strong to save

	W Whiting	1825-1878	1860	4 verses
MELITA	J B Dykes§	1823-1876	1861	8.8.8.8.8.8

Psalms 107:24   "They saw the works of the Lord, his wonderful deeds in the deep".

This is one of the most widely known hymns in English. It was written in 1860 and first appeared, after revision by the compilers, in the *First Edition of A&M* (1861). Perhaps it was inspired by the unusually stormy weather and numerous shipwrecks in late 1859, especially as Whiting had felt his life spared by God when a violent storm hit the ship, instilling a belief in God's command over the rage and calm of the sea.

Whiting's original text, beginning 'O thou, who bidd'st the ocean deep' was substantially altered by the compilers of A&M. The most striking of these changes was the rearrangement of the first stanza, so that lines 4 and 3 became lines 1 and 2 and thus arrived at the first line of the hymn we now know. Other alterations were made in the *Second Edition of A&M* of 1875. The hymn has numerous variations of text, some by Whiting himself in 1869. There is an official Royal Navy version; in the United States it is known as the 'Navy hymn'.

Whiting was born about 1825 and died at just 53. Whiting grew up near the ocean on the coasts of England and knew the perils. One unproven tale is that as headmaster of the Winchester College Choristers' School some years later, he was approached by a student about to travel to the United States, who confided in Whiting an great fear of the ocean voyage. Whiting shared his experiences of the ocean and wrote the hymn to 'anchor his faith'.

With the development of cars, aviation and even space travel – and apparently submarines - many attempts were made to extend this navy hymn . *The Book of Worship for U.S Forces: Hymns & Worship Resources for Military Personnel of the United States of America* has several such.

Psalm 107:24 is identified in the 1867 publication as the key reference for this hymn. Psalm 107:23-26 describe the power and fury of the seas in great detail:

> *"Some went out on the sea in ships; they were merchants on the mighty waters.*
> *They saw the works of the Lord, his wonderful deeds in the deep.*
> *For he spoke and stirred up a tempest that lifted high the waves.*
> *They mounted up to the heavens and down to the depths; in their peril their courage melted away.*

Each of the first three stanzas is addressed to one person of the Trinity, with all three brought together in the last stanza, giving the hymn a strong and well-rounded structure, reinforced by the refrain. The first stanza recalls God's creation of the waters (Genesis 1:9) and the powerful description of a storm at sea referenced by the Psalm. There is also an echo of *Paradise Lost VII* 166-7. The second stanza refers to the miracles of Christ's calming of the storm and walking on the water. The third stanza is more complex.

A second assessment is that the first verse refers to God the Father forbidding the waters to flood the earth as described in Psalm 104. The second verse refers again to Jesus' miracles of stilling a storm and walking on the waters of the Sea of Galilee. The third verse references the Holy Spirit's role in the creation of the earth in the Book of Genesis, while the final verse is a reference to Psalm 107.

The matching of Whiting's words to MELITA, the tune written for it by John Bacchus Dykes and first used in 1861 is an outstandingly successful pairing. The name of the tune is derived from the island of Melita (Malta), where St Paul landed after being shipwrecked (Acts 28:1). In the reaction against Dykes at the start of the 20th century it met much criticism, usually on the grounds that it falls away after a strong opening. Various alternatives were put forward. Robert Heinlein wrote a verse for astronauts, the travellers into the perils of Space.

FOLKINGHAM, VATER UNSER, LODSWORTH were all been suggested as alternatives once Dykes' style became less popular when views changed. However, Walford Davies compares the newer LODSWORTH to MELITA, "[The Dykes tune] is not bad, nor is it very good, as a setting for the words, for congregational singing, it beats LODSWORTH all ends up."

Benjamin Britten used MELITA effectively in his setting of the Chester miracle play *Noye's Fludde*. As with others, it is said to have been sung on board the Titanic on the morning before she sank. Winston Churchill had it sung on board ship before the signing of the Atlantic Charter in 1941. It is often sung at funerals.

Due to the numbers of groups to which this is a significant hymn – the words have been changed and amended very often. This is an early version of the wording.

> Eternal Father, strong to save,
> Whose arm hath bound the restless wave,
> Who bid'st the mighty ocean deep
> Its own appointed limits keep;
> O hear us when we cry to Thee,
> For those in peril on the sea.
>
> O Christ, Whose voice the waters heard
> And hushed their raging at Thy word,
> Who walkedst on the foaming deep,
> And calm amidst its rage didst sleep;
> O hear us when we cry to Thee,
> For those in peril on the sea.
>
> Most Holy Spirit, Who didst brood
> Upon the chaos dark and rude,
> And bid its angry tumult cease,
> And give, for wild confusion, peace;
> O hear us when we cry to Thee,
> For those in peril on the sea!
>
> O Trinity of love and power,
> Our brethren shield in danger's hour;
> From rock and tempest, fire and foe,
> Protect them wheresoe'er they go;
> Thus evermore shall rise to Thee
> Glad hymns of praise from land and sea.

Father, hear the prayer we offer

	Love Maria Willis	1824-1908	1859	4,5,3 verses
MARCHING	Martin Shaw	1875-1958	1915	8.7.8.7
or SUSSEX	arrgd Vaughan Williams	1872-1958		

It is not easy to understand why this hymn provoked Erik Routley to an extraordinary outburst of ill temper in 1979. It seems to be a straightforward and unexceptionable hymn, suitable for many occasions; however Routley, then best-known expert on English hymnolgy, wrote describing the hymn: (writing of himself in the third person) as "that wretched travesty of the 23rd Psalm, 'Father, hear the prayer we offer' being among the American pieces introduced to England by Garrett Horder and Percy Dearmer, [it] appeals [appears?] to him [Routley] as being by far the worst hymn of the century written in either country."

This brief American hymn comes from 1859. The first appearance was in *Tiffany's Monthly Magazine* (1859), a magazine 'devoted to the investigation of spiritual science', of which the author was at one time the editor. It was very heavily revised, probably by Samuel Longfellow. By the time of Samuel Johnson's *Hymns of the Spirit* in 1864, it was entitled 'A Prayer of Life'. The original title was 'Aspiration' and the author was Love Maria Willis nee Whitcomb, a resident of New York state. There is no strong reference to any especial Bible verse other than the obvious Psalm 23.

There are only a few hymns in this collection which derive from outside the United Kingdom. No subtle intent is meant by this. I have room for only about 75; I prefer to write about those I have already some feeling for, or for which there is clearly an interesting story.

Father, hear the prayer we offer!
Not for ease that prayer shall be,
But for strength that we may ever
Live our lives courageously.

Not forever in green pastures
Do we ask our way to be;
But the steep and rugged pathway
May we tread rejoicingly.

Not for ever by still waters   *[sometimes omitted]*
May we idly quiet stay;
But would smite the living fountains
From the rocks upon our way.

Be our strength in hours of weakness,
In our wanderings, be our guide;
Through endeavor, failure, danger,
Father, be Thou at our side!

A fifth stanza was added and printed by W G Horder in 1884 in his *Congregational Hymns*, which first introduced the hymn to Britain.

> Let our path be bright or dreary,
> Storm or sunshine be our share;
>   May our souls, in hope unweary,
>   Make Thy work our ceaseless prayer.

With its emphasis on the need for courageous living, this hymn has become a feature of many books in the USA and in Britain (where it seems especially popular, sung to the tune SUSSEX, from an English traditional melody arranged by Vaughan Williams.)

In the US, a tune by Edmund Carter of Yorkshire, (1845-1923) known simply as 'CARTER' is well-known – but then he is listed only as having composed that and one other.

Other settings include Dykes'§ ST SYLVESTER as well as his ST OSWALD; GOTT WILL'S MACHEN; STOCKWELL, MARCHING and nearly 20 others including several versions simply labelled by the first line 'Father hear the prayer we offer'.

As regards any particular Bible reference, the usage of 'green pastures' and 'still waters' makes the link to Psalm 23 very clear. Scholars will be able to attach more verses to other lines – but this is a relatively simple Victorian hymn with, as far as is known about the author's intentions, no stated claims to importance or Biblical authority.

More unusually, this hymn derives from a movement which is now seen as barely Christian in style – Spiritualism. Spiritualism then was not yet subject to the disapproval it received later.

Spiritualism first appeared in the 1840s in upstate New York (the same area where Millerism and Mormonism had emerged – all as part of the Second Awakening. This was part of the early 19th century Protestant religious revival in the United States – and linked with the much larger Romantic movement that was sweeping across England, Scotland, and Germany. The Awakening spread through charisma and emotional preaching, sparking several reform movements. Revivals especially were a key component and attracted hundreds of converts to new Protestant denominations.

The key facts of Spiritualism included a belief that contact with spirits is possible, and that spirits are more advanced than humans. These led spiritualists to accept that spirits are capable of providing useful knowledge about moral and ethical issues, as well as about the nature of God. Spiritualism developed and reached its peak growth in membership from the 1840s to the 1920s, especially in English-speaking areas. By 1897, spiritualism was said to have more than eight million followers in the United States and Europe, mostly drawn from the middle and upper classes.

Miss Whitcomb married Frederick Willis in 1858. He was at Harvard College Divinity School, but was suspended in 1857 for his interest in the Spiritualist movement, then very popular. He became a Spiritualist minister and practised as a doctor in New York state. His daughter Edith described him as a Unitarian minister. At one time Love Maria edited the Spiritualist paper *The Banner of Light* (a journal 'of Romance, Literature, and general intelligence') and also *Tiffany's Monthly Magazine* ('devoted to the investigation of spiritual science').

Fight the good fight

	John Monsell	1811-1875	1863	4 verses
DUKE STREET	John Hatton	1710-1793	1796	8.8.8.8
or PENTECOST	William Boyd	1847-1928	1864	

1 Timothy 6:12   "Fight the good fight of the faith. Take hold of the eternal life."

A fine preacher and a man of happy disposition, John Monsell urged that hymns should be fervent and joyous, and that congregations should abandon their sense of distance and reserve in singing. From this reasoning emerged those hymns for which he is best known, including 'Fight the good fight with all thy might'. This was written as an injunction to faithfulness and steadfastness based on lines from the Epistles. 'O worship the Lord in the beauty of holiness' was an Epiphany hymn with words drawn from the Psalms, and featuring imagery of the gifts brought to the baby Jesus. These are not the only hymns by him still in regular use.

The hymn, or at least the first verse, is clearly based on Paul's First Epistle to Timothy 6::12: 'Fight the good fight of faith, lay hold on eternal life, whereunto thou art also called, and hast professed a good profession before many witnesses'. The hymn lyrics urge the listener with those phrases as well as 'run the straight race', 'cast care aside', and 'faint not nor fear'. One hymnal points out that the next three verses are each based on a passage from the New Testament epistles: Hebrews 12:2; 1 Peter 5:7; and Colossians 3:11.

It was written by John Samuel Bewley Monsell and published in *Hymns of Love and Praise for the Church's Year* (1863). Irish born in 1811 he lived there, schooled there and was ordained there until he moved to Surrey in 1853 aged 42. He died in 1875 aged 64. Monsell was a prolific writer, with eleven volumes of verse, which included 300 hymns; the most important ones appeared in *Hymns and Miscellaneous Poems* (Dublin, 1837); *Spiritual Songs* (1857); *Litany Hymns* (1869) and *The Parish Hymnal after the Order of The Book of Common Prayer* (1873).

Monsell believed in spontaneity in writing and relevance to parish concerns; as he stated in his preface to *Parish Musings, or Devotional Poems* (1850), his work consisted of 'the unpremeditated aspirations and utterances of the heart of one engaged in the active service of parish labour'. He also felt a compulsion to edit; therefore various versions of his hymns exist.

John Julian described Monsell's hymns as 'bright, joyous and musical; but they lack massiveness, concentration of thought, and strong emotion'. He thought that 'a few only are of enduring excellence'. Indeed, a few of his hymns have shown sufficient powers of endurance, and so continue to be included in many modern books.

It is sung primarily to two tunes: PENTECOST, written in 1864 by William Boyd and DUKE STREET, believed to be by John Hatton.

William Boyd was born in Jamaica in 1847 and died in London in 1928. He composed PENTECOST in 1864 for the hymn text 'Come, Holy Ghost, Our Souls Inspire'. A simple chant-like tune with a range of only five tones in the melody, PENTECOST is one of the 'generic' Victorian tunes of its time. As a reminder, the Christian holiday of Pentecost is celebrated on the 50th day (the seventh Sunday) from Easter Sunday. It commemorates the descent of the Holy Spirit upon the Apostles and other followers of Jesus Christ while they were in Jerusalem. According to the text in Acts of the Apostles, there is a 'mighty rushing wind' (wind is a common symbol for the Holy Spirit) and 'tongues as of fire' appear. The gathered disciples were 'filled with the Holy Spirit, and began to speak in other tongues as the

Spirit gave them utterance'. The exact meaning of this text is subject to arguable interpretation.

Others of like measure are QUEBEC; ST CRISPIN; MORECAMBE and MARYTON. One writer says 'Sing it in harmony, perhaps unaccompanied, but with a firm pulse and not too slowly'. Therefore, as regards suitability for 'Fight the good fight', the choice has to be between the humble, meditative character of PENTECOST which stands in contrast to the spirit of rejoicing found in DUKE STREET. The text can also be sung to PUER NOBIS.

Little is known of John Hatton; he lived in Warrington, Lancashire; he died in 1793 allegedly in a stagecoach accident. His most famous setting DUKE STREET was published after his death. It was first attached to Addison's 'The spacious firmament on high' (from the 19th Psalm). Then later with C Wesley's§ 'Father, whose everlasting love' and 'Shepherd of souls, with pitying eye'. DUKE STREET also fits Montgomery's§ 'Pour out thy spirit from on high'; while in American books, it is set for Watts'§ 'Jesus shall reign where'er the sun'. Millar Patrick wrote of the tune: 'What vigour you have in it! — what magnificent movement, what superb curves, every line soaring, subsiding, like the flight of a bird!'

> Fight the good fight with all thy might;
> Christ is thy Strength, and Christ thy Right;
> Lay hold on life, and it shall be
> Thy joy and crown eternally.
>
> Run the straight race through God's good grace,
> Lift up thine eyes, and seek His face;
> Life with its way before us lies,
> Christ is the Path, and Christ the Prize.
>
> Cast care aside, upon thy Guide,
> Lean, and His mercy will provide;
> Lean, and the trusting soul shall prove
> Christ is its Life, and Christ its Love.
>
> Faint not nor fear, His arms are near,
> He changeth not, and thou art dear.
> Only believe, and thou shalt see
> That Christ is all in all to thee.

Monsell's words, combined with the customary tune, DUKE STREET, make for stirring singing, but have given problems in verse 3, where he wrote:

Cast care aside, upon thy Guide,	alters to	Cast care aside, lean on thy Guide
Lean, and his mercy will provide;		His boundless mercy will provide
Lean, and the trusting soul shall prove		Trust, and thy trusting soul shall prove
Christ is its life, and Christ its love.		.....same

A danger is that the first line will be read separately from the rest, and the comma in the middle ignored; the rhythm and syntax are not definite enough. It is not viable to 'Cast care aside upon the guide'. A number of books alter so as to ensure a more determined rendition.

For all the Saints

| | W Walsham How | 1823-1897 | 1864 | 11 verses (8or 6) |
| SINE NOMINE | R Vaughan Williams | 1872-1958 | 1906 | 10.10.10.10 |

Hebrews 12:1   "Therefore, since we are surrounded by so great a cloud of witnesses, …."

This long hymn, originally of 11 verses, was written as a processional hymn in 1864 by the Bishop of Wakefield, William Walsham How. Called both the 'poor man's bishop' and 'the children's bishop', and later the 'omnibus bishop' How was known for his work among the destitute in the London slums and among the factory workers in Yorkshire. He also wrote a number of theological works about controversies surrounding the Oxford Movement and attempted to reconcile biblical creation with the theory of evolution.

Much of its power derives from its ability to capture the spirit of the Church Militant here on earth, using imagery from the book of Revelation (see particularly its closing stanzas and their references to Revelation chapters 2, 5, 7 and 21).

Much of the text links to the Te Deum; and the whole hymn, in effect, takes the motifs described there and praises them one by one. The length of the piece, eleven verses originally, makes the singer and the audient think about the long drawn out and exhausting struggle between good and evil and then the eventual certainty of Good God triumphant against Evil Devil.

With its original title 'Saints'-Day Hymn', the text begins with a thanksgiving for the saints ('the cloud of witnesses') who confessed Christ and found in him protection and inspiration (st. 1-2). This is followed by a prayer for Christ's soldiers on earth to be 'faithful, true, and bold' (st. 3). Then the 'blest communion' of saints in heaven and on earth (st. 4). Though the holy warfare may be 'fierce and long' (st. 5), 'all the saints' may take courage from the vision of a victorious church that worships the triune God on that 'more glorious day' (st. 6-7). (Among the stanzas omitted in most hymnals are those that begin 'for all the apostles', 'for all the evangelists', and 'for all the martyrs').

The hymn was sung to the melody SARUM, by the Victorian composer J Bamby. until the arrival of the *English Hymnal* in 1906. Vaughan Williams provided a new setting called SINE NOMINE (literally, 'without name' – as which saint could one choose) in reference to its use on All Saints Day. It has been described as 'one of the finest hymn tunes of the [20th] century.' Vaughan Williams' Will forbad its use for any other text. As J R Watson writes 'to hear this sung by a large congregation with energy and joy such as in a cathedral is a memorable experience.'

Although most English hymn tunes of the Victorian era were written for singing in Soprano-Alto-Tenor-Bass 'SATB' four-part harmony, SINE NOMINE is primarily unison (verses 1,2,3,7 and 8) with organ accompaniment; three verses (4, 5 and 6) are set in sung harmony.

C V Stanford's old tune ENGELBERG was also written to be partnered with this hymn, although in the wake of SINE NOMINE it never gained popularity and is now more commonly used with other hymns, including 'When in Our Music God is Glorified'. Dibble sees Stanford's tune as a precursor to SINE NOMINE. TROYTE'S CHANT no2 was used in 1875. Since the 1990s, a tune composed by C Miner has increased in popularity.

An early version of the text :-

1. For all the saints, who from their labours rest,
   Who Thee by faith before the world confessed,
   Thy Name, O Jesus, be forever blessed.   Alleluia, Alleluia!

2. Thou wast their Rock, their Fortress and their Might;
   Thou, Lord, their Captain in the well fought fight;
   Thou, in the darkness drear, their one true Light.   Alleluia, Alleluia!

3. For the Apostles' glorious company,   *Often ommitted*
   Who bearing forth the Cross o'er land and sea,
   Shook all the mighty world, we sing to Thee: Alleluia, Alleluia!

4. O may Thy soldiers, faithful, true and bold,   *Often ommitted*
   Fight as the saints who nobly fought of old,
   And win with them the victor's crown of gold.   Alleluia, Alleluia!

5. For the Evangelists, by whose blest word,   *Often ommitted*
   Like fourfold streams, the garden of the Lord,
   Is fair and fruitful, be Thy Name adored.   Alleluia, Alleluia!

6. For Martyrs, who with rapture kindled eye,
   Saw the bright crown descending from the sky,
   And seeing, grasped it, Thee we glorify.   Alleluia, Alleluia!

7. O blest communion, fellowship divine!
   We feebly struggle, they in glory shine;
   Yet all are one in Thee, for all are Thine.   Alleluia, Alleluia!

8. And when the strife is fierce, the warfare long,
   Steals on the ear the distant triumph song,
   And hearts are brave, again, and arms are strong.   Alleluia, Alleluia!

9. The golden evening brightens in the west;
   Soon, soon to faithful warriors comes their rest;
   Sweet is the calm of paradise the blessed.   Alleluia, Alleluia!

10. But lo! there breaks a yet more glorious day;
    The saints triumphant rise in bright array;
    The King of glory passes on His way.   Alleluia, Alleluia!

11. From earth's wide bounds, from ocean's farthest coast,
    Through gates of pearl streams in the countless host,
    Singing to Father, Son and Holy Ghost: Alleluia, Alleluia!

Glorious things of Thee are spoken

	John Newton	1725-1808	1779	5 verses
AUSTRIAN HYMN§	Josef Haydn	1732-1809	1797	8.7.8.7 x2

Psalm 87:3   "Glorious things are spoken of thee, O city of God"

This text is also called 'Zion, or the City of God' which is the second line. It is an English hymn written in 1779 by John Newton. His early history was not the stuff of dreams, or nightmares – conscript; deserter; slaver; then convert. Newton's self-penned epitaph: *JOHN NEWTON, Clerk, Once an infidel and libertine, a servant of slaves in Africa was, by the rich mercy of our Lord and Saviour JESUS CHRIST, restored, pardoned and appointed to preach the Gospel which he had long laboured to destroy. He ministered near sixteen years in Olney and twenty-eight in this Church.*

Several factors contributed to Newton's conversion: a near-drowning in 1748, the piety of his friend Mary Catlett, (whom he married in 1750), and his reading of Thomas à Kempis' *Imitation of Christ*. This hymn has been called one of Newton's finest hymns, and it is certainly one of his most popular, along with 'Amazing Grace §' and 'How Sweet the Name of Jesus Sounds'. Newton's wonderful language and imagery has helped to make it one of the 'solid joys' of English hymnody for over two centuries.

This hymn was written by Newton with assistance from his friend and Olney neighbour, classical writer and poet William Cowper. Some say it was the only joyful hymn in the 1779 publication. The *Olney Hymns* are an illustration of the potent ideologies of the Evangelical movement, to which both men belonged.

The title of *Book I of the Olney Hymns*, published in 1779 by Newton and Cowper, is 'On Select Texts of Scripture,' containing hymns written on specific scripture passages, arranged in biblical order. Newton's 'Glorious Things of Thee Are Spoken', is number 60 in this book. It is written on Isaiah 33:20-21, but there are plenty of clear references to other scriptures, which Newton cited, such as Psalm 87 (the first two lines very close to Ps. 87:3; Isaiah 4:5-6 (for the third stanza); and via Olney Hymns Book 2 Hymn 24 to Jeremiah 1:5. To be thorough, other verses include Isaiah 26:1; Psalm 132:14, Psalm 46:4 and Revelation 1:6.

The theme of these stanzas is the universal church, and its story. The text begins with a vision of the new city of God (Hebrews 12:22) in the first two stanzas, and then looks back to the early journey of the Israelites, with references in the third stanza to cloud, fire, and manna (Exodus 13:21, 16:31).

The hymn is one of several in which Newton used the city of Zion to represent Christian aspiration in concrete terms. The imagery is based on some of the most visionary and poetic passages in the Bible. Newton blends something of his practical and down-to-earth imagination in lines such as 'And all fear of want remove' (his experience of actual hunger and thirst informing his spiritual application of the image). Only in the last stanza does Newton use 'I', and even then the final lines invite us to place ourselves within the community of 'Zion's children'.

Cowper is most known for his comic poem '*The Diverting History of John Gilpin Shewing how he went Farther than he intended, and came safe Home again.* Written in 1782 the ballad concerns a draper called John Gilpin who rides a runaway horse. It was very popular, to the extent that 'pirate copies were being sold all across the country, together with Gilpin books and toys'. It was republished in 1878, illustrated by Randolph Caldecott. The cover illustration is the design for the Caldecott Medal awarded annually for American Childrens' Picture-book Fiction. His poem 'Light shining out of darkness' gave us the phrase and the hymn: 'God moves in a mysterious way/ His wonders to perform §'.

'Glorious things …' was a favourite of Confederate General Stonewall Jackson. He is reported as having once awakened his soldiers in 1862 while they were in the Shenandoah Valley by singing, if that's the word, out of tune.

Three or four stanzas are sung, always including the first and second. Of the remaining three, the original fourth (beginning 'Blest inhabitants of Zion') is usually omitted, and then either the third ('Round each habitation') or the fifth ('Saviour, if of Zion's city').

From early times editors have tried re-selections and re-ordering the stanzas. Some early variations, such as adding a doxology by an unknown writer, have not lasted. However, a version made from stanzas 1, 2, and 5 is now the usual choice.

Obviously, like many others, it has suffered from the demand to alter 'thee,thou,thy' to 'you etc'. Numerous other textual tinkerings have occurred.

It is most likely that Newton's hymns were originally just chanted. The common tune nowadays is C V Taylor's ABBOT'S LEIGH setting was anecdata inaccurately states was written in response to complaints received by the BBC during the war.

For many years, the most usual setting is known as AUSTRIAN HYMN. This piece came about when several Austrians decided they must create something to stand beside the English anthem 'God save the King' written in about 1743. They felt that Austria needed something as powerful and significant, and not merely regal but imperial.

The ruler in question was Francis, born 1768, from 1792 he ruled through to 1835 as the Holy Roman Emperor, the last as the position ended in 1806, Soon after Napoleon had created the Confederation of the Rhine, Francis abdicated as the last Holy Roman Emperor. In response to Napoleon's self-enhancement to Emperor of the French, Francis assumed the title of Emperor of Austria in 1804. Francis was also King of Bohemia, Croatia and Hungary.

The poet Haschka wrote the words of the required anthem; Josef Haydn set the text to music. In January 1797, this double task was resolved, and the first performance was ordered for the birthday of the Monarch. 'Gott erhalte Franz den Kaiser' was first performed on the Emperor's birthday, 12 February 1797. It proved popular, and came to serve unofficially as Austria's first national anthem. The tune became known as AUSTRIA. As well as for this hymn and the German national anthem formerly known, popularly, as Deutschland unter alles - properly titled Das Lied der Deutschen or the Deutschlandlied - the third verse of which is the German anthem since 1922. . This has resulted in some strange outcomes.

In 1936, at Durham Cathedral, the German Ambassador to the United Kingdom, von Ribbentrop, heard the tune and -expecting 'his' anthem - gave a Nazi salute and had to be restrained by the Marquess of Londonderry. During the Second World War in a prisoner of war camp, a Protestant service was interrupted during the singing of 'Glorious things of Thee are spoken' by the POWs singing 'Sei gesegnet ohne Ende' because this was yet another hymn was set to the same tune. Therefore for some, despite it actually being an old tune dating back to the 18th century, it had uneasy reminders of Nazi Germany.

More than 40 settings suit this 8.7.8.7 D format: names include HARWELL; ST ASAPH; JEFFERSON; GREENVILLE; WORTHING; SION'S SECURITY; STOUGHTON; RIPLEY; and at least 3 just using the name of the hymn.

An early version of the words is as follows (there are many textual tweaks)

1. Glorious things of thee are spoken,
Zion, city of our God;
he whose word cannot be broken
formed thee for his own abode;
on the Rock of Ages founded,
what can shake thy sure repose?
With salvation's walls surrounded,
thou may'st smile at all thy foes.

2. See the streams of living waters,
springing from eternal love,
well supply thy sons and daughters,
and all fear of want remove;
who can faint while such a river
ever flows their thirst t'assuage?
Grace, which like the Lord, the giver,
never fails from age to age.

3. Round each habitation hov'ring,
see the cloud and fire appear
for a glory and a cov'ring,
showing that the Lord is near;
thus deriving from their banner
light by night and shade by day,
safe they feed upon the manna
which he gives them when they pray.

4. Blest inhabitants of Zion, *often ommitted*
Wash'd in the Redeemer's blood!
Jesus, whom their souls rely on
Makes them kings and priests to God:
'Tis his love his people raises
Over self to reign as kings
And as priests, his solemn praises
Each for a thank-off'ring brings.

5. Savior, if of Zion's city
I, thro' grace, a member am,
let the world deride or pity,
I will glory in thy name;
fading is the worldling's pleasure,
all his boasted pomp and show;
solid joys and lasting treasure
none but Zion's children know.

God be in my head

French c1490; then English   R Pynson   1514   1 verse; 5 lines
As per title   W Walford Davies   1910   12.10.10.10.11
Psalm 36:9   "With Thee is the fountain of Life".

This short song is a petition for God's presence; no especial verse in the bible is identified despite the strength of the prayer. 'God be in my head' is first found at the end of the 15th century; both author and provenance are unknown. The first trace of this very moving verse is in a French text dating from ca. 1490: Some spellings are old-style French.

> Jesus soit en ma teste et mon entendement.
> Jesus soit en mes yeulx et mon regardement.
> Jesus soit en ma bouche et mon parlement.
> Jesus soit en mon cueur et en mon pensement.
> Jesus soit en ma vie et mon trespassement. Amen.

The English text appears a few years later in a 1514 *Book of Hours* printed by Robert Pynson, *Hore beate marie/virginis ad vsum insignis ac prelare ecclesie Sarum* (Salisbury).

It was then printed in a *Sarum Primer* of 1558, which was a collection of prayers and worship resources developed in Salisbury, England, during the 13th century. These are sometimes referred to as the 'Sarum Use' or the Sarum Rite'. This collection developed from Saint Osmund, Bishop in 1078, and is largely the Roman rite with some extra material. Many cathedral's developed such 'Uses' but Salisbury's took a pre-eminent place. It spread, influenced and was authorized by Roman Catholic, Eastern Orthodox and Anglican churches.

In modern times the verse was revived in 1908 with a tune by T.B. Strong called POPLAR. The verse has attracted a remarkable number of tunes. CONSTANTIA, by R.O. Morris, and DAVID, by George W Briggs; LYTLINGTON by Sydney Nicholson; also FIELD, MORLICH and Nameth's version taking the hymn's title. Modern composers, notably John Rutter, have done settings for it.

The tune that has probably ensured the continued popularity of these lines is that by Walford Davies simply called GOD BE IN MY HEAD which was printed first in 1910

Hymnbooks vary in the use of 'my' or 'mine' (the 1514 text has 'myn' when the possessive pronoun is followed by a vowel – 'myn understandynge', 'myn eyen')

> God be in my head, and in my understanding:
> God be in mine eyes, and in my looking;
> God be in my mouth, and in my speaking;
> God be in my heart, and in my thinking:
> God be at mine end, and at my departing

Interestingly, after 500 years or so it has apparently been recently re-translated back into French 'Christ, soit dans mon ame' but to a setting by Coombs.

Exactly how the Proprietors chose the Psalm verse is unclear; but their theological expertise surpasses that of many.

God moves in a mysterious way

	William Cowper	1731-1800	1774	6,4,3 verses
DUNDEE	Andro Hart	d 1621	1615	8.6.8.6
John 13:7	"What I do thou knowest not …"			

J R Watson writes "This is a hymn of vivid poetic imagery conveys better than any other the mystery and impenetrability of God' by William Cowper who produced some of the finest religious verse in the English language despite a life spent in acute mental torment." The one anchor in his life was his strong evangelical faith – and perhaps the support of John Newton.

For the last two decades of his life Cowper lived in Olney, where John Newton became his pastor. There he assisted Newton in his pastoral duties, and the two collaborated on their hymn collection Olney Hymns (1779), to which Cowper contributed sixty-eight hymn texts. Despite many Olney hymns having a bible verse referenced, this does not. Careful study can attach many verses to each and every line, but such goes beyond the scope of the work here.

William Cowper (pronounced 'Cooper'); was born at Berkhampstead, Hertfordshire, England, 1731 and died at East Dereham, Norfolk, England, 1800. He is regarded as one of the best early Romantic poets as he changed the style of 18th-century nature poetry by writing of everyday life and scenes of the English countryside. To biographers he is also known as 'mad Cowper'. His literary talents produced one of the finest English hymn texts, but his chronic depression accounts for the sombre tone of many of his pieces.

Educated to become an attorney, Cowper was called to the bar in 1754, aged 23, but never practiced law. In 1763 he had the opportunity to become a clerk for the House of Lords, but the dread of the required public examination triggered depression, and he attempted suicide. His hospitalization and then friendship with Morley and Mary Unwin provided emotional stability, but the depression returned. It was deepened by a religious bent, which stressed the wrath of God, such that Cowper felt that God had predestined him to damnation.

The summary given by John Julian§ in his *Dictionary of Hymnology* is very detailed in the relationship of Cowper's mental state to the wording and style of his great hymns.

"This text was written in 1773 at a time when Cowper was soon to endure a major nervous breakdown, and it has been seen by some writers, notably Erik Routley, as the work of a man 'conquered by despair'. Its enduring appeal lies in its recognition of uncertainty and foreboding combined with a sense of trust in God whatever may happen. A threatening prospect is made endurable not through intellectual understanding but through faith."

Samuel Greatheed in his 1814 biography wrote of Cowper: "Of this sad reverse in his experience, he conceived some presentiment as it drew near, and during a solitary walk in the fields, composed that hymn, of the Olney collection, beginning, 'God moves in a mysterious way', &c. which is very expressive of that faith and hope, which he retained at the time, even in prospect of his severe distress. Mr. Cowper's relapse occurred in 1773, in his forty-second year. His spirits, no longer sustained upon the wings of faith and hope, sank, with their weight of natural depression, into the horrible abyss of absolute despair."

Particularly noteworthy is the way in which alliteration links key words within a line and between lines: 'moves' and 'mysterious', 'way' and 'wonders', 'perform' and 'plants', 'big', 'break' and 'blessings'. This device combines with rhyme and metre to produce an eminently singable text which has been used in many countries with hardly any alteration.

Some American editions change 'of' to 'with' in the second line of stanza 2. This then associates 'skill' with God rather than with 'mines' and is perhaps more logical but the image of God underground is not helpful and might well have been alien to Cowper's thought.

Such tinkering continues. Bob Kauflin, after the 2001 tsunami, added a new refrain,

'So God, we trust in You; O God, we trust in You; when tears are great and comforts few, we hope in mercies ever new; we trust in You' – and therefore a new tune as well.

This hymn appeared in John Newton's *Twenty-six Letters on Religious Subjects; to which are added Hymns*, etc. by Omicron (1774). It was also in Book III of *Olney Hymns* (1779), then entitled 'Light shining out of darkness' John 1:5. In the *First Edition of A&M* (1861) it is headed by a reference to John 13:7 (footnoted in Olney Hymns to the last stanza).

DUNDEE first appeared in the 1615 edition of the *Scottish Psalter* published in Edinburgh by Andro Hart. Called a 'French' tune (thus it also goes by the name of FRENCH), DUNDEE was one of that hymnal's twelve 'common tunes'; that is, it was not associated with a specific psalm. In the *Psalter Hymnal* the tune is in isorhythmic form (all equal rhythms) and has a harmonization that was published in Thomas Ravenscroft's Whole Booke of Psalmes (1621). The tune's name comes from the city of Dundee, known as the 'Scottish Geneva' during the era of the Scottish Reformation. DUNDEE fits well the meditative character of the text; its smooth lines invite part singing. Benjamin Britten used the hymn brilliantly in his cantata Saint Nicolas (1948), set to the tune LONDON NEW.

An early version of the text is as follows – the pairs of lines run across :-

1. God moves in a mysterious way ... His wonders to perform;
   He plants His footsteps in the sea ... And rides upon the storm

2. Deep in unknown, unfathomed mines ... Of never-failing skill
   He treasures up His bright designs ... And works His sov'reign will.

3. Ye fearful saints, fresh courage take; ... The clouds ye so much dread
   Are big with mercy and shall break ... In blessings on your head.

4. Judge not the Lord by feeble sense, ... But trust Him for His grace;
   Behind a frowning providence ... He hides a smiling face.

5. His purposes will ripen fast, ... Unfolding every hour;
   The bud may have a bitter taste, ... But sweet will be the flower.

6. Blind unbelief is sure to err ... And scan His work in vain;
   God is His own Interpreter, ... And He will make it plain.
   Amen.

This hymn is one of the most significant in the English language. In 1952, Erik Routley called it "an outstanding example of terse, epigrammatic, memorable writing. … Consider how much of its text and thought-form has found its way into our common speech." Later, in 1956, he wrote, "This hymn is of a very rare and gracious kind, the hymn of the mystery of God's being and acts. It runs so smoothly, its lines are so neat and quotable, its thought so familiar, that it is easy to miss the genius of it."

God save our gracious Queen

                           uncertain   1745   5,4,3,2,1 verses
                         Bull (uncertain)   1619   6.6.4.6.6.6.4
1 Samuel 10:24 "… Then the people shouted, "Long live the king! [Saul]"'

The origins of both the text and the tune are uncertain. It is the national anthem, with some variation, across the British Empire or many parts and ex-parts thereof: Canada, Australia; New Zealand and many others. Due to its success others, principally America, took the tune and delivered new words. A republican version is 'God bless our native land'.

Norway 'Kondesangen'; Liechtenstein, 'Oben am jungen Rhein'; Switzerland 'Rufst du, mein Vaterland'; Russia 'The Prayer of Russia [from 1816-1833]. United States has used the tune for the text 'My Country tis of thee' by Samuel F Smith from 1831.

Similarly, many countries developed their own equivalent. The French decided on the Marseillaise; the Germans on 'Deutschland unter alles' as a rebuild of ' Heil dir in Siegerkranz' to the tune AUSTRIAN HYMN by Josef Haydn.

Beyond its first verse, which is consistent, 'God Save the Queen/King' has many historic and extant versions. Since its first publication, different verses have been added and taken away and, even today, publications include various selections of verses in various orders.

In general, only one verse is sung. Sometimes two verses are sung, and on rare occasions, three. The Sovereign and the spouse are saluted with the entire composition, while other members of the royal family who are entitled to royal salute (such as the Prince of Wales or the Duke of Cambridge along with their spouses) receive just the first six bars.

Due to its speedy rise toward being the national anthem a number of claims were made. Percy Scholes points out the similarities to an early plainsong melody, although the rhythm is very distinctly that of a galliard, and he gives examples of several such dance tunes that bear a striking resemblance to 'God Save the King/Queen'. Scholes quotes a keyboard piece by John Bull (1619) which has some similarities to the modern tune; or a piece by Purcell. Others have identified an old Scotch carol 'Remember O Thou Man'.

The first published version of what is almost the present tune appeared in 1744 in *Thesaurus Musicus*; it is clearly a strong relative of the contemporary anthem. It was recorded as being sung in London theatres in 1745, with, for example, Thomas Arne writing a setting of the tune for the Drury Lane Theatre.

Scholes' analysis includes mention of 'untenable' and 'doubtful' claims for James Oswald, as well as 'an American misattribution' to Henry Carey. He does recommend the version of John Bull. Vaughan Williams states merely '17th or 18th cent'.

The earliest lyrics include these three versions of which each first line is shown: the first is as published in the Gentleman's Magazine in 1745.

                God save great George our King,
                    God bless our noble King
                        O Deus Optime

Words and tune became very popular, and the anthem was played on many occasions, most memorably and incongruously when the next monarch, George III, bathed in the sea at Weymouth in 1789.

As a 'national' anthem, the piece was subject to frequent critique by its subjects. Despite being unlike other anthems in addressing God rather than the flag or the land itself, its focus was on the Sovereign rather than the nation or the people. God and Sovereign together but without any hint of Divine Right. The third verse almost implies soe form of contract.

But national feelings also generated change – in 1851, came a verse headed 'For the use of Her Majesty's loyal subjects in their social circles and public assemblies' which called for divine protection for the anti-Catholic cause.

> Let now thine arm be seen ... Guarding our gracious Queen ... from Papal power.

There were many variations and parodies, and many attempts to re-write the text. It was sung (sometimes with modifications) on significant occasions in the lives of succeeding monarchs. Following independence, American imitations were many, from 'God save George Washington' to the famous 'My country 'tis of thee'.

The 'official' English text it is sometimes appended by two stanzas by William E Hickson beginning 'God bless our native land', in a version that explicitly rejects force and warfare:

> May peace her power extend,
> Foe be transformed to friend.
> And Britain's rights depend
> On war no more.

The most common text is that of two stanzas, beginning 'God save our gracious Queen' and 'Thy choicest gifts in store'. Some hymn books print a verse between or after:

> O Lord our God, arise,
> Scatter our enemies,
>   And make them fall;
> Confound their politics,
> Frustrate their knavish tricks;
> On Thee our hopes we fix: ... God save us all.

This ingenuous stanza has not always been found suitable for worship. An 'Official Peace Version' was drawn up in 1919 in the aftermath of the First World War, and given approval by the Privy Council. It differed from the usual version in stanzas 2 and 3 (stanza 2 line 5 has a deliberate echo of Shakespeare, Richard II):

> One realm of races four,
> Blest more and ever more,   ... God save our land!
> Home of the brave and free,
> Set in the silver sea,
> True nurse of chivalry,   ... God save our land!
>
> Kinsfolk in love and birth
> From utmost ends of earth,
>   God save us all!
> Bid strife and hatred cease,
> Bid hope and joy increase,
> Spread universal peace,
>   God save us all!

Hymns written in imitation of the original text began with 'Come, Thou Almighty King (in a tract included in George Whitefield's *A Collection of Hymns for Social Worship,* (1759) and 'Glory to God on high/ Let heaven and earth reply', by James Allen.

An early version of the text is as follows:
>God save our gracious King,
>long live our noble King,
>God save the King.
>Send her victorious,
>happy and glorious,
>long to reign over us:
>God save the King.

Note : The verse 'scatter our enemies can be placed here, peacemongers prefer it omitted.

>Thy choicest gifts in store
>On him be pleased to pour;
>Long may he reign:
>May he defend our laws,
>And ever give us cause
>To sing with heart and voice,
>God save the King.

>Through every changing scene,
>O Lord, preserve our King;
>Long may He reign:
>His heart inspire and move
>With wisdom from above,
>And in a nation's love
>His throne maintain.

optional, if not usually omitted.

Perhaps one of the most recent efforts to make changes came in 1990 taking an 1836 verse from William Hickson the early Victorian social reformer. It was strongly recommended by the Church of England's liturgical commission. Welcome the power of the modern church.

>Nor on this land alone –
>But be thy mercies known
>From shore to shore.
>Lord, make the nations see
>All me should borthers be,
>One league, one family,
>One, the world o'er.

God Save our Gracious Queen gets criticism for being too often delivered at a very slow speed; although played fast, for some it does not sound 'right'. Jerusalem is called an anthem even though Jerusalem is not even in Europe. Billy Connolly has offered the theme to the Archers ... rumpty tumpty tiddly oh, rumpty tumpty etc.

A Collage of Royalty linked with 'God save the Queen'

Great Britain
Russia
Germany
Liechtenstein

Austria
Sweden
USA

Good Christian men rejoice / In Dulci Jubilo

| French-Latin Macaronic c 1328 | trans J M Neale§ | 1818-1866 | 1837 | 3 verses |
| Zahn 4947 | c 1400 | | | 6.6.7.7.7.8.8.5.5 |

As many carols ; it is based on the Nativity scenes written by Luke – but no specific verse.

The story of this hymn has always been about accessibility to the Christmas story. In the late medieval period, there was a tradition of using folk songs to teach illiterate church-goers the Gospel story. This hymn is a good example of that practice. Written in a combination of Latin and German, it would be familiar in both the vernacular and the language of the Church. When set to a familiar folk tune, the people would be able to sing along with ease, and thus would be reminded of the story.

Over the centuries, this hymn has been translated into many different languages, so many more people could hear and sing these beautiful words that call us to praise. A missionary diary claims that on September 14, 1745, at the Moravian mission in Bethlehem, Pennsylvania, this hymn was simultaneously sung in thirteen different languages.

This is a hugely popular Carol, in fact a mainstay of the Nine Lessons and Carols. Like some carols it is also a great hymn and can be sung all year.

'In dulci jubilo' (Latin for 'In sweet rejoicing') is a traditional Christmas carol. No purely Latin version is known - so the earliest is from the Middle Ages. This medieval version is linked to the German mystic Heinrich Seuse around 1328. His story or dream is

"Now this same angel came up to the Servant (Suso) brightly, and said that God had sent him down to him, to bring him heavenly joys amid his sufferings; adding that he must cast off all his sorrows from his mind and bear them company, and that he must also dance with them in heavenly fashion. Then they drew the Servant by the hand into the dance, and the youth began a joyous song about the infant Jesus ..."

There are so many alternatives. John Mason Neale produced a looser translation in 1853 titled 'Good Christian Men, Rejoice'. It has its critics. In 1921, H J Massé wrote that it was an example of "musical wrong doing ... involving the mutilation of the rhythm of that grand tune In dulci jubilo to the English words Good Christian Men Rejoice. It is inconceivable that anyone of any real culture should have lent himself to this tinkering with a perfect tune for the sake of fitting it perforce to works of inferior merit." Masse goes on to cite a preferred English translation from 1567 by John Wedderburn as being a more 'worthy effort'.

Neale put immense effort into his translations. He was quite an enthusiast about this subject:: "It is a magnificent thing to pass along the far-stretching vista of hymns, from the sublime self-containedness of S. Ambrose to the more fervid inspiration of S. Gregory, the exquisite typology of Venantius Fortunatus, the lovely painting of St. Peter Damiani, the crystal-like simplicity of S. Notker, the scriptural calm of Godescalcus, the subjective loveliness of St. Bernard, till all culminate in the full blaze of glory which surrounds Adam of S. Victor, the greatest of them all."

Feeling thus what a noble task he had before him, it is no wonder that he spared no pains over it, or that he felt it his duty to adopt 'the exact measure and rhyme of the original, at whatever inconvenience and cramping.'

There have been a number of translations of the Latin/German poem into English [a mixture of Latin and another is known as 'macaronic']. Some have tried to retain the Latin-

and-local format; the most popular of thses dual structure versions is by R. L. de Pearsall in 1837 in retaining the Latin phrases while changing German to English.

The tune Zahn No. 4947 'Gelobt sei Gott' is first found in a manuscript of about 1400 – so possibly earlier. It is first seen in print in 1533 in a Lutheran hymnal and then in other collections. Michael Praetorius uses it for several voice-only motets around 1590-1620 and in a large festive multi-choir version with large instrumental support including trumpets and timpani; with 7, 12, 16 or 20 voices in 5 choirs (three vocal, one chapel- and one instrumental choir) and general bass. The Praetorius settings were well used in Protestant Europe.

Bach produced several pieces using the tune, as did Buxtehude for two chorale pieces. Franz Liszt included the carol in his piano suite Weihnachtsbaum in a section called 'The Shepherds at the manger' or in the German 'Die Hirten an der Krippe'. Holst included both 'Good Christian Men, Rejoice' and 'God rest you merry, gentlemen' in his 1910 choral fantasy *Christmas Day*, with accompaniment for orchestra or organ.

Together with his translation, de Pearsall (1795-1856) produced an 8-voice polyphonic version, later cut down to 4 voices. Reginald Jacques adapted this and it is now the commonest format, the first two verses are in four-part harmony, the third and fourth verses are concatenated and in eight-part harmony.

An transcription error by Thomas Helmore from the tune in *Piae Cantiones* (1582) with a caused a misread of the notation such that two long notes were added, for which Neale supplied repeated words in line 4 ie 'News, News'.

Still another 19th century English translation by Arthur T. Russell has featured in several Lutheran hymnals, entitling the work as 'Now Sing We, Now Rejoice'.

As new views become significant, words and phrases have been edited and tweaked.

Four versions are shown (first verse only)

Original Latin-German   exact translation

    In dulci jubilo,   In sweet rejoicing
    Nun singet und seid froh!   Now sing and be glad!
    Unsers Herzens Wonne   Our heart's joy
    Leit in præsepio,   lies in the manger;
    Und leuchtet als die Sonne   And it shines like the sun
    Matris in gremio,   in the mother's lap
    Alpha es et O, Alpha es et O!   You are the Alpha and Omega

Wedderburn   Now let us sing with joy and mirth
    In honor of our Lordes birth
    Our heart's consolation
    Lies in praesipio
    And shines as the sun;
    Matris in gremio.
    Alpha is and O, Alpha is and I

Neale   Good Christian men, rejoice,   ... With heart, and soul, and voice;
    Give ye heed to what we say: ... News! News!
    Jesus Christ is born to-day;   ... Ox and ass before him bow,
    And He is in the manger now   ... Christ is born to-day,
    Christ is born to-day.

Pearsall   (macaronic)
In dulci jubilo   ... Let us our homage show!
Our heart's joy reclineth ... in prasesipio
And like a bright star shineth   ... Matris in gremio
Alpha es et O

The best known text is the one by Neale – here is an early version.

Good Christian men, rejoice,
With heart and soul and voice;
Now ye hear of endless bliss:
Joy! Joy! Jesus Christ was born for this!
He has opened the heavenly door,
And man is blest forevermore.
Christ was born for this!   Christ was born for this!

Good Christian men, rejoice,
With heart and soul and voice;
Now ye need not fear the grave:
Peace! Peace! Jesus Christ was born to save!
Calls you one and calls you all,
To gain His everlasting hall.
Christ was born to save!   Christ was born to save!

In passing – Bishop Bingham goes back to Latin

It may be difficult to believe…. but after all the effort by J M Neale and his translator colleagues at translating Latin into English, the absolutely non-eccentric Bishop translated many Victorian hymns BACK into Latin – even when they were never in Latin originally.

Abide with me	O mecum maneas. Vesper adest, caligo tenebris
Angels from the Realms of Glory	Angeli, sanctae regione lucis. .
Glorious things of thee are spoken	Dicta de te sunt miranda, Zion civitas amanda.
God moves in a mysterious way	Secretis miranda viis opera omnia Numen
Hark, the herald angels sing	Audite, tollunt carmina, densae cohortes
How sweet the name of Jesus sounds	Quam dulce, quam mellifuum,
Jesus shall reign where'er the sun	Omnibus in terries Dominus regnabit Jesus
Joy to the world,	Laetitia in terris, Nam Salvator adest. .
O worship the King, all glorious above	Glorioso ferti Regi vota vetra carmine.
Rock of Ages	O rupes aeterna, mihi percussa, recondar in te
While shepherds watched their flocks	Oves dum custodientes, omnes humi considentes
When I survey the wondrous cross	Quando admirandam crucem .

These are among the 200+ he un-translated into his own especial style.

In Dulci Jubilo

Guide me, O Thou great Jehovah / Redeemer

William Williams; 1717-1791 trans. P Williams   1762/ 1771   6,5,4,3 verses
BREAD OF HEAVEN aka CWM RHONDDA   Welsh 1905   8.8.7.4.4.7.7
Psalm 48:14   "For this God is our God for ever and ever: he will be our guide …"

The origin is Welsh; the most common version is Welsh. The loudest singing is Welsh. The hymn is well known in four different ways 'Guide me, o thou great Jehovah'; 'Guide me, o thou great Redeemer; 'Bread of Heaven'; and Cwm Rhondda.

The Psalm verse is about God leading people towards Zion. The more usual link is to Exodus and the travails of the people of Israel in the desert. The text reflects the prevailing mood in the period after 1762, when the Revival was again sweeping the land being an allegory for the journey of a Christian throughout their life on earth requiring the Redeemer's guidance and ending at the gates of Heaven (the verge of Jordan) and end of time (death of death and hell's destruction). Particularly in the three stanzas in common use, the people of God are marching confidently forward.

This is well expressed in the Welsh where the pilgrim drags his way across the desert, without energy and truly needing the sustenance of the manna and the water from the rock. In the penultimate verse there is confidence that in the end Jordan will be crossed, but the hymn ends with a reference back to Calvary. The English version is far from being an actual translation; rather it is seen as a reworking.

In more detail, it thus describes the experience of God's people in their travel through the wilderness from the escape from slavery in Egypt (Exodus 12-14), being guided by a cloud by day and a fire by night (Exodus 13:17-22 to their final arrival forty years later in the land of Canaan (Joshua 3). During this time their needs were supplied by God, including the daily supply of manna 'the Bread of Heaven' Exodus 16.

The text was originally titled Gweddi am Nerth i fyned trwy anialwch y Byd (Prayer for strength for the journey through the world's wilderness) as written by William Williams 'Pantycelyn' (1717-1791) [adding his farm as an identifier]. He is generally recognised as the greatest Welsh hymnwriter. It comprised six verses, although some only show 5 verses. It originally appeared in Williams' collection *Caniadau y rhai sydd ar y Môr o Wydr* ('The Songs of those upon the Sea of Glass' 1762)

Peter Williams (1722–1796) translated part of the hymn in 1771 into the English version, with the title Prayer for Strength. This translation is the only Welsh hymn to have gained widespread circulation in the English-speaking world. A result of the translation process is that the now-familiar phrase 'Bread of heaven', which does not actually occur in the original, becomes a rewording as a reference to manna.

Despite the history of the tune and its common English text, the usual tune-&-words pairing in Welsh is quite different.

The text here eventually derives from Arglwydd, arwain.('Lord, lead me): this is usually sung to the tune CAPEL Y DDOL; or LLAN BAGLAN which both differ greatly in emphasis to the usual English setting; whereas Wele'n Sefyll Rwng y Myrtwydd ('Lo, between the myrtles standing) is the set of words paired with to CWM RHONDDA.

CWM RHONDDA is the tune is best known as the setting for the English text: 'Guide Me, O Thou Great Redeemer' or with the last word as 'Jehovah'. The Welsh word Arglwydd corresponds more-or-less to the English Lord, in all its senses. The Hebrew words in the Old Testament such as JHVH and in the New Testament as 'kyrios' are all translated as was the practice then as Jehovah. Some others and the more modern use 'Redeemer' instead.

CWM RHONDDA is the Welsh for the Rhondda Valley and became a name of popular hymn-tune written by John Hughes (1873-1932), in 1907. He wrote the first version in 1905 while the Welsh Revival was still active. The name was later changed to 'Cwm Rhondda' because M O Jones of Dowlais had his own tune called Rhondda.

The tune is used again for 'God of Grace and God of Glory' by H E Fosdick in 1930. Also for 'Full salvation! Full salvation! Lo, the fountain opened wide' by Francis Bottome.

The following are the English and Welsh versions of the hymn, as given in an early version of both texts.

Guide me, O thou great Redeemer,
Pilgrim through this barren land;
I am weak, but thou art mighty;
Hold me with thy powerful hand:
Bread of heaven, bread of heaven
Feed me till I want no more,
Feed me till I want no more.

Open thou the crystal fountain
Whence the healing stream shall flow;
Let the fiery, cloudy pillar
Lead me all my journey through:
Strong deliverer, strong deliverer
Be thou still my strength and shield,
Be thou still my strength and shield.

When I tread the verge of Jordan,
Bid my anxious fears subside;
Death of death, and hell's destruction,
Land me safe on Canaan's side:
Songs of praises, songs of praises
I will ever give to thee,
I will ever give to thee.

Welsh & Original Translation

Welsh	Original Translation
Arglwydd, arwain trwy'r anialwch,	Lord, lead me through the wilderness,
Fi, bererin gwael ei wedd,	Me, a pilgrim of poor appearance,
Nad oes ynof nerth na bywyd	I don't have strength or life in me,
Fel yn gorwedd yn y bedd:	Like lying in the grave:
Hollalluog, Hollalluog,	Omnipotent, Omnipotent
Ydyw'r Un a'm cwyd i'r lan,	Is the one who brings me to the shore,
Ydyw'r Un a'm cwyd i'r lan	Is the one who brings me to the shore.
Agor y ffynhonnau melus	Open the sweet fountains
'N tarddu i maes o'r Graig y sydd;	Flowing from the Rock that is;
Colofn dân rho'r nos i'm harwain,	Give a column of fire to lead me at night,

A rho golofn niwl y dydd;	And give a column of fog during the day.
Rho i mi fanna, Rho i mi fanna,	Give me manna. Give me manna,
Fel na bwyf yn llwfwrhau,	So that I shall not falter,
Fel na bwyf yn llwfwrhau.	So that I shall not falter.
Pan yn troedio glan Iorddonen,	When I walk the bank of the Jordan,
Par i'm hofnau suddo i gyd;	Cause all my fears to sink;
Dwg fi drwy y tonnau geirwon	Take me through the roughest waves
Draw i Ganaan – gartref clyd:	Over to Canaan, a cosy home:
Mawl diderfyn. Mawl diderfyn	Unending praise. Unending praise
Fydd i'th enw byth am hyn,	Will be to Your name for this,
Fydd i'th enw byth am hyn.	Will be to Your name for this.

The hymn has the 8.7.8.7.4.4.7.7 measure which is common in several Welsh hymns. The first and third, second and fourth match then the short fifth line has a repeat before the sixth reaches a climax – emphasised by a rising arpeggio in the alto and bass parts. The final line continues the musical development and generally repeats itself. Apparently, these vigorous characteristics caused both Welsh and English to resist the tune – and thus the text - in their collections. That attitude has now passed and the hymn has long been firmly established.

In Passing – Welsh Song

The influence of Welsh tunes into the Victorian hymnody is significant. The Welsh rugby crowds of the 1970s sang for us with all the skill of the Welsh male choirs and all the power of supporting a fantastic team. Cwm Rhondda; Ar hyd y Nos (All through the night); Sospan Fach is not a hymn but only a folk song – wonderful and emotional.

One writer says 'ever since the Battle of the Hallelujahs -- near Wrexham -- when the invading Danes were driven from the field in fright by the rush of the Cymric army shouting that mighty cry, every Christian poet in Wales has had a hallelujah in his verse'.

Through the centuries, the Welsh clung to their independent faith and the heavenly song was still murmured in a few true hearts amidst the vain and vicious lays of carnal mirth. It survived even when people and priest alike seemed utterly degenerate and godless. Brave John Oldcastle, the martyr, (1417) clung to the gospel he learned at the foot of the cross.

The young vicar, Rhys Pritchard (1579) rose from the sunken level of his profession. Accustomed to drink himself to inebriety at a public-house - a socially winked-at indulgence then - he one day took his pet goat with him, and poured liquor down the creature's throat. The refusal of the poor goat to go there again forced the reckless priest to reflect on his own ways. He forsook the ale-house and became a changed man.

Later came William Williams, 'The Sweet Singer of Wales' and 'The Watts of Wales' because he was the chief poet and hymn-writer of his time. The lady he married, Miss Mary Francis, was an actual singer, with a voice so full and melodious that the people to whom he preached during his itineraries, which she sometimes shared with him, were often more moved by her sweet hymnody than by his exhortations.

Picture of the crowd at Cardiff; some people singing.

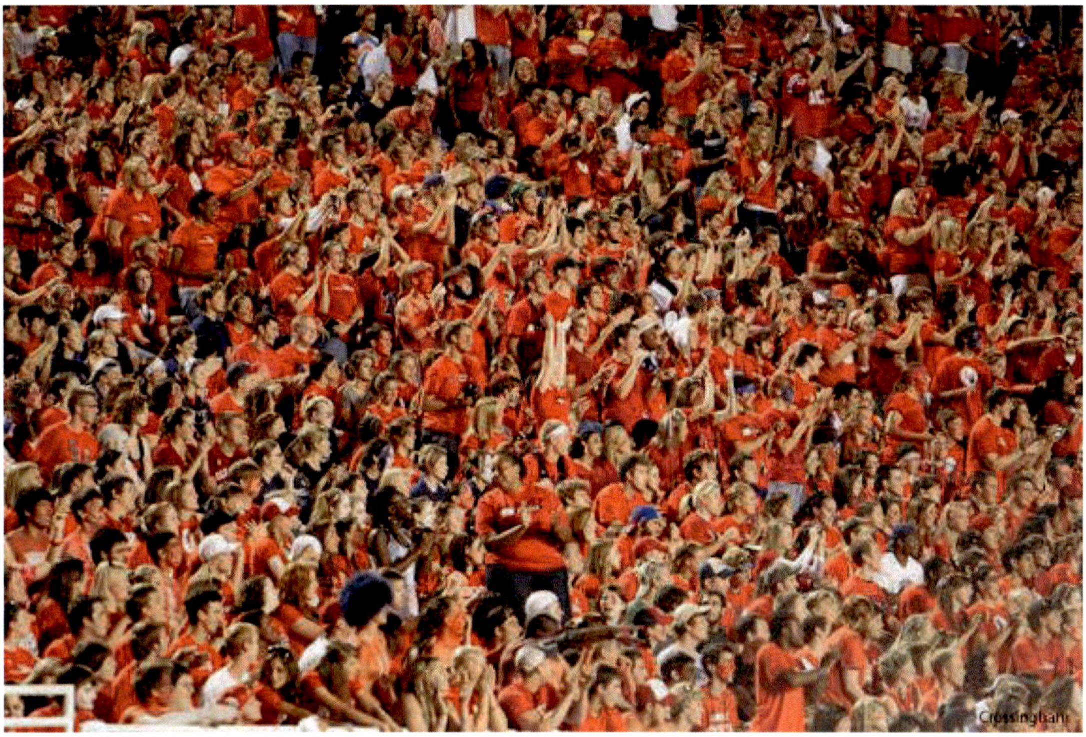

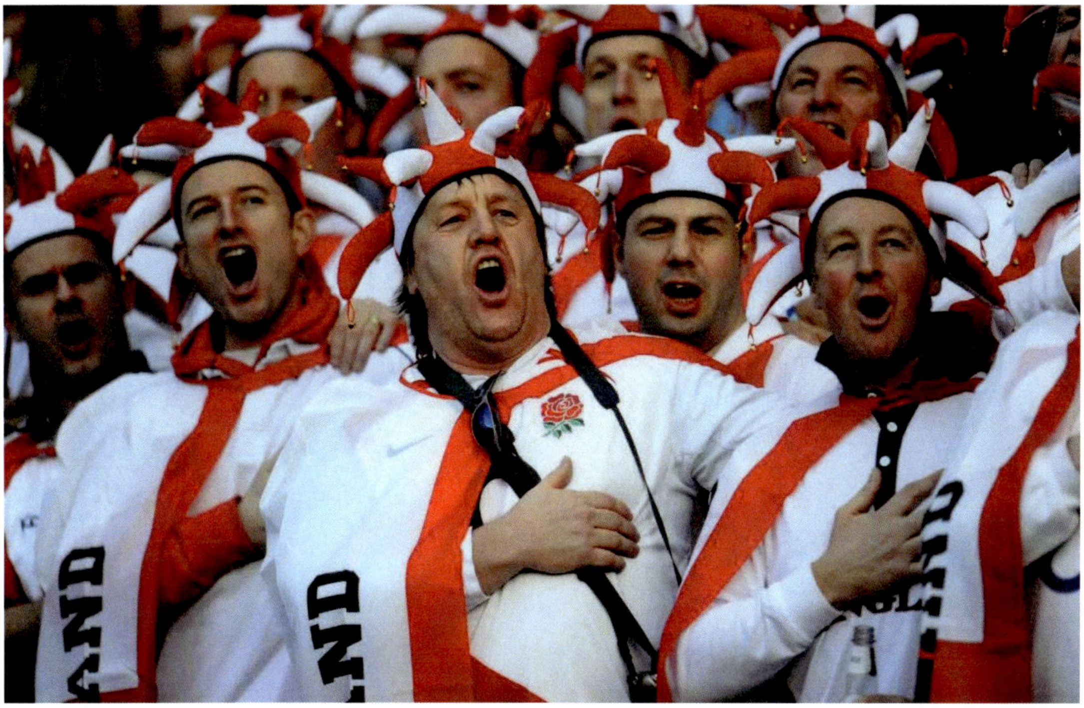

Hail the day that sees Him rise

	Charles Wesley§	1707–1788	1739	10, 6,5, 4 verses
LLANFAIR	Robert Williams	1781-1821	1837	7.7.7.7 D
Psalm 24:7	"Lift up your heads, O ye gates …"			

This was first published in Wesleys' *Hymns and Sacred Poems* (1739), under the title 'Hymn for Ascension-Day' and immediately followed 'Christ the Lord is risen today'; then republished in *Hymns on the Great Festivals* in 1746, with some changes, not all of them improvements. 'Alleluia' was added to every line in G.C. White's *Hymns and Introits* (1852) and in this form, though with a multiplicity of minor textual emendations, the hymn has been extensively used throughout the English-speaking world.

The hymn is primarily concerned with the consequences of Christ's Ascension. Wesley vividly portrays Christ's intercession as he displays the marks of his crucifixion.

Perhaps reflecting the Prayer Book (1662) Collect for Ascension Day, Wesley moves on to sound the note of devotion ('Grant our hearts may thither rise…') and concludes with the believer's hope of heaven and unity with the ascended Christ in his eternal reign.

Wesley's text (especially stanzas 4–5) continues this link: 'Grant, we beseech thee, Almighty God, that like as we do believe thy only begotten Son our Lord Jesus Christ to have ascended into the heavens; so we may also in heart and mind thither ascend …' Certainly Wesley moves on to a note of hope ('Grant our hearts may thither rise…') and ends with the believer's wish for heaven and unity with the ascended Christ in his eternal reign.

The A&M Bible reference is to Psalm 24 which rather links to the second and third stanzas. The hymn as a whole takes its cue from Luke's report of the Ascension in ch.24:50–53 and Acts 1:6–11. Stanza six echoes the promise of John 14:2–3 'And if I go and prepare a place for you, I will come again …'.

This text was soon set to the tune ASCENSION, which was composed for the Wesleys by their good friend John Frederick Lampe (ca. 1703–1751). His melodic style shows influences from both the Moravian hymn singing which the Wesleys admired and the popular style of Lampe's contemporary, G.F. Handel. This tune by Lampe has not endured, but some others by him are still extant. W H Monk also wrote a setting which suits called ASCENSION.

The usual setting is LLANFAIR which was first seen under the name BETHEL in 1837. The change of name from BETHEL to LLANFAIR is not well documented. It was given in four parts, melody in the third part, arranged by John Roberts of Henllan. The authorship of this tune has been assigned to Robert Williams (1781–1821), based on now-lost manuscript. LLANFAIR works well with other exuberant texts, including the Resurrection hymns 'Christ the Lord is risen today' and its near-equal 'Jesus Christ is risen today'. 'He is gone—beyond the skies; All the toil and sorrow done'. As a popular text in an easy metre, there are more than 20 additional hymns which match.

Having a 7.7.7.7 metre does allow other tunes to be used, such as EASTER HYMN and an astonishing 450 more. Again, the metre is not the true defining constraint when matching to text, rhyme, rhythm, intonation or emphasis.

An early version of the 5 verse text is given; showing just some of the alterations marked with ' : 'from the original.

Hail the day that sees him rise, Alleluia!
to his throne beyond the skies. Alleluia!
Christ, the Lamb for sinners given, Alleluia!   : Christ, awhile to mortals given,
enters now the highest heaven. Alleluia!   : Reascends His native heaven

There for him high triumph waits; Alleluia!   : There the glorious triumph waits
lift your heads, eternal gates. Alleluia!
He has conquered death and sin; Alleluia!   : Christ hath conquered ....
take the King of glory in. Alleluia!

                                                                Circled round with angel powers,
                                                                Their triumphant Lord, and ours,
                                                                Conqueror over death and sin,
                                                                Take the King of glory in!

Highest heaven its Lord receives; Alleluia!   : Him though highest Heav'n receives,
yet he loves the earth he leaves. Alleluia! : Still He loves the earth He leaves,
Though returning to his throne, Alleluia!   unchanged
still he calls us all his own. Alleluia!   : Still He calls mankind His own.

                                                                See! He lifts His hands above,
                                                                See! He shows the prints of love,
                                                                Hark! His gracious lips bestow,
                                                                Blessings on His church below,

Still for us he intercedes; Alleluia!   : Still for us His death He pleads,
his atoning death he pleads, Alleluia!   : Prevalent He intercedes,
near himself prepares our place, Alleluia!   unchanged
he the first fruits of our race. Alleluia!   : Harbinger of human race,

                                                                Master, (will we ever say), Alleluia!
                                                                Taken from our head to day,
                                                                See Thy faithful servants, see,
                                                                Ever gazing up to Thee

                                                                Grant, though parted from our sight,
                                                                Far above yon azure height,!
                                                                Grant our hearts may thither rise
                                                                Seeking Thee beyond the skies,

                                                                Ever upward let us move,
                                                                Wafted on the wings of love,
                                                                Looking when our Lord shall come
                                                                Longing, gasping after home,

There we shall with you remain, Alleluia!
partners of your endless reign, Alleluia!
see you with unclouded view, Alleluia!
find our heaven of heavens in you. Alleluia!

𝕳ark! 𝕿he 𝕳erald-𝕬ngels sing

                    Charles Wesley§ (adapted G Whitefield)   1739   6,5,4 verses
FESTGESANG   F Mendelssohn 1806-1847   1755   7.7.7.7 (Ref)
Luke 2 :14   "Glory to God in the highest, and on earth, peace, good will towards men."

    Charles Wesley originally penned a Christmas hymn with a curious text: 'Hark how all the Welkin rings / Glory to the King of Kings'. The original title was simply 'Hymn for Christmas Day'. A modern reader seeing the 'welkin rings' might easily think it is a bell but 'welkin' means 'sky' or 'heavens' — it was then common in English poetry. During their earlier years the Wesleys published some of their best work, especially in the first *Hymns and Sacred Poems* (1739) where this is first found.

The carol, like so many other carols, is based on the Nativity story in Luke 2; and Matthew 1 & 2. Luke 2:14, tells of the angelic chorus singing praises to God. The text, even in its truncated form, is a treasury of Scriptural and Christian theology. Verse 2 in particular moves from the eternal Son of the heavenly places, on through the timely purposes of God, and so to the virgin birth, the nature human and divine, and finally to the Jesus of the gospel story who is also Emmanuel, God with us. In the same way the final lines set out in brief parallel statements the purpose and consequence of God becoming human. There is hardly a line that cannot stand alone as expressing, sometimes by paradox, the great mystery of the Incarnation.

    Rather than simply tell the nativity story of Luke 2 & Matthew 1 & 2, Wesley pours theological truths into this text. The first verse tells the story of the angels proclaiming Christ's birth, and the second and third verse go on to make it very clear why the angels sang. Simply by describing Christ, Wesley tells us the entire Gospel story. We are told of Christ's nature, his birth and incarnation, his ministry, and his salvific purpose.

    The over-frequent tinkering with the text does mean that there can be more than one entry in books about hymns. – with the standard wording,; the second line being 'newborn' or 'th'eternal'; with or without 'Alleluia' and not forgetting the original 'welkin'.

    Martin Madan in 1760 altered verse 1 to that familiar today :-
        'Universal Nature say   ... 'Christ the Lord is born to Day!' to
        'With th'angelic Host proclaim, ...   Christ is born in Bethlehem!'

    In 1904, the editors of *Hymns Ancient & Modern* infamously changed the text back to 'welkin rings'; they were so soundly ridiculed about this and other issues, in the next edition (1906), a re-release of the 1889 edition, they returned to 'herald angels'. One version has the refrain to *Hail Him King, Hail Him King, Crown Him Lord o'er earth and sky, and Hail Him King.*

    The original – all 10 verses - was significantly adapted over the years most especially by Whitefield who changed the first line to today's version. John & Charles Wesley had an enduring friendship and connection with George Whitefield (1714–1770), beginning with their Oxford 'Holy Club' – but he changed many of their texts. Now there is the thee/thou determination of some modern commentators. The repeat of the opening line as a refrain dates to 1782. Of course, *A&M* (1861) altered verse 4:
        'Pleas'd as Man with Men t'appear ... Jesus, our Immanuel here!'
to   'Pleased as Man with man to dwell, ... Jesus, our Emmanuel.'

    Wesley was content with using the same tune as that for his Easter song 'Christ the Lord is risen today'. For that, the most frequent setting then was SALISBURY by John Lampe. The best known music now for this hymn is adapted from 'Vaterland, in deinen Gauen' by Felix Mendelssohn. In 1840—a hundred years after the hymn arrived - Mendelssohn composed a cantata; this was adapted by the English musician W H Cummings to fit the lyrics of 'Hark! the herald angels sing', which propels the carol known today.

In Britain, the Cummings harmonisation is used for the first two verses, but then a soprano descant is added and a last verse harmonisation by Sir David Wilcocks for the organ. This arrangement was first published in 1961 by OUP in their *Carols for Choirs* series. It is also the recessional hymn of the annual King's College Chapel service of Nine Lessons and Carols.

In Ireland, the connection of St Patrick's Dublin with Handel has encouraged the use of the theme from his Judas Maccabeus. Elsewhere this is used for 'Hail the Conq'ring hero comes'. The usual (first) three verses are divided into six verses, each with chorus, brass fanfare with drums and the cathedral organ, and takes about seven and a half minutes to sing.

The text here is directly from the original Wesley hymnbook of 1739 – pages 206-208. It has been edited to show the single original hymn in 10 verses of 4 lines each. The earliest version of 'Hark the Herald Angel sings' omits verse 8 & 10.

HYMN for CHRISTMAS-DAY.

I.
HARK how all the Welkin rings
" Glory to the Kings of Kings,
" Peace on Earth, and Mercy mild,
" GOD and Sinners reconcil'd !

II.
Joyful all ye Nations rife,
Join the Triumph of the Skies,
Univerfal Nature fay
" CHRIST the LORD is born to Day!
                                    CHRIST,

HYMNS and SACRED POEMS.   207

III.
CHRIST, by higheft Heav'n ador'd,
CHRIST, the Everlafting Lord,
Late in Time behold him come,
Offspring of a Virgin's Womb.

IV.
Veil'd in Flefh, the Godhead fee,
Hail th' Incarnate Deity !
Pleas'd as Man with Men t' appear
JESUS, our *Immanuel* here !

V.
Hail the Heav'nly Prince of Peace !
Hail the Sun of Righteoufnefs !
Light and Life to All he brings,
Ris'n with Healing in his Wings.

VI.
Mild he lays his Glory by,
Born — that Man no more may die,
Born — to raife the Sons of Earth,
Born — to give them Second Birth.

VII.
Come, Defire of Nations, come,
Fix in Us thy humble Home,
Rife, the Woman's Conqu'ring Seed,
Bruife in Us the Serpent's Head.

VIII.
Now difplay thy faving Pow'r,
Ruin'd Nature now reftore,
Now in Myftic Union join
Thine to Ours, and Ours to Thine.
                                    Adam's

208   HYMNS and SACRED POEMS.

IX.
Adam's Likenefs, LORD, efface,
Stamp thy Image in its Place,
Second *Adam* from above,
Reinftate us in thy Love.

X.
Let us Thee, tho' loft, regain,
Thee, the Life, the Inner Man :
O ! to All Thyfelf impart,
Form'd in each Believing Heart.

John Wesley chose not to include this hymn in the career-spanning *Collection of Hymns for the Use of the People Called Methodists* (1780). A few years later, after being entreated to produce a smaller, more affordable collection, he published *A Pocket Hymn Book*, first in 1785, then greatly revised in 1787. He included this Christmas hymn but restructured it into four stanzas of eight lines, incorporating both Whitefield's opening lines and Madan's new text, to make a new text.

Bishop Heber 1783-1826

Reginald Heber was an English cleric, man of letters and hymn-writer – and eventually for a few years, a Bishop. After 16 years as a country parson, he served as Bishop of Calcutta until his death not even 3 years later at the age of 42.

He was the first to publish sermons on the Sunday services (1822), and a writer in The Guardian has pointed out that these efforts of Heber were the germ of the now common practice, developed through the Christian Year (perhaps following Ken's Hymns on the Festivals), and by Augustus Hare, of welding together sermon, hymnal, and liturgy. The tome by Frere and Frost – *Historical Companion to Hymns Ancient and Modern* describes Heber as 'the creator of the modern hymnbook'.

The son of a rich landowner and cleric, he went to Brasenose College, Oxford. In his first year, Heber won the University Prize for Latin Verse, and made a reputation as a poet.

In 1803 he entered a long poem, 'Palestine', for the Newdigate Prize. He had been helped in composing it by Walter Scott, a family friend, before Scott's years of fame. The poem was enthusiastically received when Heber declaimed it at that year's Encaenia ceremony. It was later published; set to music by William Crotch, a professor of music at Oxford since 1797; and even translated into Welsh. Montefiore, in 1902, described it as 'the most successful and popular piece of religious verse of the first half of the 19th century'. Heber's later biographer Derrick Hughes finds its contemporary acclaim puzzling: 'It is not a good, not even a mediocre poem; it is leaden'.

After graduation he made a long tour of Scandinavia, Russia and Central Europe. Ordained in 1807, he took over his father's old parish, Hodnet, Shropshire. He wrote 57 hymns and general literature, including a 15 volume (some state 22 volumes) *Study of the works of the 17th-century cleric Jeremy Taylor*. His edition of Jeremy Taylor is still the classic.

His sixteen years at Hodnet, where he held a halfway position between a parson and a squire, were marked not only by his devoted care of his people, as a parish priest, but by literary work. He was the friend of Milman, Gifford, Southey, and others, in the world of letters, endeared to them by his candour, gentleness, 'salient playfulness', as well as learning and culture. He was helped start *The Quarterly Review*; and was appointed Preacher at Lincoln's Inn (1822). During this portion of his life he often showed a lurking fondness for missionary work and especially India. He planned long journeys on his maps and even wished himself to be Bishop of Calcutta. Perhaps somehow this became known and at the age of 40 he was called to that exact position. The new duty closed off his literary life.

Once consecrated Bishop of Calcutta in October 1823, he travelled widely and worked to improve the spiritual and general living conditions of his flock. As well as working in an area which had been bishopless, he noticed wider issues. He wrote strongly criticising the East India Company's stewardship of its Indian territories. He was concerned that few Indians were promoted to senior posts, and noted the 'bullying, insolent manner' towards Indians that was widespread amongst the Company authorities. Tempora mutantur res eadem.

Heber was a strong opponent of factional rivalry. This linked with his views on hymns and singing. At the start of the 19th century the Anglican authorities officially disapproved of the singing of hymns in churches, other than metrical psalms, although there was considerable informal hymn-singing in parishes. In October 1820 asked Bishop of London, William Howley for official recognition of his works from the Archbishop of Canterbury. Howley replied noncommittally and suggested that Heber should publish the hymns, although he proposed to withhold episcopal approval until public reaction spoke.

Heber, according to John Betjeman, was a professed admirer of the hymns of John Newton and William Cowper, and was one of the first High Church Anglicans to write his own. One critic, after considerable criticising, wrote 'But as pure and graceful devotional poetry, always true and reverent, they are an unfailing pleasure'.

Heber was unable to complete the work before his departure for India in 1823. The collection was published in 1827, after Heber's death, as *Hymns Written and Adapted to the Weekly Church Service of the Year*. In the collection were 'Holy, Holy, Holy! Lord God Almighty', which remains popular for Trinity Sunday, while 'Brightest and Best of the sons of the Morning' is frequently sung during Epiphany.

It included also 'From Greenland's Icy mountains' which has declined in popularity. Watson describes this as 'a conspicuous example of that fervent belief to convert the world to Christianity which led Heber and others to lay down their lives in the mission field'. Betjeman felt that in the modern world, the words of this hymn seem patronising and insensitive to other beliefs, with references to '...every prospect pleases and only man is vile', and to 'the heathen in his blindness [bowing] down to wood and stone'. This was certainly the view of Gandhi who was almost vehement in his antipathy.

Betjeman characterised Heber's style as consciously literary, with careful choices of adjectives and vivid figures of speech: 'poetic imagery was as important as didactic truth'. Others assess much of his work as being 'a rather obvious sermon', and to his mixing of powerful description with 'rather trite moralism'.

Heber's own view was 'I avoid all fulsome, indecorous or erotic language to HIM whom no unclean lips dare approach.' It is remarkable therefore that 'Brighest and Best' has caused offence to several generations. As noted 'Greenland's icy mountains' is now de trop and rarely included in modern hymnals. The third of Heber's great hymns is still extant – although it did suffer the indignity of parody in the First World War as the obviously popular tune gained the words 'Raining, raining, raining, Always bloody raining …'.

Julian writes of Heber's hymns 'Their beauties and faults spring from this modern spirit. They have not the scriptural strength of our best early hymns, nor the dogmatic force of the best Latin ones. They are too flowing and florid, and the conditions of hymn composition are not sufficiently understood. But as pure and graceful devotional poetry, always true and reverent, they are an unfailing pleasure. The finest of them is that majestic anthem, with on the rhythm of the English Bible, 'Holy, Holy, Holy, Lord God Almighty'.

With Victorian detail and relish, his ending is described: Arduous duties, a hostile climate and poor health led to his collapse and death after less than three years in India. Heber as planned, made trips around and across India. His second trip took him through the scenes of Schwartz's labours in Madras to Trichinopoly, where on April 3,1826, he confirmed forty-two persons, and he was deeply moved by the impression of the struggling mission, so much so that 'he showed no appearance of bodily exhaustion'. On his return from the service, he retired into his own room, and according to his invariable custom, wrote on the back of the address on Confirmation 'Trichinopoly, April 3, 1826.' This was his last act, for immediately on taking off his clothes, he went into a large cold bath, where he had bathed the two preceding mornings, but which was now the destined agent of his removal to Paradise.

In his brief life, Heber made a considerable impression, and news of his death brought many tributes. Memorials were erected in India and in St Paul's Cathedral, London.

Holy, Holy, Holy! Lord God Almighty!

	Bishop Reginald Heber	1783–1826	1826	4 verses
NICAEA	John Bacchus Dykes§	1823-1876	1861	11.12.12.10

Revelation 4:8   "They rest not day or night, saying, 'Holy, Holy, Holy, Lord God Almighty.'"

The hymn was written in the early 1800s during Heber's time as vicar at Hodnet in Shropshire (1807–1823). Coincidentally, Heber fits in this book as the previous entry – so some space can be saved. It is the author's best known and most widely used hymn, and remains popular in many denominations. It has been described as one of the rare hymns which appears 'in just about every hymnal'. The text speaks specifically of the Trinity, having been written for use on Trinity Sunday although it can also be used as a general hymn of praise at any time.

The secondary restriction based on the original words is that this is a morning hymn. Some have changed the words to 'Gratefully adoring' or the all-day 'Morning, noon and night'.

The opening line 'Holy, Holy, Holy! Lord God Almighty!' is a direct translation of the early church Sanctus. The hymn is as a 'reverent and faithful paraphrase of Revelation 4:8–11' and of the vision of unending worship in Heaven, it is an example of Heber's dutiful attempt to avoid excessive emotionalism. The text does not 'call for praise' but is rather an invitation to join in an endless song. On this occasion, such song is delivered by the Four Beasts around the throne. Despite being Revelation – these are good beasts.

The Sanctus, sometimes called the Tersanctus is a very old part of the Christian worship. Found in both Greek and Latin, the Sanctus appears in the 1540 *Book of Common Prayer* as set to music by John Merbecke in 1550: *'Holy, holy, holy, lorde God of hostes. heaven and earth are full of thy glory, Osanna in the highest.'*

The tune NICAEA was written some 40 years later by J B Dykes for the first edition of *Hymns Ancient and Modern* in 1861. The name of the setting is in tribute to the First Council of Nicaea in 325. Set up by the newly-Christian Emperor Constantine in 325, this formalized the doctrine of the Trinity. NICAEA has been noted as one of the composer's finest and has certainly contributed to the popularity of the hymn. It does have a resemblance to a 16th-century Lutheran chorale 'Wachet auf, ruff uns die stimme' by Philipp Nicolai.

One critic states: "it is a good example of Victorian hymn tune writing, with 'solid harmonies and subtle chromaticism. It begins with an ascending major third, which can be seen as symbolizing the Trinity. A few leaps and many repeated consecutive notes lend it a chant-like character. The four-part harmonisation written by Dykes is usually unchanged in hymnals, though it is frequently transposed down a tone."

Metrically, it is in the long and unusual 11.12.12.10 metre, contrasting with the shorter stanzas of most preceding English hymnody, such as that of Watts§ and Wesley§. Additionally and obviously, every single line rhymes with the initial 'holy'.

There are not many hymns that can be used as marching songs, but this is made easier by the tune given by Dykes.

The text has a wide scope, successively referencing humans, saints, angels and all living creatures, and its main theme is the 'basic belief in the Trinity', which is shared by most denominations of the Christian church despite other differences. The first stanza opens with an invitation to worship God in the morning although variants have been sometimes used to adapt the hymn for any time of day. The second stanza magnifies the opening idea, with saints joining 'in adoring the Majesty in heaven'. The third stanza describes some attributes of the Christian deity, while the final stanza is a climax of the preceding with 'earth and sky and sea' joining in praising the divine.

Variants to the original text in modern hymnals are relatively minor, except when used by non-trinitarians such as the Mormons – where the final line is changed to 'God in His glory, blessed Deity!'. Recently, of course, there has been pressure for more gender inclusive language and removal of 'thee/thy'.

Despite being in the Prayer Book, despite being a piece for singing, 'Holy, Holy, Holy', was published when Anglican authorities still strongly disapproved of the singing of hymns in churches, other than psalms, although there was considerable informal hymn-singing in parishes. Heber originally intended to win support for their inclusion.

It is almost surprising that within months of the Bishop's calculated vagueness, in 1821, the Church of England agreed to allow hymns to be sung.

> An early version of the text is as follows:
>> Holy, Holy, Holy! Lord God Almighty!
>> Early in the morning our song shall rise to Thee;
>> Holy, Holy, Holy! Merciful and Mighty!
>> God in Three Persons, blessed Trinity!
>>
>> Holy, Holy, Holy! All the saints adore Thee,
>> Casting down their golden crowns around the glassy sea;
>> Cherubim and Seraphim falling down before Thee,
>> Which wert, and art, and evermore shalt be.
>>
>> Holy, Holy, Holy! though the darkness hide Thee,
>> Though the eye of sinful man, thy glory may not see:
>> Only Thou art holy, there is none beside Thee,
>> Perfect in power in love, and purity.
>>
>> Holy, holy, holy! Lord God Almighty!
>> All thy works shall praise thy name in earth, and sky, and sea;
>> Holy, Holy, Holy! merciful and mighty,
>> God in Three Persons, blessed Trinity!

The hymn was a particular favourite of Lord Tennyson, who said that he thought it the finest hymn ever written, considering the difficulty of the subject and the devotion and purity of its diction. It was sung at Tennyson's funeral in Westminster Abbey.

The congregation of St Oswald's Church, Durham, Dykes' former church, allegedly sings the tune to these words round the composer's grave on Trinity Sunday when it is often covered in snowdrops - no snowdrops in June!

How great Thou art

	Carl Boberg 1866 -1940 revised S Hine 1958	1885	(9),4,(6) verses
O STORE GUD	possibly a Swedish folk-tune before	1891	11.10.11.10

It is also known by the first line is 'O Lord my God, when I, in awesome wonder' and the third way of recognising it is the beginning of the chorus 'Then sings my soul'. The hymn is seen as modern because it has only been known to the English-speaking world for some 70 years. And it is a well-known participant in the modern church singing style.

'How great Thou art!' is one of the most popular hymns of today. It became widely known in Britain through the work of the American evangelist Billy Graham, who said of it: "The reason I liked 'How great Thou art' was because it glorified God: it turned a Christian's eyes toward God rather than upon himself…."

This began as nine verses in Swedish 'Or storeh Gud!' in 1885 when it was written although actually not as a hymn. It then became six verses of 'Wie gross bist Du' translated by Manfred von Glehn as it was taken to German-speaking Estonia. It went onward to Russia and the Carpathians hills of Poland; then to England where it is now 'How great thou art'.

Boberg lived in south-east Sweden. Aged only 19, he wrote the nine verses of his poem after he had been going home during a storm: lightning flashing, and winds sweeping over the cornfields. The storm lasted an hour, and at its end a beautiful rainbow appeared. Once home, he opened the window overlooking the bay, which he later described as 'laying like a mirror' before him. From the far side of the water he heard a thrush singing in nearby woods. There had been a funeral that afternoon, and he could hear the tolling of the church bell in the stillness of the evening. All this inspired his poem.

A musical setting was in print by 1891; to a melody which is claimed to be a Swedish folktune, but no-one has yet been able to identify it, or to find any trace of it earlier than this printing in 1891. It is in 3/4 time. Andrew Skoog harmonised the setting the next year. In 1903, the melody reached nearly its modern form in 4/4 time in a Swedish Missionary songbook. When this was revised in 1921, inexplicably the tune was replaced with a new one, which did not prove popular, and as a side-effect the whole hymn fell into disuse. E G Johansen translated verses 1, 2, 7, 8, and 9 into English in 1925, even with the original tune restored, unforunately this version too was largely forgotten.

But in Estonia …. that little country ruled for centuries by Russia, Sweden and its other neighbours, the original Swedish poem found new popularity. Translated into German by Manfred von Glehn in 1907, the Swedish title 'Or storeh Gud!' became 'Wie gross bist Du'.

I S Prokanoff came next, perhaps due to his translation skills for German into Russian in 1914 although his result has 8 verses not just 6. The hymnbook *Kimvali* or *Cymbals* was found by Stuart Hine in the Western Ukraine in 1934.

The two missionaries entered the Carpathian mountains in the summer of 1934, and to quote directly from Hine's own account: "In the very first Carpathian mountain village to which I climbed, I stood in the street, sang a Gospel hymn, and read aloud John chapter three. Among the sympathetic listeners stood the Russian village schoolmaster. But a storm was gathering, and when it was evident I would not get any further that night, the friendly schoolmaster offered hospitality."

"Awe-inspiring again was the mighty thunder echoing through the mountains, and it was this impression which was to bring about the birth of the first verse of the hymn in English. Pushing on, I came across the young believers, 'through the woods and forest glades' I wandered, and 'heard the birds sing sweetly in the trees.' Instinctively, the young people burst into song, accompanied on their mandolins and guitars—the only song so perfectly fitting the scene: 'How great Thou art," to Prokhanoff's words.

"I was inspired by the words, the sights and the certainty that very few of these people knew of the salvation that same great God had provided—the greater work of verse three. 20 miles away, I met Dimitri 'the local man with the Bible'. Nineteen years earlier, the Tsarist army had invaded the Carpathians - a retreating soldier had left his Bible and that very year, Dimitri's wife was learning to read from it. Letter by letter, word by word she spelled out the message to the wondering villagers listened with rapt attention: 'For…God…so…lo-…ved…the… world…' Slowly she persevered, day by day, spelling out aloud the most wonderful story ever heard, right on to the crucifixion."

"It was then that the tears began to fall, and men and women dropped to their knees, crying to God aloud. About twelve were truly converted, and I arrived just in time to hear them crying out all together, each voicing aloud (unconscious of all others) the amazement brought about at seeing the revelation of God's love at Calvary for the first time."

"When a believer from a Soviet land visited refugees in Britain, and asked if there were any questions, the first to speak voiced the question in every heart, 'When are we going home?' David Griffiths and I visited a camp in Sussex, consisting entirely of Russians. Only two of them were converted, and, after the meeting, they accompanied us to the station. I asked one of them whether he had been baptised."

"Immediately he bowed his head and was evidently moved. 'In Russia', he explained, 'my wife confessed Christ as her Saviour, and was baptised. But I still loved the world, and would not take this step with her, of identification with Christ. Now I know Him, and long to tell her—but all my letters have failed to reach her in Russia. I can't tell her that I too belong to Christ— she won't know—until Christ shall come and take me home—yea, take us both home, and to see the joyful surprise on her dear face."

In 1949 Hine published the Russian and English words of the four verses then written. In 1958, the final two verses were written, completing Hine's translation, although it might be better to describe 'How great Thou art!' as a paraphrase, as Hine's experience as a missionary led directly to its creation without any reference to the original Swedish. The worldwide success of 'How great Thou art!' did bring attention back to Carl Booberg's 'Or storeh Good!' and the original once again become popular in Sweden.

Hine rejected requests to translate the remaining five verses. But he noted that German, Russian, Polish and Hungarian, however, all include Boberg's verse 8. The Polish have written a new verse 6 which has a flavour of anti-communism. Startlingly, one story of its arrival in America is via Rev Edwin Orr who heard it sung in 1954 by Naga tribesmen in Assam, India.

>The godless federation, instead   ...   of honouring, Thy holy name revile;
>Yet is Thy grace no whit diminished,   ...   And Thou with patience sufferest awhile.

Hine eventually republished and enlarged his 1953 booklet. He added two verses as below. Unfortunately, as the four-verse version had already been widely disseminated, these two verses were not taken up by any hymnal, and have mostly been forgotten until now. Some feel 'How great Thou art!' is more satisfactory with their inclusion.

Oh, when I see ungrateful man defiling
This bounteous earth, God's gifts so good and great;
In foolish pride God's holy name reviling
And yet, in grace, His wrath and judgment wait: [Chorus]

When burdens press, and seem beyond endurance,
Bowed down with grief, to Him I lift my face;
And then in love He brings me sweet assurance:
"My child! For thee sufficient is My grace":   [Chorus]

An early version of the four verse text is as follows :-

1. O Lord, my God, when I in awesome wonder
consider all the works thy hands hath made,
I see the stars, I hear the mighty thunder,
thy pow'r throughout the universe displayed;
   Refrain:
   Then sings my soul, my Savior-God, to thee:
   How great thou art! How great thou art!
   Then sings my soul, my Savior-God, to thee:
   How great thou art! How great thou art!

2. When through the woods and forest glades I wander,
and hear the birds sing sweetly in the trees;
when I look down from lofty mountain grandeur
and hear the brook and feel the gentle breeze; [Refrain]

3. And when I think that God, his Son not sparing,
Sent him to die, I scarce can take it in,
that on the cross my burden gladly bearing
he bled and died to take away my sin; [Refrain]

4. When Christ shall come with shout of acclamation
and take me home, what joy shall fill my heart!
Then I shall bow in humble adoration
And there proclaim, "My God, how great thou art!" [Refrain]

Due in part to multiple translating, paraphrasing and rewriting, as well as phrases being combined and simplified, the English-version hymn thus omits Boberg verses which begin:

When in the Bible see I all God's wonders
Which He has wrought, since Adam (came to life) .....

And *I hear deluded men, in darkened folly,*
Denying God—they mock His words (of love) .....

Also *And when I see His image coming earthward,*
Who ev'rywhere did good (showed forth His worth) ...

Old style Singing of Hymns

Hymns Ancient and Modern 1861

The real achievement of *Hymns Ancient and Modern* [H A&M] and its Proprietors was to consolidate Anglican hymnody by replacing many local books with one that was more comprehensive, less partisan, better organized, more thoroughly edited, painstakingly compiled, and supplied with more attractive music. Two streams of hymnic need met in the first 1861 collection of 273 hymns; the popular and the scholarly.

Its beginnings came from the 1858 railway journey of Rev. Denton and Rev. Murray, who had both made published collections of hymns and there talked about amalgamating the several such works then available. Hearing of this, a third hymnal author, Rev. Cosby White invited Rev. Murray, Rev. Harrison, Rev. Pulling and Rev. Baker for a meeting at St Barnabas, Pimlico. A misunderstanding seems to be the cause of Denton not being clearly invited.

Murray was the Rector of Chislehurst, and the editor, together with the Rev. Christopher Harrison, who had been his curate, of the *Hymnal for Use in the English Church* published in 1852 with some success. Denton was Vicar of St. Bartholomew's, Cripplegate, and one of the editors of the widely used *Church Hymnal*, published in 1853. The Rev. Sir Henry Baker was Vicar of Monkland, a rural Herefordshire parish where he was both squire and parson; and he became a Baronet after 1859. He had contributed to Murray's book. He was planning a hymnbook of his own, the key element of which was to have been its low price of sixpence.

Murray's *'Hymnal for use in the English Church'* had many of the features of the first edition of their combined product which became called *Hymns Ancient and Modern*; these included attribution neither of author nor composer; a Biblical quote for every hymn, arrangement by the Prayer Book Seasons of the Church and so on. This product must not be confused with the later and more successful *English Hymnal* some 50 years later.

By 1860, Denton's *Church Hymnal* had sold 32,000 reaching 6,000 copies a year; Murray's had managed 20,000 by its third edition. None of the many other hymn collections managed anything near – and there were many. Early figures are hard to find, but by 1868, H A&M had sold, or distributed at near-cost, some 4 ½ million copies.

The Committee formed after the Pimlico meeting, with Baker initially as Secretary, grew to 11 with the addition of more Reverends - Huntingford, Lyall, Maberley, Richards, Ward and Wilkins. Soon Baker placed the following advertisement in the church newspaper, the Guardian (not the larger Manchester Guardian) :-

> *To the Clergy, and others interested in Hymnology. The Editors of several existing Hymnals, being engaged, with others, in the compilation of a Book which they hope may secure a more general acceptance from Churchmen, would be very thankful for any suggestion from persons interested in the matter. Communications may be addressed to the Secretary of the Committee, Reverend H. W. Baker, Monkland Vicarage, near Leominster.*

There were some 200 replies. The response was widespread and helpful, although the advice - perhaps inevitably - was conflicting. Driven forward by Baker's enthusiasm, the Committee and its herd of Compilers acted relatively briskly, selecting, translating, editing and writing new hymns. Baker was particularly glad to have the assistance of J M Neale who was able to assist with some twenty languages.

The Compilers of the early editions of *Hymns Ancient and Modern* were moderate High-Churchmen who had very definite ideas about Christian worship in general, and the legitimate role of the hymn in particular. They distrusted emotionalism and preferred the objective to the subjective – endorsing the desire to go back to the ancient Latin and Greek churches. As a result, there was a high percentage of translations in the 1861 edition.

The core of the Committee were the Proprietors who put in the time and the funds for the new work. The Committee met frequently and corresponded hugely as at that time the Post Office operated with Victorian speed and efficiency – unlike nowadays. At all times, the final decisions lay with the Committee. A great deal of work was done by the Compilers who made their suggestions, submitted their own hymns, and commented upon the sheets sent to them. These rarely met and never as a group. There were nearly three times as many Compilers who advised regularly, though some of them withdrew after disagreements over editorial policy or doctrinal alignment. The critics of A&M wrote of them as the Forty Thieves, with slightly more accurate reference to their number than to their methods.

A specimen *H A&M* for wider review was issued in May 1859 for the words of 34 hymns. The first full edition of *H A&M* with tunes, under the musical editorship of the 'superintendent' Professor W. H. Monk appeared on March 20, 1861. This had 273 hymns. Monk arranged some 60 tunes and composed 15. Added in the 1875 edition, his most popular tune was and still is 'Eventide' for the hymn 'Abide with me' § - which in 2005 was amongst the BBC's collection *Songs of Praise Nation's 40 Favourite Hymns*. It was Monk who suggested the name of the collection as *Hymns Ancient and Modern*.

Baker's secondary contribution was more than 20 hymns of the 1861 collection; although he wrote some 40 others. Monk as the Superintendent of the music provided or adapted over 90 of the tunes. On the whole, conflicting interests were diplomatically settled.

The period can be described as 'an explosion of hymn-books'. Most were the work of individuals, reflecting particular tastes and parochial prejudices. Most of these were swept aside by A&M for three main reasons: greater range, better music, and harder selling. Although often the Compilers absorbed what they thought of value.

The Salisbury book was one such. Unusually, although a layman, Lord Nelson was a key participant. Discussion; mutual options; even mention of amalgamation; but there were cobbles on the path; what Salisbury considered 'chaste' in language and doctrine, A&M considered 'watered-down'. By 1865, the possibility was fading. The Bishop of Salisbury requested Lord Nelson's committee to complete their revision and to dissolve the amalgamation sub-committee.

Usefully, the collection matched the Dissenters' work by offering strong music with clear sound messages avoiding amateur sentimentality, vulgarity, or doggerel. The committee set themselves to produce a hymn-book which would stand with the Book of Common Prayer and also would improve congregational worship for everybody. It was the first hymnal to match words to specific tunes; and satisfying high-church pressure for ritual was a real benefit.

Comparing the sales of *Hymns Ancient and Modern* ['H A&M' or 'A&M'] to the parochial versions prior and contemporary, no others managed anything near the huge numbers of the Proprietor's efforts. From that point of view – *Hymns Ancient and Modern* was a huge success.

For wider repute, a hymn book must move from the shelves to the hands of the congregation. Each hymn within a collection has its own particular purpose and its intended use, whether to teach, to proclaim, or to give communal expression to the aspirations and emotions of the Christian life. It is certain that the contents of *H A&M* did reach the hearts, minds and souls of the users. It rescued some wonderful 'Ancient' tunes from undeserved oblivion; while some of what they delivered as 'Modern' have become true classics.

Hymns Ancient & Modern - between the lines

In selecting and editing hymns, the original Proprietors or Compilers were sensitive to contemporary theological, social, and ecclesiastical issues and developed a great skill in positive compromise. The question of copyright was rather flexible however. The Committee let itself borrow from many works, some easily, some with grudging permission. They altered words, phrases, adapted and modernised so much that for some less-approving colleagues they became known as 'the forty thieves'; despite their claim for 'ecclesiastical copyright'. Other phrases have been identified 'Altered and Modified'; and other words for A and yet other words for M: manipulated, messed, arbitrary; appalling and so on. Often quite unfairly.

As an example, the first page of the Preface to the 1861 edition, has the note to Hymn 223 'Come, ye thankful people, come. *The Compilers feel it is due to the Dean of Canterbury to state that considerable alterations were made to them in this Hymn, without his sanction; and that he wishes not to be considered responsible for it in its present form.*

Sales was the biggest signal of success. Although Rev Burrowes of Kimmeridge (Dorset) wrote in 1876 to tell Baker how H A&M had transformed his parish. *"Fourteen years ago when I came into the place in 1862 there was, in the church, an old 'Grinder' with one barrel, having three tunes. Dissent flourished. but such dissent as few can have any idea of.*
The church congregation did not amount to 12; the communicants were three! Smuggling, card playing, drinking, and gross immorality prevailed on a Sunday evening; whilst I myself and my children were even stoned in the street. I swept away Grinder, hymn book etc etc and taught the tunes in Hymns A&M. They won my people over. They had singing at church, they could join in. it was easy, musical & varied and the tunes which they took to especially were many of them those of Dr. Dykes. Now I have no Dissent here. I have no public house. I have full and even overflowing congregations and of my 150 parishioners I have generally 25, sometimes more at the Holy Table."

Less pleasing was the disagreement between Bishop Wordsworth and the Proprietors over Wordsworth's hymns being in the Appendix; this dispute reflects poorly on both parties. There was little which was self-effacing about Wordsworth. He was determined to be taken as a poet in the Romantic style and as bishop he fully endorsed himself as bard and authority. Wordsworth borrowed hymns from H A&M which after an exchange of letters was accepted by Baker because 'Wordsworth's book was different in style'. Six years later, the Proprietors asked to use 8 of Wordsworth's hymns. Wordsworth said no.

The Bishop's objections were twofold: doctrinal, and practical. He wondered with what else his own would be printed, not wishing to be associated with some 'erroneous & dangerous doctrine'. Money also mattered. His own 'The Holy Year' was five times more expensive, and Wordsworth feared that if the best and most popular.of his hymns were readily available in the cheaper collection H A&M, his own sales would decline. In compensation for this, he suggested he take a share in the profits.

Sir Henry's tone is at first incredulous: 'You don't really mean to refuse the permission I asked: do you?' and then righteous as he argued that there was a strong implication of sound theology in H A&M due to the wide acceptance which it had already met. As regards the money, Baker eventually offered a donation and things calmed down.

Letters passed also between the ex-contributor Rev. Thring and Sir Henry to within a few weeks of publication as to the correct presentation of Thring's work: Thring wrote 'words were changed, and whole stanzas redrafted, but reluctantly I suppose I must give in.'

Other collisions were more vehement. Some even threatened the perceived success of H A&M with unpleasant adverse publicity. Most of the disputes revolved around borrowing and amendments; and being well-known for both tactics, the Proprietors were not always on solid ground. But they did on occasions threaten mightily.

Rev Potts published a hymnal, about which he had written 'I am therefore sorry that you will look on it as an opposition.' Whatever had prevailed before, Baker did not reply calmly '…Not satisfied with what we gave you, you have pillaged wholesale, taken whole verses, texts, arrangements without the least compunction; some verses which are my own & which I never would have allowed you so to use; in a word if ever anyone infringed copyrights unfairly you have done it…'

Pott's explanations are a catalogue of small misunderstandings, assumptions and oversights: for example, the printer had not consulted him before selecting a type. Commented Sir Henry: 'A publisher is no judge of what a gentleman should do'. Potts was forced to limit his book to his own parish.

For Rev Chope's 1862 publication, the Committee tried to be fiercer. '[We have been] irreverently spoken of as the '40 Thieves' -- but our petty larcenies are a joke compared to Chope & Co. Their avowed principle has been to take '*Hymns A & M*' as their groundwork & endeavour to improve thereon Hymn by Hymn & Tune by Tune.' Novello stated that Chope had also infringed the copyright of another publication, their *Hymnal Noted*. Chope replied that he had not borrowed from it as it was unfit for congregational use. Chope's skill with publicity encouraged the Committee to let the matter lapse.

In August 1862, letters in the English Churchman wrote about the impossibility of any hymnbook being acceptable to all tastes. The anonymous 'Englishman' stated that even some of the compilers of A&M did not use it in their churches. Rev Trend supported this view, so when in October, Sir Henry discovered that Trend's new collection had several A&M hymns, a particularly bitter correspondence ensued. Sir Henry's first letter was extremely strong, and Trend took violent exception to it. A mutual colleague wrote 'I dare say Trend's letter [in the English Churchman] was juvenile and indiscreet. But it was nothing to the offensive terms in wh Sir H.W. Baker opened his fire upon Mr. Trend'.

Perhaps the successful sales allowed the Committee to moderate its views on copyright. By the next year, there was the occasional relaxation. As Pulling wrote '…but whilst they [the Committee] expect this permission to be asked, they would meet such applications in a friendly spirit and good reason, whenever they are similarly made'.

There were, of course, critics. Dr. Boyd Carpenter, Bishop of Ripon 'It may be confessed that in all our hymn-books there is a sad quantity of rubbish, and our congregations are often expected to sing poor stuff. The percentage of this poor stuff varies in different books, being at a minimum, perhaps, in Mr. Thring's collection, and rising to a maximum in H A&M'.

While Hymns Ancient and Modern is the most influential and very much the best-selling, by 1889, it only includes 1/10% of the figure calculated for hymns in the years of Victoria some 400,000 in 1,200 hymnals from 1837 to 1900. And there are so many new hymns.

𝕴mmortal, 𝕴nvisible, 𝕲od only wise

                        W Chalmers Smith   (1823-1897)   1867   (5),4 verses
ST DENIO (Joanna)   traditional Welsh   1800   11.11.11.11
1 Tim. 1:17   "Now unto the King eternal, immortal, invisible, the only wise God, …."

    Erik Routley has written: "Immortal, Invisible should give the reader a moment's pause. Most readers will think they know this hymn, the work of another Free Kirk minister. But it never now appears as its author wrote it, and a closer look at it in its fuller form shows that it was by no means designed to be one of those general hymns of praise that the parson slams into the praise-list when he is in too much of a hurry to think of anything else but a hymn about the reading of scripture. Just occasionally editorial tinkering changes the whole personality of a hymn; it has certainly done so here." Routley never explained what he thought was damaged. Modern singers, perhaps unaware of such intricacies, enjoy the available text, tune and associated imagery.

    Routley, the renowned late 20th century musicologist, did add: 'Immortal, Invisible' is more complex than at first hearing. This becomes especially clear when the additional, mostly unused, verses are heard'.

    Walter Chalmers Smith was a minister of the Free Church of Scotland. He wrote and, unwillingly, published this poem in 1867. Smith was less good as a poet than he believed. Several of his phrases require review in order that they fit the metre and may be sung. W Garrett Horder did the deed for his 1884 collection *Congregational Hymns*. The words became standardised in the *English Hymnal* of 1906 – subject to the thee/thy removal of current times.

    First published in Smith's own book *Hymns of Christ and the Christian Life* (1867), in the third section, 'Hymns of the Holy Trinity', this hymn had six stanzas each of four lines. This text differs considerably from the one found in most modern hymnbooks, apart from the resounding first stanza. The customary text has four stanzas, using the first three stanzas followed by two couplets taken from the last three (stanza 5 lines 1-2, stanza 6 lines 1-2).

    The text as we know it evidently owes much to Horder, who was one of the few editors to print stanza 4 ('To-day and to-morrow…'), though with an improvement to line 4 ('The same God for ever that was yesterday').

    Smith's hymn can be seen as an expansion of the Apostle Paul's doxology in 1 Timothy 1:17, conveying some of God's grander and less tangible attributes. As A E Bailey put it, "One might say that the hymn is a rather florid attempt to express the inexpressible, and so rather a stimulus to the imagination than a clarifier of thought or an incentive to action." At the same time, the hymn is rooted in scriptural ideas, making it both lofty and doctrinal – really all suitable adjectives for this sentence 'lofty, florid, inexpressed'.

    The biblical wording continues in 1 Timothy 6:16, describing Christ, 'who alone has immortality, who dwells in unapproachable light, whom no one has ever seen or can see'. The name 'Ancient of Days' refers to Daniel 7:13–14, which again describes a glorious vision of the coming Christ, presented before God the Father: as well as verses from the Psalms that suggest God as Creator and man as frail (Psalm 90), and God as the father of light (Genesis 1), hidden from us by his radiance.

    'Immortal, Invisible' is a strong text of praise to God, who created and sustains the lives of all his creatures. The text focuses on the Creator of the universe, the invisible God whose visible works in nature testify to his glory and majesty. 'Light' is the prevailing image in stanzas 1, 2, and 4 (see also Ps. 104:2); our inability to see God is not because of insufficient light but because the 'splendour of light hides [God] from view'.

It is unclear if Routley disliked the text or the setting; nevertheless to many others it is evident that ST DENIO is a splendid match for Smith's words, and must be one reason why this hymn has become so universally popular. It is hard to find an English-language hymnbook in the last 100 years in which it is not to be found.

The original setting was ST DENIO. Originally a Welsh traditional ballad tune, it became a hymn setting under the title PALESTINA in 1839. It is based on 'Can mlynedd i nawr' ('A Hundred Years from Now'), a traditional Welsh ballad popular in the early nineteenth century. It was first published as a hymn tune in John Roberts' *Caniadau y Cyssegr (Hymns of the Sanctuary*, 1839). The tune title refers to St. Denis, the patron saint of France.

ST. DENIO's bright character in a major key should put to rest the notion that all Welsh tunes are sad and in minor key, it is a sturdy tune in rounded bar form (AABA'); It bears vigorous performance with singing in harmony supported by solid organ tone. The final stanza is a jubilant profession of how God blesses all.

John Roberts was born near Aberystwyth, Wales in 1822 and died at Caernarvon 1877. He is also known by his Welsh name, Ieuan Gwyllt (Wild John) to distinguish him from many other John Roberts. Ordained in the (Calvinist) Methodist ministry in 1859, he served congregations as far apart in Aberdare and Llanberis [150 miles through the Welsh hills – which takes 4 hours even in the era of the automobile].

As editor of the *English Hymnal*, it was Vaughan Williams who selected ST DENIO for this text. There is some suggestion that it is from a Welsh folk melody and it is sometimes given the name JOANNA. The tune ST DENIO deserves a little extra emphasis as it is a tune where there are others with remarkable similarities. Nowadays, the hymn is most widely sung to the Welsh folk tune ST. DENIO even if only first paired this way in *English Hymnal* (1906).

The earliest known variant of the tune was published in Edward Miller's *Dr. Watts' Psalms and Hymns, Set to New Music* (London: 1800, paired with 'Thy mercies, my God, is the theme of my song', a hymn generally attributed to John Stocker.

For this 1800 hymnal, the tune was labelled 'An old original Welsh melody never before printed', and named ROWLANDS perhaps after the Methodist Daniel Rowlands (1713–1790), an evangelist in Wales.

In 1893, *English County Songs* found a further link between 'Green Gravel' and saw it could substitute for ST DENIO. The song belongs to a girls-only playground game. There are/were examples across the country. They began the same but varied quickly.

Green gravel, green gravel, the grass is so green,
Such beautiful flowers as ever were seen.
Oh Annie, oh Annie, your sweetheart has fled,
He's sent you a letter to turn round your head.
With 3 more amongst the many variations available
    O Betty ...... All over creation, I'm 'shamed to be seen
        O Mary ... ... The fairest young damsel that was ever seen
            O Katie ... ... And all the pretty maids are plain to be seen

In 1911, the *Journal of the Welsh Folk Song Society* identified three tunes of the same type, in which 'the opening three-note phrase is either repeated or imitated, and correspondingly the first three words (or syllables) are repeated in the text'. The last of the three was 'Can Mlynedd i 'Nawr' ('A hundred years from now'). This seemed it to be an early form of JOANNA (ST. DENIO). It also has similarities with ROWLANDS.

A version of the tune more closely following the shape of ST. DENIO first appeared in Caniadau y Cyssegr (1839), edited by John Roberts of Henllan. In this printing, the tune was called PALESTINA. Notice how the Welsh text by Morgan Rhys (1716–1776) has the characteristic repeated text, as described by the Welsh Folk Song Society.

Percy Dearmer described the tune this way: It is a straightforward tune, in triple time, which, however, gains a rather strange flavour from the impression of being in D-flat rather than the marked A-flat, then needing what feels like a modulation. In addressing this harmonic sequence, Paul Westermeyer remarked, 'That may be expected to confuse a congregation, but by leading so naturally to the dominant and then to the tonic, the result is rather to increase the interest and engender a happy surprise'.

Smith's original had several unsatisfactory variations in metre. Often trying to squeeze in an extra syllable - stanza 5 line 1 is one example among several in the poem where Smith's ear was defective. Amendments to verse 4 show the sort of changes deemed necessary.

2. Unresting, unhasting, AND silent as light,
Nor (striving)WANTING, nor wasting, Thou rulest in might;
Thy Justice like mountains HIGH soaring above
Thy clouds which are fountains of(mercy) GOODNESS and love.

3. To all life Thou givest, both great and small;
In all life Thou livest, THE true life of all;
(Thy) WE blossom and flourish (only are we(AS LEAVES ON THE TREE,
To wither and perish – but nought changeth Thee.

Smith's incompetent metrics are matched by his inadequate punctuation, which has led to attempts by editors to establish his intention. Thus stanza 2 lines 3-4 are punctuated

thy justice like mountains, high soaring above
thy clouds, which are fountains of goodness and love.

Which turns 'above' into a preposition rather than an adverb, although Smith's text is unclear on this point. In stanza 3 line 1 some hymnals insert a comma after 'all', to make it clear that 'all' is an indirect object: 'To all, life thou givest, to both great and small'.

The strong rhythms of the original ('livest', 'givest') have caused some problems for the revisers in the 'you' form. One attempt by Anthony Petti develops thusly :=

To all things, life giving, to great and to small,
In all ever living, the true life of all;

Percy Dearmer, editor of the *English Hymnal* 1906, wrote '(Our) version escapes the syllabic conundrum of the penultimate stanza by combining the first two lines of that stanza with the first two lines of the last. In this way, the text could also be set musically without visual and mental gymnastics'. His approach is clearly seen in his polysyllabic vocabulary.

The hymn was the first entry in the Horder's *Worship Hymns* of 1905 where the newly written OLRIG GRANGE by J F Bridge was its new partner.

Verse 4 is now clearly a simple cut-down using the first two lines of the original verse 4 & 5.

4. Great Father of glory, pure Father of light,
Thine angels adore Thee, all veiling their sight;
Of all Thy rich graces this grace, Lord, impart

Take the veil from our faces, the vile from our heart.

5. All laud we would render; O help us to see
'Tis only the splendor of light hideth Thee,
And so let Thy glory, almighty, impart,
Through Christ in His story, Thy Christ to the heart.

An early version, standard insofar as this can be said of any text, is as follows:

1   Immortal, invisible, God only wise,
in light inaccessible hid from our eyes,
most blessed, most glorious, the Ancient of Days,
almighty, victorious, thy great name we praise.

2   Unresting, unhasting, and silent as light,
nor wanting, nor wasting, thou rulest in might;
thy justice like mountains high soaring above
thy clouds, which are fountains of goodness and love.

3   To all life thou givest, to both great and small;
in all life thou livest, the true life of all;
we blossom and flourish as leaves on the tree,
and wither and perish but naught changeth thee.

4   Great Father of glory, pure Father of light,
thine angels adore thee, all veiling their sight;
all praise we would render, O help us to see
'tis only the splendor of light hideth thee.

This next verse is almost unknown, having been expunged for 'the usual reasons'.

Today and tomorrow with Thee still are Now
Nor trouble, nor sorrow, nor care, Lord, hast Thou
Nor passion dpth fever,nor age can decay
The same God for ever as on yesterday.

Jesus Christ is risen today   Surrexit Hodie

Surrexit Christus Hodie (Latin 14C) trans. W Walsham How   1864   11, 8,6 verses
EASTER HYMN   in Lyra Davidica   1708   7.7.7.7
Luke 24:34   "The Lord is risen indeed".

'Jesus Christ is risen today' was first written in Latin manuscripts titled 'Surrexit Christus hodie', as a Bohemian hymn in the 14th century by an unknown author. In Latin, it had eleven verses. It is rather obviously an Easter hymn about the Resurrection. The hymn is also particularly memorable for having a very extended Alleluia as a refrain after every line.

This hymn is sometimes and easily confused with Wesley's§ 'Christ the Lord is risen today'. This is because the wording is very similar and the tune of EASTER HYMN is used for both. LLANFAIR is the most common alternative – but it too can be used for both!!

It was first translated into English in 1708 by John Baptist Walsh to be included in his *Lyra Davidica (Collection of Divine Songs and Hymns)*. The verses of the hymn, then titled 'The Resurrection', were revised in 1749 by John Arnold. Initially the hymn only had three verses translated with just the first verse being a direct translation. Charles Wesley wrote a fourth verse which has become adopted. Wesley's own 'Christ the Lord is risen' has 11 verses.

This Latin resurrection text is of unknown authorship; it can be traced to three important manuscripts from the 14th century. Long after this hymn arrived, all three were compiled into a critical edition by F.J. Mone, in his *Lateinische Hymnen des Mittelalters, vol. 1* (1853). Stanzas 4, 8, and 10 in Mone's compilation can be dated to the 16th century, and thus are added later.

Two capable translations exist; neither of which have entered into common use but reflect Mone's edition well. Abraham Coles (1813–1891), produced 'For human solace, Christ today,' published in *The Light of the World* (1885); it has ten stanzas, omitting Mone's verse 11.

The other is by J M Neale§ (1818–1866), 'Today the victor o'er his foes'. It was published in *Mediaeval Hymns and Sequences* (1851), also in ten stanzas, but rather omitting stanza 10 of the Latin. Neale and Coles both retained the simple metre and rhyme of the original (iambic tetrameter). This English paraphrase reflects stanzas 1–2, 6–7, 9, and 11 of those by Mone.

Not a direct translation but very similar is Wesley's 'Christ the Lord is ris'n today'. This has the same biblical background, the same tune and is equally famed. It is however essentially a completely new hymn on the resurrection. Nonetheless, its role as an alternative to the Lyra Davidica text is clearly shown by its associated tune.

Wesley's text was first printed in *Hymns and Sacred Poems* (1739), where it was part of a cycle of hymns for the church year, beginning with Christmas 'Hark how the welkin rings aka Hark the herald Angel sings' ; then Epiphany 'Sons of men, behold from far; Resurrection 'Christ the Lord is ris'n today'; next Ascension 'Hail the day that sees him rise'; and finally Whitsunday/Pentecost 'Granted is the Saviour's prayer'.

Wesley's text imitates the rhyming couplets of the Latin, but like the *Lyra Davidica* text, its metre is trochaic rather than iambic, in four lines of seven syllables. At eleven stanzas, it is typically not printed or sung in whole. Methodist books show a shortened form.

Some churches and denominations often just use 'Jesus Christ', others use 'Christ the Lord' and some use both. Indeed, sometimes stanzas from Wesley's hymn are intertwined with the Lyra Davidica text. In some English hymnals, to avoid confusion between the two texts, Wesley's text is sometimes published starting with the second stanza, 'Love's redeeming work is done'.

The piece is a translation of part of an anonymous Latin hymn, 'Surrexit Christus hodie'; being a translation creates the reference to the 'Females' ('Mulieres o tremulae, In Galilaeam pergite'). There is an intermediary German version 'Erstanden ist der heilige Chr ist'.

A third similar text - and there's probably more - is 'Christ the Lord is risen today / Christians haste your vows to pay' by Jane E Leeson.

The hymn is set to a piece of music entitled EASTER HYMN which was composed in the *Lyra Davidica* for 'Jesus Christ Is Risen Today'. The ascription of it by some to Henry Carey is destitute of any foundation whatever, while Dr Worgan, to whom it has been assigned by others, was not born until after the publication of *Lyra Davidica*. The tune like the text has been amended. It first appeared in 1708 as a rather florid tune. Tempered to its present version by John Arnold in his *Compleat Psalmodist* (1749), EASTER HYMN is now one of the best and most joyous Easter tunes. There was a later setting again called EASTER HYMN composed by W H Monk which is also used for both texts.

In each Gospel there are chapters, verses or phrases which talk of Easter and which can be called into service as useful in analysing a hymn written for this topic. Matthew 28:6, Acts 2:32, 1 Peter 3:18 and Revelation 1:17-18 are particularly relevant here.

The basic text as generally found in hymnbooks dates from 1749. It was printed in The *Compleat Psalmodist* by John Arnold (ca. 1715-1792). There has been very little change in the last 150 years.

The original words (seldom in use today) and the 'standard' 1749 version

Jesus Christ is Risen to day, Hallelu-Hallelujah	no change
Our triumphant Holyday	no change
Who so lately on the Cross	Who did once upon the Cross
Suffer'd to redeem our loss.	no change

Hast ye Females from your Fright,	Hymns of praises let us sing
Take to Galilee your Flight:	Unto Christ our heavenly King
To his sad Disciples say,	Who endur'd the Cross and Grave
Jesus Christ is Risen to Day.	Sinners to redeem and save.

In our Paschal Joy and Feast,	But the pain that he endured
Let the Lord of Life be blest,	Our Salvation has procured
Let the Holy Trine be prais'd,	Now above the Sky he's King
And thankful Hearts to Heaven be rais'd.	Where the Angels ever sing.

Joy to the world

	Isaac Watts§	1674-1748	1719	8, 6, 5, 4, 3 verses
ANTIOCH	Lowell Mason	1792-1872	1789	8.6.8.6
Psalm 98	paraphrased by Isaac Watts			

The second consecutive entry for Isaac Watts. In 1707, Watts had a grand design for a reformation of Christian worship. At the end of the first edition of his *Hymns & Spiritual Songs* (1707), he included *A short essay toward the improvement of psalmody; or, an enquiry how the Psalms of David ought to be translated into Christian songs.* In this essay, he argued that singing the Psalms congregationally is different from reading them theologically.

Watts' 1719 preface says the verses 'are fitted to the Tunes of the Old PSALM-BOOK' and includes the instruction 'sing all entitled COMMON METRE'. In the late 18th century, 'Joy to the World' had several settings but none have survived or are in use today.

As is usual for Watts, it is a free rendering and is of only the second part of the psalm, using the final verse 'for he cometh to judge the earth…' to produce a vigorous Advent or Christmas hymn. Originally in 4 verses of 4 lines. The double repeat at line 4 came later.

Watts imitated the language of the New Testament and applied to the Christian state and worship. The paraphrase is thus a simplification, an interpretation. Consequently, he does not emphasize with equal weight the various themes of Psalm 98.

This text was written in 1719 as a Christmas carol Watts' collection *The Psalms of David*. Like so many of Watt's pieces it is based on a Psalm. This time, Watts uses Psalm 98, Psalm 96:11-12; and Genesis chapter 3:17-18.

In first and second stanzas, Watts writes of heaven and earth rejoicing at the coming of the King. An interlude that depends more on Watts' interpretation than the psalm text, stanza three speaks of Christ's blessings extending victoriously over the realm of sin. The cheerful repetition of the non-psalm phrase 'far as the curse is found' has caused this stanza to be omitted from some hymnals. But the line makes joyful sense when understood from the New Testament eyes through which Watts interprets the psalm. Stanza four celebrates Christ's rule over the nations. The nations are called to celebrate because God's faithfulness to the house of Israel has brought salvation to the world.

In 1820, Cotterill gave a much altered version, repeating verse 1 as verse 5. It was so much changed it became known by the second verse as 'Ye saints, rejoice, the Saviour reigns'. In 1870, Bingham made a version in Latin 'Laetitia in mundi! Dominus nam venit Jesus' which not surprisingly bears little relationship to the original Latin of the Psalm.

Since the 20th century, 'Joy to the World' has been the most-published Christmas hymn in North America. It is often heard in films set in America at Christmas.

The tune has a vague origin which is detailed later – it is not by Handel. One history says the tune is by Lowell Mason for the 1848 *The National Psalmist*, Mason was by that time an accomplished and well-known composer and arranger, having composed tunes such as BETHANY used for the hymn 'Nearer, My God, to Thee'. Mason had four earlier attempts to write a tune for this text; the first he called ANTIOCH and attributed it to the influence of Handel; it is quite similar to his fourth version.

Musically, the first four notes of 'Joy to the World' are the same as the first four in the chorus 'Lift up your heads' from Handel's Messiah of 1742. In the third line, a similar match is found to another Messiah piece: the arioso 'Comfort Ye'. Consequently, and with Mason's attribution to Handel, there has long been speculation over how great an influence the Messiah had on 'Joy to the World'. It is known Mason was a great admirer and scholar of Handel's music, and had in fact became president of the Boston Handel and Haydn Society in 1827. However, these apparent matches between Messiah and 'Joy to the World', have been dismissed as 'chance resemblance' by Handel scholars today.

However, several tunes have been found from the early 1830s closely resembling that of ANTIOCH, the earliest of which was published in 1832 under the title COMFORT (possibly as a nod to Handel's 'Comfort ye'). This would make it at least four years older than Mason's first publication of ANTIOCH. Other publications from the early 1830s further suggest the tune may have been around for some time before Mason's arrangement.

Thomas Hawkes published the COMFORT tune in his 1833 *Collection of Tunes*. There the attribution was simply as 'Author Unknown', suggesting it may have been older. A 1986 article by John Wilson showed what he judged as more resemblance by ANTIOCH to this piece in 1833 and also its association to another Wesley hymn 'O Joyful Sound'.

1 Joy to the world, the Lord is come!
   Let earth receive her King;
   let ev'ry heart prepare him room
   and heav'n and nature sing,
   and heav'n and nature sing,
   and heav'n, and heav'n and nature sing.

2 Joy to the earth, the Savior reigns!
   Let men their songs employ,
   while fields and floods, rocks, hills, and plains,
   repeat the sounding joy,
   repeat the sounding joy,
   repeat, repeat the sounding joy.

3 No more let sins and sorrows grow   [not original]
   nor thorns infest the ground;
   he comes to make his blessings flow
   far as the curse is found,
   far as the curse is found,
   far as, far as the curse is found.

4 He rules the world with truth and grace
   and makes the nations prove
   the glories of his righteousness
   and wonders of his love,
   and wonders of his love,
   and wonders, wonders of his love.

The third verse is modern and therefore not part of Watts' original lyrics from 1719.

Jesus shall reign where'er the sun

	Isaac Watts§	1674-1748	1719	8, 6, 5, 4, 3 verses
TRURO (et al)	Burney & Williams	1726-1814	1789	8.8.8.8

Revel. 11:15 "The kingdoms of this world are become the kingdoms of our Lord ...; and he shall reign for ever."

Despite the heading from Revelation, this text from Isaac Watts is a very free rendering, a lyrical adaptation of Psalm 72. This paraphrase of the second part of Psalm 72 (verses 8-19) appeared in *The Psalms of David* (1719), with the title 'Christ's Kingdom among the Gentiles' and Watts begins with eight stanzas. Psalm 72 is one of the 'royal psalms' and is a prayer to God for King Solomon.

In both parts of the paraphrase Watts makes the psalm refer to Christ (his usual procedure) and in the second part he begins by naming him: 'Jesus shall reign…'. He then uses the psalm as a springboard for his own very free rendering.

Psalm 72 is traditionally taken as being written by King Solomon, John Brug writes 'The heading of Psalm 72 is 'Of Solomon'. This may also be translated 'to or for Solomon'. For this reason some commentators regard this as a Psalm written by David to express his hope for Solomon'. In the Greek Septuagint version of the bible, and in its Latin translation in the Vulgate, this psalm is Psalm 71 because of a slightly different numbering system.

Some commentators see David's prayers are fulfilled in some sense pictured in the reign of Solomon, a temple will be built and there will be great peace and prosperity, yet the language is larger than Solomon. 'The whole earth is filled with his glory' is like the angel speaking from Isaiah 6. Matthew Henry sees this fulfillment in some ways in the reign of Solomon but even more in a greater than Solomon to come.

From Watts' original, stanzas 2, 3 and 7 are normally omitted in modern hymnbooks (2 and 3 describe the effects of Christian mission to the 'barbarous nations' of the world):

> 2   Behold the islands with their kings,
> And Europe her best tribute brings;
> From north to south the princes meet
> To pay their homage at his feet.
>
> 3   There Persia, glorious to behold,
> There India shines in eastern gold;
> And barbarous nations at his word
> Submit, and bow, and own their Lord....
>
> 7   Where he displays his healing power,
> Death and the curse are known no more;
> In him the tribes of Adam boast
> More blessings than their father lost.

In stanza 4 the theme of Christian mission was continued from stanzas 2 and 3:
> For him shall endless prayer be made,
> And princes throng to crown his head;

In the USA, this strong missionary content was very popular (it is found in more than one thousand hymnbooks) and there it is frequently sung to DUKE STREET.

'Princes' suggests that a ruler was responsible for the whole country turning to Christianity, as was sometimes the case. Now it is normally altered to 'praises' – in some way such that they throng. With this and other minor amendments, this energetic hymn, shortened to five stanzas, is in use in the hymnbooks of every denomination. It is frequently sung to TRURO, but also to WARRINGTON, GALILEE and DUKE STREET. Carl Wilhelm and Ralph Harrison are amongst those who have delivered settings simply named after the hymn's title.

TRURO was a tune composed by Charles Burney (1726-1814). He was apprenticed to Thomas Arne from 1744-46. While Thomas Williams is listed only as the editor of *Psalmodia Evangelica* (1789) as a contributor, there are very few details about him apart from born about 1700, died about 1800; the former date is very unlikely. TRURO's opening phrase ascends a full octave. The entire tune is influenced by George F. Handel's style and bears relationship to similar tunes.

1   Jesus shall reign where'er the sun
does its successive journeys run,
his kingdom stretch from shore to shore,
till moons shall wax and wane no more.

2   To him shall endless prayer be made,
and praises throng to crown his head.
His name like sweet perfume shall rise
with every morning sacrifice.

3   People and realms of every tongue
dwell on his love with sweetest song,
and infant voices shall proclaim
their early blessings on his name.

4   Blessings abound where'er he reigns:
the prisoners leap to lose their chains,
the weary find eternal rest,
and all who suffer want are blest.

An occasional optional verse

Where He displays His healing pow'r,
Death and the curse are known no more;
In Him the tribes of Adam boast
More blessings than their father lost.

5   Let every creature rise and bring
the highest honors to our King,
angels descend with songs again,
and earth repeat the loud amen.

John Julian 1839-1913

In the old days, long before the internet, John Julian produced a phenomenal piece of scholarship: his *Dictionary of Hymnology* which contained some 3 Million words covering some 40,000 articles. Updated in 1907, it was beyond improvement until the age of the internet. Its worth is in the biographical and historical notes which underlie any history of hymns or hymn-writers; it is not a simple accumulation of hymn texts or hymn tunes.

In any place where there is any knowledge of hymns and their history, it is likely that the name 'John Julian' will be mentioned. John Julian was born in 1839 to a Wesleyan Methodist family. Nevertheless, he was ordained into the Church of England in 1876. Appointed to Wincobank in Sheffield he remained there until 1905.

It was here he prepared his great solo production ...... *A Dictionary of Hymnology, setting forth the Origin and History of Christian Hymns of all Ages and Nations, with special reference to those contained in the hymn books of English-speaking countries, and now in Common Use; together with biographical and critical notices of their authors and translators, and historical articles on national and denominational hymnody, breviaries, missals, primers, Psalters, Sequences, &c., &c., &c.*

The First Edition was published by John Murray in 1892. It consisted of 1,616 double-columned pages: up to page 1521 there was the main body of the work, with an index, followed by an Appendix, Parts I and II, with their 'Supplemental Indices'. Murray explained that 'the ten years which have elapsed since the first pages of this Dictionary were sent to press have seen many changes and developments in hymnological history and research.' The advertisement for the work is appended as an appendix to this entry. Adding the Supplement in 1907 made it up to 1768 pages - and all this with no mention of Tunes, Settings or Composers.

But what sort of things are in the Dictionary? Fortunately, in the way of the 1890s, the language is wonderful and the willingness to add comments and opinions goes far beyond what would now be acceptable.

Some extracts have been picked by opening every 100th page and picking out a name, reference or interesting phrase; especially since the very first page has such a significant link.

p1 'A children's temple here we build' J Montgomery. This hymn was written for the opening of the first Sunday School building in Wincobank, Sheffield [Julian's own parish]. Opened on the 13th April 1841, the hymn being printed on a fly-leaf for the occasion. ... The hymn by Mrs Ann Taylor 'We thank the Lord for heaven and earth' was also written for, and sung on, the same occasion. This hymn has not come into C.U. [Common Usage].

p102   'Awake, glad soul, awake, awake' by J S B Monsell [Easter] According to his preface to the collection 'written amid the orange and olive groves of Italy, during a winter spent (for the sake of health) upon the shores of the Mediterranean Sea'. Published in 5 st. then 8 adding ii, iii & iv. In the Scottish Hymnal of st i. v, vii and viii'.
----

p200   'Calm me, my God, and keep me calm' H Bonar. [Peace] … in 8st of 4l. Its use in Britain is fair, but in America it ranks in popularity with the finest of Dr Bonar's hymns.

(p300) Dies Irae   For the use of the general reader the most accessible work on this subject is Daniel ii pp103-106. The oldest form known to the present time is that contained in a MS in the Bodleian Library [Liturg. Misc. 163f 179b) This is a Dominican Missal written at the end of the 14th cent. and apparently for use in Pisa.

…. This extensive list of 133 translations of the Dies Irae not in CU (73 English and 60 American) has been compiled ….. the total number of trs into English of this magnificent sequence is thus over 150. The nearest approach to this is Adeste Fideles.
----

p399   'From Greenland's icy mountains' Bp R Heber …. Heber was requested to write 'something for us to sing in the morning'. In a short time the Dean enquired 'What have you written?' Heber read over the first three verses. The Dean said 'that will do'. Heber added another – the Dean said enough – Heber tried to add another but the Dean was inexorable.
----

p500   'He dies! The Heavenly Lover dies. I Watts, [Passiontide].   When reprinted in Wesley's collection, Madan much amended it as was his wont. There is no evidence Wesley ever countenanced Madan's alterations much less claimed them.
----

p601   Jesus shall reign where'er the sun …. Under the spreading banyan tree sat some thousand natives from Tonga, Fiji and Samoa … men whose eyes were dim … But young and old alike rejoiced together in the joys of that day … the entire audience singing Dr Watts' hymn   …rescued from the darkness of heathenism and cannibalism …
----

p701   Ludamilia, Elisabeth born 1640, she returned in 1670 to Rudolfstadt, where she was betrothed. At this time, Measles was raging … her elder sister Sophie was seized and died. By attending on her, Ludamilia and her younger sister Christiane both caught and both died.
----

p900   Pont, Robert, son-in-law of John Knox …. Six Psalm versions are by him viz Ps. 57, 59, 76, 89, 81 & 83. Being mostly in peculiar metres none transferred to the 1565 Scottish Psalter.
----

p901   Popule meus quid feci tibi … This was appointed to be sung on Good Friday during the prostrations known by the name of 'creeping to the cross'.
----

p1000   Scandinavian Hymnody ……The plaintiveness of a large proportion of these Northern hymns is very marked, whilst the strength of their writer's personal faith is undeniable.
----

p1100   Sturm, Leonard   …. The initial letters of Sturm's eight stanzas make the acrostic Jacobina being the name of his second wife. Possibly the hymn, labelled 'For the Dying', was written at a time when she was seriously ill.
----

p1200   Urbs Beata The second part of the translation 'Christ is made the sure foundation' has been adopted as a dedication hymn with so much general favour, that it would be unthinkable not to mention the fact.

----

p1301   Zinzendorf ….his hymns are by no means free from the faults and mannerism of that sentimental and fantastic period of Moravian hymn-writing. Their burden is a deep and intense personal devotion to the crucified Saviour; the spirit being that of his favourite saying 'I have but one passion and that is He, only He'.

In the large article on Wesley and the Wesley family, the last entry is for John & Charles' sister Mehetabel.

"Here, strictly speaking, the list of hymn-writers in the Wesley family ends: but these sketches would scarcely be complete without some mention of one, who if she did not write hymns, showed plainly that she *could* have done so with a success which might have rivalled Charles' own. Mehetabel Wesley had an exquisite poetic genius, which was cultivated by a careful study of the best models, Latin and Greek as well as English, for she was an accomplished scholar. Like all the Wesleys, except Samuel and Charles, she was most unfortunate in her marriage: her husband Mr Wright was a plumber and glazier and quite incapable of appreciating her refined mind, and being a man of no principle, sought relief … in low company and pursuits. The neglected Hetty was most unhappy, but her very unhappiness lent a pathetic tenderness to her poetry. What glorious hymns might have been written. But it must be remembered that Mehetabel Wesley was a hymn-writer only '*in posse*' not '*in esse*' and can therefore claim only a passing notice.

----

p1270   When I survey the wondrous cross [Isaac Watts] … The most extensive mutilations of the text were made by T Cotterill. The mutilations by others were equally bad, and would have justified him in saying of them all, as he did of Mr Darling's text in particular 'There is just enough of Watts left here to remind one of Horace's saying that 'you may know the remains of a poet even when he is torn to pieces'.

And some dippings :

Bruce, Michael / Logan, John   ….the names are brought together by the painful controversy which has long prevailed … during the latter years of Bruce's short life he wrote various poems … immediately upon his death Logan borrowed the papers upon promise of publication … No book arrived …'The servants had singed the fowls with it'. … The verdict of 100 years shows conclusively the poetic strength of Bruce and the weakness of Logan.

Te Deum Laudamus, the 14 pages begin 'The most famous non-Biblical hymn of the Western Church, intended originally, as it appears, as a morning hymn. It is not now known in the Eastern Church in Greek form, though its first ten verses exist in Greek. Since the 6th century it has been as a Sunday service hymn for mattins before the lesson from the Gospel'.

What ails my heart? Julian writes 'When we cannot sleep at seasonable times, want of right meditating on God is frequently the cause of unrest'.

Frances Crosby (van Alstyne) … her works are written under a bewildering number of initials and noms de plume including A; C; DHW; F; FAN; FC; FJC; F J Crosby; Fanny; Jennie V; Miss Jenie Glenn; Mrs Kate Grinley; Miss V and many others. Notwithstanding the immense circulation of the millions of copies, the hymns are, with few exceptions, very weak and poor, their simplicity and earnestness their redeeming features.

Public School Hymnbooks (such as the one for Marlborough) '…the Christian ideas of faith, penitence, frailty, dependence are presented in hymns of fortitude and endeavour. The edition of 1878 recognizes that the atmosphere of culture demands a higher poetic standard, careful editing as may encourage the study of hymns'.

Julian's Dictionary was priced at two guineas (£2. 2s). John Murray's advertisement in The Athenaeum (26 December 1891) was as follows:

> The delay which has occured (sic.) in the appearance of this work and the causes which have produced that delay seem to call for some explanation.
>
> The EDITOR first began a methodical study of the subject in 1870, and in 1879 the work was undertaken for publication by MR. MURRAY.
>
> It was at first intended to annotate every Hymn published in any recognized Hymn Book in the English language in alphabetical order of first lines, and thus to form a volume of about 800 pages: further progress, however, proved that this method involved endless repetition, and would require 20 volumes instead of one. The first design was accordingly abandoned in favour of that which has since been carried out. Hymns which have a history are dealt with in separate articles: Biographical Notices of Hymn Writers are given: and minor Hymns are grouped in these Biographies, while a complete Cross Reference Index of first lines enables the reader to trace any hymn with the utmost facility.
>
> Special articles on NATIONAL and DENOMINATIONAL HYMNODY constitute a new and valuable feature in this work.
>
> The LANGUAGES and DIALECTS dealt with number nearly TWO HUNDRED, including GREEK, LATIN, SYRIAC, GERMAN, FRENCH, ITALIAN, WELSH, DUTCH, SWEDISH, &c.
>
> Most of the great Libraries of Europe have been either visited by the Editor or the Assistant Editor in the course of their researches, or direct information has been supplied therefrom by the Chief Librarians.
>
> Some 10,000 MSS have been consulted, very few of which have been used for Hymnological purposes before.
>
> The number of Hymns annotated is about 30,000: the number of AUTHORS, TRANSLATORS, &c., recorded over 5,000.
>
> The tracing out of the Mutilations and Arbitrary Changes made in many favourite Hymns, for denominational, metrical, musical, or other purposes, has of itself been a most arduous task -
>
> e.g. Seventeen changes in the first four lines of "JESU, lover of my soul", have been recorded and accounted for;
>
> and many other examples might be given.
>
> A mass of information, hitherto inaccessible to the Student of Hymnology, has been collected from many private sources, and the accepted histories of a large number of hymns, including some of the most popular, have been proved to be erroneous.
>
> The Editor has been in correspondence with upwards of One Thousand Correspondents in all parts of the world. The delay thus caused has in some instances been very great. A year and a half elapsed in one case before an answer was received to a letter of inquiry; whilst delays of six and nine months were of common occurrence.
>
> As regards the more mechanical part of the preparation of this Dictionary, it may be interesting to note that i. Of the 3,000,000 words and figures which the volume contains, more than 2,000,000 have been written originally or in revision by the Editor himself.
>
> ii. Upwards of 300£ have been spent on postage alone.
>
> iii. Sixteen different kinds of type have been employed - the total number of types set in the process being 14,027,000, or about 8 tons weight.
>
> iv. Every line of the book has been revised in proof from 5 to 10 times.
>
> v. If this Dictionary had been printed in the same type and on the same paper as the Speaker's Commentary, it would have exceeded in size the Old Testament portion (6 vols.) of that great work. It is also equal to more than vols. i .and ii. either of Dr. Smith's 'Dictionary of the Bible' or 'Dictionary of Christian Biography'.
>
> JOHN MURRAY, Albermarle Street.

King of Glory, King of Peace

	George Herbert 1593-1633	1633	7,6 verses
GWALCHMAI	J D Jones	1827-1870	1868	7.4.7.4 D

Psalm 118:21   "I will praise Thee, for Thou hast heard me, and art become my salvation."

The 266 years' interval between its publication as a poem and its transition to a hymn emphasises how the text of many a hymn stands alone and valid as a poetic piece. Having a tune of equal quality makes for a hugely different experience – the mind and heart may take in the words – a good hymn is visceral.

Here, the near-repeats from line to line – love, move; heard, spared; sing, bring; clear, hear; praise, raise; and enrol, extol – shows a skilful manipulation of language and rhyme, as with the building up of its message as each is altered by only one or two letters. Similarly, the poem cleverly uses 'love' as verb and noun. Personally, the option in the second pairing might better be sung as 'spurred'. 'Move' cannot be altered acceptably; love to dove does not work.

This text was published after Herbert's death as a poem in the collection *The Temple* (1633) under the title 'Praise (II)'. 266 years later, it was first used set as a hymn by Robert Bridges in his *Yattendon Hymnal* in 1899 (the year before he became Poet Laureate). It derives inspiration from the psalms of praise, especially Psalm 116. It was originally in seven four-line stanzas.

One of the stanzas of the original poem has been omitted and the remaining six conflated to form three 8-line stanzas in modern hymnbooks. The omitted stanza does not follow the 'thee/thee' and 'me/me' rhyme scheme of the other stanzas which gives such a clear indication of the familiar nature of the relationship between Herbert and God:

> Thou grew'st soft and moist with tears,
> Thou relentedst:
> And when Justice call'd for fears,
> Thou dissentedst.

Apparently, the image of 'King of peace' is related in Hebrews 7:2 to Melchizedek, the Old Testament king and priest who prefigures in traditional iconography the priestly role of Christ himself. This helps to establish the poem's statements of repentance and absolution, praise and worship, as a neat symbolic preparation for Holy Communion.

The simplicity of the metre, in marked contrast to the fine complexity of language and diction, has undoubtedly contributed to the lasting popularity of this piece as a hymn. The rhyme format is equally simple being A B A B C B C B for the three common verses.

There is no available data on any tune being regularly used for the first 250 years.

The Welsh tune, GWALCHMAI, has become a key contributor to the hymn's popularity. By J.D. Jones (1827-1870) and first published in 1868 it is often the tune for this text.

The next most common usage is of REDLAND.

1   King of glory, King of peace,   ... I will love Thee;
     and that love may never cease,   ... I will move Thee.
     Thou hast granted my request,   ... Thou hast heard me;
     Thou didst note my working breast,   ... Thou hast spared me.

2		Wherefore with my utmost art	... I will sing Thee,
		and the cream of all my heart	... I will bring Thee.
		Though my sins against me cried,	... Thou didst clear me;
		and alone, when they replied,	... Thou didst hear me.
3		Sev'n whole days, not one in sev'n,	... I will praise Thee;
		in my heart, though not in heav'n,	... I can raise Thee.
		Small it is, in this poor sort	... to enroll Thee:
		e'en eternity's too short	... to extol Thee.

George HERBERT (1593 – 1633) was a cousin of the Pembroke family, coincidentally perhaps his final location at Bemerton, near Salisbury which was part of the Pembroke estate. He was born in 1593 at Montgomery Castle. His godfather was John Donne.

Josiah Miller wrote in his 1869 *Singers and Songs of the Church* "His mother, to whom he was much indebted, in part because of the early death of his father, was the youngest daughter of Sir Richard Newport. From Westminster School, aged 15 he was elected to Trinity College, Cambridge. He sent his mother a sonnet, which gave promise of the peculiarities and excellences of his later style. It was sent as a testimony that his "poor abilities in poetry should be all and ever consecrated to God's glory." He graduated in 1611 aged 18; in 1619 he was appointed Orator for the University.

Favoured by James I., intimate with Lord Bacon, Bishop Andrewes, and other men of influence, and encouraged in other ways, his hopes of Court preferment were somewhat bright until they were dispelled by the deaths of the Duke of Richmond, the Marquis of Hamilton, and then of King James himself.

Retiring into Kent, he decided to take Holy Orders. In July 1626, as prebend of Layton Ecclesia, Huntingdon, he found the church in ruins, and, by the assistance of his rich kinsmen and friends, rebuilt and beautified it. After 1629, his health began to fail due to 'quotidian ague'. He was next at Woodford, Essex, but not improving in health, he removed to Dauntsey, in Wiltshire, and then as Rector to Bemerton. Inducted there in 1630, he died less than 2 years later.

Izaak Walton wrote *A life of George Herbert* which was well known. Herbert's own prose work delivered just days before his death was *Priest to the Temple*. The work became popular, and the 13th edition was issued in 1709. It is meditative rather than hymnic in character, and was never intended for use in public worship.

In 1697 a selection from The Temple appeared under the title *'Select Hymns Taken out of Mr. Herbert's Temple & turned into the Common Metre To Be Sung In The Tunes Ordinarily us'd in Churches'*. In 1739, J. & C. Wesley made a much more successful attempt to introduce his hymns into public worship by inserting over 40 in a much-altered form in their Hymns & Sacred Poems. The quaintness of Herbert's lyrics and the peculiarity of several of their metres have been against their adoption for congregational purposes. The best known are: 'Let all the world in every corner sing §'; 'My stock lies dead, and no increase'; 'Throw away Thy rod'; 'Sweet day, so cool, so calm'; and 'Teach me, my God, and King'.

Izaak Walton relates that "The Sunday before his death the poet rose suddenly from his couch, called for one of his instruments, took it in his hand, and said 'My God, My God, My music shall find Thee, And every string Shall have his attribute to sing;.

Lead, kindly Light, amid th'encircling gloom

	J H Newman	1801-1890	1833	4,5,4 verses
LUX BENIGNA (et al)	J B Dykes §	1823-1879	1865	10.4.10.4.10.10

Numbers 14:14 "In the daytime also he led them with a cloud…"

The power of this remarkable hymn is shown in part by the fact that "when the Parliament of Religion met in Chicago during the Columbian Exposition of 1893, the representatives of almost every creed known to man found two things on which they were agreed: They could all join in the Lord's Prayer, and all could sing 'Lead, Kindly Light.'" The attendees included Hindus, Buddhists, Jains, Jews, Protestants, Catholics, Unitarians, adherents of the Shinto and Zoroastrian traditions (but no one from Africa), they all met together for the first time in modern history. The Archbishop of Canterbury declined to attend because, as he put it, 'the Christian religion is the only true religion'.

As a young priest, Newman became sick while in Italy and was unable to travel for almost three weeks. In his own words: *'Before starting from my inn, I sat down on my bed and began to sob bitterly. My servant, who had acted as my nurse, asked what ailed me. I could only answer, 'I have a work to do in England.' I was aching to get home, yet for want of a vessel I was kept at Palermo for three weeks. I began to visit the churches, and they calmed my impatience, though I did not attend any services. At last I got off in an orange boat, bound for Marseilles. We were becalmed for whole week in the Straits of Bonifacio, and it was there that I wrote the lines, Lead, Kindly Light, which have since become so well known.'*

The words were written in 1833 by John Henry Newman as a poem first published in the British Magazine in 1834; it began with the title 'Faith-Heavenly Leadings'. It re-appeared in 1836's *Lyra Apostolica* with the motto 'Unto the godly there ariseth up light in the darkness'. 30 years later, in Newman's *Verses on Various Occasions* (1868) it was given its most famous title, 'The Pillar of the Cloud' (from Numbers 14: 14). Once it became a hymn, as usual the title converted to the first line.

Newman was born in 1801 and died 1890. He began as a Church of England priest, albeit of high-church tendencies. He was one of the leaders of the Oxford Movement. This group's main intent was to return to many of the Catholic beliefs and liturgical rituals of the Pre-Reformation. In 1845, he left the Church of England and was quickly ordained instead as a Catholic priest. He became a cardinal in 1879. He became a Saint in 2019.

There are several tunes for the words: It was often sung to the tune SANDON by Charles H Purday; ALBERTA by W H Harris; LUX BENIGNA composed by Dykes in 1865; LUX IN TENEBRIS by Sullivan which Ian Bradley praises as a 'much more sensitive and honest setting of Newman's ambiguity and expressions of doubt' than Dykes' 'steady, reassuring' rhythms. Newman modestly attributed the hymn's popularity: "The tune is Dykes', and Dr Dykes was a great Master". John Stainer wrote a choral anthem in 1886.

The largest mining disaster in the Durham Coalfield in England was at West Stanley Colliery, known locally as 'The Burns Pit'. Incredibly, there were still 34 men left in a pocket of clean air; sadly a few panicked, left, and died instantly from the poison gas. The remainder sat in almost total darkness, when one of them began humming. In no time at all, the rest of the miners joined in with the words of this hymn – hoping for both light and, at that moment, distant home. This was probably sung to the tune SANDON by C. H. Purday, the then popular setting. The 26 men were rescued after 14 hours and later 4 more.

On the Titanic, the soloist, Marion Wright, sang it at a hymn-singing gathering led by the Rev. Ernest C. Carter, shortly before it struck the iceberg on April 14, 1912. The hymn was also sung aboard one of the Titanic's lifeboats when the rescue ship Carpathia was sighted the following morning at the suggestion of one occupant Noelle, Countess of Rothes.

Betsie ten Boom, sister of Corrie Ten Boom, and other women sang it as they were led by the SS guards to the Ravensbruck concentration camp.

Bishop Bickersteth of Exeter added a fourth 'pirate verse' in the Hymnal Companion in 1870. Newman was not pleased, writing to the publishers: "It is not that the verse is not both in sentiment and language graceful and good, but I think you will at once see how unwilling an author must be to subject himself to the inconvenience of that being ascribed to him which is not his own." This verse is now usually omitted. The usual text is as follows :

    Lead, Kindly Light, amidst th'encircling gloom, ... Lead Thou me on!
    The night is dark, and I am far from home, ... Lead Thou me on!
    Keep Thou my feet; I do not ask to see
    The distant scene; one step enough for me.

    I was not ever thus, nor prayed that Thou ... Shouldst lead me on;
    I loved to choose and see my path; but now ... Lead Thou me on!
    I loved the garish day, and, spite of fears,
    Pride ruled my will. Remember not past years!

    So long Thy power hath blest me, sure it still ... Will lead me on.
    O'er moor and fen, o'er crag and torrent, till ... The night is gone,
    And with the morn those angel faces smile,
    Which I have loved long since, and lost awhile!

    Meantime, along the narrow rugged path, ... Thyself hast trod,
    Lead, Saviour, lead me home in childlike faith, ... Home to my God.
    To rest forever after earthly strife
    In the calm light of everlasting life.

John Julian§ called the poem 'one of the finest lyrics of the nineteenth century', writing as follows: "Angry at the state of disunion and supineness in the Church he still loved and in which he still believed; confident that he had 'a mission,' 'a work to do in England;' passionately longing for home and the converse of friends; sick in body to prostration, and, as some around him feared, even unto death; feeling that he should not die but live, and that he must work, but knowing not what that work was to be, how it was to be done, or to what it might tend, he breathed forth the impassioned and pathetic prayer, one of the birth-pangs, it might be called, of the Oxford movement of 1833."

It received some tactless alteration during the 19th century, but since that time the text has normally remained as Newman wrote it, with all its mystery and enchantment.

The last two lines, in particular, have been the topic of much debate, but Newman wisely refused to be tied to any single interpretation, quoting John Keble to the effect that "poets were not bound to be critics, or to give a sense to what they had written."

Lead us, heavenly Father, lead us

	James Edmeston	1791 – 1867	1821	3 verses
MANNHEIM	F Filitz	1804 – 1876	1875	8.7.8.7.8.7

Isaiah 48:17   "I am the LORD ….which leadeth thee by the way that thou shouldest go."

If Charles Dickens is to be believed, children were often cruelly used and badly fed in orphanages: *Oliver Twist* is dated 1837-38, not long after Edmeston's hymn. The poor and orphaned children of that time clearly needed institutions that had benevolent people such as Edmeston taking an interest. 'T'was ever so; and ever will be' said Nebuchadnezzar.

Published in Edmeston's *Sacred Lyrics, Second Series* (1821), entitled 'Hymn, Written for the Children of the London Orphan Asylum.' Edmeston took a great interest in the welfare of orphaned children, and it is significant that the metaphors he uses (stanza 1 line 3) to describe God's protection are those that might be used of an orphanage supervisor: 'Guard us, guide us, keep us, feed us'.

The hymn may have begun with the metaphors of orphanage-keeping, but it developed into a fine general hymn, its three stanzas addressing Father, Saviour, and Holy Spirit:

> Lead us, heavenly Father, lead us
> O'er the world's tempestuous sea;
> Guard us, guide us, keep us, feed us,
> For we have no help but thee;
>   Yet possessing … Every blessing,   … If our God our father be!
>
> Saviour! breathe forgiveness o'er us;
> All our weakness thou dost know,
> Thou didst tread this earth before us,
> Thou didst feel its keenest woe;
>   Lone and dreary, … Faint and weary, … Through the desert thou didst go!
> Spirit of our God, descending,
> Fill our hearts with heavenly joy,
> Love, with every passion blending,
> Pleasure, that can never cloy.
>   Thus provided, … Pardoned, guided, …   Nothing can our peace destroy!

It has become a classic for guidance in the pilgrimage of life, and a very popular wedding hymn (being used as such for the future King George VI and Queen Elizabeth in 1923).

Some have a problem with stanza 2 line 5, 'Lone and dreary, faint and weary', as a description of the temptation in the wilderness (Matthew 4:1-11), and the unnecessary substitution of 'Tempted, taunted, yet undaunted'.

One effort at rewriting was 'Son of Mary, lone and weary,/ Victor through this world didst go'. Yet another effort was 'Self denying, death defying,/ Thou to Calvary didst go'.

The rhythmic steadiness of the words was well matched by the tune chosen for it by Sir Arthur Sullivan for his collection *Church Hymns with Tunes*. Sullivan chose MANNHEIM, a German chorale arranged by Friedrich Filitz.

The *Second Edition of A&M* (1875) also included the hymn to this tune, and words and music have become closely associated since that time, although there is another tune written for the hymn, FENITON COURT, by E J Hopkins; an alternative is CORINTH.

Friedrich Filitz (1804 – 1876) was born in Schwarzburg-Rudolstadt in central Germany. He lived in Berlin from 1833, working as a music critic among other employment. In 1841, Filitz was shortlisted to be a censor of the Prussian state, although there were concerns he would be too strict. With Ludwig Erck, he published a collection of 15th & 17th Century chorales in 1845. He moved to Munich in 1847, where he left his collection of valuable church music to the Bavarian State Library. Through his collections of church music from the 16th and 17th, he made many forgotten works available once again.

======================================

In Passing – The influence of German (Lutheran) Hymns

Julian writes "German hymnody surpasses all others in its wealth."

Before the Reformation, some of the best Latin hymns were repeatedly translated. Some of them became a German-Latin meld called 'macaronic'. Later the Minnesanger of the 13th Century glorified earthly, heavenly, sexual and spiritual love after the model of Solomon's Song and the Virgin Mary as the type of pure womanhood.

The German hymnody of the Middle Ages overflows with hagiology [church] and Mariology [Virgin Mary]. Mary is even clothed in divine attributes and virtually put in the place of Christ as the fountain of all grace. This changed somewhat with the Reformation.

Luther is the St Ambrose of German hymnody. His hymns and Bible translation are characterised by simplicity and strength. They breathe the popular, joyful spirit of faith which was the heart of his theology and piety. He had an extraordinary skill of expressing profound thought in the clearest language. He is not surpassed by any uninspired writer. His power is that he never leaves the reader in doubt as to his meaning. His translation of the Bible will never lose its hold on German-speaking people. 'So rare and majestic; so full of pith and power, you will not find his equal' wrote his contemporary, Spangenberg.

Calvin's efforts put the Psalter in prime position for he wrote 'no production of man should be allowed to take the place of the Word of God'.

By about 1700, there was great reaction against the dry scholasticism and cold formalism of the Lutheran Council. From this came the Moravians, whose hymns are fresh and lively, full of devotional fervour, but sometimes degenerate into playful and irreverent sentimentalism. It is clear that some of the great Revivals were driven as well by song as by preaching.

The number of German hymns is enormous. In 1786, von Hardenberg made a catalogue of first lines for 72,733 hymns (in 5 volumes). How many are there now?

Let all the world in ev'ry corner sing

	George Herbert	1593 -1633	1633	2 verses
LUCKINGTON	Basil Harwood	1859 -1949	1908	10.4.6.6.6.6.10.4

Psalm 148:13   "His name only is excellent, and His praise above Heaven and earth".

The simple affirmation 'My God and King' is thoroughly typical of Herbert, as are the vivid contrasts of the contexts for praise. Heaven, in which 'praise' (in the singular to suggest focus) can fly, is contrasted with earth in which 'praises' (in the plural to suggest a diversity yet to be focused) may grow. The rhymes 'high/fly' and 'low/grow' emphasise the distance between heaven and earth which is crossed by singing to God, either in the shout of the Church in public worship or in the quiet privacy of worship from the heart. A familiar Herbert theme of reaching towards God through the duty and joy of praise and worship is clearly stated.

This comes from Herbert's posthumous collection *The Temple* of 1633 where it is entitled 'Antiphon (I)', this was the first of Herbert's poems to be used as a hymn without significant adaptation when it was published in *Church Hymns* (1871). In the same collection is 'King of Glory, King of Peace' §.

The hymn has been set to several different tunes, but LUCKINGTON by Basil Harwood from the Oxford Hymn Book of 1908 has been the most enduring in Great Britain. Harwood complements Herbert's words with bugle-like proclamations for 'My God and King', uses a descanting arpeggio motif to suggest the heavens and the Church with an echoing lower motif to suggest the earth and the heart.

Erik Routley delivered AUGUSTINE which lets the hymn to be sung in its original form. It has become the tune most closely associated with the hymn in the USA: indeed the hymn was not well known there until printed with AUGUSTINE. It can be sung to MACDOUGALL by Calvin Hampton. Another tune mostly only in Methodist and Baptist books in the USA is the quite recent ALL THE WORLD by R G McCutchan.

An antiphon is 'a composition, in verse or prose, consisting of verses or passages sung alternately by two choirs in worship' (*Oxford English Dictionary*). To create the antiphonal effect: so the poem runs ….. Chorus…Versicle…Chorus…Versicle…Chorus. *The Temple*, where this piece was first published, has it being performed as follows :

"Antiphone.
"Chorus: Let all the world in ev'ry corner sing,
                    My God and King.
"Vers: The heavens are not too high,
             His praise may thither flie:
             The earth is not too low,
             His praises there may grow.
"Chorus: Let all the world in ev'ry corner sing,
                    My God and King.
"Vers: The church with psalms must shout,
             No doore can keep them

Hymnbook editors have usually added an extra chorus after the first Versicle to produce two balanced hymn stanzas and dropped the designations 'Cho.' and 'Vers.'

OR more commonly and omitting the final Versicle.

> 1   Let all the world in ev'ry corner sing,
> "My God and King!"
> The heav'ns are not too high,
> God's praise may thither fly;
> the earth is not too low,
> God's praises there may grow.
> Let all the world in ev'ry corner sing,
> "My God and King!"
>
> 2   Let all the world in ev'ry corner sing,
> "My God and King!"
> The church with psalms must shout:
> no door can keep them out.
> But, more than all, the heart
> must bear the longest part.
> Let all the world in ev'ery corner sing,
> "My God and King!"

Basil Harwood (1859-1949) was born in Gloucestershire. His mother died in 1867 when Basil was eight. His parents were Quakers but his elder sister Ada, on reaching 21 in 1867, converted to the Anglican Church. Basil was allowed to attend at the Church in Almondsbury which is where he was first drawn to organ music and choral singing. His father, Edward, remarried two years later in 1869 to a lady from an Anglican family.

George Elvey's UNDIQUE GLORIA; Macalister's ST DARERCA; Martin Shaw's HIGH ROAD and apparently some 15 or more others offer alternatives to this very complex text.

'The complexity of the text is truly a mark of Herbert's skill and yet when sung to an equalt tune the complex does become easy'. This duality is part of what makes his few works so very great.

Approaching his death Miller wrote in 1869, "he played and sung the fifth stanza of his piece on Sunday—"The Sundays of man's life," &c. Thus he sang on earth such hymns and anthems as the angels and he and Mr. Ferrar now sing in heaven." Herbert's poems are sometimes difficult, because of the depth and variety of meaning they contain, and because of the quaintness of their manner, though the language is invariably clear and bold; but to the patient seeker they supply many pearls. Richard Baxter [his contemporary] said, of all the poems written up to his time, that "next to Scripture poems there were none so savoury to him as Herbert's," and that "heart-work and heaven-work made up his books."

Lift up your hearts! We lift them, Lord, to thee

	(Sursum Corda)	H Montagu Butler	1833-1918	1881	(8),5 verses
WOODLANDS		W Greatorex	1877-1949	1916	10.10.10.10

There are more than a few wonderful hymns, and many not so good, which derive from the Latin, the Greek, the Old French or other olden countries. The words here echo the English translation of the Sursum Corda, a part of the communion liturgy.

The text was written in 1881 by H Montagu Butler during his time as headmaster of Harrow School – a position he held from 1859 to 1885, a lengthy stint of 26 years. It was first published in the school magazine – for a confirmation. The hymn spread far and wide across the public school network where the meaning of the text was most sensible. Butler was once described as "the Master of Trinity, a bland Olympian in a black skull-cap with a white Jovine beard and an untiring flow of the lengthy anecdotes that are told in Heaven after the nectar has gone round twice." Another story tells how Butler fell asleep during a College meeting and awoke with the emphatic observation, 'A strong case, tellingly put'.

At Harrow, their most famous school song, but not the only one, [Ducker; 500 faces; Left, Right; The Silver Arrow etc] is 'Forty years on' which looks back to younger days :

> Forty years on, growing older and older,
> Shorter in wind, as in memory long,
> Feeble of foot, and rheumatic of shoulder,
> What will it help you that once you were strong.

In the Church of England, 'Lift up your hearts!' is usually sung to WOODLANDS, a musical setting composed by Walter Greatorex for Gresham's School in Norfolk (where he was Director of Music) in 1916. Woodlands is the name of a house at the school. It is an old school founded in 1555, by Sir John Gresham as a free grammar school for forty boys, following Henry VIII's dissolution of the Augustinian Priory of nearby Beeston Regis some 15 years before. The trustees are the Worshipful Company of Fishmongers.

Before WOODLANDS was composed, 'Lift up your hearts' was sung, in at least some of the editions of the *Harrow School Hymn Book*, to the OLD 124th. This was clearly a Psalm setting – by Loys Bourgeois (1510-1572) whose more than 20 settings for Psalms in the Geneva Psalter of 1561 still are used and sung.

> 'Lift up your hearts!' We lift them, Lord, to thee;
> Here at thy feet none other may we see:
> 'Lift up your hearts!' E'en so, with one accord,
> We lift them up, we lift them to the Lord.
>
> Above the level of the former years,
> The mire of sin, the slough of guilty fears,
> The mist of doubt, the blight of love's decay,
> O Lord of Light, lift all our hearts to-day!
>
> Above the swamps of subterfuge and shame,
> The deeds, the thoughts, that honor may not name,

> The halting tongue that dares not tell the whole,
> O Lord of Truth, lift every Christian soul!
>
> Lift every gift that thou thyself hast given;
> Low lies the best till lifted up to heaven:
> Low lie the bounding heart, the teeming brain,
> Till, sent from God, they mount to God again.
>
> Then, as the trumpet-call, in after years,
> 'Lift up your hearts!' rings pealing in our ears,
> Still shall those hearts respond, with full accord,
> 'We lift them up, we lift them to the Lord!

The original verse 5 makes clear its origin as a school hymn:
> Lift us to Thee, each boy, each master here,
> Our friends, our homes, and all we count most dear,
> Learning, and wit, grace, vigour, childish glee,
> Lift them, O Lord, and lift them all to Thee.

The other verses that are normally omitted were 4 and 7:
> Above the storms that vex this lower state,
> Pride, jealousy, and envy, rage, and hate,
> And cold mistrust that holds e'en friends apart,
> O Lord of love, lift every brother's heart.
>
> O if the hopes which thrill our hearts today
> Foreshadow aught that shall not pass away,
> And we may trust that all our days shall be
> Bound each to each by natural piety,

The comma after 'piety' indicates a long hold with a run-on to the final verse, 'Then, as the trumpet-call in after years…'. This penultimate verse 7 has a quotation from Wordsworth's 'My heart leaps up when I behold':
> And I could wish my days to be
> Bound each to each by natural piety.

It is interesting to note that the young Winston Churchill entered Harrow School in April 1888 and would have used the 1881 book. He did not mention hymns in *My Early Life* (1930), but he did describe the school songs as 'the greatest treasure Harrow possesses'. It is tempting to speculate that the singing of Butler's hymn fired him with an enthusiasm that lasted, perhaps subconsciously: he did respond to the trumpet-call in after years, and his war-time speeches consistently exhorted the British people to lift up their hearts

Lo! He comes with clouds descending

	Charles Wesley §	1707-1788	1752	4 verses
HELMSLEY	Thomas Olivers	1725–1799	1763	8.7.8.7.4.7

Revel 1:7   "Behold, he cometh with clouds…"   and other verses

---

It is considered to be one of the 'Four Great Anglican Hymns' which was a late Victorian calculation by James King (no relation) when listing which pieces were in almost every hymnal. The other 3 are shown at the end of the book.

'Lo! He comes with clouds descending' is by Charles Wesley, published in 1758 in his collection *Hymns of Intercession for all Mankind*. It is clearly based, albeit substantially reworked from 6 verses to 4, on an earlier text by John Cennick 'Lo, He cometh, countless Trumpets' from 1752; it has the same metre and deals with the same theme although with a new title changed to 'Thy Kingdom Come'; later editions had 'The Second Advent'.

It is an Advent hymn deriving its scriptural context from the Book of Revelation, the Second Coming and the Day of Judgment. As is typical for Wesleyan texts, 'Lo! He Comes' is filled with biblical imagery. Verses 1, 2, and 4 are based on the rich language of John's apocalyptic visions recorded in Revelation 1:7 and 5:11-13. The content of the text and particularly the title derived from where Revelation tells of the Second Coming of Christ..

The second verse depicts the Last Judgement with a colourful vindictiveness and objectivity which are similar to the medieval Dies Irae sequence:

Every eye shall now behold him ... Robed in dreadful majesty;
Those who set at nought and sold him, ... Pierced and nailed him to the tree,
Deeply wailing ... Shall the true Messiah see.

The third verse is of Christ's wounds and how his atoning death should lead us to greater faith and ultimately to our worship of Christ in glory (as Christ himself reminded the doubting Thomas). Verse 4 delivers a majestic doxology [hymn of praise] to Christ, our Savior.

According to Lionel Adey, it is another example of how the Methodist hymn tradition, as demonstrated by the works of Wesley, spans a wide range of texts ranging from very intimate reflections to more impersonal themes.

The text which has long been in general use is essentially Wesley's, though there have been many minor textual variations. In particular, various substitutions have been made for 'JAH, JEHOVAH' (verse 4, line 5, based on Psalm 68:4).

The tune HELMSLEY is usually attributed to Thomas Olivers, a Welsh Methodist preacher and hymn-writer. An anecdote about its composition was that Olivers heard the tune whistled in the street and derived his melody from that; a more certain source is an Irish concert song 'Guardian angels, now protect me'. The setting is sometimes called OLIVERS.

John Wesley made him editor of the Arminian Magazine; however following an 'astounding number of errata', Wesley declared in a letter that "I cannot, dare not, will not suffer Thomas Olivers to murder the magazine any longer. The errata are intolerable and innumerable. They shall be so no more" and removed him from his position in 1789. They stayed friends and eventually in 1799 Olivers was actually put in the John Wesley's grave.

Crawford rejects two other sources for HELMSLEY. He disproves the suggestion that the tune is based on a hornpipe from the burlesque Golden Pippin of c.1771; the chronology makes it such that the hornpipe comes more from the hymn or 'Guardian Angels'. Nor is it linked to Thomas Arne and his chamber opera Thomas and Sally of 1760.

By 1763, the text was in print paired with the text 'Lo! He comes with clouds descending' in Martin Madan's *Collection of Psalm and Hymn Tunes*. Madan edits, as is his wont, for a combination mostly comprising Wesley's text, but substituting some of Cennick's verses. The tune is in the familiar form with only a few variations to the modern tune.

The hymn is occasionally printed and sung with other tunes in hymnbooks including ST THOMAS; REGENT SQUARE; WESTMINSTER ABBEY; KENSINGTON NEW and CUM NUBIBUS. A more sombre choice is PICARDY.

The then Bishop of Durham, Brooke Foss Westcott, noted that in 1901, Queen Victoria was displeased after an organist played a different tune at St George's Chapel, Windsor and required, maybe requested, only Helmsley in future.

An early version of the standard 4-verse piece is :-

1   Lo! He comes with clouds descending,
once for ev'ry sinner slain;
thousand, thousand saints attending
swell the triumph of his train:
Alleluia, alleluia, alleluia!
Christ reveals his endless reign.

2   Ev'ry eye shall now behold him
robed in glorious majesty;
those who set at naught and sold him,
pierced and nailed him to the tree,
deeply wailing, deeply wailing, deeply wailing,
shall their true Messiah see.

3   Those dear tokens of his passion
still his dazzling body bears,
cause of endless exultation
to his ransomed worshipers.
With what rapture, with what rapture, with what rapture,
gaze we on those glorious scars!

4   Yea, amen, let all adore thee
high on thine eternal throne;
Savior, take the pow'r and glory,
claim the kingdom as thine own.
Alleluia, alleluia, alleluia!
Thou shalt reign, and thou alone!

Love Divine, all loves excelling

	Charles Wesley§	1707-1788	1747	4 verses
BEECHER (et al)	John Zundel	1815-1882	1870	8.7.8.7 D
Psalm 106:4	"Visit me with Thy salvation."			

This hymn by Charles Wesley on Christian perfection is among his finest: 'justly famous and beloved, better known than almost any other hymn of his'. Judging by its distribution, it is also hugely well-spread, as by the end of the 19th century, it is found in 15 of the 17 hymn books consulted by the authors of *Lyric Studies*.

It is still found in almost all general collections of the past century, including not only Methodist and Anglican but also for Seventh Day Adventist; Baptist; Brethren; Pentecostal; Congregationalist; Lutheran; Presbyterian; Reformed, and even Roman Catholic traditions. Startlingly, it is in some commercial and ecumenical collections.

It was first published in *'Hymns for those that seek and those that have Redemption in the Blood of Jesus Christ'* (1747) in four 8-line stanzas.

Digressing - the titles of some of the hymnals and collections are almost as colourful as the names taken by some Puritans – Faith-and-Joy; Abuse-Not; Zeal-of-the-Land; and the possibly invented Make-Haste-to-spread-the-Word Tomkinson.

Like many hymns, Love Divine is loosely Trinitarian in organization: Christ is invoked in the first stanza as the expression of divine love; the Holy Spirit in the second stanza as the agent of sanctification; the Father in the third stanza as the source of life; and the Trinity (presumably) in the final stanza as the joint Creator of the New Creation. Like many hymns, too, this one is a tissue of Biblical quotations, including 'Alpha and Omega' (st. 2) as an epithet of Christ, from Revelation 21:6; the casting of crowns before God's throne (st. 4), from Revelation 4:10; the promise that Christians shall be 'changed from glory into glory' (st. 2 and 4), from 2 Corinthians 3:18; as well as other, more general allusions.

It may have been intended as a Christianization of the song 'Fairest Isle' sung by Venus in Act 5 of Dryden and Purcell's semi-opera King Arthur (1691). Wesley's first stanza being modelled on what Dryden had written:

    Fairest Isle, all Isles Excelling,   Seat of Pleasures, and of Loves;
    Venus here, will chuse her Dwelling,   And forsake her Cyprian Groves.

Wesley wrote:

    Love Divine, all Loves excelling, Joy of Heaven to Earth come down,
    Fix in us thy humble Dwelling,   All thy faithful Mercies crown;

In Dryden's song, the goddess of love chooses the Isle of Britain over her native Cyprus; in Wesley's hymn divine love is asked to choose the human heart as its home rather than heaven. The last lines of the hymn are likewise adapted from existing material. Wesley has :

    Till we cast our Crowns before Thee,   Lost in Wonder, Love, and Praise!

apparently deriving from (and improving) Addison's opening for his *Hymn on Gratitude to the Deity*.

    When all thy mercies, O my God,   My rising soul surveys;
    Transported with the view, I'm lost   In wonder, love, and praise.

It may be that Wesley's words were written rather for the tune rather than as this 'Christianization'. Purcell's tune was titled 'FAIREST ISLE' as being for Dryden's text; and the hymn text fitted equally. Certainly the hymn's was later published (under the revised tune name WESTMINSTER by John Wesley in his Sacred Melody, which was the 'annex; to his *Select Hymns with tunes annext* (1761).

In current use, the hymn seems to be set most often, particularly in American hymnals, to the tune BEECHER by John Zundel and to the stately Welsh tunes HYFRYDOL by Rowland Hugh Prichard; BLAENWERN by William Penfro Rowlands and also MORIAH.

One of several tunes known, inevitably as LOVE DIVINE, one by Sir John Stainer appeared in the 1889 Supplement to Hymns Ancient and Modern. This combination has persisted into several modern British collections. Other settings – and there are many for a text this strong with a simple 8.8.8.8 metre - do include AIREDALE by Stanford; BITHYNIA by S Webbe as well as WESTMINSTER and so many others. Purcell's tune FAIREST ISLE is another obvious match. Hymnary lists an astonishing 2087, many of which may not suit.

The second stanza now is generally omitted. The 5th line, in some theological views, asks for us to no longer be given the choice to sin and thus, with no real effort, to be perfect.

> Breathe, O breathe thy loving Spirit
>   Into every troubled Breast,
> Let us all in Thee inherit,
>   Let us find that Second Rest:
> Take away our Power of sinning,
>   Alpha and Omega be,
> End of Faith as its Beginning,
>   Set our Hearts at Liberty.

Many—certainly including those of a more Calvinist persuasion, and even perhaps Wesley's brother John—found this idea troublesome. Even some fairly innocuous lines ('Let us all thy Life receive,' stanza 3) were probably read as suspiciously Perfectionist (and therefore not accessible to mere mortals), hence the common alteration to 'Let us all thy Grace receive'.

Similarly, sinless is replaced by holy or unspotted or spotless as the amender prefers; then the same avoidance of completion or perfection changes 'Finish thy creation' to 'Carry on'. It is almost astonishing how much change has occurred in this text. Words altered, phrases manipulated, lines removed and added, verses chopped and changed. Madan in particular is known for his influential hymn tinkering: Madan's knack in reconstructing the work of other hands made his book a permanent influence both for good and evil. A number of familiar hymns still bear the marks of his editorial revision.

Madan was an interesting man; Julian§ tells us he "ceased preaching after the publication of *Thelyphthora* in which he advocated the practice of polygamy. His collection of 170 hymns was thrown together without order or system of any kind … but it had a most powerful influence on hymnody for nearly 100 years."

More recent times have in general been more respectful of Wesley's original, with the exception of those collections that by policy eschew the second-person singular, replacing 'thee' and 'thou' with 'you' and sometimes introducing other changes in order to maintain metre and rhyme. As regards text-tweaking, editors (particularly Calvinists) often saw Wesleyan doctrine (freewill Arminianism) lurking in the lyrics and changed them accordingly. John Wesley responded that neither he nor and his brother could be held accountable for 'the nonsense or the doggerel' of others. Several re-phrasings of 'Love Divine' continue in circulation.

One thorough example is the recent two-stanza adaptation by C T Andrews (1969) that occurs in several Roman Catholic hymnals set to HYFRYDOL. The author of *Worship* (1971) wrote "Of the sixteen lines in Andrews' version, only three come directly from Wesley's hymn, and another four or five perhaps owe something to the original, but the theme and force of the original are wholly lost."

A 'standard' text insofar as this is a viable statement is as follows :

1 Love divine, all loves excelling,
   joy of heav'n, to earth come down,
   fix in us thy humble dwelling,
   all thy faithful mercies crown.
   Jesus, thou art all compassion,
   pure, unbounded love thou art.
   Visit us with thy salvation;
   enter ev'ry trembling heart.

2 Breathe, O breathe thy loving Spirit
   into ev'ry troubled breast.
   Let us all in thee inherit,
   let us find the promised rest.
   Take away the love of sinning;
   Alpha and Omega be.
   End of faith, as its beginning,
   set our hearts at liberty.

3 Come, Almighty, to deliver,
   let us all thy life receive.
   Suddenly return, and never,
   nevermore they temples leave.
   Thee we would be always blessing,
   serve thee as thy hosts above,
   pray, and praise thee without ceasing,
   ory in thy perfect love.

4 Finish, then, thy new creation;
   true and spotless let us be.
   Let us see thy great salvation
   perfectly restored in thee.
   Changed from glory into glory,
   till in heav'n we take our place,
   till we cast our crowns before thee,
   lost in wonder, love and praise.

Martin Luther   1483-1546

The huge majority of the hymns you know well arrive after the Reformist Protest efforts of Martin Luther. Simplifying very greatly, his attacks on the weaknesses of the then Catholic Church began the Reformation. The criticisms included the sale of Indulgences for ugly and evil deeds, both by some clerics and too many others; the need for Bibles to be available and in the vernacular; and the other behaviours which underlay the 95 Theses which were perhaps nailed to the church in Wittenberg.

Luther taught that Salvation and thence Eternal Life are NOT earned by good deeds but only as the free gift of God's Grace obtained only by Belief. He challenged the Papal view by saying the Bible is the only source of true godly knowledge and thus that all baptized Christians are, in effect, their own priests. His translation of the Bible in German presaged a surge in such new works. Remember printing had begun with Gutenberg in about 1450 and was now becoming a huge contributor to the spread of knowledge.

Luther must have had immense charisma to have driven through the changes he made in his lifetime. As well as his translations, he also wrote some 30 hymns. These were few in number but several remain with us, and the greatest include 'Ein Feste Berg' – A mighty fortress is our God; 'Christ is erstanden' – Christ the Lord is risen again;

Again in brief, in his writings, Luther made clear that his songs spread the ideas of the Reformation being about specific themes such as the Creed or Salvation;

* That a good text with a good tune in the local tongue encouraged the learning of the content and became a weapon against evil and sin.
* Singing together encouraged the community and common ground with active participation in the service.

Luther was not the only Protestant with views on singing. Probably equally emphatic in his views was Calvin (1509-1564). Originally French, he spent much time in Geneva. His views included the belief in Predestination; God's absolute sovereignty for Salvation and the avoidance of eternal damnation. His rules on singing summarise as follows :

Only psalm texts were allowed to be sung; if rewritten as verse, the text must remain as close to the Bible as possible;

Singing was unanimous, (no descants, no separation of choir and congregation);

The tune was strictly one note per syllable; allowing only a note or a half-note.

Every line had to be paused; The tunes were not allowed to exceed an octave.

The number of hymns produced in the next 100 years is phenomenal; the 5-volume listing of first lines for 72,733 hymns endorses this. How many there are by now – many more.

In the years following, especially with the Catholic counter-movement of the early 1800s, old pieces from Latin and Greek have entered the Protestant arena. Some remain current, others have slipped away. Interestingly, a list of Favourite Hymns will exclude some which are elsewhere listed in Favourite Religious Songs, as the latter will often include Ave Maria and Halleluia Chorus and others.

Henry Francis Lyte   1793-1847

Henry Lyte studied at Trinity College Dublin. Lyte's father was described as a "ne-er do-well more interested in fishing and shooting than in facing up to his family responsibilities," who deserted the family shortly after making arrangements for his two oldest sons to attend Portora Royal School, at Enniskillen, Ulster. His mother Anna moved to London, where both she and her youngest son died. The headmaster at Portora, Dr Burrowes recognised Henry's ability, paid the boy's fees, and 'welcomed him into his own family during the holidays', he was effectively adopted.

During his University course Lyte distinguished himself by gaining the English prize poem on three occasions. At one time he had intended studying Medicine; but this he abandoned for Theology, and took Holy Orders in 1815. After his curacy in southern Ireland and several appointments, he went to All Saints' Church in Brixham, Devon in 1823 which he held until his death. For much of his life Lyte was frequently ill and often went abroad.

At nearby Marazion, in 1818, he underwent a great spiritual change, which shaped and influenced the whole of his after life, the immediate cause being the illness and death of a brother clergyman. Lyte said :— *He died happy under the belief that though he had deeply erred, there was One whose death and sufferings would atone for his delinquencies, and be accepted for all that he had incurred;*' and concerning himself he added:— *'I was greatly affected by the whole matter, and brought to look at life and its issue with a different eye than before; and I began to study my Bible, and preach in another manner than I had previously done'.* His new manner of preaching followed the example of four or five local clergymen whom he had previously laughed at and considered 'enthusiastic rhapsodists'.

At Marazion, Cornwall, he met and married Anne Maxwell, daughter of a well-known Scottish-Irish family. She was 31, seven years older than her husband and a 'keen Methodist'. Strangely, it was noted, "furthermore, she could not match her husband's good looks and personal charm." Nevertheless, the marriage was happy and successful. Anne eventually made Lyte's situation more comfortable by contributing her family fortune, and she was an excellent manager of the house and finances. They had two daughters and three sons. On a Sunday, he would drive her to the Methodist Church, then go to his own. They both went to his church in the evening.

From 1820 to 1822 the Lytes lived in Sway, Hampshire, just five miles (8 km) from the sea; the house in Sway was the only one the couple shared during their marriage that was neither on a river or by the sea – Marazion; Dittisham; Charleton; Brixham; Berry Head; Crediton. At Sway they lost a month-old daughter and he wrote his first book, later published as *Tales in Verse Illustrative of the Several Petitions of the Lord's Prayer* '(1826).

In early 1824, Lyte left Charleton for Lower Brixham, a Devon fishing village. Joining the schools committee, two months later he became its chairman. He also set up the first Sunday school in the Torbay area and created a Sailors' Sunday School. As well as some religious instruction was given there, the primary object of both was educating children and seamen for whom other schooling was virtually impossible. There was an Annual Treat for the 800–1,000 Sunday school children, which included a service then tea and sports in the field.

Shortly after their arrival in Brixham, the minister attracted such large crowds that the church had to be enlarged—the resulting structure later described by his grandson as 'a hideous barn-like building'. He added to his clerical income by taking in resident pupils.

Lyte was a tall and 'unusually handsome' man, 'slightly eccentric but of great personal charm, a man noted for his wit and human understanding, a born poet and an able scholar'. He was an expert flute player and according to his great-grandson always had his flute with him. He spoke Latin, Greek, and French; was knowledgeable about wild flowers and enjoyed discussing literature. At Berry Head House near Brixham, Lyte built a magnificent library — largely of theology and old English poetry—described in his obituary as 'one of the most extensive and valuable in the West of England' – the catalogue of sale was 296 pages.

Nevertheless, Lyte was also able to identify with his parish of fishermen, visiting them at their homes and on board their ships in harbour, supplying every vessel with a Bible, and compiling songs and a manual of devotions for use at sea. In theology he was a conservative evangelical who believed that man's nature was totally corrupt. He frequently rose at 6 AM and prayed for two or more hours before breakfast.

In politics, Lyte was a Conservative who feared revolt among the irreligious poor. He publicly opposed Catholic Emancipation (which came in 1829) by speaking against it in several Devon towns, stating that he preferred Catholics to be 'emancipated from priests and from the power of the factious and turbulent demagogues of Ireland'. Lyte, a friend of Wilberforce, also opposed slavery, organising an 1833 petition to Parliament requesting it be abolished in Great Britain (as it was abolished, allegedly, that year).

Getting steadily more ill, in 1839, when only 46, Lyte wrote a poem entitled 'Declining Days'. He also grew discouraged when numbers of his congregation (including in 1846, nearly his entire choir) left him for Dissenter congregations, especially the Plymouth Brethren, after he expressed High Church sympathies and a leaning towards the Oxford Movement.

In lifelong poor health, Lyte had many respiratory illnesses and often visited continental Europe 'for the air'. he mentions medical treatments of blistering, bleeding, calomel, tartar emetic and 'large doses' of Prussic acid. In 1835 Lyte sought appointment as the vicar of Crediton but was rejected because of his increasingly debilitating asthma and bronchitis.

Lyte concentrated on Hymns based on Psalms in the main, with more than 60 texts based on the Psalms as well as 15 hymns. The best known and most widely used of his compositions are 'Abide with me, fast falls the eventide §;' 'Far from my heavenly home'; 'God of mercy, God of grace'; 'Pleasant are Thy courts above'; 'Praise, my soul, the King of heaven'§; and 'There is a safe and secret place'.

Regarding his most famous piece, obviously 'Abide with me' the story is fully told in the relevant article.

Litvack has written in the *Oxford Dictionary of National Biography* that although Lyte's "poetic energies were directed at scripturally and evangelically minded audiences, his lyric gift was universally appreciated. The example of 'Abide with me' is instructive: intensely personal and contemplative, yet nationally popular."

Mine Eyes have seen the Glory of the coming of the Lord, Battle Hymn of the Republic

	Julia W Howe	1819-1910	1861	6 verses
CANAAN'S SHORE	Traditional		c 1800	15.15.15.6 Refrain

One of the rare entries here from outside the United Kingdom. The 'Battle Hymn of the Republic', also known as 'Mine Eyes Have Seen the Glory' outside of the United States, is a popular American patriotic song by the abolitionist and writer Julia Ward Howe written in 1861, 6 months into the American Civil War (1861-1865). The chosen music was already in use for the song 'John Brown's body', but that text was barely a year old, and itself had taken the music of 'Glory, Halleluiah' from a folk hymn of the early 1800s. The first known version has the verse 'Oh brothers will you meet me, On Canaan's happy shores' then the finale 'There we'll shout and give him glory, For glory is his own'. This soon amended into 'Glory, glory, halleluiah' and the tunes spread quickly. A bible verse that nearly suits is Luke 2:30.

Howe's song refers to the judgment of the wicked and the end of the age – there are allusions to Isaiah 63:1-6 and Revelation 14:14-19 against the Southern insurrectionists.

The namesake John Brown was a jovial Scot in the Massachusetts militia; and had the same name as a recent hero of Harper's Ferry (1859). After a while, the phrase was attached to him of 'Yes, yes, poor old John Brown is dead; his body lies mouldering in the grave.' And after a while, this and similar jokes attached to the tune above known then as 'Say, brothers'.

Thence, with military humour, the most nonsensical doggerel rhymes about his fate and decomposition were, er, decomposed. The idea of his soul 'marching on' was well received. Some, feeling such humour to be coarse and irreverent, tried to urge better 'nicer' lyrics. They failed. The publishers did manage, as publishers often may, to trim the worst excesses.

Miss Howe heard the song during a review of the troops in Virginia. The review ended in some disarray, owing to a raid by Confederate forces which had to be driven off: the regiments were marched back to their lines, and the spectators sent back to Washington. The ensuing traffic jam led to the composition of one of the most famous hymns in United States history. Howe described it thus:

"My dear minister was in the carriage with me, as were several other friends. To beguile the rather tedious drive, we sung from time to time snatches of the army songs so popular at that time, concluding, I think, with 'John Brown's body lies a-mouldering in the ground; His soul is marching on.' The soldiers seemed to like this, and answered back, 'Good for you!' Mr Clarke said, 'Mrs Howe, why do you not write some good words for that stirring tune?' I replied that I had often wished to do this, but had not as yet found in my mind any leading toward it."

Regarding the actual writing – Howe remembered:

"I went to bed that night as usual, and slept, according to my wont, quite soundly. I awoke in the gray of the morning twilight; and as I lay waiting for the dawn, the long lines of the desired poem began to twine themselves in my mind. Having thought out all the stanzas, I said to myself, "I must get up and write these verses down, lest I fall asleep again and forget them." So, with a sudden effort, I sprang out of bed, and found in the dimness an old stump of a pencil which I remembered to have used the day before. I scrawled the verses almost without looking at the paper.'"

The result was published in early 1862. The sixth verse written later by Howe, which is less commonly sung, was not published at that time. Both 'John Brown' and 'Battle Hymn of the Republic' were re-published in 1874 and 1889.

In the USA the tune, and text with topical variants, have also been allied with political causes such as women's suffrage and temperance, regional and world wars, and the civil rights movement. During World War II it became a lyrical synergy of folk religion and patriotism through performances at community and national sporting events, and being sung in many churches on the Sunday nearest the fourth of July.

Several mainline USA denominational hymnals do not include the hymn, compilers citing three main objections: the musical setting trivialises the text; Second, a perceived contradiction whereby 'the Prince of Peace' leads a vengeful morally superior army into battle to crush the enemy and establish truth, with echoes of the 'crusades'; Third, the strong disapproval by some southern states of any mention of the intentional destruction of the 1864 'march to the sea'.

Most texts are made up of five stanzas:
> 'Mine eyes have seen the glory of the coming of the Lord'
> 'I have seen him in the watch-fires of a hundred circling camps'
> 'I have read a fiery gospel, writ in burnished rows of steel'
> 'He hath sounded forth the trumpet that shall never call retreat'
> 'In the beauty of the lilies Christ was born across the sea'

Various books print different selections of these stanzas. Many books omit verse 2, with its vivid portrayal of an army encamped, and verse 4, with its reminder of the bayonets or swords in the burnished rows of steel. A sixth verse, from the first draft, is sometimes added:
> He is coming like the glory of the morning on the wave;
> He is wisdom to the mighty, he is succour to the brave;
> So the world shall be his footstool, and the soul of time his slave;
> > Our God is marching on.

'Canaan's Happy Shore' has a verse and chorus of equal metrical length, melody and rhythm. 'John Brown's Body' has more syllables in its verse and uses a more rhythmically active variation of the 'Canaan' melody to accommodate the additional words.

In 'Battle Hymn', the words of the verse are packed into a yet longer line, with even more syllables than 'John Brown's Body'. The verse still uses the same underlying melody as the refrain, but the addition of many dotted rhythms allows for the more complex verse to fit correctly.

Being originally a military song, there are versions innumerable; many of which are, often only implicitly, unrepeatable and unprintable.

As an acceptable variation: a Finnish military marching song with the words 'Kalle-Kustaan muori makaa hiljaa haudassaan, ja yli haudan me marssimme näin' ('Carl Gustaf's hag lies still and silent in her grave, and we're marching over the grassy sod like this and this and this'.). A coarse and rough translation of the Finnish is not easy.

The Finnish Ice Hockey fans can be heard singing the tune with the lyrics 'Suomi tekee kohta maalin, ……itään voi' ('Finland will soon score, and no one can do anything about it').

Both Pratt Green's 'It is God who holds the nations in the hollow of his hand' as well as 'All who worship God in Jesus, all who serve the Son of Man' use the tune VISION by Walford Davies which was originally paired with 'Mine Eyes have seen…'.

1   Mine eyes have seen the glory of the coming of the Lord;
he is trampling out the vintage where the grapes of wrath are stored;
he hath loosed the fateful lightning of his terrible swift sword;
his truth is marching on.
> Refrain:
> Glory, glory, hallelujah!
> Glory, glory, hallelujah!
> Glory, glory, hallelujah!
> His truth is marching on.

2   I have seen him in the watchfires of a hundred circling camps,
they have builded him an altar in the evening dews and damps;
I can read his righteous sentence by the dim and flaring lamps;
his day is marching on.   [Refrain]

3.   I have read a fiery Gospel writ in burnished rows of steel;
As ye deal with My contemners, so with you My grace shall deal;
Let the Hero, born of woman, crush the serpent with His heel,
Since God is marching on.

4   He has sounded forth the trumpet that shall never call retreat;
he is sifting out the hearts of all before his judgment seat.
O be swift, my soul, to answer him; be jubilant, my feet!
Our God is marching on.   [Refrain]

5   In the beauty of the lilies Christ was born across the sea,
with a glory in his bosom that transfigures you and me;
as he died to make us holy, let us die to make all free,
while God is marching on.   [Refrain]

Being originally a military song, there are versions innumerable; many of which are, sometimes only implicitly, unrepeatable and unprintable.

Rather obviously, there are newer less military parodies; amongst these one may find :-

> Mine eyes have seen the glory of the burning of the school;
> We have tortured all the teachers, we have broken every rule;
> The boys are playing poker and the girls are shooting pool,
> As the school is burning down

Julia Howe was an early proponent of Peace. These strong words were penned for her *Mother's Day Proclamation for Peace* in 1870.

"Arise, then, women of this day! Arise all women who have hearts, whether our baptism be that of water or of tears!... We women of one country will be too tender of those of another country to allow our sons to be trained to injure theirs. From the bosom of the devastated earth a voice goes up with our own. It says 'Disarm, Disarm! The sword of murder is not the balance of justice'."

Russian Army 1990 and German Army 1914

James Montgomery 1771-1854

James Montgomery was born in 1771 and died 1854. His parents lived at a Moravian settlement near Ballymena, Co.Antrim in Northern Ireland and at a related site in Ayrshire Aged 9, James was sent to a Moravian school in Yorkshire; when he was 12, the parents went to the West Indies where they died in 1791.

By then, he was apprenticed to a baker in Mirfield, Yorkshire, but was more interested in writing poetry or playing and composing music. He ran away from the baker's in 1789 and went a'travelling; he trudged along, that day and the next, through Doncaster to Wentworth.

At Wath, near the latter place, he found employment in a country store—still filling up his spare moments with verse-making. The village bookseller encouraged him to make a careful selection of his poetry for publication, and forwarded it to a London publisher. Montgomery, well recommended, made his way, soon after, to the metropolis and actually worked for Harrison, the publisher. On his return to Sheffield he started work at the Sheffield Register. John Julian, the hymn historian, gives considerable detail.

The owner Joseph Gales, fled to America in fear of prosecution for sedition in 1794, Montgomery took it over, re-naming it The Sheffield Iris and it remained a radical paper. Pitt's government had passed severe sedition laws and in 1795 Montgomery was prosecuted for publishing a poem on the fall of the Bastille, and in 1796 he was imprisoned in York gaol for criticising the behaviour of the Sheffield militia at a riot. His radicalism earned him the friendship of Southey and Shelley.

His poem *The Wanderer of Switzerland* (1805) was greatly admired by Byron. His other major works were *The World before the Flood* (1812) and *Greenland* (1819), a poem celebrating the work of Moravian missionaries. He sold the Iris in 1825 but remained in Sheffield as a man of letters, a hymn writer, and a public figure.

He was closely associated with Thomas Cotterill, the perpetual curate of St Paul's, Sheffield. Cotterill was one of the pioneers of hymn singing in the Church of England especially as his *A Selection of Psalms and Hymns for Public and Private Use, adapted to the Festivals of the Church of England* was the subject of controversy.

In 1819, his own congregation appealed against its use to the Archbishop of York. It contained more than fifty of Montgomery's hymns, including 'Angels from the realms of Glory §'; 'Lord God the Holy Ghost'; 'Command they blessing from above'; and two hymns on prayer 'Prayer is the soul's sincere dream' and 'Lord, teach us how to pray aright'.

His Songs of Zion of 1822 are some of the sweetest and best sacred lyrics in the language.

In 'The Christian Psalmist of 1825, there were 103 of his hymns out of the 526 total, and a preface that may be 'the finest essay ever written on the hymn as a literary form.'

He also protested against slavery, the lot of boy chimney sweeps, and lotteries. Together with Christians of various persuasions, Montgomery supported missions and the British Bible Society. He published eleven volumes of poetry, mainly his own, and at least four hundred hymns. Some critics judge his hymn texts to be equal in quality to those of Isaac Watts and Charles Wesley. Of Montgomery's hymns (including his versions of the Psalms) more than 100 are still in common use as at 1892.

In common with most poets and hymnwriters, Montgomery strongly objected to any correction or rearrangement of his compositions. At the same time he did not hesitate to alter, rearrange, and amend the productions of others. The altered texts which appeared in

Cotterill's Selections, 1819, and which in numerous instances are still retained in some of the best hymnbooks, as the 'Rock of Ages §,' in its well-known form of three stanzas, and others of equal importance, were made principally by him for Cotterill's use. We have this confession under his own hand.

As a poet, Montgomery stands well to the front; and as a writer of hymns he ranks in popularity with Wesley, Watts, Doddridge, Newton, and Cowper. His best hymns were written in his earlier years. In his old age he wrote much that was unworthy of his reputation. His finest lyrics are 'Angels from the realms of glory §', 'Songs of praise the angels sang' (which is rather similar); 'Go to dark Gethsemane' and 'Hail to the Lord's Anointed'.

His 'Prayer is the soul's sincere desire,' is an expanded definition of prayer of great beauty; and his 'Forever with the Lord' is full of lyric fire and deep feeling. The secrets of his power as a writer of hymns were manifold. His poetic genius was of a high order, higher than most who stand with him in the front rank of Christian poets. His ear for rhythm was exceedingly accurate and refined. His knowledge of Holy Scripture was most extensive. His religious views were broad and charitable.

'To thy Temple' contains a remarkable summary of the classic form of dissenting worship, with references to hymn singing, prayer, Bible reading and sermon.

Sadly, except for those people who are well-practised or well-attending, many of Montgomery's hymns are now less well-known and even infrequent in usage.

There were two principal causes of which Montgomery was a tireless advocate: Sunday Schools and missionary work. For many years he produced hymns to be sung at Whitsuntide Festivals of the Sheffield Sunday-School Union, and he was a strong supporter of the work of missionaries overseas.

But his hymn writing transcended the occasions for which it was intended, because it concerned itself with central elements of Christian belief, the life of Christ, the church, the individual in pilgrimage and at prayer. As a result, many of them have remained in use in hymnbooks throughout the world, admired for the clarity of their doctrine and the beauty of their exposition. Lines, verses, and the hymn itself, were all skilfully crafted and shaped, as his essay in *The Christian Psalmist* said that they should be. His experience as a writer for newspapers gave him a particular facility with words, and his hymns have an energy and crispness: they go straight to the point, without losing any grace of expression.

John Julian wrote eloquently and fulsomely – ending with: 'The secrets of his power as a writer of hymns were manifold. His poetic genius was of a high order, higher than most who stand with him in the front rank of Christian poets. His ear for rhythm was exceedingly accurate and refined. His knowledge of Holy Scripture was most extensive. His religious views were broad and charitable. His devotional spirit was of the holiest type. With the faith of a strong man he united the beauty and simplicity of a child. Richly poetic without exuberance, dogmatic without uncharitableness, tender without sentimentality, elaborate without diffusiveness, richly musical without apparent effort, he has bequeathed to the Church of Christ wealth which could only have come from a true genius and a sanctified heart.'

O for a Thousand tongues to sing

	Charles Wesley§	1707-1788	1780	18 verses 4 lines;
LYNGHAM (et al)	Thomas Jarman	1776-1861	c1803	8.6.8.6
Ecclesiasticus 43:30	"When ye glorify the Lord, exult him … ye can never go far enough".			

This is yet another hugely popular piece by Charles Wesley. The hymn was the first in John Wesley's *'A Collection of Hymns for the People Called Methodists'* published in 1780. It remained the first entry in every (Wesleyan) Methodist hymnal until 1983. The apparently complex tune is of the fuguing format – with the four voices coming in sequentially – somewhat like a 'round'. Despite sounding complicated it is actually easy to sing and to enjoy.

While studying with the Moravians, Charles Wesley was suffering from pleurisy in May, 1738 and he was plagued also by extreme doubts about his faith. Wesley's bedside was attended by a group who offered him testimony and care. He read his Bible and was so affected by their words to be at peace with God. His strength began to return. He wrote this in his journal, and counted it as a renewal of his faith; when his brother John told of a similar experience days later, the two men met and sang the celebration hymn just written.

A year later, Wesley felt urged to write a hymn in commemoration of his renewal of faith. Titled 'For the anniversary day of one's conversion' this hymn began as an 18-stanza poem, with the opening lines *'Glory to God, and praise, and love, / Be ever, ever given'*. The seventh verse, which begins, 'O for a thousand tongues to sing', and which now is invariably the first verse of a shorter hymn, recalls the words of his Moravian teacher, Boehler. 'Had I a thousand tongues I would praise him [God] with them all'. This in turn may have come from a hymn by Johann Mentzner (1658-1734) beginning 'O dass ich tausend Zungen hätte'.

Today the hymn is often condensed into a smaller number (typically between six and eight) stanzas; although A&M-NS uses just verses 5,7,9,11,12, 8 and sometimes 5 again. A long alternative is beginning at verse 7 to the end but omitting 15 & 16; their omission does alter the meaning somewhat. At one time, verse 12 was omitted for the references to 'dumb' and 'lame'. While verse 17 has the now 'awful' line about 'washing the Aethiope'. The 1988 *Companion to Hymns and Psalms* notes that the verse 'He breaks the power of cancelled sin' is an apparent tautology (as the sin is already 'cancelled'); Wesley's theological intent is thus unclear.

There are complex and multiple Biblical references in this hymn. The lead reference is from the Apocrypha. For the interested and thorough, each verse has references as follows : Verse 1-2 : Ps.145:10-12; verse 2 : Luke 4:18-19, Isa. 61:1-2; verse 3 : Acts 3:16, Rom. 5:1; verse 4 : Col. 2:14; verse 5 : Heb. 2:4; verse 6 : Matt. 11:5, Isa.35:6, Acts 3:8; andverse 7 = Rev. 5:13. Without doubt there are more references for the set-aside verses.

In the U.S the hymn is commonly sung to Lowell Mason's 1839 arrangement of the setting AZMON, written by Carl G. Glaser in 1828. Mason's melody was specifically written as a setting for this hymn.

In Great Britain Thomas Jarman's tune LYNGHAM is favoured, especially in larger congregations; *Hymns Ancient and Modern* has A. J. Eyre's SELBY and J. H. Coombes' OXFORD NEW. Two well-usedl tunes are RICHMOND, by Thomas Haweis, and LYDIA, by Thomas Phillips (1735-1807) which is favoured by Methodists; although this is also used in Anglican churches. NORTHFIELD from 1889 is another fuguing tune. Robin Knowles Wallace wrote a thorough article also listing Hudson's BLESSED NAME from the late 1800s.

For many years the Anglican usage was of a tune by the Bath physician Henry Harington which earned the names HARINGTON, BATH, LANSDOWNE, ORLINGBURY as well as RETIREMENT. Whether these represent Henry's life story is not known. Yet other tunes include OXFORD NEW, SELBY and O GOD OF LOVE.

'Mortals awake, with angels join' is a different hymn also using LYNGHAM, both with and without the original fuguing. It was used in many books. To complicate things for 'O for a thousand tongues...' Jarman also wrote another tune, TRIUMPHANT GRACE for it.

It is for this text that NATIVITY survives in American shape note tradition in The Sacred Harp (1991) in non-fuguing form. The full fuguing version has survived orally as LYNGHAM, one of the pieces central to the Sheffield carol tradition, as an unexpected setting for 'While shepherds watched their flocks by night'.

The original lyrics are as follows. The modern lyrics are still similar (with less verses).

1. Glory to God, and praise and love, ... Be ever, ever given;
   By saints below and saints above, ... The Church in earth and heaven.

2. On this glad day the glorious Sun ... Of righteousness arose,
   On my benighted soul he shone, ... And filled it with repose.

3. Sudden expired the legal strife; ... 'Twas then I ceased to grieve.
   My second, real, living life, ... I then began to live.

4. Then with my heart I first believed, ... Believed with faith divine;
   Power with the Holy Ghost received ... To call the Saviour mine.

5. I felt my Lord's atoning blood ... Close to my soul applied;
   Me, me he loved - the Son of God ... For me, for me he died!

6. I found and owned his promise true, ... Ascertained of my part,
   My pardon passed in heaven I know, ... When written on my heart.

1st verse as currently sung:
7. O For a thousand tongues to sing ... My dear Redeemer's praise!
   The glories of my God and King, ... The triumphs of His grace!

Last verse
8. My gracious Master and my God, ... Assist me to proclaim,
   To spread through all the world abroad ... The honors of Thy name.

2nd
9. Jesus! the Name that charms our fears, ... That bids our sorrows cease;
   'Tis music in the sinner's ears, ... 'Tis life, and health, and peace.

10. He breaks the power of cancell'd sin, ... He sets the prisoner free;
    His blood can make the foulest clean. ... His blood avail'd for me.

3rd
11. He speaks, - and, listening to his voice, ... New life the dead receive;
    The mournful, broken hearts rejoice; ... The humble poor believe.

4th

12 Hear him, ye deaf; his praise, ye dumb,   ... Your loosen'd tongues employ;
    Ye blind, behold your Saviour come,   ... And leap, ye lame, for joy.

13 Look unto him, ye nations; own   ... Your God, ye fallen race;
    Look, and be saved through faith alone, ... Be justified by grace.

14 See all your sins on Jesus laid;   ... The Lamb of God was slain;
    His soul was once an offering made   ... For every soul of man.

15 Harlots, and publicans, and thieves,   ... In holy triumph join!   optional
    Saved is the sinner that believes   ... From crimes as great as mine.

16 Murderers, and all ye hellish crew,   ... Ye sons of lust and pride,   optional
    Believe the Savior died for you;   ... For me the Saviour died.

17 Awake from guilty nature's sleep,   ... And Christ shall give you light,
    Cast all your sins into the deep,   ... And wash the Æthiop white.

18 With me, your chief, ye then shall know, ... Shall feel your sins forgiven;
    Anticipate your heaven below,   ... And own that love is heaven.

Thomas Jarman was born on 21st December 1776 in Clipston, a small village near the northern border of the County of Northampton. His father was not only a Baptist lay preacher, but also a tailor, and Thomas was brought up in the same trade, although his brother, John, followed his father's calling to become a minister.

His natural taste for music, however, considerably interfered with his work, and he was frequently reduced to dire straits, from which only the extreme liberality of his publishers relieved him. He was a man of fine, commanding presence, but self-willed, and endowed with a considerable gift of irony, as choirs frequently found to their cost. Weston quotes from Kant that Jarman neglected his work and 'this kept him poor and soured his temper'.

In Passing : Hymns or Gospel Songs ?

Gospel songs have a longer and deeper heritage than being merely songs from the Deep South of the United States sung with huge fervour and enthusiasm, dominant vocals and strong harmonies. That is the modern view.

Gospel songs invariably have a refrain – often the second best-known way of identifying the piece. The tunes are not a church-restricted as is the case with many hymns, carefully described by one writer as 'gospel songs use a less stately cadence'. They often have many verses or a multiply-repeated format. The lack of resources led to a cappela as well as accompanying with hand-clapping or foot-stomping. Some of this persists in what is known as 'Black Gospel'; which is probably the most overt and well-known variety of 'gospel song'.

Probably due to lack of exposure, only one or two pieces are close to being 'gospel songs'. 'Abiding Grace' possibly being a halfway variant.

John Mason Neale   1818-1866

Neale's linguistic powers were enormous; he knew more or less twenty languages. Once, Neale placed before Keble the Latin of one of Keble's hymns with the words, 'Why, Keble, I thought you told me that the 'Christian Year' was entirely original.' Keble professed himself utterly confounded until Neale relieved him by owning that he had just turned it into Latin. His prose style is pure and lucid, and the range of his historical knowledge in his chosen fields was equally wide. What was unusual was that he was much less upset when his words were adapted than the majority of his colleagues.

He is most famed for his writings on a wide range of holy Christian texts, including obscure medieval hymns, both Western and Eastern. Neale is best known especially as a translator, having enriched English hymnody with many ancient and mediaeval hymns translated from Latin and Greek. He was also an Anglican priest, hymnwriter and scholar.

Neale entered Cambridge as an Evangelical, but emerged an Anglo-Catholic. He began reading the tracts produced by the Oxford Movement and developed a passionate interest in the medieval church. By 1839 his fascination with architectural antiquarianism led him and his friends to found the Cambridge Ecclesiological Society, also known as the Cambridge Camden Society, the influence of which spread quickly and widely across Anglicanism.

Unlike the Tractarians of Oxford, Neale and his associates emphasised architectural, ritualistic, and even musical principles which confirmed the Church of England as an authentic branch of the Catholic Church: their promotion of Gothic architecture, rood screens, stained glass greatly altered the fabric of Victorian churches at home and abroad.

An Anglo-Catholic, Neale's works have found the most positive reception in like-minded high-church Anglicanism. He won a scholarship to Trinity College, Cambridge in 1836, won the religious poetry prize 11 times, but his maths meant only a pass degree. Ordained in 1842, he went to Crawley in Sussex, but had to leave due to a chronic lung disease. The next winter he lived in Madeira and worked on his History of the Eastern Church. In his entire 48-year life, he received neither honour nor preferment in England; indeed his only doctorate was bestowed by Trinity College (Connecticut).

In 1846 Neale became warden of an almshouse, Sackville College, in East Grinstead, Sussex. Here, he rebuilt the college chapel, adding such ornaments as 'are now the rule rather than the exception in every well-ordered church'. As well as these ritualistic innovations, his high-church views affected his liturgical choices too. These being brought to the notice of Dr Gilbert, his bishop, began a painful controversy. Neale's accessories to worship were denounced as 'frippery' or 'spiritual haberdashery,' and he was 'inhibited' for 14 years from officiating in the diocese – until 1863.

However the Bishop did approve in 1854 of Neale's co-founding the Society of St Margaret, an Anglican sisterhood which worked primarily among the sick, the poor, and the orphaned, as well as former prostitutes. With Neale as their chaplain, the sisterhood flourished, eventually developing branches in Scotland, Canada, and India. Many Protestants then disapproved of such restorations. In 1857, he was attacked at a funeral of one of the Sisters; crowds threatened to stone him or to burn his house. Overall, Neale's responsibilities at the almshouse and convent were fairly limited; he was thus left with sufficient time to pursue his writing career.

He was also the principal founder of the Anglican and Eastern Churches Association, a religious organization founded as the Anglican and Eastern Orthodox Churches Union in 1864. One production of this organisation was the Hymns of the Eastern Church, edited by Neale and published in 1865. The same year saw his last book of Latin translations *Hymns, chiefly Mediaeval, on the Joys and Glories of Paradise' (1865).*

Neale was strongly high church in his sympathies, and had to endure a good deal of opposition, including the fourteen years' inhibition by his bishop. Neale translated the Eastern liturgies into English, and wrote a devotional commentary on the Psalms.

More than anyone else, he made English-speaking congregations aware of the centuries-old tradition of Latin, Greek, Russian, and Syrian hymns. The melody of Good King Wenceslas (his original legendary carol for Boxing Day) originates from a medieval Latin springtime poem, Tempus adest floridum. Other translations include :- All Glory, Laud and Honour §; A Great and Mighty Wonder; as well as carols such as Good Christian Men, Rejoice §; and the wonderful O come, O come, Emmanuel §; In this book, both the last and 'Christian dost thou see them §' have their own section.

J M Neale did several translations that finish as two (or more) hymns. His piece based on De Contemptu Mundi by Bernard of Cluny became 'Brief life is here our portion' as well as 'For thee, O dear, dear Country'. St Bernard's work is described by Frere as a 'long satiric poem which he relieved by passages descriptive of the joys of Paradise'

In all his translations and adaptations, he was committed to providing simple, transparent statements of the fundamentals of Christian teaching. Neale's versions of Greek hold special significance as he tried to demonstrate strong links between Anglicanism and Orthodoxy. He highlighted their shared doctrine and spirituality as expressed in hymns — particularly those used at Eastertide. Instead of precise translations (for which the original Greek cadences could not be replicated), he provided, in his *'Hymns of the Eastern Church'* (1862) carefully composed selections and adaptations.

Thus Neale's 'The Day of Resurrection' is derived from St John Damascene's Greek original, the first ode from the Golden Canon of Easter. Among the other Eastern hymns which achieved wide popularity in his translations were 'A great and mighty wonder'; 'Come ye faithful, raise the strain'; 'The day is past and over'; 'O happy band of pilgrims'. Without his work in this area, Orthodox hymnody would have remained largely inaccessible to the West. The third edition of this collection (1866) included the more complex 'Art thou weary, art thou languid?', which was not based on a single Greek original, but rather detailed a number of Orthodox ideas concerning the Transfiguration and the suffering of Christ.

The 1875 edition of the *Hymns Ancient and Modern* contains 58 of his translated hymns; the *English Hymnal* (1906) contains 63 such and six of his original hymns.

His life is a study in contrasts: born into an evangelical home, he had sympathies toward Rome; in perpetual ill health, he was incredibly productive; of scholarly temperament, he devoted much time to improving social conditions in his area; often ignored or despised by his contemporaries, he is much lauded today.

Since Neale died on 6 August 1866, the Festival of the Transfiguration, he is commemorated by the Anglican churches on the following day, 7 August. In the Episcopal Church in the United States, he shares this feast with Catherine Winkworth, who also translated hymns into English; her best-known work being that of 'Now thank we all our God' from the German.

William Henry Monk   1823-1889

W H Monk is most famous as the music editor for Hymns Ancient and Modern from 1858 through to his death in 1889. He composed and arranged settings for his employers, the Proprietors' aka the Committee for Hymns Ancient and Modern, as well as hymns for other occasions. His most famous, EVENTIDE, is used for the equally famous hymn 'Abide with Me §' was included in the first edition published in 1861, containing 273 hymns.

His youth is not well-documented, but it seems that he developed quickly on the keyboard, but perhaps less so in composition. By age 18, Monk was organist at St Peter's Church, Eaton Square (Central London). He left after two years, and moved on to two more organist posts in central London. With two years also at each of the these, they served as a stepping stone toward fostering his musical ambitions.

In 1847, Monk became choirmaster and later organist at King's College London. There he developed an interest in incorporating plainchant into Anglican services. Moving in 1852 to St Matthias, Stoke Newington, where he made many changes: plainchant was used in singing psalms, and the music performed was more appropriate to the church calendar. By now, Monk was also arranging hymns, as well as writing his own hymn melodies.

His strong sympathy for plainsong found practical expression during his 37 years as organist at Stoke Newington, where Gregorian tones were invariably used for the canticles and psalms and great stress was laid on congregational singing.

One of his earliest hymn tunes, MERTON (the usual setting for 'Hark! A thrilling voice is sounding' was first published in 1851, but from 1859 his career as a hymn tune composer, arranger and editor was inextricably bound up with the history of *A&M*, whose title he suggested to Sir Henry W Baker As musical editor he delivered the First Edition of 1861; the Appendix of 1868 and the Second Edition of 1875. It was for H A&M that Monk supplied his famous EVENTIDE tune which is mostly used for the hymn 'Abide with Me', as well as several others, including GETHSEMANE, ASCENSION, and ST DENYS.

He died only weeks before the publication of the 1889 Supplement; in all he contributed over 50 original tunes and many harmonizations of earlier melodies. Monk's was the only name to appear on the title page, and it was even sometimes referred to as 'Monk's book'.

It is well-known that this, with revisions in 1904, 1916, 1953, 1983 and so on, has become and remains one of the best-selling hymn books ever produced. Indeed, the average sales per year are regularly in excess of 1 million.

Although Monk's early compositions include several anthems and introits written in a severe, archaic idiom, he is best known for tunes employing a more overtly Victorian, but never cheap or vulgar, style. As he himself said, 'Although I enjoy Spohr and the chromatic school, I prefer diatonic harmony, especially for congregational music, where simplicity, breadth, and strength are obvious requirements'.

Some or all of these characteristics can be seen in MERTON, EVELYNS for 'At the name of Jesus'; ST ETHELWALD 'Soldiers of Christ arise'; GETHSEMANE 'Go to dark Gethsemane'; ST CONSTANTINE 'Jesu, meek and gentle', which is unusual for the conclusion of its first four verses on the dominant of the relative minor); UNDE ET MEMORES 'And now, O Father' and of course EVENTIDE 'Abide with me'.

All these possess the quality of being eminently singable. Although Monk's musical vision was limited, he occasionally achieved something more memorable, as in EVELYNS, where the combination of a well-balanced melody with strong diatonic harmonies creates a whole greater than the sum of the parts. This is certainly true of the ubiquitously popular EVENTIDE, which has found a place as a poignant funeral hymn as well as a favourite with the crowd at the Football Association Cup Final.

The same qualities distinguish his numerous, mostly anonymous, arrangements of earlier tunes, many of which have been accepted as the 'standard' version.

These include the already GETHSEMANE, adapted from Christopher Tye; CRÜGER 'Hail to the Lord's Anointed'; WÜRTEMBURG 'Christ the Lord is risen again'; and DIX 'As with gladness men of old' are just four examples, while the harmonization of the first line of ADESTE FIDELES is basically his.

His tune ALL THINGS BRIGHT AND BEAUTIFUL §, taking its label from the first line of C F Alexander's famous poem, caused the text to be even more widely sung in schools. It is now the more usual setting, having overtaken Shaw's later ROYAL OAK, an adaptation of an English traditional melody.

In 1874, Monk was appointed professor of vocal studies at King's College; subsequently he accepted similar posts at two other prestigious London music schools: the first at the National Training School for Music in 1876, and the second at Bedford College in 1878. Monk remained active in composition in his later years, writing not only hymn tunes but also anthems and other works. In 1882 Durham University awarded him an honorary Mus. Doc.

It seems very fitting that, having been so closely connected with *A&M*, he should have died the day after returning the corrected proofs of the 1889 edition. His successor as music editor, Charles Steggall completed its publication. He died on 1st March 1889 and was buried on the eastern side of Highgate Cemetery.

Details of the writing of EVENTIDE come from an article in *London Overlooked – Tales from the Smoke*. He married Hope Isidora Pillow in 1846, and their daughter Florence was born in 1849 when the family was living in Lambeth at 113 Upper Stamford Street, in a house built by the family of John Galsworthy, the novelist; soon in 1851 or 1852, they moved to Islington.

Sadly, at the age of only 2, Florence died. It was then described as 'a stroke after softening of the brain'. What the modern diagnosis would be is extremely unclear.

There were other children soon. The youngest, born in 1863, had the names Florence Hopestill Monk, to keep alive the name of her sister and to encourage the phoenix fire of hope. An article from London-Overlooked has some interesting snippets :

A letter by Hope from 1891, describes how the hymn tune arrived. She wrote that shortly after the death of Florence, that William and she had been standing at a window, hand in hand, still grieving, 'We were silently watching the glory of the setting sun until the golden hue had faded. Suddenly the words of a hymn 'Heaven's morning breaks and earth's vain shadows flee' came into William's mind. He already had a melody for Lyte's text but he was inspired anew and 'he took paper and pencilled the tune which has gone all over the world'.

One author continued 'We love it for its dignified tempo, for its sonorous restraint, for the (very specific) heartbreaking chord on the third beat of the eleventh bar.'

A discordant detractor, one Hatherly, wrote from his heights as a musical purist in 1865 '… we find a double minor seventh, an ill-sounding discord, and throughout the tune, wherever a discord will stick, there will such be found, thus in 16 chords out of 40'. Opinions vary as much as recollections.

Now thank we all our God

Nun danket all Gott 1637 Rinkart trans C.Winkworth   1827-1878   1858   2 verses
Zahn 5142 Cruger 1647   adapted F Mendelssohn   1840   6.7.6.7 x2
Psalm 47:1 "Clap your hands together, all people; sing unto God with the voice of melody."

    This is a hugely popular hymn in both the English-speaking and German-speaking world. The German 'Nun danket alle Gott', written in 1637 by the Lutheran pastor Martin Rinkart was translated by Catherine Winkworth in 1858. Its strong, almost martial hymn tune, Zahn No. 5142, was published by Johann Crüger in the 1647 edition of his *'Praxis pietatis melica'*. Once thought to be also by Rinkart, the modern view is that the setting is by Cruger. The hymn is probably the most famous of all those English ones derived from German.

    It is not surprising that Rinkart was able to write these powerful words. He was born in 1586 near Eilenburg, Saxony, Germany [20 miles south of Berlin]. Due to family poverty and low standing he only managed an education through sheer persistence in hard work, frugality, and using his natural musical talents to pay his own way through the University of Leipzig. His heart's desire was to be a pastor.

    When a position as deacon came open in 1610, he applied but was not accepted. His perseverance earned him a diaconate in 1611 in nearby Eisleben. Proving his value through his giftings and hard work, his hometown of Eilenburg invited him to come home and be the archdeacon of their parish. By 1617, his life dream was fulfilled when he became their full pastor. Grateful then, no one expected the Thirty Years War to change everything.

    The next year, in 1618 the Thirty Years' War broke out. Because Eilenburg was a walled city, refugees from the countryside poured in for safety, especially after a siege began in 1632. The overcrowding, combined with the consequences of war, led to serious food shortages. History records fights in the streets over the bodies of dead cats and crows. In 1637, plague followed and wreaked havoc on the weakened bodies. Of the four pastors, one, overwhelmed, simply ran away. When the remaining two pastors died from plague, it was up to Martin to bury them and continue to provide pastoral care to the entire town and the refugees it held. In that last year more than 4,480 people died and Martin Rinkart often buried as many as fifty people a day, including his own wife. More than 8,000 in the city died.

    Martin survived the entire ordeal despite spending his days among the sick and dying. He gave away all he owned except for the meagre necessary provisions for his own children, even mortgaging any future income he would receive. Amidst all this suffering the Swedes continued to besiege their city. When an impossible tribute of 30,000 florins was demanded by the Swedish general, it was Pastor Rinkart who was sent to lead the city delegation to beg mercy from the commander. When his pleas were refused, he turned to the citizens behind him and said, 'Come, my children, we can find no hearing, no mercy with men, let us take refuge with God'. He fell to his knees and spoke to God with such a desperate earnestness that the general relented, lowering the demand to 2,000 florins.

    At the possibility of relief, and even the beginnings of peace, Martin wrote a hymn for his children to sing 'Nun danket alle Gott'. He taught it also to his congregation and it was later translated into English by Catherine Winkworth as 'Now Thank We All Our God'.

    The melody is used in J.S. Bach's cantatas, such as BWV 79, 192 (although the music is lost!), then harmonized for four voices in BWV 252 and 386, and finally set in a chorale prelude, BWV 657, as part of the Great Eighteen Chorale Preludes. The now-standard harmonisation was devised by Felix Mendelssohn in 1840 when he adopted the hymn, sung in the now-standard key of F major and with its original German lyrics, as the chorale to his Lobgesang or Hymn of Praise (also known as his Symphony No. 2)

Catherine Winkworth was an English hymnwriter and educator. She translated the German chorale tradition of church hymns for English speakers. She also worked for better education for girls, and translated biographies of two founders of religious sisterhoods. The first two verses in German are almost a paraphrase of Ecclesiasticus 1:22-24.

A modern German edition of the text   and the Winkworth translation

    Nun danket alle Gott   :   Now thank we all our God
    Mit Herzen, Mund und Handen :   with heart and hand and voices
    Der große Dinge tut   :   Who wondrous things has done
    An uns und allen Enden   :   in Whom this world rejoices
    Der uns von Mutterlieb   :   who from our mothers' arms
    Und Kindesbeinen an   :   has blessed us on our way
    Unzählig viel zu gut   :   with countless gifts of love
    Bis hierher hat getan   :   and still is ours today.

    Der erwig reiche Gott   :   O may this bounteous God
    Woll uns in unserm Leben   :   through all our life be near us,
    Ein immer fröhlich Herz   :   with ever joyful hearts
    Und edlen Frieden geben   :   and blessed peace to cheer us;
    Und uns in seiner Gnad   :   And keep us in His grace
    erhalten fort und fort,   :   and guide us when perplex'd
    und uns aus aller Not   :   And free us from all ills,
    erlösen hier und dort.   :   in this world and the next.

A third verse, a doxology (hymn of praise, does occur in some hymnals.

    All praise and thanks to God
    the Father now be given,
    the Son and Spirit blest,
    who reign in highest heaven
    the one eternal God,
    whom heaven and earth adore;
    for thus it was, is now,
    and shall be evermore.[1]

It was said that after the Battle of Leuthen in 1757, the hymn was taken up by the entire assembled Prussian army. This narrative is not even anecdata, but a later invention. of Prussian propaganda. Nevertheless, this story means the melody has been called the Leuthen Chorale.

The chosen A&M bible verse is Psalm 47:1, elsewhere there is a link to ' … Therefore my heart exults, and with my song I shall thank Him', from Psalm 27:8.

O come, all ye faithful: Adeste Fideles

Adeste Fideles	via Wade 1711-1786 et at	1743	4,8 verses
Per title	(via Wade)	1743	irregular
Luke 2:15	"Let us now go even unto Bethlehem."		

The history of this great carol is uncertain – survival of ancient texts being poor from the days of parchment and manuscript. What is certain is that there is a Latin precursor called Adeste Fideles; that John Wade made copies and often signed them because his calligraphy was so splendid and he also had copies printed as a collection *'Cantus Diversi pro Dominicis et Festis per annum'* in 1761. Perhaps because it simplifies the history, Wade is often attributed as the origin of the work, even if probably neither author nor composer.

Suggestions have been of pre-Wade existence attributed to St Bonaventure in the 13th century, Cistercian monks in Spain, Portugal or Germany, or John IV of Portugal. King John IV of Portugal has his supporters as author as he was a writer on music and composer; although more likely as patron or collector. During his brief reign (1640-1656) he collected one of the largest music libraries of the era – destroyed in the 1755 earthquake; and two manuscripts with a precursor of Wade's version have been found there dated to1640.

The Duke of Leeds was so impressed by a performance of the hymn at the Chapel of the Portuguese Embassy in London in 1782, it that he commissioned an arrangement from Thomas Greatorex (1758-1831), director of the Concerts of Antient Music. This took some time, and apparently it was not performed until 1797. This was the beginning of its wider dissemination, usually under the misleading title, the 'Portuguese Hymn'.

There were 4 original Latin verses; the French priest J F E Borderies wrote 3 more and another 2 arrived from source unknown. The recognised English translations have come through Frederick Oakeley in 1841, just before he joined Newman in converting to Roman Catholic; and W T Brooke, who also converted but from Baptist to Anglican. Obviously changes and amendments are numerous. Even Oakeley's first translation was amended, by him, from 'Ye Faithful, approach ye'.

As regards the music, Wade is credited as his manuscripts include the tune. John IV returns as another suggestion of course. These early settings are set in the traditional square notation used for mediaeval liturgical music. John Reading, Handel, Gluck and Arne, who knew Wade, have been mentioned as having had influence or for having made arrangements. Taking the Andre Previn view, there are still only 12 notes available and nearness or similarity is not always a sufficient indicator of connection.

In the United Kingdom and United States it is often sung today in an arrangement of the 'one and only' traditional setting by Sir David Willcocks, which was originally published in 1961 by OUP in the first book in the Carols for Choirs series. This arrangement makes use of the basic harmonisation from The English Hymnal but adds a soprano descant in verse six (verse three in the original) with its reharmonised organ accompaniment, and a last verse harmonisation in verse seven (verse four in the original), which is sung in unison.

In Canterbury Online, Professor Watson concludes 'This hymn is unusual in that it has no rhyme and an irregular metre, and its final stanza is properly sung on Christmas morning only; but this has not prevented it from being one of the most popular of all Christmas hymns, found in books of every denomination and sung (often as the climax) at carol services everywhere. It has ensured Oakeley's immortality.'

This carol has served as the penultimate hymn sung at the Festival of Nine Lessons and (Many)Carols by the Choir of King's College, Cambridge after the last lesson from John chapter 1. The Catholics at the Vatican have the Latin traditionally as the final anthem during Midnight Mass at St Peter's Basilica.

Verses are often omitted – either because the hymn is too long in its entirety or because the words are unsuitable for the day on which they are sung;. For example, the eighth anonymous verse is only sung on Epiphany, if at all; while the last verse of the original is normally reserved for Christmas (Midnight) Mass. Mostly, the first four are sung.

Needless to say, variants exist of word, phrase, line, verse, tune; in numbers too many to select or to identify the most interesting. Julians'§ *Dictionary of Hymnology* lists only 30 or 40 differences in just the first line 'Come hither'; 'Be present'; 'O Hie ye'; 'Approach'; 'Believers, assemble'; 'Come, Faithful all'; Draw nigh, ye faithful'; 'Draw near, ye faithful Christians'; Ye faithful, come triumphant'; 'Ye faithful souls, approach and sing'; 'O come, all faithful, and your homage bring' and very many more.

These are the original four Latin verses as published by Wade, along with their English translation by Frederick Oakeley.

Adeste fideles læti triumphantes,	O come, all ye faithful, joyful and triumphant!
Venite, venite in Bethlehem.	O come ye, O come ye to Bethlehem;
Natum videte	Come and behold him
Regem angelorum:	Born the King of Angels:
Venite adoremus (3×)	O come, let us adore Him, (3×)
Dominum.	Christ the Lord.
Deum de Deo, lumen de lumine	God of God, light of light,
Gestant puellæ viscera	Lo, he abhors not the Virgin's womb;
Deum verum, genitum non factum.	Very God, begotten, not created:
Venite adoremus (3×)	O come, let us adore Him, (3×)
Dominum.	Christ the Lord.
Cantet nunc io, chorus angelorum;	Sing, choirs of angels, sing in exultation,
Cantet nunc aula cælestium,	Sing, all ye citizens of Heaven above!
Gloria, gloria in excelsis Deo,	Glory to God, glory in the highest:
Venite adoremus (3×)	O come, let us adore Him, (3×)
Dominum.	Christ the Lord.
Ergo qui natus die hodierna.	Yea, Lord, we greet thee, born this happy morning;
Jesu, tibi sit gloria,	Jesus, to thee be glory given!
Patris æterni Verbum caro factum.	Word of the Father, now in flesh appearing!
Venite adoremus (3×)	O come, let us adore Him, (3×)
Dominum.	Christ the Lord.

And later verses, with English prose translations, (not from Oakeley).

En grege relicto, humiles ad cunas,	Lo! The flock abandon'd, the summon'd shepherds
Vocati pastores adproperant:	Hurry lowly to the cradle:
Et nos ovanti gradu festinemus,	May we too make haste with exultant gait!
Venite adoremus (3×) Dominum.	O come, let us adore Him, (3×) Christ the Lord.

Stella duce, Magi Christum adorantes,   A star leading, the Magi, worshipping Christ,
Aurum, tus et myrrham dant munera.   give gifts: gold, frankincense, myrrh.
Iesu infanti corda præbeamus   May we proffer our hearts to the infant Christ!
Venite adoremus (3×) Dominum.   O come, let us adore Him, (3×) Christ the Lord.

Æterni parentis splendorem æternum   We shall see the eternal splendour
Velatum sub carne videbimus   Of the eternal father, veiled in flesh,
Deum infantem pannis involutum   The infant God wrapped in cloths.
Venite adoremus (3×) Dominum.   O come, let us adore Him, (3×) Christ the Lord.

Pro nobis egenum et fœno cubantem,   May we warm him, needy and lying on hay,
Piis foveamus amplexibus.   With our pious embraces:
Sic nos amantem quis non redamaret?   Who does not love him who loves us thus?
Venite adoremus (3×) Dominum.   O come, let us adore Him, (3×) Christ the Lord.

Cantet nunc hymnos chorus angelorum   Sing now choir of angels hymns!
Cantet nunc aula cælestium,   Sing now halls of the heavenly!
Gloria in excelsis Deo!   Glory to God in the highest!
Venite adoremus (3×) Dominum.   O come, let us adore Him, (3×) Christ the Lord.

One startling new interpretation, perhaps driven by the date of Wade's work, is that there is a Jacobite connection. Professor Bennett Zon at Durham University postulates that the secret codes of Jacobite interest are present. Faithful - the Jacobites; Bethlehem – England; Rex Angelorum – a pun on Rex Anglorum or England.

He also notes that early forms of Wade's carol appear in Roman Catholic liturgical books of that period close to prayers for the exiled Old Pretender; and that these books are decorated with florid Jacobite imagery and other Jacobite codings.   John IV was unavailable for comment.

In Passing : Carols

The period of Advent and Christmas, even all the way through to Candleman at the end of January, is the time for carolling. This book includes a few of the so-called 'caroline' variety. It would be easy to have many in English. At deepest winter, there are carols in almost every known language, some are truly wonder-full and awe-full.

A collector could make a fascinating collection in Spain, Italy, France, Germany and find gorgeous songs which, even if translated in English, might remain truly inspirational. Sadly, most such songs do not travel. In Britain, a very few have travelled from Germany 'O Tannenbaum' and 'Stille Nacht' being the best known.

O God, our help in ages past

	Isaac Watts§	1674-1748	1708	9 verses
ST ANNE	William Croft	1678-1727	1708	8.6.8.6 CM

Psalm 90:1   "Lord, thou hast been our refuge from one generation to another".

This hymn is often sung as part of the Remembrance Day service in the UK and some Commonwealth countries. It is perhaps unfortunate that in Britain this great hymn has become so firmly associated with services for Remembrance Day such that it is less frequently sung on other occasions. In the USA and Canada, free from this 20th- and 21st-century association, it has appeared in more than a thousand hymnals.

'Our God, Our Help in Ages Past' is a hymn from 1708 that takes the 90th Psalm and paraphrases it. Watt's original text had nine stanzas; however, in present usage the fourth, sixth, and eighth stanzas are commonly omitted to leave a total of six (Methodist books also include the original sixth stanza to leave a total of seven).

It was very common for Isaac Watts to write texts based on or as paraphrases the Psalms of David. In the first stanza, Watts took the first word of the Psalm, "Lord," a simple word of address, and expanded it in five ways: "Our God," "our help," "our hope," "our shelter," and "our eternal home."

It is remarkable that Watts, who regularly brought Christ into his metrical versions of the psalms, makes no mention of him here. It contrasts the greatness of God with human frailty, which is 'borne away' and 'forgotten, as a dream'; with superb poetic economy, it emphasises that the great God is indeed 'Our God' and 'our eternal home'. After the awe-inspiring contemplation of 'Man frail, and God eternal', it very appropriately ends in a prayer: 'Be thou our guard while troubles last/ And our eternal home.'

The hymn was originally part of *The Psalms of David Imitated in the Language of the New Testament*, published by Watts in 1719. In this book he paraphrased in Christian verse the entire psalter with the exception of twelve Psalms which he felt were unsuited for Christian usage. In that book this piece was headed 'Man frail, and God Eternal'.

In my family bible of 1733 are three different examples of the Psalms: the Psalms of the Bible; the Psalms as according to the *Book of Common Prayer* and the *Psalms in Metrical Form (Old Version) by Sternhold and Hopkins*. This arrangement was very common, even though the parts were often printed separately and then bound together.

Hymn historian John Julian§ in his 1892 *Dictionary of Hymnology* praised the overall quality of Watts' text, writing, 'Of Watts' original, it would be difficult to write too highly. It is undoubtedly one of his finest compositions, and his best paraphrase'.

There are many eminent admirers of this hymn, and George Sampson too had the opinion that it is 'the greatest of all English hymns'.

Julian also includes 'His theological as well as philosophical fame was considerable. His *Speculations on the Human Nature of the Logos*, as a contribution to the great controversy on the Holy Trinity, brought on him the charge of Arian opinions [Arianism holds that the Son is distinct from the Father and therefore subordinate to Him].

His hymn 'Behold the glories of the Lamb' is said to have been the first he composed, and done as an attempt to raise the standard of praise. The 454 *Hymns and Versions of the Psalms* are all in Common Use at the present time (1892).

The setting ST ANNE ('Common Metre' 86.86) to which the text is most often sung was composed by William Croft whilst he was the organist of St Anne's Church in Soho, London: hence the name of the tune. It first appeared anonymously in the Supplement to the New Version of the Psalms in 1708. Originally intended to be used with a version of Psalm 62, it took some years until the setting was fitted to Watts' text and the tune gained recognition.

After centuries, it is a guess as to whether Bach and his ilk created pieces freely, from something overheard, or borrowed from a nearly-similar tune. Just consider how much non-repeatable music was then being created. J S Bach's Fugue in E-flat major BWV 552 is often called the 'St. Anne' in the English-speaking world, because it begins similarly to the first line of the hymn tune. Young Bach's mentor Buxtehude in Lubeck again used the hymn's first line as a theme for the (first) fugue of his organ piece 'Praeludium-pedaliter'. Handel used the tune in an anthem entitled, 'O Praise the Lord'.

Arthur Sullivan did the same in the first and last sections of his Festival Te Deum, first in a relatively standard setting, but eventually pairing it with a military march accompaniment. Others too: Carl Ruggles; Vaughan Williams and others have worked with the melody.

In 1738, John Wesley's hymnal, *Psalms and Hymns*, changed the first line of the text from 'Our God' to 'O God'. Both Watts' wording and Wesley's rewording are in current use. Wesley's preference for 'O God' over 'Our God' may have been because he thought that five 'ours' in one 4-line verse were too much, or that 'Our God' was too familiar. But Watts was deliberately emphasising that this Eternal God, though contrasted with us in his greatness and permanence, is nevertheless 'our God': the God who is for us as frail human beings, and not simply as good Puritan and Dissenting Christians, God's chosen people.

Wesley made other alterations, substituting 'still may we dwell secure' for 'thy saints have dwelt secure' (stanza 2, line 2) and 'be thou our guard while life shall last' for 'be thou our guard while troubles last' (the original stanza 9, line 3).

A thorough textual analysis is as follows: 'In the first stanza, Watts took the first word of the Psalm, 'Lord', a simple word of address, and expanded it in five ways: 'Our God', 'our help', 'our hope', 'our shelter', and 'our eternal home'. Poetically, the repetition of the word 'our' is called anaphora. In spite of the period at the end of the first stanza, these four lines are an incomplete thought, carrying over into the second stanza, where the first operative verb of the paraphrase is 'dwelt', preceded by four lines of salutation and one line describing where this has happened ('Under the shadow of thy throne').

The second stanza, then, is where the substance of the first verse of Psalm 90 is expressed. The second verse of the psalm is reworded in stanza 3, the third verse translates to stanza 4, and the fourth verse to stanza 5. The flood of the fifth verse is expanded into Watts' stanzas 6 and 7, and the rest of the fifth and sixth verses on the grass is conveyed in stanza 8.

In modern hymnals, some stanzas are omitted, for example, leaving just 6 after omitting the original stanzas 4 and 8 and often 6.

4	Thy word commands our flesh to dust,	...	'Return, ye sons of men':
	All nations rose from earth at first,	...	And turn to earth again...
8	Like flow'ry fields the nations stand	...	Pleased with the morning light;
	The flowers beneath the mower's hand	...	Lie withering ere 'tis night.
6	The busy tribes of flesh and blood,	...	With all their lives and cares,
	Are carried downward by thy flood,	...	And lost in following years.

Leaving the original 1,2,3,5,7th and 9th verses as follows :

1   O God, our help in ages past,
Our hope for years to come,
Our shelter from the stormy blast,
And our eternal home;

2   Under the shadow of thy throne
Thy saints have dwelt secure;
Sufficient is thine arm alone,
And our defence is sure.

3   Before the hills in order stood,
Or earth received her frame,
From everlasting thou art God,
To endless years the same.

5   A thousand ages in thy sight
Are like an evening gone,
Short as the watch that ends the night
Before the rising sun.

7   Time, like an ever-rolling stream,
Bears all its sons away;
They fly forgotten, as a dream
Dies at the opening day.

9   O God, our help in ages past,
Our hope for years to come,
Be thou our guard while troubles last,
And our eternal home.

As a humorous aside, yet simultaneously stern, the facsimile pages on Hymnologyarchive show the previous Psalm and its verse 6.

     Our age to seventy years is set;   ... how short the Term! How frail the State!
     And if to eighty we arrive   ... we rather sigh and groan than live.

     But O how oft thy wrath appears,   ... and cuts off our expected Years!
     Thy Wrath awakes our humble Dread: ... We fear the Power that strikes us Dead!.

In 1964, J.B. Priestley, taking the flood analogy a bit beyond its limits, offered a curious criticism: "Our favourite images of Time are of course all these tides, floods, rivers, streams: perhaps the most familiar of all, from Isaac Watts's famous hymn: 'Time, like an ever-rolling stream, bears all its sons away'. This seems fine until we begin to think about it (though to be fair to Watts, he probably never intended us to think about it). These sons that are being borne away—where are they going?"

O Jesus I have promised

	John Ernest Bode	1816-1874	1866	6 verses
WOLVERCOTE	W H Ferguson	1874-1950	c1910	7.6.7.6 D

John 12:26   "If any man serve me, let him follow me; …"

Unlike most other hymns, this one was written for a very specific family occasion – the confirmation of the author's children. John Bode's children, a daughter and two sons, were all being confirmed in 1866. There is no evidence that he ever wrote 'we have promised'.

Confirmation is a Church rite or service especially where infant baptism occurs. It is a choice by the adult or nearly-adult child that they wish to 'confirm' the promises made on their behalf that they will 'be a good Christian'. In effect, it completes their membership of that church. In many Protestant churches, those who are unconfirmed may take communion; the unconfirmed are asked merely to take a blessing.

The first publication of this text was in a leaflet about Confirmation by the SPCK (*Society for the Propagation of Christian Knowledge* – founded 1698). It was entitled 'Hymn for the newly confirmed'. It has rarely been absent from any major hymn book since its arrival.

Originally there were 6 verses, but has mostly been presented as 5 or even 4. The omitted stanza 4 concerned with discipleship, and (using the example of Peter) with sin and forgiveness:

O let me see Thy features	… The look that once could make
So many a true disciple	… Leave all things for Thy sake;
The look that beam'd on Peter	… When he Thy Name denied;
The look that draws Thy loved ones	… Close to Thy piercèd side.

Some believe it is a most appropriate hymn for Confirmation, inviting the singer to renounce the world, the flesh, and the devil (in stanzas 2 and 3); however Percy Dearmer noted that 'Bishops have been known to implore their clergy that this should not be sung at all the Confirmations they attend'. The logic behind this suggestion that renouncing such issues is not suitable for confirmation is not completely clear to the layman.

It is found in books of all denominations throughout the English-speaking world, and has spread to some other countries and languages.

Several tunes are frequently sung in Britain: most often WOLVERCOTE by W H Ferguson, but other tunes have been used including Harwood's THORNBURY; MUNICH by Mendelssohn; DAY OF REST; NYLAND; HATHEROP CASTLE ABERRHONDDU; and ANGEL'S STORY by A H Mann, (the director of the first Nine Lessons and Carols from King's College); for example.

Mann's story is typical of a chorister, born in 1833, he sang as a child-chorister in the Leamington Parish Church. Then, choristers were given lessons in all facets of church music, including organ lessons, counterpoint studies, and more in exchange for providing an extraordinary level of service to their parish church (services throughout the week, all holidays, extra services, etc.). The result is that most choristers who completed their studies received an excellent music education, and James was no exception.

An early version is as follows (as usual omitting the original verse 4)

1. O Jesus, I have promised
   to serve thee to the end;
   be thou for ever near me,
   my Master and my Friend:
   I shall not fear the battle
   if thou art by my side,
   nor wander from the pathway
   if thou wilt be my guide.

2. O let me feel thee near me:
   the world is ever near;
   I see the sights that dazzle,
   the tempting sounds I hear;
   my foes are ever near me,
   around me and within;
   but, Jesus, draw thou nearer,
   and shield my soul from sin.

3. O let me hear thee speaking
   in accents clear and still
   above the storms of passion,
   the murmurs of self-will;
   O speak to reassure me,
   to hasten or control;
   O speak, and make me listen,
   thou guardian of my soul.

4. O Jesus, thou hast promised
   to all who follow thee,
   that where thou art in glory
   there shall thy servant be;
   and, Jesus, I have promised
   to serve thee to the end:
   O give me grace to follow,
   my Master and my Friend.

5. O let me see thy foot-marks,
   and in them plant mine own;
   my hope to follow duly
   is in thy strength alone:
   O guide me, call me, draw me,
   uphold me to the end;
   and then in heaven receive me,
   my Saviour and my Friend.

O praise ye the Lord

| | Sir Henry Williams Baker § | 1821-1877 | 1875 | 4 verses |
| LAUDATE DOMINUM | C H Parry | 1848-1918 | 1894 | 10.10.11.11 |

Psalm 148:1   "Praise ye the LORD from the heavens: praise him in the heights".

This is an enthusiastic 'doxology' or Hymn of Praise – and perhaps the most powerful expression of that intention in the last 200 years. It is considered to be one of finest pieces written by Sir Henry Williams Baker. It was published in the 1875 *Hymns Ancient and Modern Second edition*. Baker was editor of both the *1861 edition* [273 hymns], the *1868 Appendix* [386] and the *1875 Second edition* [473]. Others took over for the 1889 supplement [638] and 1916 [779].

In effect, this entire text is an amplification in hymn form of the 'alleluia' phrases that frame Psalm 148 and 150. While stanzas 1-3 are based on various verses in those psalms, stanza 4 is a summary: 'For love in creation, for heaven restored, for grace of salvation, sing praise to the Lord!'   This paraphrase is based firstly on Psalm 150 and pats of Psalm 148, and an allusion in verse 2 to 1 John 3:1-2 which gives a Christian character to the text.

It was set in 1875 to a tune written for it by Henry J Gauntlett entitled LAUDATE DOMINUM ('praise ye the Lord'), to which it is sometimes still sung.

However, it is now more commonly set to the spectacular tune, also called LAUDATE DOMINUM, by C H Parry. This was written to be sung to Baker's words as part of an anthem, 'Hear my words, O ye people', composed in 1894 for the Festival of the Salisbury Diocesan Choral Association.

1   O praise ye the Lord! Praise him in the height;
    rejoice in his word, ye angels of light;
    ye heavens adore him by whom ye were made,
    and worship before him, in brightness arrayed.

2   O praise ye the Lord! Praise him upon earth,
    in tuneful accord, ye sons of new birth;
    praise him who hath brought you his grace from above,
    praise him who hath taught you to sing of his love.

3   O praise ye the Lord, all things that give sound;
    each jubilant chord re-echo around;
    loud organs, his glory forth tell in deep tone,
    and, sweet harp, the story of what he hath done.

4   O praise ye the Lord! Thanksgiving and song
    to him be outpoured all ages along:
    for love in creation, for heaven restored,
    for grace of salvation, O praise ye the Lord!   (Amen, amen.)

O Thou who camest from above

	Charles Wesley §	1797 – 1788	1762	2 verses
HEREFORD	S S Wesley	1810-1876	1872	8.8.8.8

Levit.6:13   "..The fire shall ever be burning upon the altar, it shall never go out."

Is it possible to write a series of 21 hymns on the Book of Leviticus?

Charles Wesley proved that it could be done. The hymn takes a relatively uninteresting verse from Leviticus, describing the duties of Aaron and his sons, and turns it into a remarkable expression of Christian experience. Indeed, when John Wesley was asked about his own faith he said that 'his experience might almost any time be found in the following lines', quoting the first two stanzas. At another time, asked to speak in a class meeting about his own state of sanctification, he is recorded as quoting the second two stanzas.

First published in *'Short Hymns on Select Passages of the Holy Scriptures* (1762), this is the fourth hymn out of the 21. The majority are just a single verse. This is in two 8-line stanzas, prefaced by the text 'The fire shall ever be burning upon the altar, it shall never go out' [Levit.6:13] which is clearly the topic for verse 2. Of the hymns from this series, the only other occasionally sung example from the 21 is 'A charge to keep I have'.

As a reminder - there are 27 chapters in Leviticus, which is the third in the Bible. Most of the chapters are Yahweh's speeches to Moses which are to be passed on to the tribes. This is within the timetable of Exodus up to the completion of the Tabernacle – and Leviticus details how to make offerings and perform rituals correctly. Chapter 26 actually gives a thorough expression of the curses resulting from failure. The book is a lengthy and detailed series of instructions emphasizing the ritual, legal and moral practices Israelites they must perform as required by Jehovah rather than any more casual beliefs they might consider. Must not May.

In Wesley's 1780 Collection he included this hymn in the section *'For Believers, Working',* which suggests that he saw it as beginning with the Holy Spirit and ending with practical religion ('acts of faith and love'). His response was that of congregations, and hymnbook compilers, throughout the world: the hymn is a classic expression of heartfelt aspiration.

As a 'holy spirit' song, this also echoes such hymns as 'Come, Holy Spirit, heavenly dove' by Isaac Watts.

As with other Charles Wesley hymns of this period – but not often mentioned - it is indebted to Matthew Henry's multi-volume *Commentary* of 1708, but it also has an astonishing number of New Testament references, which transform the Old Testament source.

To some hymnbook compilers the opening lines of stanza ii.,
'There let it for Thy glory burn ... With inextinguishable blaze,'
have presented difficulties which have caused its omission from many collections. Bishop E. H. Bickersteth, in his *Hymnal Companion,* amened this this difficulty by rendering the lines :-
'There let it for Thy glory burn ... Unquenched, undimmed in darkest days.'

An early version of the text is :-
1   O Thou who camest from above
    the fire celestial to impart,
    kindle a flame of sacred love
    on the mean altar of my heart!

2   There let it for thy glory burn
with inextinguishable blaze,
and trembling to its source return
in humble prayer and fervent praise.

3   Jesus, confirm my heart's desire
to work, and speak, and think for thee;
still let me guard the holy fire,
and still stir up the gift in me.

4   Ready for all thy perfect will,
my acts of faith and love repeat;
till death thy endless mercies seal,
and make the sacrifice complete.

WILTON, WAREHAM, EISENACH, ONTARIO and others fit the required metre.

The setting HEREFORD is by Samuel Sebastian Wesley (b. London, England, 1810; d. Gloucester, England, 1876) the English organist and composer. The grandson of Charles Wesley, he was born in London, and sang in the choir of the Chapel Royal as a boy. He learned composition and organ from his father, Samuel, completed a doctorate in music at Oxford, and composed for piano, organ, and choir.

He was organist at Hereford Cathedral (1832-1835), Exeter Cathedral (1835-1842), Leeds Parish Church (1842-1849), Winchester Cathedral (1849-1865), and Gloucester Cathedral (1865-1876). Dismayed by the low musical standards prevalent in provincial cathedrals and at the lack of support for cathedral music, he also embarked on a life-long campaign to improve matters; among his publications was an outspoken pamphlet, *A Few Words on Cathedral Music and the Musical System of the Church* (1849).

For much of his career S S Wesley was better known as an organist than as a composer, and his playing, which was compared favourably with that of Mendelssohn, invariably attracted large audiences. Although seen now as the pre-eminent figure in mid 19th-century church music, his published compositions, many of which reflect contemporary German music, met with some hostility in the press. This, coupled with growing disillusionment at the lot of a cathedral musician, led to a steady, albeit gradual, loss of the will to compose.

That this decline should have taken place at just the time — the early 1860s — that he was immersed in the composition of many new hymn tunes for a huge collection, eventually published as *The European Psalmist* (1872), is paradoxical. But in one way it had a happy outcome, not least because the small scale and concentrated expression required in a hymn tune seemed exactly to match his reduced ability to conceive extended works. In its 733 hymns, 130 were by him.

O worship the King all glorious above

	Sir Robert Grant	1780-1838	1833	6,5 verses
HANOVER	William Croft	1678-1727	1708	10.10.11.11

Psalm 104:1-2 "Bless the Lord, O my soul, O Lord my God, thou art very great; thou art clothed with honour and majesty. Who coverest thyself with light as with a garment .... "

For hymnologist Erik Routley (1917–1982), this hymn ranked among his favorites:
"For sheer literary grace and beauty this may be one of the six finest hymns in the language. We all love it for its combination of effortless energy, high-spirited innocence, and the occasional touch of superb dignity. Almost every word in it is a word in the common man's vocabulary— both of its own day and of ours. Yet in the first and last verses there rise two towering lines, built in monolithic style, which give a grand sweep of structure to the whole— Pavilion'd in splendour, and girded with praise .... O measureless might, ineffable love.

This highly wrought and eloquent simplicity gives the whole hymn a texture which very happily reflects that of the psalm on which it is founded. For the 104th Psalm is, even among the psalms, an astonishing piece of writing .... The total message of the hymn is that all that is set down in Psalm 104 is a pageant not merely of God's power but also of his love. This takes us to the heart of the Christian teaching on creation."

The outcome of a series of rewrites and changes is this text by Sir Robert Grant. It is a magnificent hymn of praise to God as Creator, Preserver, and Redeemer and was first published in Edward Bickesteth's *Christian Psalmody* (1833). Grant's text is a free paraphrase of Psalm 104, roughly covering verses 1–13 and 24–33. He patterned the metre after the traditional setting of 10.10.11.11 established by William Kethe's version in '*Foure Score and Seuen Psalmes of Dauid*' (Geneva, 1560). Others soon translated the remaining hymns and the full 150 were available within the year.

It is necessary to point out that the sequence of the 150 Psalms is not always simple and agreed; in the old Sternhold and Hopkins edition (1562) it holds place as Psalm 104.

This rendering of Psalm 104 follows the version by William Kethe in the *Anglo-Genevan Psalter* of 1561 by using the same metre. That text begins:
>My soule praise the Lord, speake good of his Name:
>O Lord our great God how doest thou appeare!
>So passing in glorie, that great is thy fame,
>Honour and maiestie, in thee shine most cleare.

Kethe's metrical version is in three parts, containing 24 verses. Grant's six-stanza hymn takes Kethe's literal rendering and makes it metaphorical. Thus stanza 9 was follows:
>He sendeth the springs to strong streams or lakes,
>Which run do full swift among the huge hills;
>Where both the wild asses their thirst often slakes,
>And beasts of the mountains thereof drink their fills.

Then Sir Robert Grant's beautiful adaptation turns it into God's 'bountiful care' :
>' which streams from the hills and descends to the plain,
>and sweetly distils in the dew and the rain'.

After being first set to H J Gauntlett's' fine tune HOUGHTON, it is now customarily sung to HANOVER, by William Croft, a tune whose splendour matches that of the text. Tune and words together have appeared in books of every denomination throughout the world. In the

US, LYONS is now a common option. And with a metre of 10.10.11.11 there are yet others. J R Watson is fulsome in his praise 'a magnificent and strong tune which carries the words with great conviction and sureness'.

Croft also wrote the tune for 'O God, our help in ages past§'. He took over as at the Chapel Royal after Jeremiah Clarke's suicide. His 'Musica Sacra' was the first church music collection to be printed as a score. It contains his 'Funeral Sentences', 'a glorious work of near genius' which takes 7 sentences from the Book of Common Prayer to be said at a funeral.

'O Praise ye the Lord §' [two entries earlier in this book] has the same metre too, so either version of Laudate Dominum will suit, provided the melody's contour also fits.

This hymn which begins 'O worship the King' is very different from Monsell's offering which continues '… in the beauty of holiness'.

An early version of the text is as follows :

1   O worship the King all-glorious above,
     O gratefully sing his power and his love:
     our shield and defender, the Ancient of Days,
     pavilioned in splendor and girded with praise.

2   O tell of his might and sing of his grace,
     whose robe is the light, whose canopy space.
     His chariots of wrath the deep thunderclouds form,
     and dark is his path on the wings of the storm.

3   The earth with its store of wonders untold,   (often omitted)
     Almighty, Thy power hath founded of old;
     Established it fast by a changeless decree,
     And round it hath cast, like a mantle, the sea.

4   Your bountiful care, what tongue can recite?
     It breathes in the air, it shines in the light;
     it streams from the hills, it descends to the plain,
     and sweetly distills in the dew and the rain.

5   Frail children of dust, and feeble as frail,
     in you do we trust, nor find you to fail.
     Your mercies, how tender, how firm to the end,
     our Maker, Defender, Redeemer, and Friend!

6   O measureless Might, unchangeable Love,
     whom angels delight to worship above!
     Your ransomed creation, with glory ablaze,
     in true adoration shall sing to your praise!

Onward, Christian soldiers

	S Baring-Gould	1834-1924	1865	(6) 5, 4 verses
ST GERTRUDE	Sir A Sullivan	1842-1900	1871	11, 11, 11, 11 D

Deut.31:8   "And the Lord, he it is that doth go before thee."

The vicarage at Horbury has a letter from Baring-Gould about the event making it clear that it was written on Whitsun Eve, 1865 for the 'Brig [Bridge] children':

It had been resolved that the Brig children should come up to the parish church on Whitsun Tuesday; & Mr Fred Knowles came to me at the Vicarage and asked what they were to sing on the long walk. We dismissed one thing & then another & I said, I would write a processional. 'You must be sharp about it" said Mr Knowles, 'For this is Saturday & there will shortly be no printing done'

So I set to work & knocked off the hymn in about ten minutes. We got it printed, & practised on Sunday afternoon at school, & it was sung to a tune by J Haydn on the Tuesday. I sent it to the 'Church Times' & it was therein printed & published.

I dare say you have heard the story of my bidding the choir alter the lines of the hymn from 'With the Cross of Jesus going on before' to 'With the Cross of Jesus, left behind the door', when the Archbishop of York objected to the cross being carried in procession when he was present at Darton. The story is apocryphal. He never was at Darton. The story was invented by my oldest son, when an American interviewer called on him in New York for some 'copy' about the hymn; & he invented the story to humbug the interviewer.

S. Baring-Gould   May 31 1910

'Onward, Christian Soldiers' is a 19th-century English hymn. The words were written by Sabine Baring-Gould in 1865, and the music was composed by Arthur Sullivan in 1871.

The lyric was written as a processional hymn for children walking from Horbury Bridge, where Baring-Gould was curate, to Horbury St Peter's Church near Wakefield, Yorkshire, at Whitsuntide in 1865. It was originally entitled, 'Hymn for Procession with Cross and Banners'. Baring-Gould reportedly wrote the whole text in about 15 minutes, later apologising, 'It was written in great haste, and I am afraid that some of the lines are faulty'. He later allowed hymn-book compilers to alter the lyrics. For example, the phrase 'one in hope and doctrine' to 'one in hope and purpose'; then 'We are not divided' to 'Though divisions harass'. In most modern hymnals, Baring-Gould's original words are used.

Baring-Gould originally set the lyrics to a melody from the slow movement of Joseph Haydn's Symphony in D, No. 15. This was printed in 1871 in the English church periodical, the Church Times. His works are numerous, the most important of which are, *Lives of the Saints*, only 15 vols., 1872-77; *Curious Myths of the Middle Ages*, 2 series, 1866-68; *The Origin and Development of Religious Belief*, 2 vols., 1869-1870.

The hymn did not receive wide acceptance, however, until Sullivan wrote the tune ST GERTRUDE for it. Sullivan quoted the tune in his Te Deum for the Boer War, first performed in 1902, after his death. Sullivan named the tune 'St Gertrude' after the wife of his friend Ernest Seymer, at whose country home he composed the tune. The Salvation Army adopted the hymn as its favoured processional. The piece became Sullivan's most popular hymn.

Another hymn sung to the St. Gertrude tune is 'Forward Through the Ages', written by F L Hosmer (1840–1929) in 1908. There are obviously others.

When Churchill and Roosevelt met in 1941 to agree the Atlantic Charter, a Prime Minister Churchill chose the hymns for the service. He chose this and later he said 'We sang 'Onward, Christian Soldiers' indeed, and I felt that this was no vain presumption, but that we had the right to feel that we were serving a cause for the sake of which a trumpet has sounded from on high'.

An attempt was made in the 1980s to strip 'Onward, Christian Soldiers' from some Methodist and Episcopal Hymnals due to perceived militarism. Outrage among church-goers caused both committees to back down.

The hymn's tune has also been used as the basis for many parodies, including 'Lloyd George Knew My Father' and ' Like a mighty tortoise, / Moves the Church of God; / Brothers, we are treading / Where we've always trod.' Or the more recent 'Onward Christian Pilgrims Put your Sandals on' – a silly hymn-mix which appears to try to equate the modern Christian over-woke view with earlier views of liberal hippy vegetarians.

It appeared in the *Appendix* (1868) to the first edition of A&M, set to a tune called ST ALBAN arranged by Dykes from the Haydn setting used by Baring-Gould; it is called HAYDN. The famous tune to which it is normally sung, ST GERTRUDE, by Arthur Sullivan appeared in The Musical Times in November 1871.

The hymn's theme is taken from the New Testament as to the Christian being a soldier for Christ, for example II Timothy 2:3: 'Thou therefore endure hardness, as a good soldier of Jesus Christ'. The image of the Christian soldier is used to great effect in this hymn, combining the traditional images of the Church Militant with a straightforward appeal to children who love dressing up and playing soldiers.

The apostle Paul recognized the reality of spiritual warfare when he wrote, 'Put on the whole armour of God, that you may be able to stand against the schemes of the devil. For we do not wrestle against flesh and blood, but against the rulers, against the authorities, against the cosmic powers over this present darkness, against the spiritual forces of evil in the heavenly places'. (Ephes. 6:11-12).

It is important to recognize a distinction between spiritual warfare and physical, political warfare. The church universal should oppose war that is sought for human, political reasons, but it cannot avoid fighting evil in all its forms through the armour of God: truth, righteousness, peace, faith, salvation, the Word of God, and prayer (Ephes. 6:14-18).

In spite of 2 Timothy 2: 3, this hymn is disapproved of by those who reject militaristic imagery in worship. It became the occasion of a nation-wide controversy in the USA in 1986, fanned by television and radio networks, when the United Methodist committee compiling their new hymnal proposed to omit it, concerned that the language of the hymn was perceived to be contrary to their social principles. The outcome has been described as a 'furore'!

The committee later also restored 'Isaac Watts' 'Am I a soldier of the Cross' and withdrew its proposed alterations to 'The Battle Hymn of the Republic', 'Mine eyes have seen the Glory of the Coming of the Lord'. All these steps were widely perceived as a victory for the majority of ordinary members of the UMC, who had been vocal in their opposition to change. It is remarkable that a hymn written in ten minutes for children to sing on a march should have caused such an uproar. It has been hugely popular in many countries, as well as in the USA and Canada, where it is found in more than 1,500 hymnals.

A standard 4-verse text is

1 Onward, Christian soldiers, marching as to war.
 With the cross of Jesus going on before:
 Christ, the royal Master, leads against the foe;
 Forward into battle, see His banners go.
  Refrain:
  Onward, Christian soldiers, marching as to war,
  With the cross of Jesus going on before.

At the sign of triumph Satan's host doth flee; (generally omitted)
On, then, Christian soldiers, On to victory!
Hell's foundations quiver At the shout of praise;
Brothers, lift your voices, Loud your anthems raise! [Refrain]

2 Like a mighty army moves the church of God;
 brothers, we are treading where the saints have trod;
 we are not divided, all one body we,
 one in hope and doctrine, one in charity. [Refrain]

3 Crowns and thrones may perish, kingdoms rise and wane,
 But the Church of Jesus constant will remain,
 Gates of hell can never 'gainst that church prevail;
 We have Christ's own promise, and that cannot fail. [Refrain]

What the saints established that I hold for true. (not included by author)
What the saints believed, that believe I too.
Long as earth endureth men that faith will hold, -
Kingdoms, nations, empires, in destruction rolled. [Refrain]

4 Onward, then, ye people, join our happy throng;
 Blend with ours your voices in the triumph song.
 Glory, laud, and honor unto Christ the King:
 This through countless ages men and angels sing. [Refrain]

In passing - The Verse of Lord Calvin

From   Precautionary Tales for Grandparents   © by James Muirden 2008

Lord Calvin thought that Bishops should not sit On working groups that <u>rewrote</u> Holy Writ.
The Bible sanctioned by the first King James Sublimely justified its noble aims,
Giving the Word in words that thrilled the ears. It had done so for some 400 years!
How gross, to pander to the modern fashion For so-called clarity instead of pashion!
How can we <u>clarify</u> the Most Divine? Is He revealed in the Written Line?
No, no. To seek him tread the Lakeland hills – Observe him in a host of golden daffodils
Or in the sunrise breaking through the mist (Lord Calvin was, you'll guess, a pantheist).
When a committee struggles to convey What they suppose the Scribe had <u>meant</u> to say
Out of the window goes the hallowed verse, And we are left with gibberish – or worse!
Before this licensed meddling occurred, John wrote 'In the beginning was the Word',
Which they <u>improved</u> to 'When all things began, The Word already was.' Laugh if you can,
Howl if you must, at such a travesty; But that's how John starts in the N.E.B
(New English Bible nineteen-sixty-one) On reading this and other things they'd done,
Lord Calvin to his Library retired, Drafted his Epitaph, and then expired.
'Dear Lord', it ran, 'What I had hoped to do Was come to thee; now I must come to You'.

===

   additional lines - unauthorised (as yet)

At his funeral, there was no hymn There was a car, some sort of herss.
No comfort there, while the waiting few Sat on worn-out chairs, no ornate pew.
The family listened to the chosen verse and quite suddenly felt so much worse.
They turned to hear the final word and, all as one, said 'that's absurd',
The priest in sweaty t-shirt, grubby jeans Said, we have the way, but not the means.
The murmurs grew, the feelings bitter What must be said, would be on Twitter.

Perhaps now dead Lord Calvin smile(d) not smile like the crocodile
But happy, glorious, fulsome, freed for there was no mention of his deed.
He had, just once, sinned so bad but, seemed ignored, he was so glad.
Could he, would he, should he, tell? He'd heard of likely torments fell.
But, here, alone he knew his place so, sighed, quite happy and fill'd with grace
Just then, a voice, so deep did roar; Alarmed, Lord Calvin fell to t' floor.
"I know what you have done - so vile Be grateful, many sins can wait awhile."
Silent now, Lord Calvin cursed But quietly, for he knew the worst.
His punishment – long torture meant to wait and wait and wait, intent.
But time did pass, Lord Calvin learned That what he got was truly earn'd.
The world could be so very nice If he and his avoided vice
So now in somewhere fair at last Lord Calvin consider'd his misspent past.
Do as you should would be his law Not spend his years on bullying more.

salms

Psalms, in whole or in part, are a huge factor in the creation of many of the hymns here. In this microtome, there are a noticeable number – some 20% - of the 70 or more entries which are either a direct quote or else paraphrase of a Psalm or are clearly based on verses from a Psalm. These include the following :-

Ps.72:	Jesus shall reign where'er the sun
Ps.87:	Glorious things of thee are spoken
Ps.98:	Joy to the World
Ps.100:	All People that on earth do dwell;
Ps.104:	O Worship the King all glorious above;
Ps.103	Praise to the Lord, the Almighty, the King of Creation;
and Ps.103	Praise, my soul, the King of Heaven.
Ps.116:	King of Glory, King of Peace
Ps.136:	Praise, o praise, my God and King
Ps.148:	Ye holy angels bright
Ps.150	O Praise ye the Lord

Any hymn with 'shepherds' is often linked to Psalm 23; although this is definitely obvious for 'The Lord's my shepherd' and 'The King of Love my shepherd is', but also there is :

Ps.23	Father hear the prayer we offer.

The history of the Psalms before they were translated into English is two-fold. The Psalms as a component of the Hebrew Bible being the first; second, is the usage of those same Psalms within the early Christian Church. Needless to say, the actual evidence for some of the theories, suggestions and calculated guesses put forward by others is quite fragile.

Miles Coverdale published his translation of Luther's versions of the Psalms as early as 1535. By 1540, Marot's versions were known at the court of Francis I. Soon these passed into Protestant use at Geneva. Coverdale, Marot and Sternhold all wished to substitute their versified Psalms for the ballads of the court and people.

For his 40 translations, Sternhold used only one metre – the Common Metre – except for Psalm 120. This choice of metre became the predominant form not only of the old and new versions of England and Scotland, but of other metrical psalters and English hymns in general. The exact sequence from these 40 to a complete set within 100 years is unclear. And, by then, some had two versions: Psalm 23 'Dominus Regit me' by WW & TS; Psalm 100 'Jubilate Deo' by JH twice, and others too such as Ps.125 'Qui confidunt'.

Much of this summary is extracted from John Julian's *Dictionary of Hymnology* of 1892.

The first step towards modern hymnody in the vernacular came with the Psalms being translated and then put into verse. There were pre-Reformation examples: Bishop Aldhelm in about 700; Bede perhaps; Coverdale who wrote JJ Coverdale … 'Would God … our carters and ploughman had none other thing to whistle upon save psalms … and if women … spinning at the wheels had none other songs … they should be better occupied than with hey nony, hey troly loly, dawoobop dawoobop'.

In France Marot offered a popular set of Psalms. Perhaps the most significant collections were those produced in Geneva around 1550-1565 in German, French and English. By 1696, there were two particularly significant complete versions of the Psalms in English.

There was the OLD Version known as 'Sternhold and Hopkins' and there also was the NEW Version known as 'Tate and Brady'. With the history of every church for allowing schism and counter-schism, it is admirable that these two continued side-by-side in print and in use. The Old Version was first printed in 1550; the New Version first in 1696. The Sternhold & Hopkins version remained in use during through to the early-Victorian era. However, nowadays 130 years after Julian, it is rare to hear the Psalms sung at all whether as their unversed, unrhymed originals or otherwise.

A review of the first lines does not instantly see the usual phrasing. In Sternhold & Hopkins, two obvious examples, has the first line of #23 as 'My Shepherd is the living Lord' and #100 in two forms as 'All people that on earth do dwell' as well as 'In God the Lord be glad and light' – which is rather different. In the New Version, the first line for #23 is 'The Lord himself, the mighty Lord'; and for #100 'With one consent let all the earth'.

Within 2 years of the first edition 'New' in 1696, there was the both the New Version (Hodgkin) and the 'Second Edition corrected' by Clark. There were considerable changes between the two. Julian writes 'It was natural to expect that the publication of one would cease the other. This, however, did not take place for 200 years.'

Julian later writes 'the New Version had a large quantity of spiritless CM as poor in language as the literal originals and a few examples of sweet and simple verse. Those who tread the waste of metrical Psalters will consider it an advance on its predecessors.'

Tate was born in Dublin, son of Faithful Teate, in 1652. He succeeded Shadwell as Poet Laureate (who succeeded the first, one Dryden), earning his annual 'Sack of Canary' now 720 bottles of Sherry – at least 2 every day!! Very few such poets are still renowned.

There were some strange examples of enversed psalms along the years. Abraham France did a version in hexameters – which did not succeed. Pike offered *Lyrics without rhyme* (1751); Cotton Mather delivered *Psalterium Americanum* which was 'merely the Authorized Version thrown into unrhymned Common Metre for singing.'

Loys Bourgeois is worthy of mention as the composer behind many of the best-known metrical Psalm arrangements. In 1549 and 1550 he worked on a collection of tunes. A long-lost copy of the *Genevan Psalter* of 1551 made it clear to what extent to which he was composer, arranger or compiler. In an Avertissement (note) to the reader Bourgeois specifies exactly what his predecessors had done, what he had changed and which were his own contributions. He is one of the three main contributors to the *Genevan Psalter*.

Unfortunately, he fell foul of local musical authorities and was sent to prison on 3 December 1551 for changing the tunes for some well-known psalms 'without a license'. He was released on the personal intervention of Calvin but the controversy continued: those who had already learned the tunes had no desire to learn new versions, and the town council ordered the burning of Bourgeois' instructions to the singers, claiming they were confusing. Shortly after this incident, Bourgeois left Geneva never to return: he settled in Lyon, his Geneva employment was terminated, and his wife tardily followed him to Lyon. While in Lyon, Bourgeois wrote a fierce piece of invective against the publishers of Geneva.

Sternhold is credited with the authorship of thirty-nine psalms in the *Old Scottish Psalter* [1564] which followed on from the *Geneva Psalter* of 1560. Hopkin's contribution was thirty-seven psalms. It has been said of his psalms and those of Sternhold: 'They are very faithful, but somewhat coarse and homely in phraseology'. As Fuller well said, 'their authors' piety was better than their poetry, and they had drunk more of Jordan than of Helicon'.

Kethe contributed twenty-five psalms to the Psalter, noted for the easy flow and variety of their metres, and must have given brightness to the congregational singing.

Whittingham contributed sixteen psalms, written in a great variety of metres.

Thomas Norton contributed 26 psalms of which 8 reached the *Scottish Psalter*. He also wrote several tracts on the religious controversies of the age.

John Daye printed a set by Archbishop Parker in 1562 which included the Canticles, as well as the Doxology in all available metres: CM, LM, SM. Apparently 'his rhythms and stresses are entirely distinct from Sternhold, so as to facilitate singing'.

Julian tells in considerable detail 'Of a different order is the version by Sir Philip Sidney, completed by his sister. The metres are 'more rare and excellent for method and varietie' the fantastical and capricious measures of the lighter Elizabethan style. They have frequent freshness and spirit ... and now that a higher music no longer chains us ... the 84th, 92nd and more regular 96th full of grace and charm'.

To the psalm-loving Puritan, the perfection of the metrical version was a matter of supreme moment. The version by Rous, later Provost of Eton under the Commonwealth, was an attempt to satisfy the new and stronger demands. The House of Commons ordered it 'to be sung in all churches and chapels within the kingdom'. But ... the House of Lords preferred their own versifier, William Barton. But the Assembly of Divines did not authorise Mr Barton's work. In the end, there is no evidence that the House of Commons completed their approval of Rous. And the Scots did not like it either; they suspected Rous of heterodoxy as being an adherent of Cromwell. They introduced considerable variations to suit their requirements.

John Milton, the poet and also Secretary for Foreign Tongues (that is translator and propagandist), attempted Psalms 80 to 88, translating direct from the Hebrew, which was printed in the margins. Every word added and thus not in the original was in italics. No better illustration of the literal principle in Puritan translation is needed – and no one can say it was successful.

Julian continues 'The dreariness of these efforts now produced a demand for some literary excellence. The lack of adequate music did not help. Patrick in 1692 had a version which adopted a mode of evangelical interpretation but it had little success'.

'Some of the great names of hymnody presented better and more interesting and more useable productions, Isaac Watts§ (1719); Montgomery§ (1822); Keble (1839). Watts saw and was bold enough to say that there were parts of the Psalms which could never be sung, and which were therefore useless as hymns. His renderings were often paraphrases rather than translations. He broke Psalms into pieces; not surprisingly Ps 119 is thus split [in the BCP, the 174 verses are in 22 parts – each linked to one letter of the Hebrew alphabet]. Watts' new method was divergent from literalism, but a legitimate and fruitful one. But, when he tried to push this method beyond the guidance of scripture, Watts was betrayed into such vulgarity as the substitution of 'Britain' for 'Israel'.

'Keble knew that Hebrew chanting and English metre were irreconcilable, yet he persevered despite his anticipation of Pusey's adverse criticism. But in the judgement of the present writer [ie JJ] no other version has such refinement of diction, sustained merit, lyric force and fire, and flashes of imaginative energy.

Julian concludes 'The reader will have observed that this is the history of a long tenacious struggle of the Metrical Psalter against the growing power of original hymn as the material of praise. For the worship of the masses certain grand and simple psalms are unequalled. Nowhere is the Glory of God in his works so magnificently exhibited as in the Psalms … Nowhere is the jubilance of praise so majestic – even while checked by the chilling and irrelevant thought of the sinfulness and inadequacy of our utterances.

The influence of the Psalter is by no means worked out. It may take new forms but it is impossible that the Psalms can cease to inspire many of the deepest, tenderest, most intense utterances in future hymns.

There are extra pieces in the full Sternhold and Hopkins variety of Psalter and its descendants. These include the versified Ten Commandments, Creed, Magnificat and so on.

Readers of this sketch, Julian writes, will have observed that in one aspect this is the history of the long tenacious struggle of the Metrical Psalter against the growing power of original hymns as the material of praise. But fresh efforts are made under freer conditions.

A version of considerable freshness, freedom and spirit appeared in 1863 with irregular verse structure by Mr Malet. Mr Birks delivered in 1874 the *Companion Psalter* with his own development of the meditative psalms. His lyric measures are often soft and melodious; he introduces freely Evangelical ideas: but they are not always the legitimate unfolding of the psalm and sometimes the groundwork is scarcely perceptible.

In the later Supplement, Julian adds extra detail on the Psalters developed from 1561 to 1570 and relevant activity in Germany. He goes as far as noting the four different prefaces 1561, 1562, 1566, 1567 of the Genevan Psalter. The language is wonderful.

1561 'Psalmes of David in Englishe metre, by Thomas Sterneholde and others: conferred with the Ebrue, & in certain places corrected (as the sense of the Prophet required) and the Note ioyned with all. Veri mete to be used of all sortes of people privately for their godly solace and comfort: laying aparte all ungodlye Songes and Ballades, which tend only to the nourishing of vice and corrupting of youth. … Let the words of God dwell plenteouslye in all wisedome teaching & exhorting one another in Psalmes, Hymnes & spirituall songs, and sing unto the Lord in your herts.

1566 …. Newlye set fourth all allowed to be sung of the people together, in Churches, before and after Morning and Evening Prayer: as also before and after the Sermon. And moreover in private houses ….

At this date the use in Public Worship of the Psalms and the Hymns had the cordial approval of the Queen's Censors [The Archbishops, Bishop of London, the Chancellors of both Universities, the Bishop being Ordinary and the Archdeacon of the place of printing.].

Julian then looks at Lutheran practice with the Psalms, noting … 1688-1754 …the tendency was to found hymns on portions of the Psalms rather than to versify the entire Psalter. 1766-1816 … the tendency was to write moral hymns rather than to attempt Psalm-versions. Concluding his main article 'The metrical psalms still contribute largely to our hymnals. The least successful renderings have been the Messianic psalms. Nor have the penitential psalms yielded much. In one or two instances the dauntless trust of the Psalmists has been nobly reproduced'.

'Nowhere is the jubilance of praise so majestic, unchecked by the chilling and irrelevant thought – true and sad as it is – of the sinfulness and inadequacy of our utterances. These characteristics are impressed deeply on Watts for example; and they are of abiding value as a counterpoise to the morbid emotion, effeminacy, self-consciousness and anodyne of motives which make some modern hymns so sickly. …. It may take new forms, select and develop more freely from the ideas, but it is impossible that the Psalms can cease to inspire many of the deepest, tenderest, most intense utterances of future hymns.'

Praise, O praise our God and King

	Sir H W Baker §	1821-1877	1861	8 verses
MONKLAND	John Antes / (John Wilkes)	1740-1811		7.7.7.7 Refrain

Psalm 136:25 "Who giveth food to all flesh, for his mercy endureth for ever."

END Baker gave very detailed notes for the singing of this at Monkland Church Harvest Festival. 'The first and last verses to be sung in Chorus, the others with the first two lines of the tune as 'Semi-Chorus' and the second two as 'Chorus'.'

The text was written for the *First Edition of Hymns A&M* by the chief editor Sir Henry Williams Baker and printed there in the 'Harvest' section. It appeared beneath the text: 'Who giveth food to all flesh; for His mercy endureth for ever' (from Psalm 136:25).

It is an imitation of John Milton's paraphrase of Psalm 136, 'Let us with a gladsome mind'. Baker modernised Milton's 'aye endure' to 'still endure' and, after three verses, turned the general thankfulness of the psalm into a harvest hymn. He then took the idea one stage further with food becoming a metaphor, and the promise of 'richer Food than this', the pledge of heaven (suggesting the meditation on spiritual food in John 6: 26-58).

The tune was named Monkland by W H Monk, after the village in Herefordshire in which Baker was vicar. Monk attributed it to J.B. Wilkes, who was in Baker's time organist at Monkland. However in 1960 the particular melody was discovered in the Moravian Church archives in London in a manuscript book by John Antes in about 1800 for a Christmas hymn, 'What good news the angels bring', in printed later in a Moravian hymnal of 1824. The story traces further back to being rooted in a tune for the text 'Fahre fort' in J A Freylinghausen's famous hymnal *Geistreiches Gesangbuch* (1704). Antes then significantly altered it.

Antes was a missionary, watchmaker, business manager, and composer. Born near the Moravian community of Bethlehem, Pennsylvania, he was trained at the Moravian boys' school and later received religious education and further training as a watchmaker in Herrnhut, Germany. From 1770 to 1781 he served as a missionary in Egypt and from 1783 until his death was the business manager of the Moravian community in Fullneck, England. Although music was his avocation, Antes was a fine composer and musician. Among his compositions are a number of anthems, several string trios, and over fifty hymn tunes.

John Julian wrote of Baker in his *Dictionary of Hymnology*:

Sir Henry's name is intimately associated with hymnody. One of his earliest compositions was the very beautiful hymn, "Oh! what if we are Christ's," which he contributed to Murray's Hymnal for the Use of the English Church, 1852.

His hymns, including metrical litanies and translations, number in the revised edition of Hymns Ancient & Modern, are 33 in all (eventually 59). Others were contributed at various times to Murray's Hymnal, Hymns Ancient & Modern and the London Mission Hymn Book, 1876-7. The last contains his three latest hymns. These are not included in Hymns Ancient & Modern. Of his hymns four only are in the highest strains of jubilation, another four are bright and cheerful, and the remainder are very tender, but exceedingly plaintive, sometimes even to sadness. Even those which at first seem bright and cheerful have an undertone of plaintiveness, and leave a dreamy sadness upon the spirit of the singer.

One version of the text is as follows. The simple structure and refrain make it easy to learn and sing – perhaps especially so for exhausted agricultural labourers and their children.

1   Praise, O praise our God and King;
    hymns of adoration sing:
        Refrain:
          For his mercies still endure ever faithful, ever sure.

2   Praise him that he made the sun
    day by day his course to run: [Refrain]

3   And the silver moon by night,
    shining with her gentle light: [Refrain]

4   Praise him that he gave the rain
    to mature the swelling grain: [Refrain]

5   And hath bid the fruitful field
    crops of precious increase yield: [Refrain]

6   Praise him for our harvest-store;
    he hath filled the garner-floor: [Refrain]

7   And for richer food than this,
    pledge of everlasting bliss: [Refrain]

8   Glory to our bounteous King;
    glory let creation sing:
        Glory to the Father, Son,
          and blest Spirit, Three in One.

In passing – Local names for hymns

Starting with the birthplace of Hymns Ancient and Modern – Monkland near Leominster in the Hereford Diocese … Hymnary reveals that the following named for nearby places.

MONKLAND	by Antes, adapted by J Wilkes, organist at Monkland for H W Baker
KINGSLAND	Lord, be thy word my rule by William Boyce c 1791
EARDISLEY	Anon (but apparently collected by R Vaughan Williams)
DILWYN	Anon, but listed as arranged by Vaughan Williams in about 1920
LEOMINSTER	George Martin 1862 founder of the National Choral Society
LEOMINSTER	Unknown - in St Albans Hymn Book 1867
LEOMINSTER	by Samuel Holyoke fl 1800 of Massachusetts - – 700 hymns
HEREFORD	O Thou who camest from above by S S Wesley 1872
HEREFORD	Lift up your heads, ye gates by Henry Gauntlett 1872
HEREFORD	We come to be confirmed, Lord by William Hayes fl 1750

   and 5 more Herefords.

Going further afield to larger towns, there are 10 Gloucesters and 21 Worcesters.

Praise, my soul, the King of heaven

| | H F Lyte § | 1793-1847 | 1834 | (5) 4 verses |
| LAUDA ANIMA | John Goss | 1800-1880 | 1868 | 8.7.8.7.8.7 |

Psalm 103:1 "Praise the Lord, o my soul, and all that is within me…"

In theology Lyte was a conservative evangelical who believed that man's nature was totally corrupt. He frequently rose at 6 AM and prayed for two or more hours before breakfast. There is more of his story on his Page§ and on the page for 'Abide with Me'§.

Lyte explained in his preface his intention of paraphrase rather than equivalence:

Instead, therefore, of attempting a new version of the Psalms, he has contented himself with endeavouring to condense the leading sentiments of each into a few verses for cong-regational singing. The modern practice of using only three or four verses at a time would render the great majority of the Psalms, if literally translated, unfit, on the score of length, for public worship; and a few ill-connected verses detached from the rest can scarcely give a more just view of the harmonious whole, than a few bricks can of the building of which they may have formed a part. The author has therefore simply endeavoured to give the spirit of each Psalm in such a compass as the public taste would tolerate…'.

The words for the hymn were first published in Lyte's *The Spirit of the Psalms* (1834), a publication for the use of his own congregation in Devon. It appeared in multiple influential publications, such as the *First edition of Hymns Ancient and Modern* (1861) and the first *English Hymnal* (1906). The usual setting of LAUDA ANIMA by John Goss was attached in 1868 and the pairing endures in modern hymnals. It then became an 'instant' success, a report in the 1869 Musical Times stating that 'it is at once the most beautiful and dignified hymn tune which has lately come under our notice'. It remains extremely popular and J R Watson notes that 'it is hard to find a major hymnbook that does not include it'.

The text is a free paraphrase of Psalm 103. While, in the mid-nineteenth century, hymn writers usually kept their metrical settings of psalm texts as close as possible to the original, he instead decided to maintain the spirit of the words while freely paraphrasing them. The result speaks, in an imaginative fashion, with 'beautiful imagery and thoughtful prose', of themes such as the Love of God, healing and forgiveness, including the repeated exclamations 'Praise Him!', in what is a spectacular rhetorical statement of praise.

For his 1834 book, he included four paraphrases based on Psalm 103 – this is the second. The original fourth stanza ('Frail as summer's flower'), corresponding with verses 15–17 of the Psalm, was noted for optional omission and many modern hymnals exclude it. The text of the omitted stanza shares a 'valedictory but hopeful tone' with the other well-known hymn by Lyte, 'Abide with me §'.

Other more modern changes, including more gender-neutral language, are relatively minor. An alternate text, written as part of the 1980s and 1990s attempts to reduce the omnipresence of masculine metaphors for God begins 'Praise my soul, the God of heaven'.

The hymn is most commonly sung to the tune LAUDA ANIMA ('Praise, my soul'), written as a setting for Lyte's words by John Goss in 1868. Paul Westermeyer notes that it has 'been praised as one of the finest' hymn tunes from the Victorian period and remains much a favourite of congregations. The first stanza is marked to be sung in unison with harmonies from the organ. The second is in four-part harmony, while the remainder is again in unison.

In modern versions, Lyte's text has been frequently altered. One common variant, which originates in the 1861 H A&M collection, is replacing the line 'Praise Him! Praise Him!' with 'Alleluia!' or perhaps more accurately A-a-a-a-a-a-a-a-a-a-a-a-Alleluia.

One alternative tune amongst the many in 8.7.8.7.8.7 metre is REGENT SQUARE, originally written by Henry Smart for 'Glory be to God the Father' by Horatius Bona.

With or without these and other minor changes, the hymn is a spectacular piece of praise rhetoric. It compresses a great deal into its five stanzas, and combines a powerful statement of God's grandeur as the king of heaven with a recognition of his tenderness to frail humanity. It is also suitable for many different occasions, and can be sung by people of all denominations.

1. Praise, my soul, the King of heaven;
to his feet thy tribute bring;
ransomed, healed, restored, forgiven,
who like me his praise should sing?
Praise him! Praise him!   Praise the everlasting King.

2. Praise him for his grace and favour
to our fathers in distress;
praise him, still the same for ever,
slow to chide, and swift to bless:
Praise him! Praise him!   glorious in his faithfulness.

3. Father-like he tends and spares us;
well our feeble frame he knows;
in his hands he gently bears us,
rescues us from all our foes:
Praise him! Praise him!   widely as his mercy flows.

4. Frail as summer's flower we flourish;   (optional)
blows the wind and it is gone;
but, while mortals rise and perish,
God endures unchanging on.
Praise him! Praise him!   Praise the high eternal One.

5. Angels, help us to adore him;
ye behold him face to face;
sun and moon, bow down before him;
dwellers all in time and space.
Praise him! Praise him!   Praise with us the God of grace.

Praise the Lord! ye heavens, adore Him

	Foundling Hospital		c 1796	2 (3) verses
AUSTRIA §	Josef Haydn	1732-1809	1797	8.7.8.7 D
Psalm 148:1	"Praise ye the LORD from the heavens: praise him in the heights".			

The two verses of this hymn were found in a leaflet, containing five hymns and a Sanctus, pasted in to the 1796 edition of *Psalms, Hymns and Anthems of the Foundling Hospital*. There is no marker as to when the pasting in was done. It was entitled 'Hymn from Ps. 148. Haydn. Anon.' The reference to Haydn suggests that the tune may have been AUSTRIA, with which the hymn has been associated since that time.

Hymns Ancient and Modern has Kempthorne as the author – but there is no better evidence to that effect. The Haydn melody is also known as 'Gott erhalte Franz den Kaiser' and was the Austrian national anthem. It has been paired with a significant number of texts.

An alternate setting was by Geoffrey Shaw called PRAISE. With a metre of 8.7.8.7 there are numerous others, insofar as a mere metric similarity is sufficient for rhythm, rhyme, tone and texture. Hymnary.org suggests that a mere 56 other tunes have been identified as being settings for this text; HYFRYDOL; FABEN; PEREZ; ESSEX; and more.

It has become universally popular, sometimes in two verses, and sometimes as here with a doxology at the third verse by Edward Osler.

1. Praise the Lord! ye Heav'ns, adore him;   ... Praise him angels, in the height;
   Sun and moon, rejoice before him;   ... Praise him, all ye stars of light.
   Praise the Lord! for he has spoken;   ... Worlds his mighty voice obeyed;
   Laws which never shall be broken... For their guidance he has made.

2. Praise the Lord! for he is glorious;   ... Never shall his promise fail;
   God has made his saints victorious;   ... Sin and death shall not prevail.
   Praise the God of our salvation!   ... Hosts on high his pow'r proclaim;
   Heav'n, and earth, and all creation,   ... Laud and magnify his name.

3. Worship, honor, glory, blessing,   ... Lord, we offer unto thee;
   Young and old, thy praise expressing,   ... In glad homage bend the knee.
   All the saints in heav'n adore thee,   ... We would bow before thy throne;
   As thine angels serve before thee, ... So on earth thy will be done.

Squeezing in – before the next page

Isaac Watts in his Song for Children managed the Ten Commandments in 10 lines:

Thou shalt have no more Gods but me   ... Before no idol bow the knee
Take not the Name of God in vain: ... Nor dare the Sabbath-day profane.
Give both they parents honour due.   ... Take heed that thou no murder do.
Abstain from words and deeds unclean: ... Nor steal, though thou are poor and mean.
Make no wilful lie, nor love it.   ... Of thy neighbour's dare not covet.

In Passing - The Ten Commandments in verse

One startling side-effect of the versification of the Psalms was the extra effort put in to do the same to the 'important' pieces of the Old and New Testaments. Many of the Bibles and especially the collections of Metrical Psalms included these extras.

Specific texts include the 3 Canticles from Luke – Magnificat, Nunc Dimittis and Benedictus; also the Te Deum, Benedicite, Lord's Prayer; and the 10 Commandments.

There were more than a few translations and rewrites of these BUT, strangely and sadly, their success as sung pieces has diminished to almost zero. This transcribed example is simple – but not sung any more, despite there being many 8.8.8.8 tunes.

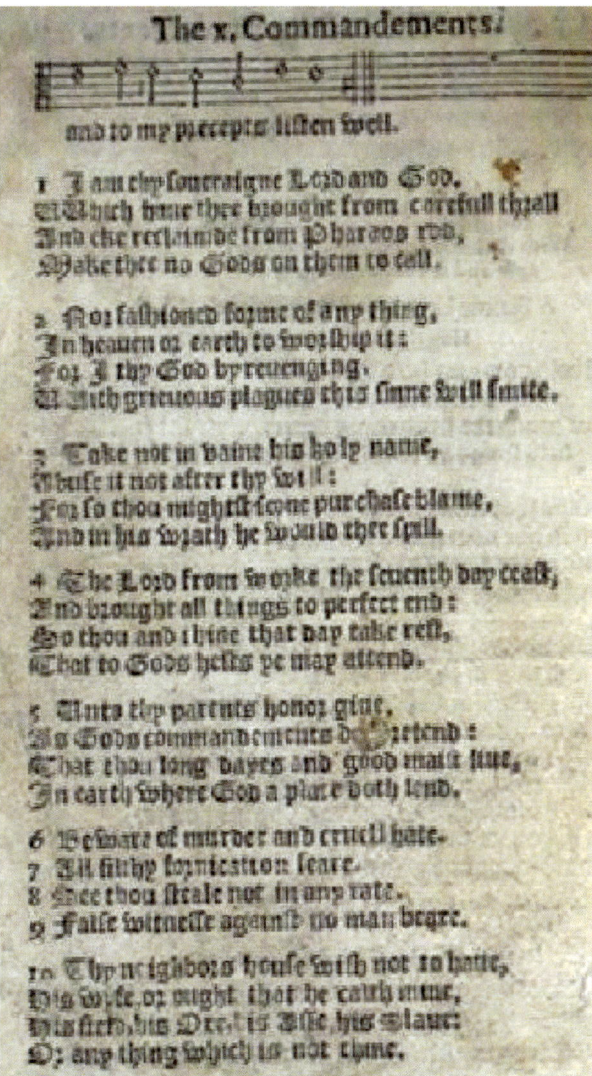

[first three lines missed on facsimile]
(and) to my precepts listen well.

I am thy Sovereigne Lord and God.
which have thee brought from carefull thrall
And cke reclaimde from Pharaos rod,
Make thee no Gods on them to call.

Nor fashioned forme of any thing,
in heaven or earth to worship it:
For I thy God by revenging
with grievous plagues this sinne will smite.

Take not in vaine his holy name,
Abuse it not after thy will:
For so thou might come purchase blame,
And in his wrath he would thee spill.

The lord from worke the seventh day ceas'd,
And brought all things to perfect end:
And thou and thine that day take rest,
That to God's tests ye may attend.

Unto thy parents honor give,
As god's commandements do intend
That thou long days and good may live
In earth where God a place doth tend

Beware of murder and cruell hate.
All filthy formication feare.
See thou steale not in any rate.
False witness against no man beare.

Thy neighbors house wish not to have,
 his wife or ought that he calls mine,
His herd, his Oxe, his Ass, his slave;
or anything which is not thine.

Several versions exist of the metrical Ten Commandments; Isaac Watts even produced a 10-line version. The Hopkins and Sternhold version has two examples; Tate and Brady have another two. There is a modern Anglo-Geneva version most recently updated in 2010. There are French versions from their Geneva Psalter equivalents.

Praise to the Holiest in the height   (Gerontius)

Dream of Gerontius adapted   J H Newman   1801-1890   1865   7 verses
GERONTIUS   J B Dykes §   1823-1876   1868   8.6.8.6
1 Cor.15:47 "The first man is of the earth, earthy; the second Man is the Lord from heaven."

This hymn is an extract from the much larger work 'The Dream of Gerontius' an 1865 poem written by John Henry Newman. He was by then some 20 years converted to Catholic from Anglican high-church. The form is the prayer of a dying man, and the angelic and demonic responses; sequentially exploring the Catholic-held beliefs of the journey from death through Purgatory, thence to Paradise, and to God.

Only a very few of Newman's poems have become into use as hymns. Other than this, the most notable is, 'Lead, kindly Light'. He did also made nearly 40 Latin hymn translations.

The text beginning 'Praise to the Holiest in the height' is sung by 'the Fifth Choir of Angelicals' in Part II as the soul of Gerontius ('old man') crosses the threshold of death into Purgatory. It is an extract from John Henry Newman's *Dream of Gerontius* published in 1865. The hymn first appeared in the 1868 *H A&M Appendix* to the setting by Dykes called, perhaps unsurprisingly, GERONTIUS.

The repeat of verse 1 at the end has become traditional; without it the poem ends 'to suffer and to die', which is less satisfactory as a conclusion. Elgar endorses the arrangement in his magnificent oratorio of 1900 composed on Newman's words. The setting NEWMAN, by R R Terry (sometimes known as BILLING) arrived in 1912 but is not greatly used.

The hymn is a profound meditation on 1 Corinthians 15: 20-47, in which God in Christ, the second Adam, restores the world which had been lost by the sin of the first Adam. He does so by his Incarnation: his becoming human is an even higher gift than grace. In human form he undergoes the 'double agony' (the agony in the garden, and the suffering on the cross) which will teach and inspire, and demonstrate the power of 'generous love'.

The actions of the Incarnate God are appropriately enclosed within the 'praise' motif of the first and last verses. 'The phrase 'a higher gift than grace' has caused problems to some evangelical Protestants, who would argue that there can be no higher gift than grace. However, in the context of *The Dream of Gerontius* it would seem to refer to the Incarnation, and Newman's argument is that God in Christ the Incarnate Word is an even higher gift than grace. One effort to avoid controversy is by printing instead 'the highest gift of grace', but this does not adhere to Newman's carefully argued thesis

Whatever Newman's inspiration, *The Dream of Gerontius* remains one of the pivotal works on death and the soul of the Victorian era and one of Newman's most famous works.

A version suitable as a standard text is as follows :

1	Praise to the Holiest in the height, in all his words most wonderful,	... and in the depth be praise: ... most sure in all his ways.
2	O loving wisdom of our God! a second Adam to the fight	... When all was sin and shame, ... and to the rescue came.
3	O wisest love! that flesh and blood, should strive afresh against the foe,	... which did in Adam fail, ... should strive and should prevail;
4	And that a higher gift than grace God's presence and his very self,	... should flesh and blood refine, ... and essence all-divine.
5	O generous love! that he, who smote the double agony in Man	... in Man for man the foe, ... for man should undergo;
6	And in the garden secretly, should teach his brethren, and inspire	... and on the cross on high, ... to suffer and to die.
7	Praise to the Holiest in the height, in all his words most wonderful,	... and in the depth be praise: ... most sure in all his ways.

Digression   Cardinal John Henry Newman

John Julian§ writes thus (somewhat edited) in his *Dictionary of Hymnology* (1907):

The barest outline only is possible as the hymnological side of Cardinal Newman's life and work is so small compared with the causes which have ruled, and the events which have accompanied his life as a whole, that the barest outline of biographical facts and summary of poetical works comprise all that properly belongs to this work. 'His influence on hymnology has not been of a marked character. Two brilliant original pieces, and little more than half a dozen translations from the Latin, are all that can claim to rank with his inimitable prose.'

John Henry Newman was born in 1801 in London; educated at Ealing then Trinity, Oxford, he graduated in 1820 and became a fellow at Oriel in 1822. He took Holy Orders in 1824, was appointed to St. Mary's, Oxford, in the spring of 1828. In 1830 he became one of the Select University Preachers.

His association with Keble, Pusey, and others, in what is known as The Oxford Movement, together with the publication of the Tracts for the Times, are matters of history. Tract 90, entitled *'Bernards on Certain Passages in the Thirty-nine Articles'*, in 1841, was followed by his retirement to Littlemore. His formal recantation, in 1843, of all that he had said against Rome; his resignation in September of the same year of both St. Mary's and Littlemore; and of his formal application to be received into the Church of Rome in October 1845 – from a documentary viewpoint - are matters of factual record.

He progressed through and upwards in the Roman Catholic hierarchy. In 1879 he was created a Cardinal, the level immediately below Pope, and as such bestowed by the Pope.

Digression   'Dream of Gerontius'

The Dream of Gerontius was written by Newman some 20 years after he officially moved to the Catholic church. As a reminder, it is the prayer of a dying man with the angelic and demonic responses as the old man 'Gerontius' journeys from death through Purgatory, thence to Paradise, and to God. The poem begins as he nears death and then reawakens as a soul, preparing for judgment, following one of the most important events any human can experience: death.

Newman uses the death and judgement of Gerontius as a prism through which the reader is drawn to contemplation of their own fear of death and sense of unworthiness before God. His depiction of the overwhelmed Gerontius in Phase Seven of the poem, who begs to be taken for purgatorial cleansing rather than diminish the perfection of God and his courts of Saints and Angels by his continued presence, has become a popular expression of humanity's desire for healing through redemptive suffering. Indeed this scene of the poem has done much for the endorsement of the doctrine of purgatory which had previously come to be seen as a fearful terror rather than a state of final purification essentially positive in nature.

Newman said that the poem 'was written by accident – and it was published by accident'. He wrote it up in fair copy from fifty-two scraps of paper between 17 January and 7 February 1865 and published it in May and June of the same year, in two parts in the Jesuit periodical The Month. The poem inspired a choral work also called Dream of Gerontius by Elgar in 1900.

Gerontius owes much to the *Divine Comedy* of Dante Alighieri, a much older Italian or rather Tuscan allegorical depiction of travelling through the realms of the dead, completed in 1320. It is best known for the Nine Circles of Damnation with Treachery as the worst.

Newman's poem is divided into seven individual 'phases', and is Newman's longest written poem. The first details the Old Man's final minutes in this world with the later phases illustrating his journey through the courts of Heaven.

<u>First Phase</u>   Gerontius is a dying man, he isn't confident with where he's going in the afterlife and acknowledges he could be going to hell. Finally a priest intones the 'Proficiscere' and bids Gerontius to go forth to the inexpressible joys that await him.

<u>Second Phase</u>   Gerontius' disembodied soul awakens; uncertain of being alive or dead - he is disoriented. – his angel betimes guided him – Gerontius accepts he is dead.

<u>Third Phase</u>   The angel explains that time and space are mere human constructs; thus the only thing keeping Gerontius from God is his own thinking. The soul no longer fears but feels joy. The angel explains that the joy will help the soul through the next temptations.

<u>Fourth Phase</u>   The soul of Gerontius and the Angel arrive at 'the judgment-court' where demons have assembled. Satan's legions now run this area in hopes of 'gathering souls for hell'. The demons mock those who turn to religion merely because of fear of the unknown.

<u>Fifth Phase</u>   The soul and the angel move past the many Choir of Angels singing the Praises of God. The angel promises joy but that Gerontius will be horrified at his own sins.

<u>Sixth Phase</u>   They are now very near to the 'veiled presence of our God'. The Angel of Agony is asking Jesus to be merciful to all mankind, and adds mention of Gerontius. Gerontius now feels ready to face God and 'intemperately' rushes forward – it is too much. Sick with love and sick at his ins – he realizes he is not ready;and asks his angel for respite.

<u>Seventh Phase</u> The Angel asks that the 'golden prison open its gates' and allow the soul of Gerontius to Purgatory; and hopes for his release to Heaven 'Farewell, but not forever'.

Digression   'Dante's Divine Comedy'

This work by Dante Alighieri is seen as the pre-eminent work in Italian literature and one of the greatest pieces of world literature. It was begun in 1308 and published in 1320, the year before Dante died. The poem also reflects the real-life issues between the Florentine Guelphs and the Ghibellines in Central Italy / Tuscany. Dante's White Guelphs lost; Dante was exiled.

This is a narrative poem giving an imaginative view of the Afterlife according to the 14th century Catholic church's medieval worldview. It comes in three parts – Inferno, Purgatorio, Paradiso. The core of the tale is the state of the soul after death and a medieval view of how divine justice is meted out as due punishment or reward.

The poem represents the soul's journey towards God, beginning with the recognition and rejection of Sin (Inferno), followed by the penitent Christian life (Purgatorio), which is then followed by the soul's ascent to God (Paradiso) – all in accord with the general philosophy derived from the Summa Theologica of Thomas Aquinas.

Written in the first person, the poem tells of Dante's journey through the three realms of the dead, lasting from the night before Good Friday to the Wednesday after Easter in the spring of 1300. The pilgrim Dante is accompanied by Virgil (who represents humans reason, and who guides him for all of Inferno and most of Purgatorio); Beatrice (who represents divine revelation, theology, faith and grace, guiding him at the end of Purgatorio and for most of Paradiso); and finally Saint Bernard of Clairvaux (who represents contemplative mysticism and devotion to Mary to Mary the Mother, guiding him in the final cantos of Paradiso).

The poem is composed of 14,233 lines that are divided into three cantiche; each consisting of 33 cantos. The number three is prominent in the work, 3 sections, 33 cantos, 3 guides, 33 syllables per line; triple-rhyme pattern and so on. Each of the 3 realms is a pattern of 9 – Circles of Inferno; Rings of Purgatory and the Celestial bodies of Paradise. The number 7 occurs too – 7 moral elements, 7 deadly sins and so on. To ensure further patterns – the 9 are linked to a 1; and the 7 to another 2 to make, yes, 9.

Each sin's punishment in Inferno is a form of poetic justice. The Inferno represents the Christian soul seeing sin for what it really is, and the three beasts represent three types of sin: the self-indulgent, the violent, and the malicious. The nine circles are first Limbo for those ignorant of Christ, then the circles of Lust, Gluttony, Avarice, Anger, then Violence, Heretics, Abusers, finally Fraud and Treachery.

Purgatorio is not a valid concept in the Anglican arena where there is no place to assess one's own sinfulness. Mount Purgatory has seven terraces, corresponding to the seven deadly sins [Wrath, Envy, Pride, Sloth, Lust, Gluttony and Greed]. Sin here is more psychological than that of the Inferno, being based on motives, rather than actions.

One notable element is that Dante shows the medieval knowledge of a spherical Earth. Dante talks of the stars visible in the south, the altered position of the sun, and the idea of time-zones; with sunset at Jerusalem, midnight on the Ganges, and sunrise in Purgatory.

In Paradiso Dante works through the Four Cardinal Virtues [Prudence, Fortitude, Justice and Temperance] and the three Theological Virtues [Faith, Hope and Love]. The vision of heaven found is Dante's personal vision. The Divine Comedy finishes with Dante seeing the Triune God. In a flash of understanding that he cannot express, Dante finally understands the mystery of Christ's divinity and humanity, and his soul becomes aligned with God's love: L'amour che move il sole e l'altre stelle.

Praise to the Lord, the Almighty,

Lobe den Herren: Neander 1680   trans. C Winkworth   1863   (5) 4 verses
Zahn 1912c Traditional German   1665   14.14.4.7.8
Nehemiah 9:6 "Thou hast made heaven, the earth, the sea and all that is within them…"

Apparently, this translation is an example of translators' reshaping a text to their own era's tastes. Although Lionel Adey, the hymnologist, praises other translations by Catherine Winkworth, and describes this one as a 'classic'; but he critiques her changes to the sense of Neander's text as an example of 'muscular Christianity' tinged with Philistinism'. The critic notes the discarding the German Renaissance flavour of psaltery and harp to introduce a mention of 'health' more typical of 19th-century Christianity. Inconveniently, there are no details of which bits are viewed as so discrepant.

The 5-verse text text and tune both are found together in Joachim Neander's German-language hymn 'Lobe den Herren, den mächtigen König der Ehren', published in 1680. John Julian in his 1892 *Dictionary of Hymnology* calls the German original 'a magnificent hymn of praise to God, perhaps the finest creation of its author, and of the first rank in its class'.

The melody traces back to 1665; there are many versions and it may be a folk tune. It is catalogued as Zahn 1912c and with variants. After 1665, when the tune was used for ('Hast thou, beloved, completely concealed thy face?'); that poem was adapted as a hymn, beginning 'Hast du denn, Jesu…'. The tune was in Crüger's *Praxis Pietatis Melica* of 1668, and then used by Neander for his hymn in 1680 book. The common setting today is by W S Bennett and O Goldschmidt from 1863.

The original German in 1680 has five stanzas. Catherine Winkworth's translation, in the same metre of the original, was first published in *The Chorale Book for England* (1863). It had only four stanzas, her verse 2 combining parts of Neander's verses 2 and 3.

Bach adapted the traditional setting for his cantata *Lobe den Herren* BWV 137 in 1725. Again in 1729 he used it for *Herr Gott, Herr Gott, Beherrscher aller Dinge*, BWV 120a. Then for a third time, as the last of his *Schübler Chorales* for solo organ, BWV 650. But Bach and his equivalents had to produce work every week for their church and court employers. Reproduction was merely by printed copies when these eventually arrived. The speed of every choir and instrumentalist must have been astonishing especially for genuinely new works. Pieces that were like another would have been significantly easier to learn.

It was the favorite hymn of King Frederick William III of Prussia who first heard it in 1800. John Julian's *Dictionary of Hymnology* lists more than ten English translations of 'Lobe den Herren' printed in various 19th-century hymnals. The one most commonly appearing nowadays is by Catherine Winkworth, with various editorial alterations then and recently.

The text has proved seductive to alterers and those who like to provide their own additions. Remarkably English Hymnals added three extra stanzas, 'Praise to the Lord, who, when tempests their warfare are raging', 'Praise to the Lord, who when sickness with terror uniting', and 'Praise to the Lord, who when darkness of sin is abounding'. Two Lutheran additions can be 'Praise thou the Lord, who with marvelous wisdom hath made thee!' from 1913, or 'Praise thou the Lord, who hath fearfully, wondrously made thee', by Jeremiah H. Good from the *Evangelical Lutheran Hymnal* (1880).

Despite such efforts, the success of the hymn, which in some form is found in books of every denomination throughout the world, must be owing in part to the tune.

   The German verses   The Catherine Winkworth translation

1 Lobe den Herren, den mächtigen König der Ehren,
   meine geliebete Seele, das ist mein Begehren.
   Kommet zuhauf,   ... Psalter und Harfe, wacht auf,
   lasset den Liesegang hören!
        1   Praise to the Lord, the Almighty, the King of creation;
                 O my soul, praise him, for he is thy health and salvation:
                 Come ye who hear,   ... Brothers and sisters draw near,
                 Praise him in glad adoration.

2 Lobe den Herren, der alles so herrlich regieret,
   der dich auf Adelers Fittichen sicher geführet,
   der dich erhält,   ... wie es dir selber gefällt;
   hast du nicht dieses verspüret?
        2   Praise to the Lord, who o'er all things so wondrously reigneth,
                 Shelters thee under his wings, yea, so gently sustaineth:
                 Hast thou not seen   ... All that is needful hath been
                 Granted in what he ordaineth?

3 Lobe den Herren, der künstlich und fein dich bereitet,
   der dir Gesundheit verliehen, dich freundlich geleitet.
   In wieviel Not   ... hat nicht der gnädige Gott
   über dir Flügel gebreitet!
        3   Praise to the Lord, who doth prosper thy work, and defend thee;
                 Surely his goodness and mercy here daily attend thee;
                 Ponder anew   ... All the Almighty can do,
                 He who with love doth befriend thee.

4 Lobe den Herren, der deinen Stand sichtbar gesegnet,
   der aus dem Himmel mit Strömen der Liebe geregnet.
   Denke daran,   ... was der Allmächtige kann,
   der dir mit Liebe begegnet.
        4   Praise to the Lord! Oh let all that is in me adore Him!
                 All that hath life and breath, come now with praises before Him!
                 Let the Amen   ... Sound from His people again,
                 Gladly for aye we adore Him!

5 Lobe den Herren, was in mir ist, lobe den Namen.
   Alles, was Odem hat, lobe mit Abrahams Samen.
   Er ist dein Licht,   ... Seele, vergiss es ja nicht.
   Lobende, schließe mit Amen!

As noted Winkworth produced only 4 verses.

Ride on! ride on in majesty

	Henry Hart Milman	1791-1868	1820	5 verses
WINCHESTER NEW	W H Havergal	1793-1870	1864	8.8.8.8

Matthew 21:9 'And the multitudes that went before … saying Hosanna' (Palm Sunday)

Stanley L Osbourne describes this hymn as 'Objective, robust, confident, and stirring, it possesses that peculiar combination of tragedy and victory which draws the singer into the very centre of the drama. It is this which gives the hymn its power and its challenge'. The hymn proved popular: in 1907, John Julian§, in his *Dictionary of Hymnology*, stated it was the most popular Palm Sunday hymn in the English language at that time.

The hymn, while short, is used as a Processional on Palm Sunday to celebrate Jesus' triumphal entry into Jerusalem. The relevant verses are at the beginning of Matthew 21.

A hymn can be worded and this can be seen as 'poor'; in particular, the third line of the first verse 'Thine humble beast pursues his road' has been disliked by some hymn book editors. Perhaps they dislike the word humble appearing next to the ass or in the vicinity of Jesus. Whatever their reasoning, always unpublished, this phrase has often been replaced. Examples include: in 1852 'O Saviour meek, pursue Thy road'; 1855 'With joyous throngs pursue Thy road' and others. Both attempts received little popular attention. Remarkably, this led to some hymn books omitting the first verse as a concession to Victorian woke-ness.

While Milman wrote 'Ride on, ride on in majesty!' in 1820, it was not published in a hymn book until 1827 when it was published in Bishop Heber's *'Hymns Written and Adapted to the Weekly Church Service of the Year'* apparently after Milman had met Heber.

The *First Edition of A&M* (1861) changed Milman's original text 'Thine humble beast pursues his road' (stanza 1 line 3) to 'O Saviour meek, pursue thy road'. The picturesque 'wingèd squadrons' (stanza 3 line 2) was also changed to 'angel armies'. This has been followed by others, although A&M itself restored the original in 1904.

The hymn has its place in hymnals throughout the world as one of the greatest modern hymns for Palm Sunday. As already noted, there have been many minor adjustments to the text, and the hymn has not escaped the 'you' treatment in some modern books.

As regards the setting, the most common are ST DROSTANE by J B Dykes§ and WINCHESTER NEW by William Henry Havergal. The latter actually derives from a German tune traced back to *Musikalisches Handbuch der geistlichen Melodien* (Hamburg, 1690). The Wesleys used the melody several times. This was reworked into a long-metre setting by Havergal in an 1864 publication, *Old Church Psalmody*. Named after the town of Winchester, it has 'new' affixed to distinguish it from Winchester Old. The 'old' version is most commonly sung to the Christmas hymn 'While shepherds watched their flocks by night'.

In the US, CANONBURY is used adapted from Robert Schumann's Nachtstücke 4. There are, of course, a number of others that suit not just the metre but the style.

It was the first hymn in Milman's own *Selection of Psalms and Hymns* (1837), and it has remained the hymn by which he is chiefly remembered. The original text is as follows :

1. Ride on! ride on in majesty!
   Hark, all the tribes hosanna cry;
   Thine humble beast pursues his road
   With palms and scattered garments strowed.

2. Ride on! ride on in majesty!
   In lowly pomp ride on to die:
   O Christ, thy triumphs now begin
   O'er captive death and conquered sin.

3. Ride on! ride on in majesty!
   The wingèd squadrons of the sky
   Look down with sad and wondering eyes
   To see the approaching sacrifice.

4. Ride on! ride on in majesty!
   Thy last and fiercest strife is nigh;
   The Father, on his sapphire throne,
   Expects his own anointed Son.

5. Ride on! ride on in majesty!
   In lowly pomp ride on to die;
   Bow thy meek head to mortal pain,
   Then take, O God, thy power, and reign.

The author, Henry Milman was one of the great 19th-century churchmen and he was a man of immense industry and energy. Ordained in 1816, he was first appointed to St Mary's, Reading, in 1818, during his incumbency he also wrote widely as a dramatist (his verse drama, Fazio, 1815, produced at Covent Garden, 1818, was a great success), a poet (*The Fall of Jerusalem*, 1820, *The Martyr of Antioch*, 1822, *Belshazzar*, 1822) and a notable historian. His *History of the Jews* (1830) was controversial, because it applied modern methods of historical enquiry to the Bible.

Later he became a Canon of Westminster and rector of St Margaret's, Westminster, in 1835, and Dean of St Paul's in 1849. A major innovation of his time as Dean was the introduction of evening services under the dome in 1858. It was followed by *The History of Christianity from the Birth of Christ to the Abolition of Paganism in the Roman Empire* (1840). Several years were next given to the production of his last great work, *The History of Latin Christianity, including that of the Popes to the Pontificate of Nicholas V,* which was published, three volumes in 1854, and three volumes in 1856.

After these years of literary labour and incessant activity, he was overtaken with paralysis and died in 1868, at Sunningfield, near Ascot, aged 78. As a preacher he was less known than as a writer. His sermons were elegant and classical, but passionless—well read, but strangely destitute of the energy.

Rock of Ages, cleft for me

	Augustus Toplady	1740-1778	1775	4,3 verses
REDHEAD 76	Richard Redhead	1820-1901	1853	
TOPLADY	Thomas Hastings	1784-1872	1832	7.7.7.7.7.7

1 Corinthians 10:4 "That rock was Christ."

It is a puzzle to some as to why and how this particular text and tune should be so hugely popular. The Hymnary survey has it as one of the very very few in more than 2,000 hymnals. There are stories about this hymn, its origin and always more to learn about the theological pressures between Toplady and Charles Wesley in their passion for truth and certainty.

As regards the text and tune themselves – the core of each of these hymn-pieces – Rev Toplady delivered 4 different versions between October 1775 and July 1776. Taking their example from him and their own whims, the text is and has been and will be altered with great enthusiasm creating a large number of different versions in a multitude of churches. Thus, not too surprisingly, an early line 'When my eye-strings break in death' was changed to 'When my eyes shall close in death'. The most popular text is still very close to the original.

122 years after publication, an unevidenced story arrived about its arrival. Sir H W Wills asserted that Toplady was triggered by an incident at Burrington Combe near his curacy at Blagdon. He was caught in a storm and sheltered in a gap in the rocks. The event inspired the first line and then the whole text. That fissure is now identified, labelled and has its own nearby teashop. Most hymnologists find this near-fable unbelievable.

The first full text came in *The Gospel Magazine* (March 1776), where Toplady was the editor. It was there titled 'A living and dying PRAYER for the HOLIEST BELIEVER in the world'.

Much more interesting as an insight into Toplady's views is the essay which preceded. This essay was remarkable as an example of Toplady's evangelical mode: *'A remarkable Calculation: Introduced here, for the sake of the spiritual Improvement subjoined. Questions and Answers, relative to the National Debt'.* Noting that the National Debt was so large that it would never be paid off, Toplady applied this idea to the Christian state. Because human beings live in a fallen world, each one sins every day, every hour, every minute, and every second, resulted in what Toplady called 'our dreadful account'. At a rate of one per second he calculated :- at ten years old each of us is chargeable with 315 millions and 360 thousand sins. By three-score-and -ten a mere 2.2 billion. Toplady gives no guide as to how he makes this rule nor how such sins can be lessened, amended, avoided or repented.

By self-question and answer he asks about Mankind's debt *Answ. The arithmetic of angels would be unable to ascertain the full amount.* Fortunately, he adds *'Christ's redemption will not only counter-balance, but infinitely over-balance, ALL the sins of the WHOLE believing world.'* Then he quoted Isaac Watts – *'Believing Sinners free are set, For Christ hath PAID their dreadful debt.'*

Other than Rock of Ages, Toplady is less famous. Other than the bitter pamphlet battle between Toplady and John Wesley over the suitability and correctness of Calvinist/Reformed theology (Toplady) versus Arminian theology there is some suggestion that his own text betrays uncertainty. His own words 'be of sin the double cure, save from wrath and make me pure' are much closer to a Methodist teaching. John Wesley certainly preached the 'double cure'; by which the atonement of Jesus saves the sinner yet the Holy Ghost delivers the cleansing from sin. Toplady's later text was 'Be of sin the double cure, Save me from its guilt and power'. His reason for altering the rhyme to a poor one must have been significant.

A fifth verse is added in one or two hymnals; some omit verse 2 or verse 3,

1. Rock of Ages, cleft for me.
   Let me hide myself in thee!
   Let the water and the blood,
   From thy wounded side which flow'd,
   Be of sin the double cure;
   Cleanse me from its guilt and power.

2. Not the labour of my hands
   Can fulfil thy law's demands:
   Could my zeal no respite know,
   Could my tears for ever flow,
   All for sin could not atone:
   Thou must save, and thou alone.

3. Nothing in my hand I bring,
   Simply to thy cross I cling;
   Naked, come to thee for dress;
   Helpless, look to thee for grace;
   Foul, I to the fountain fly,
   Wash me, Saviour, or I die!

4. While I draw this fleeting breath,
   When mine eye-strings break in death,
   When I soar to tracts unknown,
   See thee on thy judgment throne,-
   Rock of Ages, cleft for me!
   Let me hide myself in thee!

A verse occasionally added is :

Should my tears for ever flow,   ... Should my zeal no languor know,
This for sin could not atone;   ... Thou must save, and Thou alone;
In my hand no price I bring,   ... Simply to Thy cross I cling.

Richard Redhead became organist at All Saints Church, London aged 19. He and his rector, Rev Oakely, were strongly committed to the Oxford Movement; together they produced the first Anglican plainsong psalter, *Laudes Diurnae* (1843).

Hastings was a prolific composer, writing some 1,000 hymn tunes over his career, and the "simple, easy, and solemn" style of his music remains a major influence on the hymns of the Protestant churches to this day. Hastings' 1822 *Dissertation on Musical Taste*, the first full musical treatise by an American author, was a notable voice in the shift in American music toward the models of German music rather than British; as 'one of the first spokespersons for the cultivated tradition of American music', he emphasized the science and philosophical mission of music above the looser and more folk-based music of his predecessors.

Soldiers of Christ, arise

	Charles Wesley§	1707-1788	1747	16,12,3 verses
ST ETHELWALD	W H Monk§	1823-1889	1861	6.6.8.6
DIADEMATA §	G J Elvey	1816-1893		

Ephesians 6:11 "Put on the whole armour of God."

Wesley initially wrote this poem titled 'The Whole Armour of God' Ephesians VI' in 1747 and it was used to defend himself, colleagues and followers against the weight of criticism of Methodism in the United Kingdom. During their evangelical careers, both Charles Wesley and his brother John received physical abuse because of their work. This hymn was one response. It became known as 'The Christian's bugle blast' because of the military references and the apparent call to arms when it was set to music.

The whole poem is written in what G.H. Findlay called Charles Wesley's 'fighting metre… the hammer-headed iambic six or eight', beginning and ending on an accented syllable. Similarly Percy Dearmer noted 'the mastered simplicity' of this hymn: 'its faultless technique, its sagacity in the use of imperfect rhymes'.

The hymn was published as 'Soldiers of Christ, Arise' in 1749 in *Hymns and Sacred Poems* with 16 verses of 8 lines. By 1780, it was published as a hymn in John Wesley's *A Collection of Hymns for the Use of the People Called Methodists* with 12 verses. Since 1847, the hymn is usually only performed hugely truncated with 3 verses.

The poem began as sixteen 8-line verses, John Wesley used 12 in his 1780 collection. He made them into three separate hymns: 'Soldiers of Christ. Arise] using verses 1-4; 'But above all, lay hold' verses 7,8,11,12; and finally 'In fellowship alone' 13-16. Later another was made 'Pray without ceasing, pray'.

Hymns A&M 1861 chopped 'Soldiers of Christ; into a much reduced set of 5 4-line verses with an added doxology – all to the tune ST ETHELWALD by their tame composer W H Monk. This means that the best known version of a 128-line poem is just 20 lines long.

Elsewhere, 3 of the original verses are sung to Edward W Naylor's FROM STRENGTH TO STRENGTH.

The hymn is based on a detailed reading of Ephesians 6:10-18, with references to the whole armour ('panoply', verse 2), the girdle of truth and the breastplate of righteousness (verse 5), the feet shod with the gospel (stanza 6), the shield of faith (stanza 7), the helmet of salvation (stanza 9), and the sword of the spirit (stanza 10).

A recent author suggests that the opening line is possibly a reminiscence of the words of Pope Innocent III at the Albigensian crusade of 1208, 'Up, soldiers of Christ!'. But the metaphor of the Christian soldier is so common, from Ephesians 6 (and 2 Timothy 2:3) that the hymn needs no specific occasion as a starting point.

There are some fourteen imperfect rhymes in the sixteen stanzas, yet the whole effect is unmarred. Strength is added by repetition: 'believe' four times in stanza 8, and 'pray' six times (plus 'prayer') in stanza 12. The hymn also has its full share of Charles Wesley's fine polysyllables: 'indissolubly'; 'panoply' (from the Greek of Ephesians 6); 'unutterable' (from Romans 8: 26, but also from Milton). It is stirring work.

In the hymn, the words 'adamant and gold' are used. This is speculated to be Wesley making reference to John Milton's poem, Paradise Lost where it says 'Satan, with vast and haughty strides advanced, Came towering, armed in adamant and gold'. It has been suggested that Wesley intended for the hymn to be for Christians to use Satan's ways against him.

Wesley himself wrote the first setting for this text; and it too was titled 'Soldiers of Christ'. It is not the most common setting now. Its place has been taken by DIADEMATA written by George Job Elvey. William P Merrill wrote another, and there are more.

It is one of only a few Methodist hymns that overtly referred to battles or the notion of Christians as soldiers. It is almost astonishing to be told that in the United Methodist Church's current hymnal there is one, and only one, hymn therein which was originally in John Wesley's *A Collection of Hymns for the Use of the People Called Methodists* – and it is this hymn suggesting that Christ's soldiers should arise, stand against their foes.

With any great text, there are changes, amendments and worse. For example the omission of the splendid lines:

> Stand then against your Foes,　In close and firm Array,
> Legions of wily Fiends oppose　Throughout the Evil Day;

This is the 5-verse version of the early text :-

1　　Soldiers of Christ, arise,
　　And put your armor on,
　　Strong in the strength which God supplies,
　　Through His eternal Son;
　　Strong in the Lord of Hosts,
　　And in His mighty pow'r,
　　Who in the strength of Jesus trusts
　　Is more than conqueror.

With the other verses, reset to a 4-line format, as is sometimes the case.

2　　Stand then in His great might,　With all His strength endued;
　　And take, to arm you for the fight,　The panoply of God,
　　That, having all things done,　And all your conflicts past,
　　Ye may o'ercome through Christ alone,　And stand complete at last.

3　　Leave no unguarded place,　No weakness of the soul,
　　Take every virtue, every grace,　And fortify the whole.
　　To keep your armor bright　Attend with constant care,
　　Still walking in your Captain's sight　And watching unto prayer.

4　　Pray, without ceasing pray,　Your Captain gives the word;
　　His summons cheerfully obey,　And call upon the Lord:
　　To God your every want　In instant prayer display;
　　Pray always; pray, and never faint;　Pray, without ceasing pray.

5　　From strength to strength go on;　Wrestle, and fight, and pray;
　　Tread all the powers of darkness down,　And win the well-fought day:
　　Still let the Spirit cry　In all His soldiers, "Come!"
　　Till Christ the Lord descend from high,　And take the conquerors home.

The Church's one Foundation

	Samuel John Stone	1839-1900	c1866	7,5,8 verses
AURELIA	Samuel S Wesley	1810-1876		7.6.7.6 D

Coloss. 1:18   "He is the head of the body, the Church…"

Not many hymns have been written as a direct result of an argument between churchmen. This one was written in the 1860s by Samuel John Stone, unusually, as a direct response to the schism within the Church of South Africa caused by J W Colenso, first Bishop of Natal. Colenso had published *The Pentateuch and the Book of Joshua Critically Examined* (1862), which had expressed doubts about traditional biblical authority. When the bishop was deposed by Bishop Gray of Cape Town for his teachings, he appealed to the higher ecclesiastical authorities in England.

It was then that Samuel Stone became involved in the debate. The author composed a set of hymns titled '*Lyra Fidelium; Twelve Hymns on the Twelve Articles of the Apostles' Creed (1866)* - in tribute to the orthodoxy and steadfastness of Bishop Gray. Also headed 'He is the Head of the Body, the Church' – the hymn text 'The Church's One Foundation' is included there in respect of the ninth article, '*The holy Catholic Church; The Communion of Saints*'.

The controversy is alluded to in the hymn's fourth verse: 'Though with a scornful wonder men see her sore oppressed, by schisms rent asunder, by heresies distressed'. The original text is even more blunt.

The Church shall never perish!	… Her dear Lord, to defend,
To guide, sustain, and cherish,	… Is with her to the end;
Though there be those who hate her,	… And false souls in her pale,
Against or foe or traitor	… She ever shall prevail.

The words also served as inspiration for Rudyard Kipling's 1896 poem, Hymn Before Action, during his time in Africa. Another hymn inspired by this controversy was H W Baker's 'Lord, thy word abideth'.

The strength of the hymn lies in the simplicity and directness of its message, the vividness of its metaphor, and the deliberate and distinct echoes of words and phrases from scripture. In Lyra Fidelium there are no less than four biblical quotations annotated to each stanza; in one, seven. It was hailed in Stone's own time as 'the battle-song of the Church'.

The hymn came into its own at the time of the Lambeth Conference in 1888, when it was sung at all the major services. It is recorded that at St Paul's Cathedral its effect was so powerful that the singers were physically overwhelmed: 'it made them feel weak at the knees, their legs trembled, and they really felt as though they were going to collapse' (quoted in Wesley Milgate, *Songs of the People of God*, 1982). It has never lost its wide appeal, and has rarely been absent from major hymnbooks.

Despite appearances, it is not linked to 'Christ is the sure foundation'.

The popularity of the hymn is due in part to the fusion of the words with S S Wesley's magnificent and stately tune, AURELIA, originally written for 'Jerusalem the golden' but set to this hymn in the *H A&M Second Edition* 1875.

The hymn originally had seven stanzas, of which the first runs:

> *The church's one foundation ... is Jesus Christ, her Lord;*
> *she is his new creation ... by water and the Word:*
> *from heav'n he came and sought her ... to be his holy bride;*
> *with his own blood he bought her, ... and for her life he died.*

When the hymn came to be added to *Hymns Ancient and Modern* it was rewritten to include only five stanzas. In 1885, three more stanzas were added to the original seven for use as an ecclesiastical processional hymn in Salisbury Cathedral; this longer version was used again during the 1888 Lambeth Conference.

The original version of Stone's hymn was greatly improved by combining the first four lines of the two last stanzas to form a new final stanza, thus removing some sentimental words and phrases. In the penultimate stanza, after the second line 'With those whose rest is won',

there was: With all her sons and daughters who, by the Master's Hand
            Led through the deathly waters, repose in Eden-land.

and the final stanza describes the 'happy ones and holy' who 'On high may dwell with Thee',

followed by: There, past the border mountains, where in sweet vales the Bride
              With Thee by living fountains for ever shall abide!

A 4 or 5 verse example of an early version is as follows :

1   The Church's one foundation is Jesus Christ her Lord;
    she is his new creation, by water and the word:
    from heaven he came and sought her to be his holy bride;
    with his own blood he bought her, and for her life he died.

2   Elect from every nation, yet one o'er all the earth,
    her charter of salvation: one Lord, one faith, one birth;
    one holy name she blesses, partakes one holy food,
    and to one hope she presses with every grace endued.

(often omitted)   Though with a scornful wonder this world sees her oppressed,
    by schisms rent asunder, by heresies distressed,
    yet saints their watch are keeping; their cry goes up: "How long?"
    and soon the night of weeping shall be the morn of song.

3   'Mid toil and tribulation, and tumult of her war,
    she waits the consummation of peace forevermore,
    till with the vision glorious her longing eyes are blest,
    and the great Church victorious shall be the Church at rest.

4   Yet she on earth hath union with God, the Three in One,
    and mystic sweet communion with those whose rest is won:
    O happy ones and holy! Lord, give us grace that we,
    like them, the meek and lowly, on high may dwell with thee.

The day Thou gavest, Lord, is ended

	John Ellerton	1826-1893	1870	5,(4) verses
ST CLEMENT	Clement Scholefield	1839-1904	1874	9.8.9.8

Psalm 113:3   "… from the rising of the sun to the going down of the same."

It is significant how tastes have changed. Writing in 1896, Henry Housman, Ellerton's biographer, gives it sparse mention compared with other hymns now totally forgotten. 'The day thou gavest' is now thought of as one of the great hymns of the church, regularly appearing in lists of most popular hymns. Underlying the words is the grand conception of the world-wide church, expanding 'till all thy creatures own thy sway', as opposed to 'earth's proud empires' which will disappear. In the middle three stanzas it presents a vision of the globe, spinning through space, with the praise of God arising from country after country, wherever darkness turns into light.

Rev John Ellerton (1826–1893) wrote it in 1870 for inclusion in *A Liturgy for Missionary Meetings*. When written, the theme focussed on the worldwide fellowship of the church and its continual offering of prayer and praise to God. While written as a missionary song, the text taken literally is now used at Evensong, at funerals and at endings generally. The hymn has an enduring popularity, coming in third place in a *BBC Songs of Praise* poll of favourite hymns in 2005. Surprisingly, two different translations are included in German official hymnals.

Ellerton wrote or translated eighty-six or more hymns of which this is now by far the best-known. He was co-editor with William Walsham How and others of the Society for Promoting Christian Knowledge (SPCK) publication *Church Hymns*, 1871.

John Julian writes, in the wonderful language of the late Victorian, '…of his translations, 'Sing Alleluia forth in duteous praise', and 'Welcome, happy morning, age to age shall say', are the most successful and popular. The subjects of his hymns, and the circumstances under which they were written, had much to do with the concentration of thought and terseness of expression by which they are characterized.

'The words which he uses are usually short and simple; the thought is clear and well stated; the rhythm is good and stately. Ordinary facts in sacred history and in daily life are lifted above the commonplace rhymes with which they are usually associated, thereby rendering the hymns bearable to the cultured, and instructive to the devout'.

Although the words have been sung to S S Wesley' RADFORD and to the tune LES COMMANDEMENTS DE DIEU by Loys Bourgeois, much of its popularity may be owed to the marriage of the words to ST CLEMENT which is a popular British hymn tune used for several hymns. The tune was written specially for it by Ellerton's younger contemporary Rev Clement Scholefield (1839–1904) and it first appeared in Sir Arthur Sullivan's *Church Hymns with Tunes* (1874).

However, in 2000 the Rev. Ian Bradley of St Andrews University and author of *The Daily Telegraph Book of Hymns* identified a strong connection between Sullivan and Scholefield and then looked at the quality of the music. His starting-point was the fact that this tune stands head and shoulders above the quality of Scholefield's other work. None of the 41 other hymn-tunes penned by this self-taught musician show anything like the craftsmanship, originality or melodic sweep of St Clement. He concluded 'Sullivan almost certainly had a larger hand in St

Clement than has been or can ever definitely be, credited to him.'   The calculation was made easier by Professor Bradley being at expert both at hymns and at Gilbert & Sullivan.

Following on – it has been suggested that the name of the tune may have been a joke on the composer's first name. Without further detail the reasoning must be Gilbertian.

A version of the text is as follows with the original 'thou' etc converted to 'you'.

1   The day you gave us, God, is ended;
the darkness falls at your request.
To you our morning hymns ascended;
your praise shall sanctify our rest.

2   We thank you that your church, unsleeping
while earth rolls onward into light,
through all the world its watch is keeping,
and never rests by day or night.

3   As o'er each continent and island
each dawn leads on another day,
the voice of prayer is never silent,
nor do the praises die away.

4   The sun that bids us rest is waking
Our brethren 'neath the western sky,
And hour by hour fresh lips are making
Your wondrous doings heard on high.

5   So be it, Lord, your throne shall never,
like earth's proud empires, pass away.
Your reign endures and grows forever,
until there dawns your glorious day.

John Ellerton has a particular significance to this volume. Again, the best source is John Julian : 'Interestingly, Mr Ellerton is best known as a hymnologist writing for the general audience. This is especially evident in his *Notes and Illustrations of Church Hymns, their authors and translators,* published in 1881'.

'The notes on the hymns which are special to the collection, and many of which were contributed thereto, are full, accurate, and of special value. Those on the older hymns are too general for accuracy. They are written in a popular form, which necessarily precludes what a hymnological expert would wish for as extended research, fulness, and exactness of detail. What he did produce was well accepted by the general public as delightful and very useful'.

The King of love my Shepherd is

| | Sir Henry W Baker§ | 1821-1877 | 1868 | 6 verses |
| DOMINUS REGIT ME | J B Dykes§ | 1823-1876 | 1868 | 8.7.8.7 |

Psalm 23:1   "The Lord is my shepherd."

Some argue that it was bold of Baker to undertake a metrical version of a psalm that was so well known and frequently paraphrased: he had George Herbert, Addison and Isaac Watts, and many metrical psalters, as predecessors. There are certainly many other versions.

His particular contribution was to give an Anglican slant to Psalm 23, interpreting it as a psalm of love and care, but stressing these qualities as evidenced in the Eucharist. The spread table of stanza 5 becomes the altar on which the elements are displayed, and the delight comes as the believer takes the 'pure chalice'; the unction, or anointing (from 1 John 2: 27), while bestowing grace in a spiritual sense, also has suggestions of a rite. This stanza spreads its meaning through the whole hymn, allowing the words of Psalm 23 to acquire an extra significance: so that the last stanza suggests that the length of days of a person's life can be spent, figuratively, 'within thy house for ever', in the service and under the influence of the church, and then later in heaven.

This is an 1868 hymn with lyrics written by Henry W Baker, and based on the Welsh version of Psalm 23 and the work of Edmund Prys. It was part of the *Appendix to Ancient and Modern* in 1868.

It is one of several hymns based around Psalm 23. Another very well-known example is 'The Lord's my shepherd, I'll not want'. This is commonly attributed to the English Puritan Francis Rous and sung to the tune Crimond by David Grant. It first appeared in the *Scots Metrical Psalter* in 1650. Its modern popularity derives greatly from being an early and regular broadcast on the wireless and also for being used at the marriage of Queen Elizabeth.

A third hugely well-known version is George Herbert's which is the similar only at the first line.   "The God of love my Shepherd is,   ... And He that doth me feed:
    While He is mine and I am His,   ... What can I want or need

Some prefer this for its 'restrained simplicity'; but as has been mentioned, the preference for any hymn is subjective and often personal.   One past the first line – there is no similarity. 'The King' has a metre of 8.7.8.7   while 'The Lord' has 8.6.8.6.

There are yet many others pieces linked to Psalm 23, over 400 by one count. Joseph Addison gave us 'The Lord my pasture shall prepare' in 1712; Isaac Watts wrote 'My shepherd will supply my need'; 'My shepherd is the living Lord, as well as 'The Lord my shepherd is' in 1719; James Montgomery 'The Lord is my shepherd' in 1822.   Joseph Gelineau recently wrote 'My shepherd is the Lord' and the list will grow.

Baker's words are sung to at least five different melodies:
    DOMINUS REGIT ME   arranged by John Bacchus Dykes
    ST COLUMBA,   the traditional Irish tune
    ICH DANK' DIR SCHON   Michael Praetorius
    and   REMSEN   Welsh traditional.

Vaughan Williams, while definitely no great admirer of Victorian tunes, regretted that he had been refused permission to use Dykes' in the *English Hymnal* - 'such a beautiful tune'. So he used the traditional Irish tune, ST COLUMBA; this is a frequent alternative tune.

J R Watson (*The Victorian Hymn*, 1981) considers 'The King of Love' 'one of the finest' of Victorian hymns; while Pollard, a few years before in 1960, considered Baker's version 'too florid, exuberant and elaborate'.

A E Bailey (*The Gospel in Hymns*) says 'Such a fusion of the old and new, metaphor with parable, the physical with the spiritual, the Judaic with the Ecclesiastical, is well nigh a work of genius'. He then gives very comprehensive detail as to the wealth of scriptural inspiration in the hymn (as well as Psalm 23) John 10, 1 – 5; and James, Luke, and so on.– that's a great deal of cross-checking in the bible.

One can reflect back, and conclude that the first stanzas suggest the ransomed soul, sought out in love and rescued from sin (Baker's version of 'he restoreth my soul'). The beautiful use of the 'shepherd' metaphor in stanza 3, as the shepherd carries the lamb gently on his shoulder, is an illustration of the tenderness which J Julian noted in Baker's work

An early version of the text is as follows :

1. The King of love my Shepherd is,
   whose goodness faileth never.
   I nothing lack if I am his,
   and he is mine forever.

2. Where streams of living water flow,
   my ransomed soul he leadeth;
   and where the verdant pastures grow,
   with food celestial feedeth.

3. Perverse and foolish, oft I strayed,
   but yet in love he sought me;
   and on his shoulder gently laid,
   and home, rejoicing, brought me.

4. In death's dark vale I fear no ill,
   with thee, dear Lord, beside me;
   thy rod and staff my comfort still,
   thy cross before to guide me.

5. Thou spreadst a table in my sight;
   thy unction grace bestoweth;
   and oh, what transport of delight
   from thy pure chalice floweth!

6. And so through all the length of days,
   thy goodness faileth never;
   Good Shepherd, may I sing thy praise
   within thy house forever.

This hymn shows the enormous divergence of opinions on hymnography and how very subjective views on suitability and general hymn-icity may be compared to the much less changeable Bible text or Prayer Book.

The Lord's my shepherd

	Francis Rous	c1581-1659	1650	5 verses
CRIMOND	(David Grant) / Jessie Irvine	1836-1887	1871	8.6.8.6 CM

The Psalters produced in Geneva around 1560 by the French and Scottish have been the source of many hymns. In particular they have been used for the writing of metrical or versified Psalms, which have then been edited into hymns. It is a psalm that is greatly loved for its brevity, beauty and its power to comfort, and it is not surprising that this version is now frequently used at funerals. However, its late 20th-century fame is almost entirely owing to the tune CRIMOND, which has only recently become associated with these words

The hymn being based on the words of Psalm 23; it is helpful to find a reasonably current version of the Bible text: *The LORD is my shepherd; I shall not want. He maketh me to lie down in green pastures: he leadeth me beside the still waters.*

The text delivered by Rous in 1638 is quite different *'My Shepherd is the Living Lord And He that doth me feed, How can I then lack anything whereof I stand in need?*

In this particular hymn-ified version the text becomes: *The Lord's my shepherd, I'll not want: he makes me down to lie in pastures green: he leadeth me the quiet waters by.*

Looking and comparing, it is not surprising that one estimate is that only 10% of Rous' original text was retained in the final version. It was after all being reviewed by a committee.

There is a complex Scottish v English divergence in the background to this hymn. The Church of Scotland determined as part of their views on the Protestant Reformation that exclusive psalmody was their rule as a central part of public worship. John Knox introduced the *Book of Common Order* into the Church of Scotland in 1564. This contained metrical versions of all the Psalms, adapted from Calvin's *Geneva Psalter* of 1539. Calvin and Knox were sternly intent that all such Psalms were to be sung to the Genevan setting in unison only.

After some decades, so many amendments, corrections and alterations had been made that a new translation was seen to be advisable. Francis Rous was an English lawyer and politician. It was felt that the poetry in the existing versified Psalms could be better. Rous (1580/1–1659), a long-serving member of the English Parliament (1620–1659) and Provost of Eton College (1644–1659), set about the task. By 1638, his first attempt came out anonymously as *The Booke of Psalmes in English Meeter* (1638). In his preface, he expressed his doubts about the old, and his belief in the undeniable need for change. Phrasing his aims as carefully as possible he 'assayed only to change some pieces of the usual version, even such as seemed to call aloud, and as it were undeniably for a change.'

He delivered a second set in 1641. He had a fellow translator, William Barton – now a rival. A committee of translators was appointed to approve a new translation. The Scottish committee took just 6 years to come to a conclusion. During their deliberations, they hugely altered Rous' text. In 1650, the General Assembly of the Church of Scotland, the church's ruling body, did approve their amended-Rous version for the new *Scots Metrical Psalter*.

Although Rous was the choice in Scotland due to its perceived accuracy in translating source texts, in England, Barton's version found favour with the English Parliament.

Boyd in 1646/8 delivered his version. A colleague, Baillie, said 'Our good friend, Mr. Zachary Boyd, has put himself to a great deal of pains and charges to make a psalter, but I ever warned him his hopes were groundless to get it received in our churches, yet the flatteries of his unadvised neighbours makes him insist in his fruitless design'. But at least his wording was preferred for at least the beginning of Psalm 23.

There is some indication that BELMONT was used from around 1812, but no earlier setting is documented. Implicitly, it was chanted or used with a local tune.

CRIMOND is the most common setting nowadays. There is still uncertainty as to the authorship. David Grant is the name currently attached, but Jessie Irvine was the daughter of the minister at Crimond and claimed that she had merely asked Grant for help in 1871 with the harmonisation. At the time, Grant was working on a hymnal with the precentor at Crimond, Rev Clubb, and others. When it was complete, Grant was listed as the composer and claimed that Jessie's request was for another tune BALLANTINE.

There has been considerable research ongoing on this issue; my view tends to Irvine.

CRIMOND was used for the text by a remarkable choir, the Glasgow Orpheus Choir, under Sir Hugh Roberton, in the early years of broadcasting on what was then called 'the wireless'. It was also chosen for the wedding of Princess Elizabeth in 1947 and for the Silver Wedding of King George VI and Queen Elizabeth in 1948, and became widely known and loved from that time on. The *Scottish Psalter* of 1929 also had settings of WILTSHIRE and MARTYRDOM.

An early version of the text is as follows. A few hymnals do a quasi-repeat of the last two lines of each verse as a refrain.

1	The Lord's my shepherd, I'll not want:	... he makes me down to lie	
	in pastures green: he leadeth me	... the quiet waters by.	
2	My soul he doth restore again,	... and me to walk doth make	
	within the paths of righteousness,	... even for his own name's sake.	
3	Yea, though I walk through death's dark vale,	... yet will I fear none ill;	
	for thou art with me, and thy rod	... and staff me comfort still.	
4	My table thou hast furnished	... in presence of my foes;	
	my head thou dost with oil anoint,	... and my cup overflows.	
5	Goodness and mercy all my life	... shall surely follow me;	
	and in God's house for evermore	... my dwelling-place shall be.	

There is a green hill far away

	C F Alexander	1818-1895	1848	5 verses
HORSLEY	William Horsley	1774-1858	1844	8.6.8.6 CM
Romans 5:8	"While we were yet sinners, Christ died for us."			

'There is a green hill far away' was originally written as a children's hymn but now usually sung for Passiontide. The words are by Cecil Frances Alexander, and the most popular tune by William Horsley. It was first published in her *Hymns for Little Children* (1848) written originally for her godson; and the profound but simple text reflects well as being for children. Despite the apparent simplicity, the text remains well known today due to its 'clear presentation of the redemptive work of Christ'. There is often a smile when the original is sung and people think about 'without' a city wall.

A recently found story is that as a child, the daughter of a stern military officer, she hid her poems. Once discovered, her father made a box with a slit, and each Sunday evening, the box was opened and that week's poems were read aloud. Perhaps this was why some of her best hymns were written early; *Hymns for Children* was published when she was just 25.

The writer's husband, Bishop of Derry, considered it among the best of those written by his wife. Others noted the fine poetic skill and proclaimed that 'she surpassed all other writers of sacred song in meeting a growing demand for children's hymns'. The hymn became popular as part pf the 1868 appendix to *Hymns Ancient and Modern*, paired with the tune HORSLEY. French composer Charles Gounod, who wrote a setting for it in 1871, reportedly considered that it was 'the most perfect hymn in the English language', due in part to its striking simplicity.

The hymn delivers a 'clear summary of the redemptive work of Christ'. It remains popular to this day, appearing in most compilations. Indeed since its first publication, 'it would be hard to find it missing from a major hymn book'.

It is a simple but profound hymn, explaining the doctrine of the Atonement in language that can be easily understood by a child, and ending with a suggestion that comes from a unday-school teacher and is also tender and practical – 'And try his works to do.' The progression of the hymn from its slightly mysterious opening to this ending is a fine example of Alexander's pedagogical method: narrative is followed by explanation and then precept.

The text is in five common-metre verses. Its basis is the words 'Suffered under Pontius Pilate, was crucified, dead, and buried', of the Apostles' Creed, and is a metric paraphrase of the Creed with each article extended to form a complete hymn. It is a 'touching' description of Christ dying for the sins of men and giving his 'redeeming blood' to 'save us all'. It is less clear why *H A&M* chooses the text given above.

For many centuries, the Apostles' Creed has been a vital tool for instruction in Christian doctrine. For just as long, it has been sung, either in chanted form in Latin or versified metrically into other languages. Metrical hymns based on the Creed sometimes encapsulate the entire text in a single hymn, or they are made in an extended form, with separate hymns for each of the twelve articles of the Creed as has been done by Mrs Alexander.

The first stanza refers to Golgotha (Calvary). According to legend, the author often went past a 'green hill' when walking from her home to Derry, and she might have associated this with the distant – both physically and temporally – location of the Crucifixion. 'Without' in the second line is an old-style 'outside' contrary to 'within'. The final line refers to passages such as 1 John 2 and Isaiah 53:6. The second stanza speaks of the mystery of the cross and of atonement through the sacrifice of Christ, based on Isaiah 53:5 and 2 Corinthians 5:21.

The third stanza talks of the forgiveness of sin (Hebrews 9:22 & Ephesians 1:6–7), through which Man is made good (2 Cor 5:17), framing this as the gateway to Heaven, an imagery continued in the fourth stanza.

The final stanza is a fitting emotional conclusion to the text, and the repetition of the word 'dearly' here refers has a double meaning: 'that Christ loved mankind dearly, and in a way that cost Him dearly'. The final line is a clear call to the instruction to 'love the Lord your God with all your heart and with all your soul and with all your might' (Deuteronomy 6:5).

The original opening in 1848 was 'There is a green hill far away,/ Beside a ruined city wall'. Dearmer's commentary on the hymn includes the statement 'The opening line is of course untrue.' He went on to argue that there was no evidence in the Gospels that our Lord was crucified on a hill, and that 'the sun-bitten hills of Judaea are not green.' This and other objections in his commentary have had no effect on the popularity of this hymn. Perhaps Dearmer was too easily able to 'put away childish things' in favour of high-church Socialism.

Many books have altered 'without' (the Scottish 'outwith') in verse 1 line 2 to 'outside a city wall' or even 'beside', which clarifies the picture although it probably lessens the mystery. Dearmer also opined that 'it turns the line into a jingle.'

HORSLEY was first found in 1844 as a four-part setting with figured bass in collection *Twenty Four Psalm Tunes and Eight Chants*. It has remained unchanged ever since. William Horsley was organist at Ely Chapel, Holborn and at the Asylum for Female Orphans. He assisted Calcott, married his daughter and succeeded him for 52 years until he died in 1858. He founded the London Philharmonic Society, and became a close friend of Mendelssohn.

In the United States, the hymn is also frequently sung to the tune GREEN HILL by gospel composer George C Stebbins; and this uses the final stanza as a refrain. Another alternative is MEDITATION by John H Gower; and this is also used for 'There is a fountain filled with blood' by William Cowper.

	There is a green hill far away,	... outside a city wall,
	where the dear Lord was crucified	... who died to save us all.
2	We may not know, we cannot tell,	... what pains he had to bear,
	but we believe it was for us	... he hung and suffered there.
3	He died that we might be forgiven,	... he died to make us good,
	that we might go at last to heaven,	... saved by his precious blood.
4	There was no other good enough	... to pay the price of sin,
	he only could unlock the gate	... of heaven, and let us in.
5	Oh, dearly, dearly has he loved,	... and we must love him too,
	and trust in his redeeming blood,	... and try his works to do.

Thine be the glory, ris'n conquering Son

	E Budry	trans Richard B Hoyle	1875-1939	1923	3 verses
MACCABEUS	G F Handel		1685-1759	1747	10.11.11.11
I Corinthians 15:57	"Thanks be to God, which giveth us the victory:"				

À toi la gloire, O Ressuscité is the original French-Swiss title of this hymn written by the Swiss Protestant minister, Edmond Budry (1854–1932). It was translated into this fine hymn, now most often heard around Easter. The standard English translation is that of 1923 by Richard Birch Hoyle. Edmond Louis Budry was a minister of the Swiss Eglise Evangélique du Canton de Vaud. Reportedly, he was inspired to write it after the death of his first wife in Lausanne, Switzerland.

'Thine Be the Glory' is sung to the hymn tune called MACCABAEUS. This was originally written by the German-British composer G F Handel; initially for his 1747 oratorio Joshua, in which it features as a chorus, 'See, the Conquering Hero Comes!', celebrating the military victories of the Biblical figure Joshua. The chorus is sung there three times, and its final rendition is accompanied by a military side drum. It is thought that Handel may have taken inspiration from a march in *Componienti musicali* written by Georg Muffat.

Handel was confident that the tune would prove popular, and claimed to the music historian John Hawkins that 'You will live to see it a greater favourite with the people than my other fine things'. So confident was Handel of its popularity that he added the chorus to his other oratorio Judas Maccabaeus, written the previous year. 'See, the Conquering Hero Comes!' was thus repurposed to celebrate the military victory of another Old Testament figure, Judas Maccabaeus. Handel's tune bears some historic anti-Jacobite associations.

The German Advent hymn *Tochter Zion, freue dich* uses the same tune. In 1796 Beethoven wrote 12 variations on 'See, the Conquering Hero Comes!' for both piano and cello.

Handel's popular chorus tune was first put to use as a hymn tune in *Harmonia Sacra*, a hymnal compiled in 1754 by Thomas Butts, where it is a setting for Charles Wesley's hymn 'Christ the Lord Is Risen Today'. His use of Handel's militaristic theme aimed to reinforce the view of the resurrected Christ as a warrior victorious over death and the powers of evil.

Budry's text also celebrates the Resurrection of Jesus with references to the appearance of angels in the scene of the empty tomb and his text adds elements of Isaiah 25:8. The hymn makes particular reference to verses of the First Epistle to the Corinthians ch.15. The central theme of the victorious Christ is drawn from v:57: 'But thanks be to God, which giveth us the victory through our Lord Jesus Christ', while in the second verse of the hymn is taken directly from v:55: 'O death, where is thy sting? O grave, where is thy victory?'. The line 'No more we doubt thee' may also be a reference to Doubting Thomas.

Since 1957, in the Netherlands, Calvin Seerveld used 'Thine Be the Glory', with his favourite hymn tune, as a basis to write 'Praised Be the Father' for his wedding. This combination is now a regular wedding hymn.

In Germany the Advent hymn Tochter Zion, freue dich (Zion's Daughter) was written by Friedrich Ranke to the same tune; it may be that Thine Be the Glory was actually based on this hymn; there is some confusion over the exact chronology.

The frequent use of 'thee,thine,' has triggered the modern amount of correction.

An early version of the text is as follows

> 1   Thine is the glory, risen, conqu'ring Son;
> Endless is the victory, Thou o'er death hast won;
> Angels in bright raiment rolled the stone away,
> Kept the folded grave clothes where Thy body lay.
>> Refrain
>> Thine is the glory, risen conqu'ring Son,
>> Endless is the vict'ry, Thou o'er death hast won.
>
> 2   Lo! Jesus meets us, risen from the tomb;
> Lovingly He greets us, scatters fear and gloom;
> Let the church with gladness, hymns of triumph sing;
> For her Lord now liveth, death hath lost its sting. [Refrain]
>
> 3   No more we doubt Thee, glorious Prince of life;
> Life is naught without Thee; aid us in our strife;
> Make us more than conqu'rors, through Thy deathless love:
> Bring us safe through Jordan to Thy home above. [Refrain]

In terms of date, this is a 20th century song and therefore by most assessments 'modern'. But 1923 is nearly a century ago and the style, rhythm and especially tune are sufficient to make it 'proper' for this book.

Below are the first verse's original lyrics in French; a direct translation and the 'official' hymn.

> À toi la gloire, O Ressuscité!
> À toi la victoire pour l'éternité!
> Brillant de lumière, l'ange est descendu,
> Il roule la Pierre du tombeau vaincu.

> Thine [be] the glory, Oh resurrected One!
> Thine [be] the victory, for eternity!
> Shining with light, the angel descended,
> He rolled the stone from the conquered grave.

> Thine be the glory, risen, conqu'ring Son;
> endless is the vict'ry Thou o'er death hast won.
> Angels in bright raiment rolled the stone away,
> kept the folded grave-clothes where Thy body lay.

Isaac Watts 1674-1748

Isaac Watts was an English Congregationalist Christian minister, hymn writer, theologian, and logician. He was a prolific and popular hymn writer and is credited with some 750 hymns, including 'When I Survey the Wondrous Cross§', 'Joy to the World§', and 'Our God, Our Help in Ages Past§'. He has been called the 'Godfather of English Hymnody'.

Watts was one of the first to write hymn words based on personal feelings and testimony. When he used the word 'I' in the opening line of his great hymn, 'When I survey the wondrous cross' he was actually part of a revolution in the way people express their faith in music.

As well as the hymns, Watts wrote some significant books. His joyful hymns expressed wonder, praise and adoration covering the whole range of Christian experience. They prepared the way for the great revival under the Wesleys and Whitfield. In its way, this was a step towards the Anglican reaction and the Victorian Revival.

Watts spoke candidly about the irreligon of his time, regretting 'the decay of vital religion in the hearts and minds of men'. He held religious opinions that were more nondenominational or ecumenical than was common for a nonconformist Congregationalist. Watts had a greater interest in promoting education and scholarship than preaching for any particular sect.

He began rhyming as a child – his poem when not praying with his eyes shut:

A little mouse for want of stairs, ran up a rope to say its prayers.

For this he was punished and responded

O father, father, pity take And I will no more verses make.

He began to learn Latin at four, Greek at nine, French at ten, and Hebrew at thirteen years of age. On another occasion his mother, finding some verses by the seven-year old, doubted his authorship because of their quality. He therefore composed an acrostic on his own name, in the process demonstrating a Calvinism that suited his time and background:

> **I** am a vile polluted lump of earth,
> **S**o I've continued ever since my birth,
> **A**lthough Jehovah grace does daily give me,
> **A**s sure this monster Satan will deceive me,
> **C**ome therefore, Lord, from Satan's claws relieve me.
> **W**ash me in Thy blood, O Christ,
> **A**nd grace divine impart,
> **T**hen search and try the corners of my heart,
> **T**hat I in all things may be fit to do
> **S**ervice to Thee, and sing Thy praises too.

Following his father who was incarcerated twice for his views; and similarly unable to take Oath to the King as a nonconformist, he was thus blocked from university, law, military and many other jobs. He went to the Dissenting Academy at Stoke Newington in 1690 and his life then centred there (now part of Inner East London).

Around 1700, Watts became pastor at Mark Lane Congregational Chapel, where he helped train preachers, despite his poor health. He was very ill in 1702 and asked for respite; he continued as minister of Mark Lane, but in 1703 the congregation appointed Samuel Price as his assistant. There must have been something remarkable about the ailing Watts, because the

Mark Lane congregation not only kept him on as minister but also continued to provide his stipend.

Horae Lyricae (1706), *Hymns and Spiritual Songs* (1707-9), and *Psalms of David Imitated* (1719) contain nearly 500 hymns and versions, of which many remain amongst the cherished treasures of English devotion. It is enough to name but these: 'There is a land of pure delight', 'Jesus shall reign where'er the sun', 'When I survey the wond'rous cross', and 'O God, our help in ages past'. These are remarkable collections, rich with the fruit of much study in both classical and modern literature, and full of exuberance and confidence. The preface to the 1709 work stated firmly 'The whole Book is confin'd to three Sorts of Metre'—i.e., Common, Long, and Short Metres, these being the format for all the Psalm collections of the previous 60 years.

Watts took work as a private tutor and lived with the nonconformist Hartopp family at Fleetwood House in Stoke Newington. Through them, he became acquainted with their immediate neighbours Sir Thomas Abney and Lady Mary. His health was throughout infirm; and in 1712 he was prostrated by illness so violent that he never fully recovered. A visit which he paid to Sir Thomas Abney at Theobalds 'for a change of air resulted in his domestication in the establishment till his death', thirty-six years afterwards, on November 25th, 1748. After Sir Thomas died in 1722, his widow Lady Mary and Elizabeth her unmarried daughter moved to Abney House from Hertfordshire, and Watts moved with them.

'Divine Songs *Attempted in Easy Language for the Use of Children'* was written by Watts in 1715 (also known as *Divine and Moral Songs for Children* and other similar titles) is a collection of didactic, moral poetry for children. The inclusion of the Ten Commandments in ten lines is particularly interesting – even if now no versions are sung.

Though Watts' hymns are now better known, *Divine Songs* was ubiquitous for nearly two hundred years and some 1,000 editions as a standard child's textbook. These include 'Against Idleness' or 'How doth the little busy bee'; and also 'Tis the voice of the sluggard'. Watts makes it clear by showing the metre, that these are to be sung not merely recited.

. Both meant to teach children the importance of hard work, and were extremely well known in the nineteenth century. Walter de la Mare wrote that 'a childhood without the busy bee and the sluggard would resemble a hymnal without 'O God, our help in ages past'. Lewis Carroll wrote parodies of both – 'How doth the Little Crocodile' and 'Tis the Voice of the Lobster'.

In 1724, Watts published a textbook on logic; its full title was, *Logick, or The Right Use of Reason in the Enquiry After Truth With a Variety of Rules to Guard Against Error in the Affairs of Religion and Human Life, as well as in the Sciences.*
**See Digression on Logic*

Though hardly over 5 feet high, and feeble physically, he was counted among the best preachers of his time, and his sermons by no means belie his reputation. His theology was marked by a large charity and catholic spirit then uncommon amongst Dissenters. His theological works were numerous, but are now quite forgotten.

Like all young men Watts pined for feminine company, but the ladies tended to judge him on his looks rather than his character. On one occasion, hopefully somewhat apocryphal, Watts plucked up the courage to propose to a beloved. In refusing his matrimonial proposal, she responded, 'I like the jewel but not the setting'. Remaining unmarried, books were Watt's chosen companions in his many times of illness, and he maintained a wide correspondence.

It is, however, as a hymn writer that Isaac Watts is at his finest. According to tradition, during the time that he was living at home after leaving the Academy in 1694 Isaac, aged 20, complained to his father about the 'uncouthness' of the Psalms that were sung in the worship at the Above Bar Meeting House. His father suggested that he might compose something better. His first attempt seems to have been 'A new Song to the Lamb that was slain', based on verses from Revelation 5, with a grand and confident first verse:

> Behold the glories of the Lamb   Amidst his Father's throne:
> Prepare new Honours for his Name,   And songs before unknown.

This is considered by some to be 'the birth of the English hymn'. Before this book, only Psalms or adaptations of existing poems were sung in churches but Watts saw no reason why Christians shouldn't sing God's praises in the form of good poetry specifically written for that purpose.

Watson says of this, "…the verse parades its originality. It was written by a young man who had been trained in rhetoric and classical prosody at school; Watts would have absorbed the tradition of rhetoric as the art of persuasive communication' but 'one source of Watts' strength is his ability to… find his own voice". This hymn rightly became the first text in *Hymns and Spiritual Songs* (1707). The collection, which went through 16 editions, with many revisions in his lifetime, eventually contained a total of 365 texts.

Watts' unerring sense of the right way of saying things, with economy and strength, was the foundation of his skill as a hymn writer. Watson has noted that "his hymnody is not difficult or spectacularly metaphorical so much as attentive to the need to find the correct word 'in the discourse in which it stands' without destroying the rhyme or the rhythm".

He continues: "Watts' hymns depend for their effect not just on their crisp vocabulary and their clarity, but on their 'numbers': on the way in which the words, punctuation, stress and rhythm become elements in the line, with the lines constituting the verse". Watts' decision to exclude from his hymns the more spectacular flights of poetic language found in 'The Adventurous Muse' is part of a Puritan restraint that gives his work a seriousness that tempers and mixes with the evident joy.

As Donald Davie wrote about the worship of 'Old Dissent': "Art is measure, is exclusion; is therefore simplicity (hard-earned), is sobriety, tense with all the extravagances that it has been tempted by and has denied itself. Watts' Puritan principles also led him to celebrate the particular blessings of God on his own country in ways that seem tactless to modern sensibilities".

The teachings of 16th-century Reformation leaders such as John Calvin who translated the Psalms in the vernacular for congregational singing, followed this historic worship practice. Watts was not the first Protestant to promote the singing of hymns; however, his prolific hymn writing helped usher in a new era of English worship as many other poets followed in his path.

Watts led the change in practice by including new poetry for 'original songs of Christian experience' to be used in worship. The older tradition was based on the poetry of the Bible especially the Psalms.

Watts also introduced a new way of rendering the Psalms in verse for church services, proposing that they be adapted for hymns with a specifically Christian perspective, that is New Testament rather than Old (Jewish) Testament. As Watts put it in the title of his 1719 metrical Psalter, the Psalms should be 'imitated in the language of the New Testament'.

As part of Watts' design, his hymns could be sung to familiar melodies, and he made this clear in his preface to *Hymns and Spiritual Songs* by pointing out how 'The whole Book is confin'd to three Sorts of Metre' — i.e., Common, Long, and Short Metres.

To end: he wrote the most dignified and noble of all hymns for great national occasions, 'O God, our help in ages past'. At his best, he combined such nobility and dignity with joy and with what Erik Routley correctly identified as 'wonder': "of all our hymn writers he scaled the greatest heights and plumbed the most bathetic abysses... Watts was the father, and also the liberator, of English hymnody, and the manner in which he used his new freedom was characteristic. He used it to express wonder... whether he was on the mountain top or whether he was floundering in the bog, he remained wondering... the liberation of English hymnody was, for him, the setting free of the English Protestant Christian to wonder and adore".

Watts was described as "pious without ostentation; devout without enthusiasm; humble without disguise; patient without fainting or complaint; faithful without morosity; firm without rigour; zealous without fury; and studious without gloom or stiffness".

Davis suggests that 'in his quiet compromising way, Watts was at heart a rebel. His questioning attitude was not confined solely to things spiritual. His innovations in education, poetry and hymnody show that he was not willing to accept things because usage had made them sacrosanct'

Digression   Watts' Logick

Logick, or The Right Use of Reason in the Enquiry After Truth With a Variety of Rules to Guard Against Error in the Affairs of Religion and Human Life, as well as in the Sciences.

Watts wrote this textbook on logic, first published in 1724, which ran for twenty editions to about 1850. The book was for beginners of logic, so it was in four parts: Perception, Judgement, Reasoning, and Method, and then built a detailed structure for each section.

Each part is divided into chapters, and some of these chapters are divided into sections. The content of the chapters and sections is subdivided by the following devices: divisions, distributions, notes, observations, directions, rules, illustrations, and remarks. Every contentum of the book comes under one or more of these headings, and this methodical arrangement serves to make the exposition clear.

Watts was careful to distinguish between judgements and propositions., unlike some other logic authors. For Watts, judgement is "to compare... ideas together, and to join them by affirmation, or disjoin then by negation, according as we find them to agree or disagree".

He continues, 'when mere ideas are joined in the mind without words, it is rather called a judgement; but when clothed with words it is called a proposition'. Watts' Logic follows the scholastic tradition and divides propositions into universal affirmative, universal negative, particular affirmative, and particular negative.

In the third part, Watts discusses reasoning and argumentation., with particular emphasis on the theory of syllogism. This was considered a centrally important part of classical logic. According to Watts, and like other logicians of his day, Watts defined logic as an art rather than a science. This emphasis on logic as a practical art distinguishes his book from others.

By stressing a practical and non-formal part of logic, Watts gave rules and directions for any kind of inquiry.

We plough the fields, and scatter

M Claudius [1782] trans. J M Campbell		1817-1878	1869	17 or 13 verses
WIR PFLUGEN	J A P Schulz	1747-1800	1800	7.6.7.6, 7.6.7.6 D
Psalm 145:15	"…. Thou givest them their meat in due season."			

'We plough the fields, and scatter' is a hymn of German origin commonly associated with harvest festival – reached in the third verse. Written by poet Matthias Claudius, 'Wir pflügen und wir streuen' was published in 1782 and with some verses translated into English by Jane Montgomery Campbell in 1861. It appears, abbreviated, in the musical Godspell, as the song, 'All Good Gifts'. It is among the most performed of hymns in the United Kingdom.

In 1777, Matthias Claudius had become ill and returned to Christianity after leaving it in his 20s. During his illness he wrote a number of poems. In 1782, a friend invited him over for dinner and asked him to bring one of the Christian poems he had written. Claudius delivered his 17 verse piece 'Im Anfang war's auf Erden' ('In the beginning on earth, there was…') based on Psalm 144. The poem was then published in *Asinus omnia sua secum portans – Vol 4* as a peasant's song.

The poem describes a fictitious harvest festival in the countryside under the title Paul Erdmann's Fest. In it, Claudius contrasts the somewhat arrogant noble lords with the human nobility of the agricultural workers. As a highlight of the festival, the spokesman for the peasants asks the Lord if they can sing their peasant song. This is an alternating song between the lead singer, to whom Claudius gives the name Hans Westen, and the choir 'alle Bauern'. In the end, everyone toasts to the landlord.

The peasant song differs from today's version in that it begins differently – the original beginning refers to Genesis 1:2– with a total of 16 four-line verses is considerably longer and the chorus is slightly different. This German version spread widely. Many hymnals cut down the 17 verse poem and began at verse 3 'Wir pflügen und wir streuen'.

In 1800, it was set to music attributed to Johann A. P. Schulz to a tune which, tidily, he labelled 'Wir pflugen'.

Schulz 1747-1800, in 1768 Schulz started as music teacher and accompanist to the Polish Princess Sapieha Woiwodin von Smolensk. Schulz moved to Berlin and traveled with her for three years performing throughout Europe, where he came in contact with many new musical ideas. The harmonization by Dykes§ was in the 1861 *Hymns Ancient and Modern*.

The tune is noted for its opening phrase, which encompasses a very wide range, but that doesn't appear to discourage most congregations from singing it. Sing the stanzas in unison (note that lines 1 and 4 are unison) and the refrain in harmony. Change the organ registration before stanza 3 to highlight the change of focus in the text: as we sing stanzas 1 and 2, we address each other, but in stanza 3 we address God.

In 1862 in England, Jane Campbell, who was proficient in the German language, started to translate a number of German hymns into English. She translated the German original; however, she did not make a strict translation but did ensure retention of the hymn's original focus of giving thanks to God for the harvest. She taught the hymn to the children at the Church of England parish school in London where her father was the rector. The hymn was later published in Charles Bere's *Garland of Songs* and *Children's Chorale Book*.

The hymn is predominantly used as a hymn to give thanks to God for the harvest and it thus is used in the United States as a hymn for Thanksgiving.

Updates, almost parodies, include John Betjeman who parodied the hymn as 'We spray the fields and scatter/the poison on the land' published as a protest against modern farming methods and new planning legislation. There are other near-parodic re-writes.

Brian Wren's revised text was published in 1983; it was criticised as for some it looks to worldwide sinequity rather than being a harvest hymn.

> We plough the fields with tractors, With drills we sow the land;
> But growth is still the wondrous gift. Of God's almighty hand.
> We use our fertilisers. To help the growing grain;
> But for its full fruition, It needs God's sun and rain. All good gifts around us.
>
> Then why are people starving, when we have life so good?
> And some in crowded cities search dustbins for their food;
> And even some go hungry who farm in distant lands;
> Lord, help us learn more swiftly to share with open hands.

An early version of the text is as follows :

1. We plow the fields, and scatter
the good seed on the land,
but it is fed and watered
by God's almighty hand.
God sends the snow in winter,
the warmth to swell the grain,
the breezes, and the sunshine,
and soft refreshing rain.
   Refrain:
   All good gifts around us are sent from heav'n above.
   We thank you, God, we thank you, God, for all your love.

2. You only are the Maker
of all things near and far.
You paint the wayside flower,
you light the evening star.
The winds and waves obey you,
by you the birds are fed;
much more to us, your children,
you give our daily bread.   [Refrain]

3. We thank you, then, Creator,
for all things bright and good,
the seed-time, and the harvest,
our life, our health, our food.
Accept the gifts we offer
for all your love imparts,
and what you most would welcome:
our humble, thankful hearts.   [Refrain

Charles Wesley 1707-1788

Hear the name 'Wesley' and what do you think? You'd probably answer either Methodist or hymns, I hope. Charles Wesley is most widely known for writing the words for over 6,500 hymns. His works include 'Christ the Lord is ris'n today' 'Lo! He comes with clouds, descending' and the carol 'Hark! The herald angels sing'. Here you will have found several others which have spread and been sung across the world – not always just in English.

Charles was born in Epworth, Lincolnshire, the 16th child of Samuel and Susannah. Samuel was an ex-dissenter now Anglican cleric and poet. He was a younger brother of both Methodist founder John and Samuel the younger, and he became the father of musician Samuel and grandfather of musician Samuel S. The majority of the males in the family became clerics; some as Methodists, some as Anglicans.

He was educated at Oxford University, where his brothers had also studied, and he formed the 'Holy Club' among his fellow students in 1729; also known as the Sacramentariasn' or the 'Methodists' for being so methodical and detailed in their Bible study, their opinions and disciplined lifestyle John Wesley later joined this group, as did George Whitefield. Charles followed his father and brother into the church in 1735, and he travelled with John to Georgia in America, returning a year later. Even at this time, both brothers adhered strictly to the high-church principles (as then understood) of their parents.

Following their evangelical conversions in 1738 - Charles first, John three days later - the brothers travelled throughout Britain, converting followers to the Methodist revival through preaching and hymn-singing. Despite their closeness, Charles and John did not always agree on questions relating to their beliefs. In particular, Charles was strongly opposed to separating from the Church of England into which they had been ordained.

In 1749 aged 41, he married Sarah Gwynne, aged 26, daughter of a Welsh gentleman who had been converted to Methodism by Howell Harris.

From about 1738 aged 30, Charles began to write the poetic hymns for which he would become known. In January 1739, he was appointed as curate at St Mary's Islington, but was forced to resign when the churchwardens objected to his evangelical preaching.

Later that same year, finding that they were unwelcome inside parish churches, the Wesley brothers took to preaching to crowds in open fields. From 1740, John and Charles were the joint leaders of the Methodist Revival and they evangelised throughout Britain and Ireland. They were opposed by many Anglican clergy, especially when their appointed lay preachers began to preach in parishes without seeking permission Charles established first Methodist society at Newcastle in September 1742, and he faced mob violence several times.

Following a period of illness, after 1756 Charles made no more journeys to distant parts of the country, mainly just moving between Bristol and London. Increasingly in his later years Charles became the mouthpiece of the so-called 'Church' Methodists'—he was strongly opposed to a separation of Methodism from its Anglican roots. In the 1780s, he was especially dismayed by his brother's ordination of Methody priests to serve in America and Charles criticised this in a published poem.

In April 1749 aged 41, he married the much younger Sarah Gwynne (1726–1822), also known as Sally. They lived first in Bristol, then after 1771 in both Bristol and London, after 1778 in London only. Of their 8 children 3 survived to adulthood – lower than the typical ratio. Young Samuel and Young Charles were both musical prodigies: Charles became organist to the Royal family; Samuel became 'the English Mozart'. Samuel Wesley's son, S S Wesley, was one of the foremost British composers of the 19th century.

The family moved to London in 1771 when Charles was in his mid-60s. One official history of Methodism describes him as almost an institution. *He was a Methodist preacher who had ceased to itinerate, the acknowledged pastor of the principal chapels in the Metropolis, a venerable figure who could pray, preach and administer the sacraments with all the freedom and impressiveness of a city rector, while himself acknowledging none of the limitations imposed by an Episcopal authority.*

Another biographer, John Hampson, writing in 1791, gave this description of Charles: *This gentleman was of a warm and lively disposition, of great frankness and integrity, and there was a warmness in his nature which some would perhaps call precipitancy and imprudence. He had a great regard for men of principle in all persuasions, and with all his heart abhorred a hypocrite. His conversation was pleasing and instructive and often seasoned with wit and humour. His religion was of the right sort: not gloomy and cynical, but cheerful and benevolent.*

In figure, Charles was stocky, stouter than John, and often in indifferent health. There were periods in his life when he was sick after every meal; perhaps this helps to explain his vegetarianism. He was a home-lover with no desire to be in the public eye, an affectionate husband and father, concerned for every aspect of the temporal and spiritual welfare of his children. He was open, courageous, impetuous, large-hearted to his friends, and a good if sometimes wary judge of character.

Henry Moore in his Life (1825) has provided a vivid description of how his colourful style continued even into old age: *'When he was nearly fourscore, he retained something of this eccentricity. He rode every day (clothed for winter even in summer) a little horse, grey with age. When he mounted, if a subject struck him, he proceeded to expand, and put it in order. He would write a hymn thus given him, on a card, (kept for the purpose) with his pencil, in short-hand. Not unfrequently he has come to our house in the City-road, and, having left the poney in the garden in front, he would enter, crying out, 'Pen and ink! Pen and ink!' These being supplied, he wrote the hymn he had been composing. When this was done, he would look round on those present, and salute them with much kindness, ask after their health, give out a short hymn, and thus put all in mind of eternity.*

On his deathbed he sent for the Rector of St Marylebone Parish Church, John Harley, and purportedly told him *'Sir, whatever the world may say of me, I have lived, and I die, a member of the Church of England. I pray you to bury me in your churchyard'*. At the age of 80, he died on 29 March 1788, in London. Such was his life – what can be said of his Hymns.

He found his style — passionate, fervid, lucid, forceful, direct — early in his hymn writing; and (as has often been remarked) it hardly changed for the next fifty years. In his career, Wesley published the words of between 6,500 and 10,000 hymns, many of which are still popular. In this volume are found several of high repute :

- 'Christ the Lord is risen today' § which is an Easter hymn;
- 'Hail the Day That Sees Him Rise' § - another Easter hymn
- 'Hark! The herald angels sing' § - this one is for Christmas

As well as 'Jesu, lover of My Soul'; 'Love Divine, all loves excelling' §; 'O for a thousand tongues to sing' §; 'Soldiers of Christ arise' §;'Lo! He comes with clouds descending' §; 'And can it be' §; there are still so many others such as 'Arise, My Soul, Arise'; 'Christ, Whose Glory Fills the Skies'; 'Rejoice, the Lord is King'.

Wesley's other work included poems, epistles, elegies as well as both political and satirical verse. A collected edition requires 15 volumes supplemented by the 3 volumes of *The*

Unpublished Poetry. The words to the hymns are found in the plethora of his own publications and many many modern hymnals.

His hymns are marked by their strong doctrinal content (notably the Arminian insistence on the universality of God's love; a richness of scriptural and literary allusion, and the wide variety of his metrical and rhythmic forms. These hymns have had a very significant influence not only on Methodism, but on Christian worship and modern theology as a whole.

He communicates several doctrines: the personal indwelling of the Holy Spirit, the sanctifying words of the Spirit, the limitless depravity of mankind, and humanity's personal accountability to God.

Wesley's hymns are notable as interpretations of Scripture. He also produced paraphrases of the Psalms, contributing to the long tradition of English metrical Psalmody. A notable feature of his Psalms is the introduction of Jesus into the Psalms, continuing a tradition of Christological readings of the Psalms evident in the translations of Kethe and Isaac Watts. The introduction of Jesus into the Psalms was often the source of controversy, even within his own family. Charles' brother Samuel Wesley wrote a poem against such practice

John was his faithful editor and we owe to John the singable form of some of the best known Charles Wesley hymns. However, with the quantity supplied, it is not surprising that John should describe these lyrics as 'some bad', some average, and some 'excellently good'.

Charles was thought of, as he has been ever since, as 'the sweet singer of Methodism'; so that is not surprising to find that on his death an unidentified old London woman asked despairingly, 'Who will poetry for us now?'

John Julian§, the hymn historian, described Charles Wesley as 'perhaps … the great hymn writer of all ages'. There are other claimants, of course, and hymn writing is not a competitive art; but it is an assessment that continues to command wide assent. One recent computation suggests that he wrote over 8,900 hymns or poems (the distinction is often blurred – and so is the count). This is three times the output of Wordsworth, an average of ten lines of verse a day for fifty years.

In 1953, the historian Flew wrote: ' Using his skills, Charles Wesley builds a careful structure: he knows what he wishes to say, and plans his pathway to a distinct goal, often with an eternal dimension in the heavenly places ('ceaseless glory'; 'perfect day'; 'that heavenly land') and grounded in love ('wonder, love and praise'; 'everlasting love'; 'thy new, best name of Love'). Newton Flew demonstrates with numerous examples the hidden skeleton on which the body of a hymn is built and yet with such cunning that the framework seldom obtrudes. Charles Wesley then clothes this framework with a lyric, classical in its proportions, vigorous in its language, and animated by what has been aptly called 'passionate orthodoxy': 'We may not see God. We cannot fail to see that Wesley saw him.'

The range of his hymnody is as wide as the quantity might suggest, so that he deals with all the pastoral concerns which John used as divisions in his 1780 Collection (believers rejoicing, fighting, praying, watching and so on) and with every season of the Christian year.

For Advent he (with others) gives us 'Lo! He comes …'; for Christmas (with alterations) 'Hark! The herald angels sing'; for Easter, 'Christ the Lord is risen today'; 'Love's redeeming work is done' (altered) for Ascension; 'Hail the day …' for Pentecost; and 'Come. Holy Ghost, our hearts inspire'. — and the list could be multiplied. Often what he has to say is for a specific occasion ('on deliverance from a mob'; 'after preaching in church'; 'for one in prison') and certain themes constantly recur.

Second to content, structure and range, must be set skill and craftsmanship. Charles Wesley is often thought of as a herald of the Romantic revival in his lyrical freedom and revolt against too mechanical a regularity. Yet this was only possible because the ordered discipline of verse, the constraints of rhyme and metre, were the natural outcome of his classical training and his own precocious talent, refined by constant practice.

To this natural bent must be added his wide reading (Henry Bett, among others, traces some of his sources: cf. the line 'Love divine, all loves excelling' linking with Dryden's Song of Venus in King Arthur, 'Fairest Isle, all isles excelling'); and also the literary climate of his day.

Art conceals art: and the modern reader, as Wesley would wish, seldom notices technique. Yet beneath a verse 'so simple it could be understood, and so smooth that it could be used, by plain men' lies a combination of classical and Anglo-Saxon vocabulary, often in a kind of counterpoint; a single thought frequently complete within the line, carried home by the strength of the chosen verb and clinched by the rhyme; and a range of metrical form perhaps unique for his day.

Frank Baker writes of the in which the hymns employ the arts of Rhetoric and chiasmus, now an epizeuxis or perhaps an epanadiplosis, here an oxymoron, there a metaphor. — and a wide range of tropes and figures, of which a few are now identifiable.

All these aspects of craftsmanship, so carefully analysed by Wesley scholars, contribute to the power and vitality of the writing. But the whole is greater than the sum of its parts. Charles Wesley's work is sung today because he offers in a way which diverse congregations recognize, even if often below the level of the conscious mind, hymns in which we can express together the movements and aspirations of the heart towards the God who is known to us in Jesus Christ.

As a tangent – here is John Wesley's own introduction to his 1780 *Collection of Hymns for the use of people called Methodists*:

May I be permitted to add a few words with regard to the poetry? Then I will speak to those who are the judges thereof, with all freedom and unreserve. To these I may say, without offence, 1. In these hymns there is no doggerel, no botches, nothing put in to patch up the rhyme, no feeble expletives.

2. Here is nothing turgid or bombast, on the one hand, or low and creeping, on the other.

3. Here are no cant expression, no words without meaning. Those who impute this to us know not what they say. We talk common sense, both in prose and verse, and use no word but in a fixed and determinate sense.

4. Here are, allow me to say, both the purity, the strength, and the elegance of the English language, and, at the same time, the utmost simplicity and plainness, suited to every capacity.

Lastly, I desire men of taste to judge, (these are the only competent judges) whether there be not in some of the following hyms the true Spirit of Poetry, such as cannot be acquired by art and labour but must be the gift of nature. By labour, a man may become a tolerable imitator of Spenser, Shakespeare or Milton, and may heap together pretty compound epithets such as pale-eyed and the like, but unless he be *born* a poet, he will never attain the genuine Spirit of Poetry.

When I survey the wondrous Cross

| | Isaac Watts § | 1674-1748 | 1707 | 5,4,3 verses |
| ROCKINGHAM | Edward Miller | c1731-1807 | 1790 | 8.8.8.8 LM |

Philip 3:7   "What things were gain to me, those I counted loss for Christ."

While it did not fit to have the first entry in this book to be by Wesley, when the ending came in sight, there was a chance and a choice to end with three giants of that era – Wesley§ again, Watts§ and Richard Baxter; but Bunyan got in the way as did the German harvest.

'When I survey…' is found in hymn books of all denominations throughout the world. It received an extended study in J R Watson, *The English Hymn, A Critical and Historical Study* (1997).

This hymn first appeared in Hymns and Spiritual Songs (1707), Book III, *'Prepared for the holy Ordinance of the Lord's Supper'*, with the title *'Crucifixion to the World by the Cross of Christ*; Gal. 6.14.' It then began as follows but the second line was amended by Watts within 2 years.

'When I survey the wondrous Cross…   no change
'Where the young Prince of Glory dy'd   became On which the Prince of Glory died'

This is one of the greatest hymns on the Passion of Christ, almost certainly the greatest hymn in English on that subject. The singing 'I' surveys the crucifixion of Christ, as though from a distance; though reference is made to the blood which is shed, what flows down from 'his head, his hands, his feet' as 'sorrow and love.' Perhaps in no other English hymn is the use of 'I' and 'me' less egotistical. The self here is totally centred on the crucified Christ, in whose dying presence gain is loss and pride is contemptible. At the last line, the singer leaves the scene knowing that this 'amazing' love demands nothing less than 'my soul, my life, my all'. That last line should surely be sung, not with confident gusto, but almost silently, with profoundest and almost incredulous reverence.

Stanza 4 has often been omitted:
  His dying crimson, like a robe,   … Spreads o'er his body on the tree;
  Then am I dead to all the globe,   … And all the globe is dead to me.

The omission is sanctioned by its appearance in square brackets in early printings, but the stanza is not only beautiful in itself: it paraphrases the second part of Galatians 6: 14: 'by whom the world is crucified unto me, and I unto the world.' The hymn gains much by its inclusion. It was also omitted from the *First Edition of A&M*, which added an inappropriate doxology, continued until *A&MR*. The 'dying crimson' stanza came into that tradition only with *A&MCP*. A&M also amended verse 5-L2 to 'offering' instead of 'present'; 'Offering', for some reason thought to be more dignified, became accepted in many books.

One of the most remarkable structural features of the text is its use of chiasmus (the crossing of words or ideas) in the third stanza, where 'Sorrow and Love' is reversed to become 'Love and Sorrow'. The Greek letter chi (X), which gives this rhetorical figure its name, has often been used as a symbol of the cross; it is also the first letter in the word 'Christ'. Since this chiasmus occurs in the exact center of the hymn (the middle lines in the third of five stanzas), it appears Watts has placed a symbol of both the cross and the Man who was crucified on that cross at the very heart of the hymn. Chiasmus also appears in the last two lines of the original fourth stanza: 'Then am I dead to all the Globe, / And all the Globe is dead to me'.

Other poetic devices also appear in the text, including paradox ('My richest Gain I count but Loss / And pour Contempt on all my Pride'), hypotyposis (using vivid imagery to bring a scene to mind; stanza three and the opening lines of the original stanza four), and climax ('Demands my Soul, my Life, my All'). 'Prince of Glory' does not appear in the Bible but seems to combine ideas from Isaiah 9:6 ('Prince of Peace') and Psalm 24:7 ('King of glory').

In Britain it is most frequently associated with the tune ROCKINGHAM, adapted by Edward Miller from an earlier tune maybe TUNBRIDGE. In some parts of Britain it is sung to JOB, by William Arnold; another setting was the English traditional melody O WALY WALY daringly set as an alternative tune. In the USA it is sung to HAMBURG, by Lowell Mason in 1825; this simple tune has only five tones, thus putting the focus solely on the text.

The first publication of Watts' text with a tune occurred in book two of William Tans'ur's *Heaven on Earth; or, the Beauty of Holiness* (1738). However, Tans'ur had previously published it several times with different texts under the titles EVENING HYMN and SARUM.

1   When I survey the wondrous cross,
    On which the Prince of glory died,
    My richest gain I count but loss,
    And pour contempt on all my pride.

2   Forbid it, Lord! that I should boast,
    Save in the death of Christ, my God;
    All the vain things that charm me most
    I sacrifice them to His blood.

3   See, from His head, His hands, His feet,
    Sorrow and love flow mingled down;   X
    Did e'er such love and sorrow meet,
    Or thorns compose so rich a crown?

4   His dying crimson, like a robe,
    Spreads o'er His body on the tree;
    Then I am dead to all the globe,   X
    And all the globe is dead to me.

5   Were the whole ream of nature mine,
    That were a present far too small;
    Love so amazing, so divine,
    Demands my soul, my life, my all.

In what Albert Bailey has called a 'combination of imagery, insight, and passion', Watts captured the essence of Christ's sacrifice on the cross and the appropriate Christian response to that sacrifice. It is a vivid reminder of the debt owed to the 'Prince of Glory' whose love demands our 'All'. Erik Routley has written: 'Yet it surely must be agreed that this is the most penetrating of all hymns, the most demanding, the most imaginative. It these things precisely because its style is so simple. It is drawn throughout in strong, clear, simple lines and colours.'

Who would true valour see

	John Bunyan	1628-1688	1684	3 verses
MONKS GATE	Vaughan Williams	1872-1958	1906	11.11.12.11

1 Hebrews 11:13: "...and confessed that they were strangers and pilgrims on the earth."

'Who would true valour see' is the best known hymn using words of John Bunyan. In his *Pilgrim's Progress* written in 1684; it appears in Part 2 of Christina's travels. These words were sung by Mr Valiant-for-Truth, 'a man with his Sword drawn, and his Face all bloody' still in company with Mr Greatheart near the end of their pilgrimage.

AS with many other of the fine pieces of 17th century devotional verse, it took years before this became a hymn, indeed it is only in the last 150 years that it has been treated as a hymn.

There is another hymn which is very often confused with this; entitled 'He who would valiant be' for the *English Hymnal*. Despite their source being identical, it is almost as if these are two separate hymns – different text, different settings – same origin. Actually the second is a direct rewrite in 1906 because a group of people so disliked the phrasing and wording of the original. Percy Dearmer and his group so disliked some of the words and intentions of the early text that they insisted on a revision then a complete rewrite.

The first inclusion of these words, unchanged from Bunyan's original text, was in a hymn book was in 1873 in a selection compiled by a Congregational minister in Brighton, E. Paxton Hood. The words were set to a tune, VALOUR, by Josiah Booth,

Bunyan's three verses have survived in many books, in spite of the strong competition from Dearmer's words. Successive editions of *A&M* avoided 'Hobgoblin' and used 'No goblin'! Many other major books have stood by Bunyan's original text. The apparently artless words of that text conceal a consummate skill, expressing a powerful blend of tough courage and serene assurance. The first part of each verse is that of a warrior; so it is rough and awkward in its language and rhymes; the second part moves into a triple rhyme which is much smoother and more easily read or sung, until each verse ends with the unrhymed word 'pilgrim', the most important word in the song. The rhyme scheme reflects this format as ABAB CCC D.

The metre may appear regular but the reality of intonation, accent, rhythm make it often actually irregular, and the syntax is unusual. Every verse, however, moves through these various processes to come out at the end with a simple statement, 'To be a pilgrim'.

Bunyan almost certainly did not intend for his text to be sung in public worship. For one, the standard tunes of the day would not have accommodated his unique metre. More importantly, congregational hymn singing was very strongly discouraged among Puritan dissenters of his time, but the practice of it would be championed by Benjamin Keach in his treatise *The Breach Repaired in God's Worship* (1691) and then brought to greater fruition through the works of Isaac Watts § (1674–1748) – the Godfather of English hymn-singing.

For a time, Bunyan's original version was not commonly sung in churches, perhaps because of the references to 'hobgoblin' and 'foul fiend'. However, one commentator has said: 'Bunyan's burly song strikes a new and welcome note in our Hymnal. The quaint sincerity of the words stirs us out of our easygoing dull Christianity to the thrill of great adventure.'

Recent hymn books have tended to return to the original. It is perhaps the tricky decision as to whether to take the author's text using his language or to accept a later generation's prissiness.

John Bunyan born 1628, died 1688 aged 60, came from the village of Elstow, near Bedford. He had some schooling and at the age of sixteen joined the Parliamentary Army during the first stage of the English Civil War. After three years in the army he returned to Elstow and took up the trade of tinker, which he had learned from his father. He became interested in religion after his marriage, attending first the parish church and then joining the Bedford Meeting, a nonconformist group in Bedford, and becoming a preacher. After the restoration of the monarch, when the freedom of nonconformists was curtailed, Bunyan was arrested and spent the next twelve years in jail as he refused to give up preaching. During this time he wrote a spiritual autobiography, *Grace Abounding to the Chief of Sinners*. Bunyan a Puritan preacher and a writer best remembered as the author of the Christian allegory *The Pilgrim's Progress*, which was not published until some years after his release. In addition to this, Bunyan wrote nearly sixty titles, many of them expanded sermons.

The words of 'Who would true valour see' were modified so extensively by Percy Dearmer for the 1906 *English Hymnal* that the new piece is now known as 'To be a Pilgrim' or, at least as often, 'He who would valiant be'.

Both hymns have been sung to the melody NOAB (John Roberts, 1870) and ST DUNSTANS (Charles W. Douglas, 1917). Modern composers have also written new settings.

At the same time, in 1906 it was given a new tune by Ralph Vaughan Williams, who used a melody based on the traditional song 'Our Captain Cried All Hands'. He heard this at the hamlet of Monks Gate in West Sussex – hence the name of the melody. The new work is generally treated as a new hymn. In *English Hymnal* Vaughan-Williams included some 35 folk-songs or traditional tunes he or others had collected and adapted.

Dearmer was remarkably forthright on this occasion. 'To include the hobgoblins would have been to ensure disaster; to ask the congregation of St Ignotus, Erewhon Park [Nowhere Park] to invite all to come and look at them, if they wished to see true valour, would have been difficult... no one would have been more distressed than Bunyan himself to have people singing about hobgoblins in church'. It is not easy to know what Bunyan would have been distressed about, but he would have been robust enough in his belief to sweep aside such objections if necessary. If a work such as *The Pilgrim's Progress*, or a song from it, could be of use to a believer on pilgrimage, then Bunyan would surely not have minded when or where it was sung.

Dearmer, who was usually so good at responding to poetry in worship, seems to have become strangely literal-minded here. And certainly congregations since that time have sung about the hobgoblins and their valour without feeling any difficulty or embarrassment. Bunyan's words have a strong appeal because they recognise skill and courage, and the importance of those qualities in the pilgrimage of life.

Percy Dearmer 1867 – 1936.

Percy Dearmer was clearly a very determined man, eager to show his disapproval and willing to amend words, texts and meaning to suit. He did so for this hymn; he did it for 'All things bright and beautiful'§ – accusing C F Alexander from his own ivory folly.

He combined his high-church views and a great admiration for both Roman ritualism and Poetry with being a life-long socialist.

Dearmer defended his substantial revisions on the grounds that the original was never for congregational singing. The more modern view is that the original has more potency and directness; and that these values are rather subdued in the Dearmer-Hutton version

Whatever the wording - there can be no doubt that Vaughan Williams' choice of tune made Bunyan's text – in either form – not only singable but immensely popular.

    1   Who would true valour see, Let him come hither;
          One here will constant be, Come wind, come weather
          There's no discouragement Shall make him once relent
          His first avowed intent To be a pilgrim.

    2   Whoso beset him round With dismal stories
          Do but themselves confound; His strength the more is.
          No lion can him fright, He'll with a giant fight,
          He will have a right To be a pilgrim.

    3   Hobgoblin nor foul fiend Can daunt his spirit,
          He knows he at the end Shall life inherit.
          Then fancies fly away, He'll fear not what men say,
          He'll labor night and day To be a pilgrim.

And Percy Dearmer's rewritten hymn.

    1   He who would valiant be 'gainst all disaster,
          let him in constancy follow the Master:
          there's no discouragement shall make him once relent
          his first avowed intent to be a pilgrim.

    2   Who so beset him round with dismal stories
          do but themselves confound — his strength the more is:
          no foes shall stay his might, though he with giants fight;
          he will make good his right to be a pilgrim.

    3   Since, Lord, thou dost defend us with thy Spirit,
          we know we at the end shall life inherit:
          then, fancies, flee away! I'll fear not what men say,
          I'll labour night and day to be a pilgrim.

Pictures from Pilgrims Progress.

THE
Pilgrim's Progreſs
FROM
THIS WORLD,
TO
That which is to come
Delivered under the Similitude of a
DREAM
Wherein is Diſcovered,
The Manner of his ſetting out,
His Dangerous JOURNEY,
AND
Safe Arrival at the Deſired Countrey.

By *JOHN BUNYAN.*

The Fourth Edition, with Additions.

I have uſed Similitudes. *Hoſea*, 12. 10.

Licenſed and Entred according to Order.

LONDON,
Printed for *Nath. Ponder*, at the *Peacock* in the *Poultrey* near the Church, 1680.

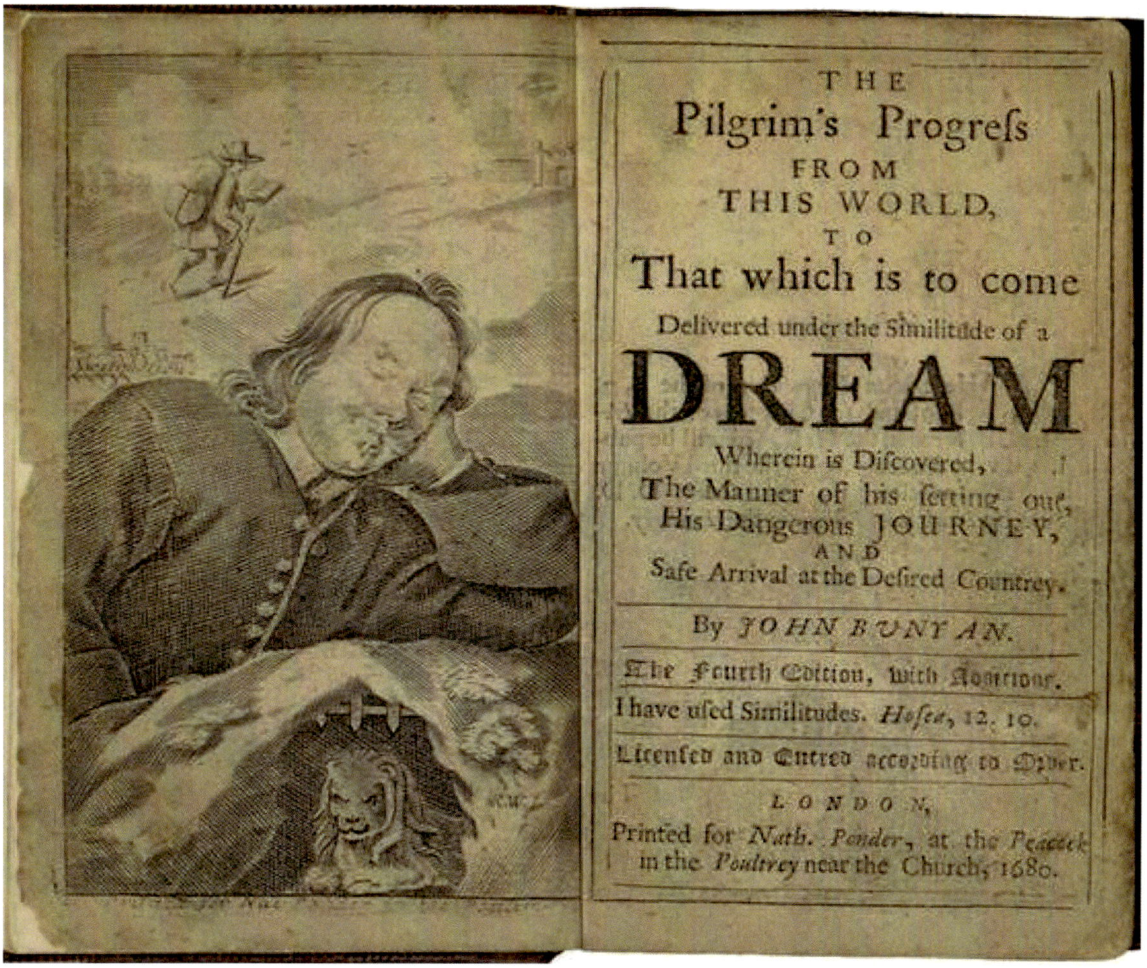

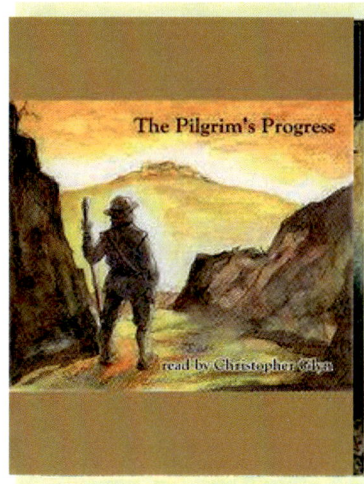

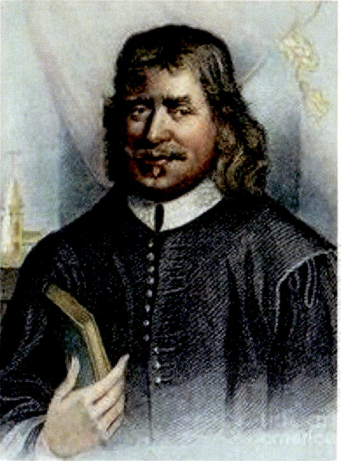

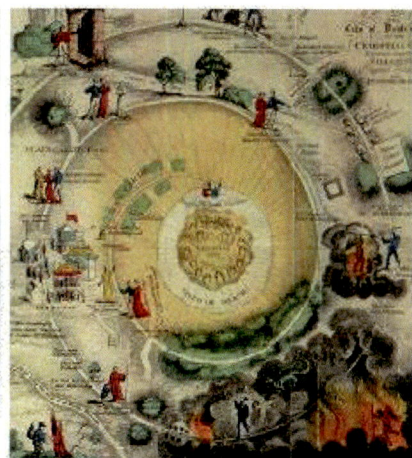

Ye holy Angels bright

	Richard Baxter	1615-1681	1674	16 ...3 verses
DARWALL'S 148th	John Darwall	1731-1789	1773	12.12.8.8

Psalm 148:1   "Praise ye the LORD from the heavens: praise him in the heights".

Richard Baxter was a Puritan with strong and definite views – sufficient to put him at odds with many of his fellows. He refused the offer from Charles II of the bishopric of Hereford. After the Act of Uniformity in 1662, he left the Church of England and became a non-conformist. By 1685, he was condemned by Judge Jeffries for sedition. A contemporary of Bunyan, his hymns are part of the rich accumulation of 17th century religious verse. Baxter was a firm believer that singing should not be limited to metrical psalms.

It is astonishing how this text has changed from the original of 1674. The traditional form of this hymn seems now to have settled down at just verses 1,2 & 5, although sometimes verse 4 is included. With its invariable tune, known in most books as DARWALL'S 148th, it has become a standard and much-loved hymn of praise. It was first published in Baxter's *The Poor Man's Family Book* (1674), entitled 'A Psalm of Praise, To the Tune of Psalm 148'.

This began as an enormous 16 verse piece. Even in the first year of publication, it was divided into two parts, the second beginning at Stanza 9 ('Let not the fear or smart/ of his chastizing Rod'). Even as early as 1681, the second half of Baxter's stanza 1 was altered:

'You there so nigh Are much more meet' became

'Than we the feet For things so high'.

As well as being cut in two, it has been cut further, amended, changed, edited. Sometimes 8 of the verses are supplied; strangely not all of these are sung. The 16-verse hymn is too long and is not in modern books or printed here, but it has a magnificent last verse :

The Sun is but a spark from the Eternal Light;
Its brightest beams are dark, to that most Glorious Sight.
There the whole Chord [choir] With one accord
Shall praise the Lord For evermore.

The Historical Edition of A&M (1909) notes, 'the alterations are considerable' to Baxter's original. Christopher Idle wrote in 2006 'The textual history would fill at least a booklet'.

A second hymn began 'Ye saints with sounding voice' (a stanza not in Baxter's hymn, and probably amended by Gurney), subsequently using Baxter's second part, stanzas 8, 11, 15 and 16. It is not of note, except for the fact that its first stanza ended with lines which are now frequently moved to replace the finale of the last verse.

Let all thy days Till life shall end, Whate'er he send Be filled with praise.

The very much most common setting for this hymn is known as DARWALL'S 148th. John Darwall was a Staffordshire, born there in 1732 and died there in 1789. His fame rests on his effort in composing a soprano tune and bass line for each of the 150 psalm versifications in the *Tate and Brady New Version of the Psalms of David* (1696).

In an organ dedication speech in 1773 Darwall advocated singing the 'Psalm tunes in quicker time than common [in order that] six verses might be sung in the same space of time that four generally are'.

There are some other settings, partly because there was considerable similarity in the rhythms of some of the versified psalms. From the modern view, because this is a wonderful and popular hymn so some wish to put their own stamp on it. Old settings include CROFT'S 136TH; ST GREGORY; LAUS DEO; ST JOHN and HOWARD.

Strangely, with the re-numbering of Psalms that occurred at this time, Psalm 148 at that time was 'Ye boundless realms of joy'.

A version with 8 verses as per the original is as follows :-

1   Ye holy angels bright, Who stand before God's throne
    And dwell in glorious light, Praise ye the Lord each one.
    Assist our song, or else the theme
    Too high doth seem for mortal tongue.

2   Ye blessèd souls at rest, That see your Savior's face,
    Whose glory, e'en the least Is far above our grace.
    God's praises sound, as in His sight
    With sweet delight you do abound.

3   Ye saints, who toil below, Adore your heavenly king,   [added]
    And onward as ye go Some joyful anthem sing;
    Take what He gives and praise Him still,
    Through good or ill, who ever lives!

4   All nations of the earth, Extol the world's great King:
    With melody and mirth His glorious praises sing,
    For He still reigns, and will bring low
    The proudest foe that Him disdains.

5   Sing forth Jehovah's praise, Ye saints, that on Him call!
    Him magnify always His holy churches all!
    In Him rejoice and there proclaim
    His holy name with sounding voice.

6   My soul, bear thou thy part, Triumph in God above,
    And with a well tuned heart Sing thou the songs of love.
    And all my days let no distress
    Nor fears suppress His joyful praise.

7   Away, distrustful care! I have Thy promise, Lord:
    To banish all despair, I have Thine oath and Word:
    And therefore I shall see Thy face
    And there Thy grace shall magnify.

8   With Thy triumphant flock Then I shall numbered be;
    Built on th'eternal rock, His glory shall we see.
    The heav'ns so high With praise shall ring
    And all shall sing in harmony.

REFERENCES - Publications and Websites

The sources for this microtome include :-

John Julian's *Dictionary of Hymnology* (1892)
    (and betimes its descendant, the Canterbury (Online) Dictionary of Hymnology)

Frere's *Historical Edition of Hymns Ancient and Modern*	1906	
Frost's *Historical Companion to Hymns Ancient and Modern*	1962	
Chamber's Encyclopedia	1892	
Arnold's *New Oxford Companion to Music* 'Hymns' edited Scholes	1983	
Hymns Ancient and Modern (reproduction)	1861	236 hymns
Hymns Ancient and Modern with Appendix	1868	349 hymns
Hymns Ancient and Modern 2nd Edition	1875	473 hymns
Hymns Ancient and Modern 2nd Edition with Supplement	1889	638 hymns
Hymns Ancient and Modern 1916 Standard Edition		779 hymns
Hymns Ancient and Modern 1953 Revised Edition		636 hymns
English Hymnal	1906	

Many other Hymnals – for which the introduction is often the most interesting section.

Olney Hymns facsimile	Copper & Newton Trustees	2009	ISBN	0-95-055301-8

Hymns and Faith	Erik Routley	1955		
The Leon Valley	Norman Reeves	1980	ISBN	0-85033-347-4
Great Christian Hymn Writers	Smith & Carlson	1997	ISBN	978-0-89107-944-6
Songs of Praise	Andrew Barr	2001	ISBN	0-7459-5085-3
Anthology of Hymns	Prof. J R Watson	2003	ISBN	0-19-926583-6
Songs of Praise – Favourite Hymns		2004	ISBN	0-7459-5143-0
Awake my Soul	Prof. J R Watson	2005	ISBN	0-281-05768-0
The Telegraph Book of Hymns	Ian Bradley	2008	ISBN	978-0-571-25959-5
Forty Favourites	Aled Jones	2009	ISBN	978-1-84809-101-1
Hear my Song	Pam Rhodes	2010	ISBN	978-0-281-06193-8
Hymns Ancient & Modern & H W Baker		2013	ISBN	978-0-953-63145-2
Stories of Favourite Hymns	William Hunton	2020	ISBN	979-8-60193-079-6
Precautionary Tales for Grandparents	J Muirden	2008	ISBN	978-1-84024-707-7
Divine and Moral Songs for Children	I Watts		ISBN	978-1-53350-291-9

Websites

archive.org/details/cu31924021638071   'Internet Archive' offers some remarkable documents including Middle English, Sternhold & Hopkins from the 17C and many others, such as the annotated Methodist Hymnal 1904.

Hymnary.org is splendidly helpful on hymns, biblical verses as well as giving extracts from Victorian 'Lives' although much leaning towards the American user;

Hymnologyarchive.com delivers very through articles on authors, composers, texts and tunes.

hymnology.hymnsam.co.uk is the actual site for Canterbury Dictionary of Hymnology

Wikipedia has been looked at while bearing in mind that is occasionally poorly sourced.

Other websites include :
   St Augustine's Lyre aka ToSingistoPrayTwice.

   Stempublishing.com   has some useful listings.

Many entries are enhanced by viewpoints from other occasional sources and friends,
Any errors or omissions, any missing references or attributions are solely the fault of the author in delivering an enthusiastic work rather than an academic paper.

Afterwords

Chambers Encyclopedia 1892 – on Hymns

Each of the entries is a direct quote from 'HYMNS' – with only occasional minor editing.

The usually accepted definition of a hymn is that of St Augustine in about 415: 'Do you know what a hymn is? It is singing to the praise of God. If you praise God and do not sing – you utter no hymn. If you sing and praise no God – you utter no hymn.'

In Greek, the mother-tongue of Christianity (?), it is natural to search for early forms of sacred song .... there are few ... some which are more oriental in character, with affinity to the Hebrew modes'. These include the hymns and poems of Gregory of Nazianzus, written after 381. They number about 240, 38 dogmatic, 40 on moral subjects, 99 on his own life and 60 more ... amongst are some splendid hymns, we know not one in a modern hymn-book.

The link with the Jewish ... is most obvious in the use of the Psalms, then next, the use of Halleluiah and Hosanna, finally in the use of antiphons and versicles.

No name is associated with Latin hymns until after the Council of Nicaea in 333. ... Prudentius wrote poems from which extracts were taken admirably suited to the service. The 63rd edition of his Poems was printed in 1836 – a splendid testimony to his worth.

The first English hymn book was Hymns and Songs of the Church (1623) by George Wither. The king granted him a patent to bind up the book with the Metrical psalms. Julian tells us 'But for the Puritan reaction that then set in, the development of original hymns might have then begun. Instead of fame and profit, it brought him persecution and loss, notwithstanding the approbation by many members of Convocation.'

John Wesley's work for the Church of England remained a dead-letter until 1760 when Martin Madan published his collection, gathered from Watts and Wesleys, altered to his own Calvinist views without permission and published without leave.

Usually it is said that Methodist hymnody has had a great influence on English hymnody; this is, however, only true of the hymns of John and Charles Wesley.

From the outset of Christianity throughout the nations of the earth, it has become a necessity to preach and to supply them with hymns. This has resulted in a great variety of subject, metre, language and style. We have seen how at an early stage, reverent strophes to praise the Holy Trinity and a few others formed the staple of sacred song.

We have seen how the expansion of church life and the development of doctrine and practices called forth a fuller and more extended hymnody, until every incident of importance in the Bible story, every conceivable shade of Christian doctrine and ritual, every epoch in the church's history, every experience in her children's life have been enshrined in sacred song.

John Henry, Cardinal Newman, began as a Calvinist due to his mother, and his belief in the doctrine of eternal punishment from his own reading. From reading John Newton, he biased his mind that Rome is the Antichrist. He believed in celibacy with certain brief intervals of 'a month now, and a month then'. After writing 'Lead, kindly light' while at sea, he raced from Marseilles to Oxford to Keble's Assize sermon on National Apostasy, which he always regarded as the date at which the Tractarian movement began [July 14th 1833]. He strongly believed in discipline; he prevented a fellow cleric from attending the marriage of his own sister who had seceded from the Anglican church. ….. There is much more to be said about Newman

---

Carols – some of these ancient ones 'Cherry Tree' and 'St Stephen' preserve curious legends that have descended from the remote past. Many … were much corrupted when they found their way into print. Beside sacred carols, there were jovial carols for Christmas feasts.

… and hymn-related people and subjects

… The practice of singing carols in church instead of in the open air and in consequence the quaint fantastic carols of old days are falling out of remembrance. There are carols from France, Russia, Manx and Wales.

Chambers is strangely mute on certain entries – J B Dykes is listed but not W H Monk nor H W Baker. The nearest 'Baker' is Sir Richard, …. author of *The Kings of England* a work without which no gentleman's library is complete … Notwithstanding its reputation, however the book had no lack of errors, and now is all but forgotten.

John Bacchus Dykes does get a mention of bare facts as well as noting that he was joint-editor of Hymns Ancient & Modern – next comes 'Dymoke' a Lincolnshire family who for nineteen generations held the office of Champion of England whose rights, mounted on horseback and armed to the teeth, were exercised at each Coronation.

When it comes to W H Monk who is absent, Chambers has as its nearest entry - 'Maria Monk – a woman of bad character who pretended in 1835 to have escaped from a nunnery, and who, coming to New York, found a good many credulous adherents and published *Awful Disclosures* and *Further Disclosures*, which had an enormous sale.

Next to James Montgomery 'a minor poet' is Robert Montgomery 'poetaster' … of his thirty-one works, two 'The Omnipresence of the Deity' and 'Satan' are still remembered but only for Macaulay's onslaught in the Edinburgh Review for April 1830.

John Mason Neale …a preposterous adaptation of Pilgrims Progress, and a long series of stories for the young, intended to popularise church history, but the value is almost exclusively other than historical…. There is no modern author to whom hymnology owes a greater debt than to this inspired writer whose own ecclesiastical sympathies were so narrow'

Isaac Watts … 'This childless saint and scholar assured the perpetuity of his name by his Divine and Moral Songs for Children (1715) which, in spite of metrical defect and much hopeless prose, show strength, sanity and the right simplicity without weakness'.

Charles Wesley has a tiny piece compared to John, for whom Chambers delivers a lengthy text, referring to his failed marriage in some detail.

Oxford Dictionary of Music – Scholes: Hymns

After some 6 years work, and over a million words – surpassing the length of the Bible at less than 800,000 - in 1938 Percy Scholes delivered his huge one-volume first edition of **The Oxford Companion to Music;** the article on Hymns remains mostly his work.

He wrote virtually all the text himself. The only exceptions were the article on tonic sol-fa (for which he was dissatisfied with his own article) and the synopses of the plots of operas (which he regarded as too boring). Although the Oxford Companion to Music was (and is) regarded as authoritative, the text is enlivened by Scholes' own anecdotal and quirky style.

In his writing for this work, and elsewhere, Scholes never believed in holding back his personal opinions in favour of a neutral point of view. He is credited with the description of harpsichord music as sounding like "a toasting fork on a birdcage" Certainly the 2nd edition still retains many appallingly attractive quotes - even in the 108 pages on Hymns (out of over 2000). Almost no hymnists get a mention as Scholes does not see them as 'significant'.

"… All existing books are open to criticism – and receive it."

"…'Lining-out' [reading a psalm line then the congregation, then another line] was seen as a temporary concession to ignorance …but came to possess that sanctity that oft attaches to ecclesiastical custom'

"Organ accompaniment: This was for long very crude and extremely slow.

"… A peculiarity of Highland life was the extraordinary way the psalm tunes have been lengthened with roulades and grace notes as to be unrecognizable.

"Charles Wesley protested the 'scandalous doggerel' of his predecessors.

'The best of the tunes of Monk, Dykes and Stainer are worthy, but their second-best ….depend overmuch rather than on melody but on sweetness of harmony (they have been brutally called 'the strawberry jam of music')."

" …some of the more 'sugary' Victorian tunes were banished to an Appendix known in the 1904 A&M edition, not always affectionately, as the Chamber of Horrors'.

"… In 1960, a collection of hymns arrived, mainly with well-known words, set to tunes in an idiom previously virtually unknown in church music, which could broadly be called 'pop'. … though (often) much derived from folk or musical stage show. …. Some have added words reflecting current Christian thinking and social concerns, an example being 'when I needed a neighbour, were you there'.

"… Modern hymns have been of variable quality …from the fine to banal verses of simplistic theological content and doubtful value…'

"… the most enduring hymns tend to be the well-worn favourites of the Victorian period 'Abide with me §' or 'Onward Christian Soldiers §'. …with the wording staying, preferably, with the fervent original rather than the tame 'Onward Christian Pilgrims, put your sandals on…'

As neither Charles Wesley§, Watts§, Monk§ or Dykes§ get a mention, in passing one notes 'Charles Wesley -nephew of John, eldest son of Charles, in his youth showed immense musical promise… However, having learnt his craft … his imagination ceased to function, his talents withered and with his appointment as organist to George III (who would hear only Handel) his absorption in the past prevented any further creative development.

Please read this book or maybe it's online – so opinionated, such fun.

Canterbury (OnLine) Dictionary of Hymnology

John Julian's *Dictionary of Hymnology* came out in 1892 and was republished, revised and so on just once in 1907. The 1,768 pages covering some 40,000 articles in a 3 inch tome of more than 3,000,000 words was not able to be redone until the age of the internet.

Others attempted to update, revise and expand his work but this was barely possible, and when attempted incomplete, until the arrival of the Internet. Professor Richard Watson of Durham was persuaded – once he had officially retired - to take the lead of the enormous task, together with Professor Emma Hornby. His colleague, Professor Jerry Dibble took on the major task of being Music Editor.

The new, modernised version is now the Canterbury [Press] (Online) Dictionary of Hymnology [generally abbreviated in this book to 'CODH']. It is nearly impossible to get the story of and behind most hymns and most hymnic people without reference to it. Albeit that there are other sources, some are strongly biased to the American, others – and I may mean Wikipedia – must be used with as much care as necessary. As an example, today, Wiki describes John Julian as mixed-blood pirate in the Caribbean around 1720-1730 and his death aged 32! [The necessary new entry will be dealt with via the Dictionary of National Biography and the CODH itself.]

Fortunately, deliberate mis-entry seems rare and neither 'fake' nor excessive 'woke' have invaded all the Wiki output. This is not to say that 'Christian Soldiers' and the like do not get critique – which is fair. Criticism for merely or primarily being the output of a different era is, from some aspects, uncalled for.

There are currently well over 6,000 articles in the CODH – and it continues to grow. After a gap of 110 years, some of the older 'Julian' entries have lost their value and importance. Some 10 to 20 articles are now being added per month.

The conclusion of the CODH article for John Julian lets him tell the tale; he wrote :... *'The pursuit of this aim has very frequently demanded, for the production of even one page only, as much time and attention as is usually expended on one hundred pages of ordinary history or criticism.'* Over 10 years, ten thousand manuscripts were consulted; 43 others contributed; and over a thousand people wrote letters assisting in the research into more than 4,000 hymns.'

New hymns and new tunes for old hymns rarely become part of an dictionary until they have reached some suitable level of repute or popularity. John Rutter as a modern author and primarily as composer is listed; but Leonard Cohen's 'Hallelujah' is not; despite being well-known and with some 200 different covers. The much more secular words in Cohen's own alternative may make a difference.

Completeness might have been missed by John Julian omitting the composers, e.g J Bacchus Dykes and their settings. Adding these would have massively expanded his task. For reasons unclear, Hymns Ancient and Modern is not mentioned. Whatever criticism can now be mounted, Julian's huge book was and is a phenomenal piece of research.

The Introduction to CODH concludes *'John Julian's research and achievement were truly magisterial, and his Dictionary remained at the forefront of hymnological research for over a hundred years.'*

The 'Four Great Hymns' in James King's survey were All Praise to Thee, my God, this Night, by Thomas Ken; Hark! The Herald Angels sing and Lo! He comes with clouds, descending; both by Charles Wesley; and Rock of Ages by Augustus Toplady.